Decision Analysis for Creating the Future

Individuals and groups often find themselves in problematic situations not knowing what to do next. They may experience a sense of unease that things aren't quite right, with no clear path to a better future. This book shows how decision analysis and the social skills of the decision analyst can enable us to explore the future before having to live it. The author is a senior decision analyst sharing his lived experience with many clients in numerous private, public and voluntary organisations. The book sets out a five-step process to choose, define and assemble the 10 key ingredients of any problem into one model. Changes to the ingredients representing possible futures provide new glimpses into the future, stimulate creativity and lead to new solutions. Readers will gain a sound theoretical foundation with an understanding of process consultancy skills and the types of problems for which decision analysis is appropriate.

Lawrence D. Phillips is Emeritus Professor in the Department of Management, London School of Economics and Political Science. In 2005, he received the Frank P. Ramsey Medal for distinguished contributions in Decision Analysis. In 2021, Dr Phillips was given the Society of Decision Professionals' Pioneer Award.

Decision Analysis for Creating the Future

LAWRENCE D. PHILLIPS
London School of Economics and Political Science

CAMBRIDGE
UNIVERSITY PRESS

Shaftesbury Road, Cambridge CB2 8EA, United Kingdom

One Liberty Plaza, 20th Floor, New York, NY 10006, USA

477 Williamstown Road, Port Melbourne, VIC 3207, Australia

314–321, 3rd Floor, Plot 3, Splendor Forum, Jasola District Centre,
New Delhi – 110025, India

Cambridge University Press is part of Cambridge University Press & Assessment,
a department of the University of Cambridge.

We share the University's mission to contribute to society through the pursuit of
education, learning and research at the highest international levels of excellence.

www.cambridge.org
Information on this title: www.cambridge.org/9781009622875

DOI: 10.1017/9781009622899

First published 2026

A catalogue record for this publication is available from the British Library

A Cataloging-in-Publication data record for this book is available from the Library of Congress

ISBN 978-1-009-62287-5 Hardback
ISBN 978-1-009-62284-4 Paperback

Cambridge University Press & Assessment has no responsibility for the persistence
or accuracy of URLs for external or third-party internet websites referred to in this
publication and does not guarantee that any content on such websites is, or will remain,
accurate or appropriate.

For EU product safety concerns, contact us at Calle de José Abascal, 56, 1°, 28003 Madrid,
Spain, or email eugpsr@cambridge.org

To Dr Cameron R. Peterson
With thanks for showing me early in my career that good decision
models are simple, but not simplistic.

Contents

Chapter Summaries

relationships between the act-event-outcome ingredients are
emphasised by relevance diagrams.

17   Manage Risk

Event trees show decisions to take now that can mitigate
subsequent unfavourable events defining the risk of a situation,
whereas fault trees assume an unfavourable event has occurred,
with decisions to be taken that reduce the undesirable consequences
and their likelihood of occurring if a fault occurs in a complex system.
Two case studies provide examples. Scenario analysis provides a way
to understand deep uncertainty.

18   Revise Opinion

A brief introduction to Bayesian statistics is provided here, showing
how uncertainty expressed as probabilities should be revised as more
information is received, and is illustrated with an example of how
data revised a researcher's degrees of belief about the effects of
medical cannabis on epilepsy in children. This is followed by a
major project showing how Bayesian Belief Networks can assist
underwriters to assess risk premiums.

19   Think Strategically

Thinking strategically means considering what and why before
deciding how and when, shaped by context, the organisation's
mission and vision, focused by strategic intent, and made practical
by intermediate goals or challenges. A case study shows how an
umbrella organisation reshaped its future to better serve its
members in providing health care. A final case study integrated
three model types enabling the US response to unrest in the
Middle East.

Part III Epilogue

Preface

It is said that the present is pregnant with the future.

Voltaire, borrowing from Leibnitz[i]

Badness of memory everyone complains of, but nobody of the want of judgement.

François de La Rochefoucauld, 1666[ii]

It is only through our sustained, good judgement and decision making that we create a better future, whether acting for ourselves, our family, the workplace, the nation or beyond. Every chapter of this book contributes to some aspect of how we could make decisions that are good enough to help us move forward, creating a better future. Usually, there are no 'right' decisions, but there are always better and worse ones, and often becoming certain about what not to do is more important than making the best choice.

This book is a practical guide to applying decision analysis: the many ways of formulating future-oriented decisions, the ingredients of good decisions, and recipes for creating quantitative models that enable decision makers to explore different pathways to the future. Up until 1984, I had thought that the purpose of decision analysis was to build a model and apply an algorithm that would show which of many possible decisions was best.

But that usually isn't what decision makers require, as I learned at a meeting in 1984. I was seated next to Robb Wilmot, the Managing Director of International Computers Ltd (ICL), then the UK's largest computer company, just the two of us looking at the screen of a desktop computer. He explored the results from a decision-analytic model I helped his top team create a few days earlier about decisions for allocating resources to the company's development products, made more difficult by considerable worldwide uncertainty about the future for mainframe computers.

Robb tried out different assumptions about the future, changing some of the numerical judgements made by his team. I typed in the new numbers, and we saw the results. 'Oh, that's not a good outcome,' he said, and tried different assumptions, which gave a better result. He continued this process, many times over, and eventually said, 'OK, you can

---

[i] H. I. Woolf (trans.). (1924). Concatenation of events (p. 99). In *The Portable Voltaire, Philosophical Dictionary*. Knopf.

[ii] The phrase was first published in the 1666 edition of F. de La Rochefoucauld, *Reflections; Or Sentences and Moral Maxims*.

close the computer. Now I know what to do!' He turned to me and exclaimed, 'This model is really helpful. It allows me to try out the future before I have to live it!'

That's what this book is about: how to create models that enable decision makers to explore possible futures, mobilising our unique human ability to anticipate the future and construct narratives about the expected consequences of our decisions.

Robb taught me something I hadn't known, as so many clients have done, and this book passes on much of what I have learned, divided into three parts: Part I provides the technical principles of decision analysis; Part II presents the social principles for developing a helping relationship with your client; and Part III blends the technical and social principles for you to choose and apply decision modelling as a 'socio-technical' approach to your client's problem.

Chapters 1–6 provide practical knowledge about the 10 ingredients of good decisions and how the three key ingredients of these 10 combine, a short history of decision theory and its applied discipline, and decision analysis, along with chapters that show how to make valid quantitative measurements of values, trade-offs among the values and uncertainty, with detailed practical methods for measuring the ingredients.

Chapters 7–11, in Part II, present the skilled knowledge about how to interact with an organisation's key problem owners so we can work together in a helping relationship to create models that cover all the conflicting issues which are making it difficult for your client to reach consensus among his or her colleagues about what to do. I start by describing the process of decision conferencing, a special type of workshop that provides a structure for groups to model and explore the important issues, identify possible ways forward, and support the accountable decision maker.

In succeeding chapters, I discuss interpersonal relationships among people in organisations, how managers exercise leadership within the limits of their authority and are held accountable for the consequences of their decisions, how teams of people can work more effectively and constructively together to make recommendations and advise the decision maker, and how you as a facilitator of a group can work as a process consultant to help participants accomplish their primary task.

Chapters 12–19, in Part III, provide six general-purpose recipes for structuring many types of problems: comparing options, determining priorities and allocating resources, bargaining and negotiating, choosing alternatives, analysing risk, and revising uncertainty as data becomes available. Fifteen case studies show how this was done. The final chapter focuses on strategic thinking.

***

There is one outstanding critical issue for you to consider if you want to create a helping relationship with your client, which I'll illustrate with a story of my experience fresh out of university, as an ensign (one stripe), in the US Navy.

I was on duty in the ship's Combat Information Center (CIC) during a training exercise in which the USS John Paul Jones (DD-932) was the lead ship of a squadron of six destroyers. The Commodore (four stripes, a Navy captain) of the squadron and his lieutenant (two stripes) were quartered on the JPJ, and they were both present nearby in the CIC. The training exercise simulated how a 'screen' of five ships sailing ahead of an aircraft carrier (simulated by the sixth destroyer) could protect the carrier against an attack by a submarine. Our five ships formed a spread-out arc ahead of the carrier so our sonars could pick up the presence of a submarine before it was close enough to fire a torpedo at the carrier.

A submarine constituted the seventh ship of the training exercise, and we were sailing ahead in zig-zagged courses to make it difficult for the submarine to find and track us. We had no idea where the submarine was because our sonar screens showed no contact. Suddenly, the ship simulating the carrier reported a simulated attack on it. The Commodore was horrified and furious. 'How could this happen?!' he shouted. When I looked at the positions of our five screening ships, I could see that our position as the middle ship was not along an equally spaced arc – we were considerably ahead of the other four ships.

I had a hunch. I called down to the sonar room and asked them to tell me today's sonar range and they replied that difficult water conditions limited the maximum range to about 1,500 yards. I plotted the positions of our ships on a navigation chart (yes, a paper chart; not automated in those days), then used a compass to draw a circle of a 1,500-yard radius around each of our five ships. As our ship was well ahead of the screening ships, I could see that our sonar range didn't overlap at all with the ranges of the ships behind us, leaving gaps on both our starboard and port sides through which the submarine must have attacked the simulated carrier.

Very pleased with myself, I went over to the Commodore, showed him the chart and suggested that if we pulled our ship back to make a smoother arc of overlapping sonar ranges, that would go some way to preventing any further attempt at an attack. At which point, he stood erect, looked me in the eye and roared, 'Are you telling me how I should run this exercise, *Ensign*?' I quickly backed off, said, 'Not at all, sir, just thought I could be helpful,' apologised, and returned to my position. Fortunately, it was near the end of my watch and within ten minutes I left the CIC after briefing my relief.

Never again during my three years in the US Navy did I deign to tell a more senior officer how to do his job. It didn't occur to me until writing this book what I could have said to the Commodore. It might have been to show my plot and ask if this could have any relevance to the attack, without suggesting what to do. Better yet, I should have shown it first to his lieutenant, for it was he who had suggested the formation of our five-ship screen.

What is the relevance here of this experience? Very simple:

NEVER TELL DECISION MAKERS WHAT THEY SHOULD DECIDE.

We decision analysts are filled with 'shoulds': you should do this, or you should do that. But prescription isn't our role; rather, we are in a position to work with decision makers and their colleagues to help them use decision analytic modelling by engaging in structured discourse, assisting them to create narratives that clarify difficult situations in which values may conflict and uncertainty attends the future, not to tell them what to do. It will be clearer in Part III how the results of modelling can be presented in such a way that accountable decision makers can see a way forward without undermining their authority.

Many years ago, Detlof von Winterfeldt, a decision analyst at the University of Southern California, told me how pleased he was about a project he had completed for the US Department of Energy (DOE), but later discovered that the DOE hadn't implemented the results of his modelling. When he became better acquainted with the head of the Agency, he asked what was wrong with his analysis. 'You did nothing wrong,' he replied, 'it was a good project, but you made the mistake of telling us what to do.'

I'll have more to say about this in Chapter 10, but for now, take that as gospel, while recognising it is a rule that sometimes can be broken. Your job as a consultant is to help your client make a good decision, not to tell him or her what to decide. (By the way, two hours after I left my watch, the Commodore ordered our ship back to form a tight arc and no further simulated attacks occurred. A little later, we established a good relationship.)

Now, I have a positive suggestion. It is this: try to identify the source of your client's initial discomfort that led them to ask you for help. Were they preparing to make an important decision, but didn't feel confident about it? Was the problem they faced complex, with no agreement among the key players about how to resolve it? Had the organisation changed direction, but lacked guidance on how to adapt to changing circumstances? Was the organisation's performance deteriorating for no discernible reason?

In short, what were the reasons for your client's sense of unease? I ask because only rarely has a client acknowledged they needed help to choose between the available alternatives. We may ask for help from coaches to improve our golf or tennis, or to learn a new language, or play a musical instrument, but we don't seek help for making decisions. Decision making seems as natural as breathing, so it would be absurd, even demeaning, to seek help.

It's possible that decisions themselves aren't the real problem; it is a perceived gap by the decision maker between where they or their organisation is now, and where they wish to be in the future. That's why it is important to explore a client's sense of unease first, to ensure that it is within your competence to assist; and, second, to locate what aspect of the problem is bothering them.

For Commercial Union Assurance Company, in the early 1970s, it was to improve the decisions of their underwriters because the company was becoming unprofitable. Mars Confectionery in Slough, UK, wanted to enter the snack bar market in the 1980s, but needed to decide with what product. For International Computers Ltd (ICL), in the 1980s it was to expand the company's products beyond mainframe computers. In the 1990s, the UK's Ministry of Defence (MOD) wanted to do a better job prioritising spending on military equipment to provide improved capability for their operating forces. For the European Medicines Agency (EMA), in the 2000s, it was to improve the transparency and communicability of their decisions about medicinal products. In the 2010s, the charity Drug Science, an independent scientific committee on drugs in the UK, was concerned to publicise the harm of psychoactive drugs and other substances.

Models developed to close those gaps always included options, only a few of which were decisions. For example, in the Mars example, the options were possible snack bars evaluated against a variety of benefits and costs, but in the end, the model's results were interpreted as demonstrating why the original decision to expand their offerings to include snack bars was not feasible for the Slough factory, so the original decision to move into snack bars was dropped. For ICL, the options for over seventy decision conferences were often strategies, *what* could be done to realise the corporate mission and vision, but not decisions about *how* to do that. For the MOD, the options were often systems that could deliver cost-effective capability to achieve a mission. For the EMA, we modelled the benefit-risk balance of new drugs compared to placebos, not the decision about approving the drug. For Drug Science, the options were the substances, evaluated for their physical, psychological and social harms, based mainly on the lived experience of specialists in treating addictions as data about drugs was sparse.

These six organisations appear again in Part III, along with many others that illustrate issues which arise when applying decision analysis. This book's emphasis is on analysing a problematic situation and developing one or more models that will help decision makers to act even though alternative decisions may not appear in the model. The decisions themselves may be a step beyond the model, although the model will in some way help the decision maker to decide, as it did for Robb Wilmot.

Acknowledgements

The first people to thank are my clients, for it is they who have enabled theory to be turned into practice. Peter Hall at ICL taught me about the importance of mission, objectives and strategy, and the two of us managed to deploy portable white boards to our client meetings back in the 1980s as the only way to show model structures and content in decision conferences because projecting computer outputs was not then feasible.

Malcolm Kree patiently and convincingly persuaded more senior UK Navy officers to apply decision conferencing in prioritising armed forces equipment purchases, deftly persuading others, often senior officers, who had never done this before to have a go. As Peter Jacobs moved from Mars to British Sugar and then to BUPA, he persisted in learning from modelling with his senior colleagues, even though he didn't always agree with the results. George Greener was the first operational senior researcher of my acquaintance to focus on the future rather than just maximising current performance.

Without Roger Miller's support, risk managers in the City of London might never have heard about how decision analysis could help them. My early acquaintance with the pharmaceutical industry owes much to Stuart Walker, the founder of the Centre for Medicines Research, whose extensive contacts in the industry enabled us to test various approaches to modelling the benefit-risk balance of drugs. Eventually, pharmaceutical companies began to use decision-analytic prioritisation of medicinal products at all stages of development, and many people in those organisations supported it. In particular, I owe a lot to David Kreuter, Peter Ringrose and Nancy Hutson for helping me to understand and absorb the cultures of their organisations.

The support of Thomas Lönngren and Hans-Georg Eichler at the European Medicines Agency enabled my LSE colleague Barbara Fasolo and Nikos Zafiropoulos, and me to see how decision analysis concepts could be applied to improve the transparency and communicability of approving new medicines, and with the help of five LSE MSc students, to learn how to model the benefit-risk balance of drugs, all guided by Francesco Pignatti's wise counsel.

I am greatly indebted to George Wright's steady help in the 1970s as our cross-cultural research found replicable differences in East–West handling of uncertainty and risk. Elliott Jaques provided support during some early difficult times and taught me about organisations and role relationships that to this day I find useful. Jonathan Rosenhead's support at the LSE came at an appropriate time, and I thank him for that.

David Nutt has many times shown me how decision modelling can be applied in medicine, and, of course, initially to the harm of drugs.

Facilitating a group with the help of a colleague does more than relieve the strain of constantly attending to the group life. Scott Barclay cleverly used our work together to develop Hiview and Equity, trying out and revising the programs in response to the demands of a live case. Mara Airoldi proved to be an excellent co-facilitator, able to think and do very quickly and well. My late wife, MaryAnn, was good at sensing what was going on under the surface of the group's behaviour, and we used that particularly well in training new facilitators.

I helped to found Catalyze with Bob Kitchen in 2002, now a successful and growing consultancy company of more than 30 people in the UK, with active branches in Australia and New Zealand. I co-facilitated many decision conferences with Bob, who contributed to establishing decision conferences in the UK's MOD. Their work continues today under the watchful eye of Kevin Bossley, their current managing director.

Long overdue is a proper acknowledgement of the support by Dennis Lindley, when I was writing my 1973 book, *Bayesian Statistics for Social Scientists*. He read every chapter and certainly improved my ability to explain then what were very new concepts in statistics. He has now passed, but I hope this will set the record straight; there is much in that book that I learned from him in his English gentlemanly way.

Here, too, is a place to thank the late Athol Hughes and Ana Sauma for their psychoanalytic help, which enabled me to write both the 1973 book and this one, and in many other ways, too.

Finally, how can I adequately convey how much I have benefited from the gentle comments of Charlotte Doyle, a fellow graduate student at the University of Michigan in the early 1960s, now a professor of psychology at Sarah Lawrence College, who has written wisely about creativity. And I gained from the book-publishing experience, lightly leavened with humour, of Lee Roy Beach, a post-doctoral fellow at the University of Michigan then, now a retired emeritus professor at the University of Arizona. Two dear friends with whom I participate in separate virtual meetings every week as I have been writing this book. Remaining errors are, of course, mine.

Part I

The Technical Principles

The first chapter establishes the decision framework, beginning with an elementary problem that introduces the 10 ingredients of good decisions, how the key ingredients, probabilities, preference values and trade-off weights, are combined, and the five steps for creating a decision analysis model. It is this framework that connects all the subsequent chapters. Chapter 2 gives a brief history of decision theory and decision analysis, which makes clear how the three key ingredients were identified and why they are logically inevitable. Chapter 3 explores their meaning as subjective constructs, while Chapters 4, 5 and 6 detail methods for quantifying them.

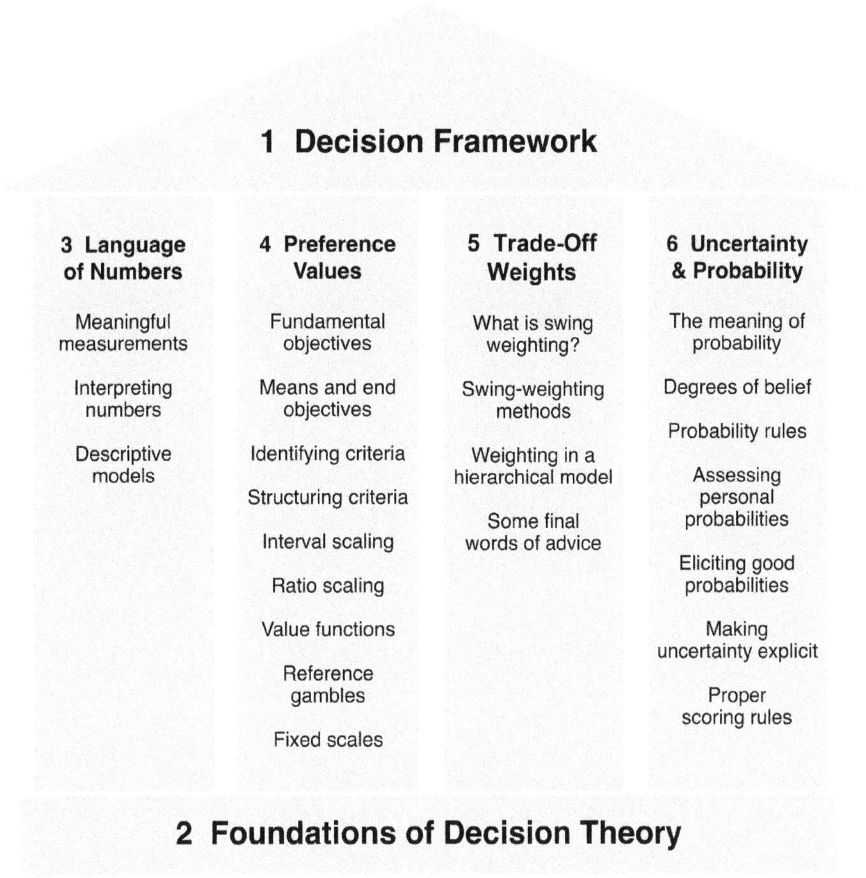

1 Decision Framework

3 Language of Numbers	4 Preference Values	5 Trade-Off Weights	6 Uncertainty & Probability
Meaningful measurements	Fundamental objectives	What is swing weighting?	The meaning of probability
Interpreting numbers	Means and end objectives	Swing-weighting methods	Degrees of belief
Descriptive models	Identifying criteria	Weighting in a hierarchical model	Probability rules
	Structuring criteria	Some final words of advice	Assessing personal probabilities
	Interval scaling		Eliciting good probabilities
	Ratio scaling		Making uncertainty explicit
	Value functions		Proper scoring rules
	Reference gambles		
	Fixed scales		

2 Foundations of Decision Theory

Figure 1.0

1　A Decision-Making Framework

The beginning of knowledge consists of learning to call things by their names.

Confucius

At a party, I meet someone who asks, 'What do you do for a living?'

'I'm a decision analyst,' I reply. 'I teach decision science and I apply it to help people make better decisions.'

'A *science* of decision making. Is that possible?'

'Yes,' I reply, 'And it's really quite simple.'

'OK, explain it to me, in just one minute.'

'Right. First, think about what you want to achieve by taking a decision. Second, identify different alternatives for achieving the objectives. Third, judge the consequences of taking a decision – the good and bad things that might occur, and how much you might be willing to trade-off between the good and the bad. And fourth, assess the degree of uncertainty about realising the consequences.'

'That's it?'

'Not quite. Those four steps take the problem apart into pieces, and for each decision alternative, reduce the attractiveness of the consequences if they are uncertain: the more uncertain, the less attractive they are. Then you choose the decision for which the overall adjusted attractiveness is best.'

'That took more than one minute.'

'I know. The curse of being a university professor. It's hard to reduce a 50-minute lecture into only a few minutes.'

That's why I've written this book.

Let's take it one step at a time. The dialogue above introduces most of the steps in making good decisions using language that is familiar. But what are the ingredients? There are just 10 ingredients, which we will discover by working through a hypothetical problem, and along the way I'll show how to combine the ingredients using 'logical glue', the term coined by Howard Raiffa in his ground-breaking 1968 book, *Decision Analysis*.[1] Once the ingredients and logical glue are made clear, you will be prepared for the framework, which I'll present at the end of the chapter. That framework will provide you with the ability to take a fresh look at any decision.

The Blind Problem

We start with a simple decision, for if we can understand how decision theory works for a simple problem, we are more likely to apply it correctly for real small-world decisions. Imagine that you have been suffering difficulty seeing clearly and your optician suggests you consult an ophthalmologist. After a careful examination, she tells you that you have a rare eye disease, which if left untreated, will cause you to become permanently blind in both eyes. However, an operation could restore your full sight, but that is not guaranteed as it is a new treatment and is not always successful, in which case the operation will leave you ... dead.

At this point, most people would ask questions to see if other alternatives would reduce the risk, but let's stay with this example because it is perhaps the simplest sort of choice under uncertainty, an uncertain event compared to a certainty, and it easily portrays elements of the vocabulary you will need to make sense of many difficult problems. Figure 1.1 shows a simple decision tree of the eye problem.

What more would you like to know? Most people to whom I've posed this problem ask what the chance of success is. The ophthalmologist says about 70 per cent. I will discuss probabilities in Chapter 6, and we will examine the basis for assigning a probability. For now, assume 70 per cent, shown properly on a decision tree as decimal numbers between 0 and 1.0, inclusive (Figure 1.2).

For now, consider what you think you would do. Agree to the operation with a 70 per cent chance of success leading to your sight restored and a 30 per cent chance of dying on the operating table, OR reject the operation and go blind in both eyes within the next three months?

Now, set aside your choice and let's work through the problem. I presume that you would prefer to be fully sighted rather than blind, and you would prefer being blind in

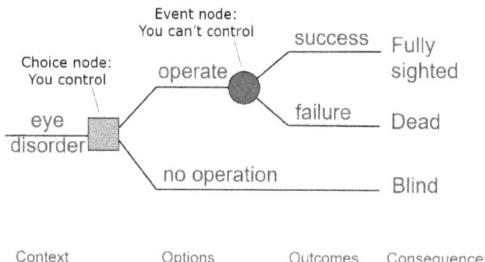

Figure 1.1

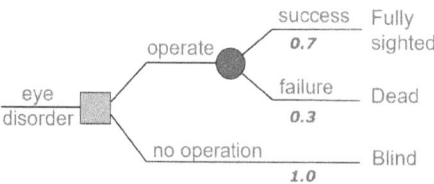

Figure 1.2

both eyes to being dead. Two simple comparisons which lead me to suppose you therefore prefer being fully sighted to being dead. If so, then your order of preference would be fully sighted, blind, dead. What you probably didn't say was, 'I don't know' for one of the comparisons, although some people do and tell me they would have to think more deeply about it.

You might have asked, 'What do you mean by "preference"?' The *Oxford Dictionary* definition – 'liking of one thing better than another' – will do, and in plain English means desirability, worth or value. In other words, it's the preference for a consequence regardless of its probability, a *preference value*. We'll now analyse the problem further to construct your preferences between the options.

Let's start by assigning a pair of arbitrary numbers to represent the preference value to you of the two extreme consequences: 100 to fully sighted and 0 to dead. Relative to those two numbers, what would you assign to being blind? Is it closer to 100 or to 0? If you say '50', then I would ask, 'Since 50 is halfway between 100, then does it follow for you that being fully sighted is as much better than being blind as being dead is worse?'

This is a comparison of preference values based on the added value to you of being fully sighted instead of blind, compared to the added value of being blind rather than dead. Most people say those increments of value are not the same: the dead-to-blind increment is quite a bit larger than the blind-to-fully-sighted increment. If I ask how much bigger, some might say four times bigger, which suggests that blind could be given an 80 since 0 to 80 is four times the 20-point difference between blind and fully sighted (Figure 1.3).

As I'm sure you appreciate, there is no correct answer here; the number you assign depends on many things that are personal to you, so others might assess different numbers for themselves. The context of the decision is crucial, for it will influence this assessment and all those to follow. Let's proceed with the 80. All the consequences are now located on a 0–100 preference value scale whose numbers represent your relative strengths of preference for the consequences.

The updated decision tree is shown in Figure 1.4. Is it possible to place the decisions on the 0–100 preference value scale? Since 'don't operate' leads to certain blindness, which was scored at 80, that number also represents the relative value of the decision. But 'operate' could lead to either of two differently valued consequences, so how can a single number represent the preference value of that decision?

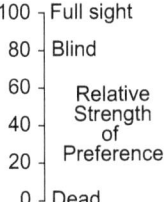

Figure 1.3

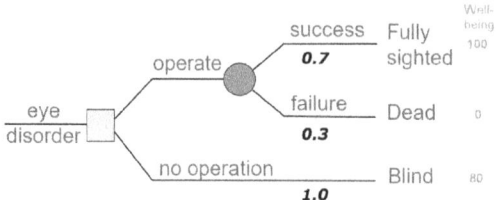

Figure 1.4

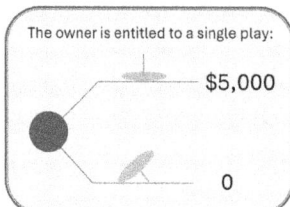

Figure 1.5

Certainty Equivalents

Let's see how we can find that single number. Imagine I gave you the ticket shown in Figure 1.5.

You now own it. A third person will toss the thumbtack (drawing pin in the UK) onto a hard tabletop, where it will land either with its point up or down. If it lands point up, I give you $5,000, but if it lands point down, nothing. Before the toss, you can examine the thumbtack, which I randomly selected from a package of them from a stationer's store, but you aren't allowed to gather data by tossing it many times. I think you would agree this a good deal. You don't have to pay for the toss, so you might be better off by $5,000, but no money lost if point down is the outcome.

If for any reason you wouldn't like to play this gamble, you might consider selling it. What would you consider to be a fair selling price? If the chances of the two outcomes were equal, then you would have a 0.5 chance of winning $5,000 and 0.5 of winning nothing. So, it's clear that, at best, the monetary value of the gamble might be $2,500, which is £5,000 times 0.5. 'Yes,' you say, 'If someone offered me $2,500, I would take it.' Let's define that as the certain monetary equivalent. It's the single certain equivalent that you judge would be fair. And if you are pretty sure the probability is less than 0.5, say 0.4, then the certain monetary equivalent would be $2,000. In general, the lower the probability of success, the less attractive the wager.

The wager would also be less attractive if there was a penalty for the drawing pin landing pin down. For example, suppose that outcome would cost the owner of the wager $1,000. Multiply that loss by the probability of failure, 0.5 if success is also 0.5, and the weighted monetary value of –$1,000 is –$500. Now, add that to the +$2,500 and the fair value of the wager becomes less attractive at $2,000. This summing of weighted values is referred to as an 'expected' value, so the $2,000 is considered as an *expected monetary value*, or EMV, although you 'expect' either $5,000 or nothing. That's the idea we'll now take forward for the blind problem.

Obviously the operate option must be valued higher than zero and lower than 100. By taking a weighted average of those two numbers, we arrive at an expected preference value (EPV) of 70 (Figure 1.6).

Now we're ready to compare the options: 'operate' is at 70, 'don't operate' is at 80, so choose not to operate. The cross-off mark indicates that the operate option is not the best choice. That's only a 10-point difference in value, half the 20-point difference between blind and fully sighted, so maybe it's worth thinking more deeply about that 80 for being blind. Best to talk to some blind people (as I have done in a project for the UK charity, Guide Dogs for the Blind, where I learned that many blind people don't even feel particularly disadvantaged).

Now I want to ask you another question. What were you thinking of when you assigned the preference values of 100–80–0 to the consequences? Perhaps you were focused on your *physical well-being* and how well you could continue your present life. Fair enough. But if you were married, with children, perhaps you might also consider how well off your family would be as a separate consideration alongside your physical well-being. We'll call it *family well-being*, defined as the extent of financial, social and psychological well-being for your family until your children have grown and left home. Now things get more complex, but see it through, back-tracking and reading again after seeing the final result, which comes later. It's really all just simple arithmetic.

For this family criterion, what would your preferences be for the three consequences? If you remain fully sighted, you will continue as now, a score of 100, and being blind might well be the worst, a score of zero. If you die, your insurance could help your family to adapt after you die, perhaps sufficiently to sustain the family until the children are grown, but their social and psychological well-being will certainly be disrupted. You might take account of your spouse's income, if you both work, the ages of your children, how your death might affect the children and the impact on grandparents, and any other considerations. For the purposes of illustration, let's assume a score of 60. The new decision tree, expanded to take account of both criteria – your physical and family's well-being – is shown in Figure 1.7.

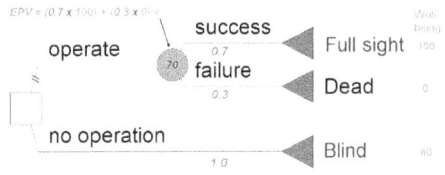

Figure 1.6

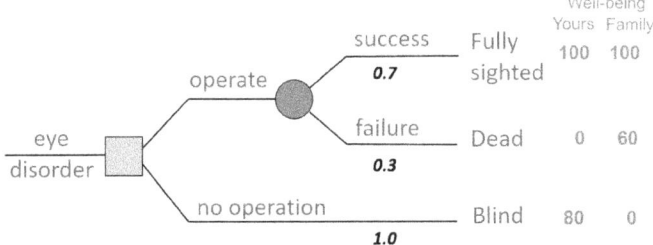

Figure 1.7

Considering *only* the scores under the family criterion, weight them by their probabilities:

$$EPV(Family) = (100 \times 0.7) + (60 \times 0.3) = 88$$

Thus, operate is valued at 88, while 'don't operate' is valued at 80. Now the operate option looks slightly more attractive. Obviously, the choice depends on which criterion you take into consideration. Can both be accommodated? Common sense and decision theory both say 'yes': by weighting the criteria, but they differ in how this is done.

Common sense might suggest more weight on your well-being and less on your family because your life is at stake. Indeed, if you consulted your family, they might tell you to ignore the financial consequences and express more aversion to risk than you feel. More generally, we take several criteria into account when choosing a place to live, buying a car, selecting a job or finding a school for our children.

Let's see how in decision analysis it is done properly for the blind problem, as the method applies to all decisions in which multiple criteria, however dissimilar they seem to be, are a prominent feature of the choice problem.

We're going to weight the scales so we can add together the two weighted scores at the end of each branch of the decision tree. Then, we can repeat the above calculation, multiplying the new weighted values by the probabilities of the two events and adding the products. First, let's look at the tops and bottoms of each scale, shown in Figure 1.8.

The best positions on both scales are Fully Sighted, but the worst position on the left scale is Dead, while it is Blind on the right scale. Which of those differences would you consider to be the biggest? That is, which swing in value is greater, from Dead to Fully Sighted for your own well-being, or from Blind to Fully Sighted for your family's well-being? If that feels like comparing apples to oranges, it is actually the *values* of apples and oranges for the problem at hand that are being compared. Waldorf salads include apples, but not oranges, so oranges don't add value for that kind of salad. As we will see for all decision models, it is the *context* of the decision that influences and establishes value.

So, now I ask, which scale represents the greatest swing in preference value from the worst to best position? To answer the question, consider now how big your difference in personal physical well-being is between being dead or fully sighted, compared to the well-being difference for your family between you being blind and

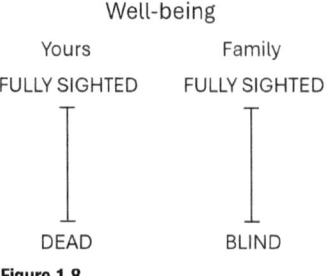

Figure 1.8

fully sighted. In short, compare the worst-best difference on each scale *and* how much you care about those differences. That's the key question for eliciting weights.

Many people to whom I've posed this problem don't hesitate to say it's the personal difference in well-being that matters most to them, a lot, so I give that a weight of 100. Compared to that, I ask, how big is the other increment of preference value? A typical answer is 25. In decision analysis, we call these numbers *swing-weights* (see Figure 1.9).

With those weights, when expressed as decimals that sum to 1.0, 0.8 and 0.2, a process called *normalisation*, we can now combine those 0–100 scales by weighting the preference values of the options, with the results shown in Figure 1.10 in the Total column. The weighted score at the end of each branch in the decision tree is then multiplied by the branch probability and summed, the EPV calculation, to give 73.6 (round up to 74; these aren't precise figures). Compared to the 64 for Blind, this result now favours the operation.

The original preference value for operate has increased from 70 to 74, but the value for being blind has decreased from 80 to 64, leaving a value difference for this two-criteria model of only 10 units of preference value, and now operate is more preferred. Taking account of your family's preferences changed the preferred option; multiple criteria and swing weights are indeed important ingredients. I'll say more about swing-weighting in Chapter 5.

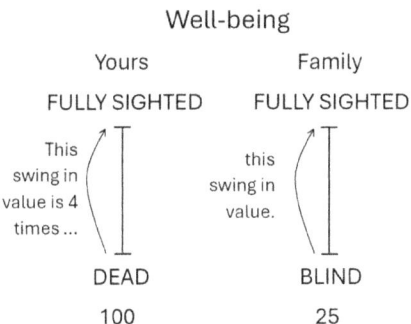

Figure 1.9

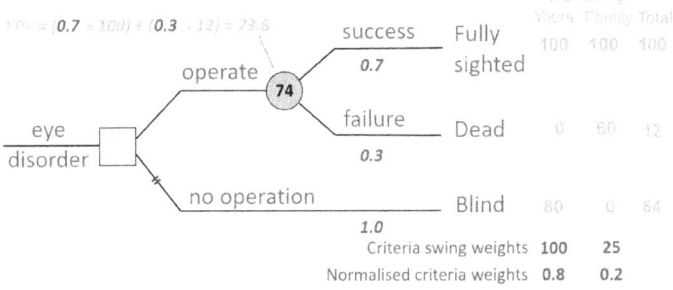

Figure 1.10

That completes the analysis of the blind problem. If it were your problem for real, I would now suggest you think about it for at least a couple weeks before making any decision and talk to those who might be affected by the consequences of your decision. Discuss it further with your family. Consider how you feel about the risk of an operation, how comfortable you are with the 70–30 chances, how much you would dread exposing yourself to the risk, and how others might feel about it.

The Ingredients of Good Decisions

Now let's take stock of what we've learned as I summarise the ingredients used in modelling the blind problem. Some or all of 10 ingredients characterise every decision you take. That is the beauty of decision analysis, for it can be applied to any decision, whatever the topic. Even if you never construct a model of a decision, it will be helpful to keep in mind each of these ingredients, for they all play different roles, depending on the context and type of problem, in any final decision. The way we go about choosing the ingredients is often referred to as framing the problem.

The relative importance of the ingredients in framing is a matter of judgement and may change as a model develops. It's wise to keep an open mind about which ingredients are appropriate for any given problem, because once you are committed to a particular combination of ingredients, it can be difficult to see you might be ignoring important issues, especially for experienced decision analysts who have learned which ingredients to use for certain problems. Bread requires yeast – unless it's banana bread.

For now, let's focus on the 10 ingredients of good decision making, five each for structure and content, all influenced by context (see Table 1.1).

This list of 10 ingredients is silent about the *process* of putting the ingredients together. Similar ingredients appear in many recipes, like flour, milk, eggs, sugar and salt for bread, pancakes and waffles. So different problems require different combinations of ingredients. Selecting the right ingredients and combining them properly is a matter of process, the subject of the chapters in Part III.

There are different ways of organising the structure and content of a decision model depending on the context of the problem, which is discussed in Chapter 12. Also, sometimes the options are given, while for other problems, the objectives and criteria are given. Uncertain events might need to be considered first, or a need to avoid disastrous consequences.

However, to begin helping your client, you start by exploring their sense of unease resulting from a growing concern about the discrepancy between the current situation and a desired future. Your role as a decision analyst is to help your client take decisions that will close or lessen the gap. The approach you take to develop the helping relationship is discussed in Part II.

Table 1.1 The 10 ingredients of good decisions

The 10 ingredients of good decisions		
	Definition	**Blind problem Example**
Structure		
Objectives	The aims or purposes to be achieved	Stay as healthy as possible
Criteria	Standards against which achievement of the objectives are assessed	Personal well-being Family well-being
Options	Alternatives, decisions, choices or courses of action for achieving the objectives	Operate Don't operate
Events	Happenings that can influence achievement of the objectives	An operation
Outcomes	Ways by which the happenings influence achievement of the objectives	Success Failure
Content		
Consequences	The results or effects of the event's outcomes	Fully sighted Blind Dead
Preference values	Extent to which the consequences are judged to achieve the objectives	100 for fully sighted 80 for being blind 0 for death
Trade-offs	The extent to which more value on one criterion can be balanced by less on another	0.8 for personal well-being 0.2 for family well-being
Probabilities	Degrees of belief about the occurrence of the outcomes	70% for success 30% for failure
Risk attitude	Extent to which the possibility of harm is judged to be tolerable	Must think more because the two options are close in value

The Grammar of Decision Making

At this point, I need to generalise the two calculations that gave a preference value of 74 to the operate option when both your physical well-being and your family's well-being were being considered.

The point of this excursion is to show that decision modelling isn't restricted to simple two-outcome uncertain events. I've found that when students are introduced to decision theory with the blind problem, or something similar, this can create the impression that all problems can be reduced to this simple form of choosing between an uncertain event versus a sure thing. Real problems are more complex, as we shall see in Part III.

When statisticians or decision analysts multiply values by probabilities, they call the sum of the products an 'expected' value, with the abbreviation 'EV'. It doesn't represent anybody's psychological 'expectation', so I avoid the term when working with clients and will mostly not use it in this book, but when I do it means 'weighted average'.

Statisticians also use the term 'random variable' as a generic term for a quantity whose numerical value is not yet known. Again, this term isn't helpful in work with clients if you refer to preference values as random variables because there is nothing random about the numbers at the end of a decision tree, and clients don't usually think of them as variable. Except for constants, any number in a decision analysis starts off as an *uncertain quantity*, a term that is self-explanatory, so I frequently use it.

If this were a problem with many options, events and criteria, it would be necessary to keep track of when to calculate what. The decision tree is a great way to visualise what to do and when, and I'm happy to report that computer programs are available to help you create the tree, populate it with the uncertain quantities we use, probabilities, weights and values, and then let the program do the calculating.[2] If you are a do-it-yourself sort of person and are familiar with spreadsheets, you could draw the tree on paper and then instruct the program to do the calculations. Many examples are given in Kirkwood's excellent book.[3]

The Mathematics of Decision Analysis

Skip this section if you intend to rely on a decision tree program to do all the work for you. If you would like to see how to express the blind problem calculations in a single formula, read on. The following formulas constitute the grammar of decision analysis and can be generalised for any number of options, events and criteria. It's done in four steps.

Step 1: Create the tree and convert it to a table with rows and columns that include the probabilities, values and swing weights. It would look something like Table 1.2 for

Table 1.2

Step 1		CRITERIA		*Step 2*	*Step 3*
OPTIONS	CONSEQENCES and j probabilities	Well-being $k = 1$	Family $k = 2$	Weighted value sum	Sums × probabilities
Operate $i = 1$	FULLY SIGHTED $p_1 = 0.7$	100 v_{111}	100 v_{112}	100 V_{11}	73.6 V_1
	DEAD $p_2 = 0.3$	0 v_{121}	60 v_{122}	12 V_{12}	
Don't operate $i = 2$	BLIND $p_3 = 1.0$	80 v_{231}	0 v_{232}	64 V_{13}	64 V_2
	swing weights:	$w_1 = 0.8$	$w_2 = 0.2$		

the blind problem (check out the pattern of subscripts on the preference values; I'll use these in the equations).

Step 2: For each of the consequences, multiply the values associated with the criteria by the column swing weights and sum the products.

$$V_{ij} = \sum_k w_k v_{ijk}$$

This step combines the preference values for each consequence into a single value. In the algebraic notation, it eliminates the k subscript.

Step 3: For each of the options' consequences, multiply the weighted value sum calculated in Step 2 by the probability for each consequence and sum the products.

$$EV_i = \sum_j p_{ij} V_{ij}$$

This step combines the single weighted preference value associated with each consequence into a single value for each option; it eliminates the j subscript. Because several values are multiplied by probabilities and summed, I've shown the result as an expected value as is common in statistics and decision theory.

Those two equations can be combined into one, which in application requires the doubly weighted sum to be carried out in the sequence of step 1 then 2:

$$EV_i = \sum_j \sum_k p_{ij} v_{ijk}$$

You might have noticed that the equations for the first two steps have one feature in common: they both weight a preference value with a number that extends from 0 to 1. If I were using a spreadsheet to do the computations, the computer wouldn't know whether the number represented a probability or a swing weight. I take advantage of this feature in Chapter 5 for benefit-safety models of pain-killer drugs.

Step 4: Choose the option with the highest expected value. The equation for that is simple:

$$\max_i EV_i, \text{for i} > 1$$

You 'maximise' the *EV* by choosing the bigger one. Note that to do that there must be two or more options. I have sometimes been asked to create a decision analysis model to justify a single option, which I explain can't be done unless at least two options are being considered. A persuasive argument might do the job, but beware if someone introduces a new option that might be better.

A Framework for Creating Decision Models

You've now learned the fundamentals of decision analysis. The next step is to gain experience in applying that knowledge; learning the fundamentals of decision analysis is akin to learning a new language – it takes practice to become skilful. You've learned enough to apply it to simple situations, like the blind problem, perhaps with more options, more events and more criteria. The principles remain the same for larger problems.

Start with something small, just to practise. Something you could do entirely intuitively, which will most likely give you the answer you expected. Or perhaps not, in which case, go back and see why the model and your intuition disagree. A PhD graduate in decision theory whom I knew had received several job offers, and was about to decide on one, when I suggested to him that he try modelling it by using a software package developed by the staff of my Decision Analysis Unit. When he did, the best option was not the one he intuitively preferred. He then applied the software again, each day for a week, receiving the same result, and he finally realised this was caused by a fundamental conflict in his core personal values. He then thought more deeply about his life's goals, resolved the value conflict, and chose an option he had originally dismissed.

Whatever you find from your initial attempts at modelling, keep at it and soon you will become fluent in this new language. I no longer have to look up familiar recipes in *The Joy of Cooking*, as I now know the ingredients, their amounts, and how to combine them to produce results. Even better, I now have the experience to know how to change the recipe to produce new and different results. That's the main topic of Part III.

You may feel that the numbers for the blind problem were excessively precise, and I agree with you. I'll say more about this in the next three chapters, but we are bound to accept imprecision in the numbers when making decisions about the future because the solid data we would like to have is not yet available; subjective judgement is required in assessing preference values, trade-off weights and probabilities. Those three quantities are not sitting in your client's head, waiting to be plucked out. Rather, they are formed in the process of building and exploring the model, as Lichtenstein and Slovic pointed out in their important research compendium, *The Construction of Preference*.[4] As we will see in Chapter 3, numerical quantities are the language of decision theory, and the intellectual effort of expressing preferences in numerical form helps one to form the preferences, making them explicit, finding inadequacies and inconsistencies, then changing or revising them.

A rough rule of thumb, derived mainly from experience, is that the precision of probabilities, scores or weights, expressed on a 0–100 scale, is about ±5. I applied that rule of thumb in considering the final results for the blind problem in comparing the 74 for operate and 64 for don't operate. As an engineering student, I was taught to limit displays of results to significant figures that are within the limits of precision, so I mentally added 5 to 74 and subtracted 5 from 74, a range of 69 to 79. Then I did the same for the 64, giving 59 to 69. The low of 69 on the former is identical to the high on the latter, so I suggested more thinking about the problem for a couple of weeks before deciding (or revising the model).

Let's now be explicit about the process for creating any decision model, which is shown here.

The Five Steps for Creating Any Decision Model

1. **Consider context**: What has given rise to your client's sense of unease? What is the problem? What is going on now? What aspects of the physical and social environments are relevant to any decision model that could help to resolve the problem? At this stage, the options and criteria are not necessarily known. Understanding the context will influence assessment of preference values, trade-off weights and probabilities.

2. **Frame the problem**: Can the problem be represented by a decision model (including a model in which the options aren't decisions)? Which of the 10 ingredients should be represented in the model? Is the problem more one of resolving uncertainty, or of conflicting values, or a combination of those two main features?

3. **Provide content**: Where is the information that is relevant to judgements of preference values and probabilities? What expertise is needed for assessing preference values and what potentially different expertise for judging value trade-offs? Data may be relevant to future outcome probabilities, but expert opinion will also be required.

4. **Explore results**: What results might change when considering different assumptions or judgements about the future? Computer-based sensitivity analyses show the extent to which results are robust, that is, they may not change substantially to differences in experts' judgements and imprecision in the data.

5. **Agree the way forward**: What can be agreed by those engaged in the modelling that would be helpful to the decision maker? Consensus about the way forward may be possible when sensitivity analyses show that the results are robust. Can a narrative be constructed based on the modelling that points to possible ways forward? If the results are not robust, then include in the narrative the key differences in judgements or assumptions so the accountable person can resolve the differences and take a decision.

I'll use these five process steps in the six recipes of Chapters 13 to 18, where the 10 ingredients of good decisions are applied in different ways and combinations for each type of problem. In the meantime, you might start honing your decision-making skills by applying what you've learned so far on a real problem of your own, or one of a friend or colleague.

It's best if this is a real problem, otherwise it will be difficult or impossible to make the required assessments because the problem is hypothetical. You might help someone who is thinking of changing jobs, a young person looking for a job or a family needing a new kitchen appliance. It's best to avoid the question of what car to buy, as cars are often expressions of the purchaser's personality, which can cloud rational analysis!

The occasional client wants to know the origins of the concepts you use in modelling their decision problem, or you might be curious about the origins of the key ingredients for all decisions. If so, move on to Chapter 2 to discover the origins of decision analysis and learn why the three ingredients, preference values, trade-offs and probabilities, were not just arbitrarily chosen concepts.

Chapter 3 takes up the issue of how to establish that the numbers associated with the three ingredients can be said to meaningfully represent the property being measured. Or you could move to any of Chapters 4 to 6 for more information about the three ingredients and how to assess them. If you have a particular problem in mind, you might skip to Chapter 12, which describes the six types of decision models, to see if one of the other chapters in Part III could help you address your problem.

And since strategy is a continuing theme throughout the book, you could read Chapter 19 to learn more about strategic thinking.

Whichever chapter you go to next, I recommend that, at some point, you come back and read all six chapters of Part 1. A sound understanding of these chapters will provide a boost to your growing confidence in using this new language of decision analysis.

Summary

This chapter introduced the 10 ingredients to be considered if you are constructing a model that could help to resolve your client's sense of unease, enabling him or her to take a decision. In modelling the blind problem, we've identified the 10 ingredients that are common to all decisions: five for the structure of the problem – objectives, criteria, options, events and outcomes; and five for the content – consequences, preference values, trade-offs, probabilities and risk attitude. All 10 require a degree of judgement for analysing a decision. The five structure ingredients establish what content must be considered, while the five content ingredients give magnitude and direction to the options.

The blind problem also introduced the 'logical glue' that enables preference values on the different criteria to be brought together. For problems dominated by multiple criteria, the logical glue is trade-off weights for the criteria that create a common unit of preference value, enabling them to be compared. If a problem is dominated by uncertainty, the logical glue is the probabilities of an option's preference values that adjust the option's preference values and combine them, enabling the options to be compared.

In applying the ingredients to a real problem, a framework can prevent errors of omission. The five-step framework for creating a decision model is a distillation of many frameworks reported in books and papers about decision analysis. In practice, a few more steps may be needed,[5] depending on the type of problem, as you can see in Chapters 13 to 18.

At this point, you may well wonder how it is possible to reduce the complexity of taking decisions to just three numerical quantities. Where did they come from? Why these three and not others? What is the justification for the expected preference value model? These issues are addressed in the next chapter.

2 The Foundations of Decision Theory

> The person who truly knows a thing sees the reasons why the thing was determined to be and could not have been otherwise.
>
> Attributed to Baruch Spinoza, Dutch philosopher, 1632–77[6]

This chapter explains the foundations of modern decision theory and its offspring, the applied discipline of decision analysis. I think it is important to be aware of this background, for if you know how decision theory came into being, you can see it couldn't have been different. I know of no other theory in the social sciences which is so firmly rooted in such sound foundations.

The concepts we used to analyse the blind problem are derived from the characteristics of coherent preferences. The theory starts by describing the principles that define coherent preferences, then shows that together they logically imply that the key ingredients of all decisions are probabilities and utilities and that utilities multiplied by probabilities are the basis for identifying the best decision. An extension of the principles establishes the basis for describing a third ingredient, trade-offs among multiple objectives quantified as weights, along with a justification for applying the theory to preference values, which are used throughout this book.

Some critics believe our actual preferences often are not coherent, that is, they don't follow the principles that are assumed in decision theory, so the theory is useless. However, this criticism fails to recognise that just as coherent preferences logically imply the features of good decisions, so the logic can work in reverse order: good decisions imply coherent preferences, with only the latter justified in different ways by different theorists. That's how the theory is used – analyse a problem by applying the concepts of decision analysis and that will create coherence of preferences. Indeed, it is clarity about preferences that enables the decision maker to act. Howard Raiffa said this eloquently in his classic exposition of decision analysis:

The spirit of decision analysis is divide and conquer: decompose a complex problem into simpler problems, get one's thinking straight on these simpler problems, paste these analyses together with logical glue, and come out with a program of action for the complex problem.[7]

Sometimes it is useful to explain a little theory to clients if they are worried about the subjectivity of decision theory and would prefer more objective ways of modelling. I sometimes point out that there is no objective theory of decision making, as 'objective' means independent from human thought, and it is people who make decisions, so all decisions include some elements of subjectivity. This is true even when preference values and probabilities are based on available data; someone must judge the extent to which data is relevant for the future.

The Founders

Modern-day decision theory began in 1926 with the modest musings of a bright young man, Frank Plumpton Ramsey (Figure 2.1), a British mathematician, philosopher and economist, who was a Fellow and Lecturer at King's College, University of Cambridge. His starting point was to assume an idealised decision-maker:

The theory I propose to adopt is that we seek things which we want, which may be our own or other people's pleasure, or anything else whatever, and our actions are such as we think most likely to realize these goods.[8]

He applied his mathematical prowess to the exploration of what the idealised decision maker should logically consider in choosing a course of action. His focus was on the decision maker's degrees of belief, and he developed a set of principles to guide the logical analysis. He proposed several principles (axioms) and derived their logical implications (theorems), much as the basic assumptions in plane geometry, such as the shortest distance between two points is a straight line, which most people would agree are obvious, to prove the non-obvious Pythagorean theorem, which applies to all right-angled triangles.

Ramsey suggested several 'agreeable principles' which show that the laws of probability apply to the logical decision maker's degrees of belief. He also extended his axioms to include the measurement of utility (which I will usually refer to as preference value) and the usefulness of expected utility, thus laying the foundations of decision theory.

Figure 2.1

He clearly felt he was on the right track, but modestly said this was only a beginning:

I have not worked out the mathematical logic of this in detail, because this would, I think, be rather like working out to seven places of decimals a result only valid to two. My logic cannot be regarded as giving more than the sort of way it might work.[9]

Sadly, Ramsey suffered from chronic liver problems, and died from complications of an operation in 1930 at the age of only 26. Lytton Strachey, the author of *Eminent Victorians*, wrote: 'I always thought there was something of Newton about him – the ease and majesty of the thought – the gentleness of the temperament – and suppose Newton had died at – how old was he? – twenty-six?'[10] The late, eminent Bayesian statistician Professor Dennis Lindley considered that probabilities, utilities and expected utility were as important to our subjective world as Newton's three laws are to the physical world.

One of Lindley's teachers was Sir Harold Jeffreys (Figure 2.2), a Cambridge don known to Ramsey. In 1939, Jeffreys published his *Theory of Probability*, with his own system of axioms and theorems about degrees of belief, which included several chapters on how the theory could be used to quantify statistical significance and hypothesis tests.[11] Sadly, his equations are not easy to calculate even with a modern-day calculator. As far as I know, these were hardly ever applied, particularly as simpler classical statistical methods were adopted. In my view, Jeffreys was ahead of his time.

Unknown to these two native speakers of English, Bruno de Finetti (Figure 2.3), an Italian statistician and actuary, was also exploring the meaning of probability and its laws. This was published in French in 1937, and its translated title, *Foresight: Its Logical Laws, Its Subjective Sources*,[12] nicely summarises his view that logic demands probabilities to be interpreted as subjective. Those views were expanded and elaborated in his 1970 two-volume book, translated in 1974 as *Theory of Probability: A Critical Introductory Treatment*.[13]

Figure 2.2

Figure 2.3

Figure 2.4

In 1944, von Neumann and Morgenstern published their landmark book, *Theory of Games and Economic Behavior*, to provide, in the book's Appendix, an axiomatic treatment of utility. They assumed objective probabilities and then explained four axioms of coherent choice that led logically to utilities and the expected utility principle.[14]

Influenced by the work of Ramsey, de Finetti and Jeffreys, those three strands were woven together by Leonard 'Jimmie' Savage (Figure 2.4) in his 1954 book, *The Foundations of Statistics*.[15] His intention was to provide a solid theoretical grounding for the classical Neyman-Pearson approach to hypothesis testing, which treats probabilities as relative frequencies. His approach considered probabilities as degrees of belief, which can be revised as new data becomes available, by the application of one of the probability laws know as Bayes' rule. However, he admitted in the second edition of his book[16] that he had failed to register many contradictions and inconsistencies between the two systems.

But it was a magnificent failure, for Savage's book laid the foundations for modern decision theory and established Bayesian statistics as a logically coherent approach to statistical inference. He started with three principles about a decision maker's preferences and showed that personal probabilities, utilities and the expected utility calculation are the logical characteristics of coherent preferences. This formulation is now often referred to as Bayesian statistical decision theory.

The Axioms and Theorems of Decision Theory

In words, here are Savage's principles, although I've split his first principle into two separate ones. Remember, these are principles to which you might aspire in your everyday decision making. They might describe your preferences as you would like them to be for any decision problem you are facing, but they don't necessarily describe how you actually experience them. Think of them as principles of an ideal decision maker, which I mean when in the following I address 'you'. In decision theory, they are treated as axioms, assumptions about an ideal decision maker.

Principle 1: Ordering of acts. In considering act A and act B, you can state that you prefer A to B, or B to A, or you are indifferent between them. What you wouldn't say is 'I don't know,' for actually making a choice with that state of mind could have undesired consequences. For example, imagine that you walk into a betting shop with no clear preferences for any horse, so you make several bets on the horses running in the next race and give your bets to the bookie behind the window. He looks at them and asks you if you are sure about these bets because they show that whichever horse wins you are certain to lose money. That's called a 'Dutch book', but my Dutch friends call it an 'English book'.

Principle 2: Transitivity of preferences. This is about consequences A, B and C. If you prefer A to B, and B to C, then you should prefer A to C. Sometimes people exhibit intransitivity of their preferences, but it is usually because they use different bases for comparison for each pair. Imagine you are looking at a restaurant menu and have narrowed down the alternatives to three specials, each of which is three courses. You might prefer A to B for their main dish, B to C for the dessert, and C to A for the price. Best to balance all three characteristics in making the comparisons. Failure to do so could result in an unscrupulous restaurant making a money pump out of you. They could offer C for free, but since you prefer B to C, they ask you to pay £1 to trade C for B. Then they offer A as a trade for B by paying another £1. Then, since your preferences are intransitive, you prefer C to A, and they ask you for another £1 to trade A for C. You're back where you started, they are £3 richer, and with another few rounds they have made you into a money pump.

Principle 3: Dominance. Back to acts A and B. If all the consequences of A are at least as good as the consequences for B, and at least one consequence of A is better, then choose A. Imagine you have narrowed the choice of a new car to just two alternatives, A and B. A General Motors senior salesman once told me that all their salesmen are trained to use the acronym SPACER, which stands for a car's Safety, Performance, Appearance, Comfort, Economy and Reliability, in chatting to a potential buyer so they can determine which characteristics to emphasise in their sales pitch. If you use the acronym and see that the cars A and B are identical on all those characteristics, except that car A's comfort feels better, than choose car A (provided that the SPACER criteria are your basis for deciding among A and B, but if not, this principle should apply to whatever criteria you apply).

Principle 4: Sure-thing (as Savage named it). In thinking about choosing to purchase a house in a new city, you might consider whether its citizens generally support conservative or liberal candidates. You ask yourself if you would choose the house if you knew it were a conservative city, and decide you would buy the house. You then ask yourself if you knew it were a liberal city, and again decide you would buy the house. Knowing that the political slant of the city wouldn't affect your choice, you recognise that you would buy whatever the political leaning might be. Formally, your choice between either X or Y would be unaffected whatever the outcome of uncertain event E. Whereas Principle 3 applies to consequences, this principle is about courses of action.

By themselves, these principles usually won't be of much help for anyone wanting to make coherent decisions. Mathematicians call these principles 'axioms' and they apply logic to the axioms to prove 'theorems'. And the theorems are indeed useful:

1. **Probabilities exist**. That is, the choice of an option is in part characterised by numbers between 0 and 1 which obey the laws normally associated with probabilities, such as, if an event's probability of occurring is judged to be p, then its probability of not occurring must be 1 − p. Savage called these numbers personal probabilities and they are often referred to as subjective probabilities, though Bayesian statisticians who typically believe that all probabilities are subjective just refer to these numbers as *probabilities*.

2. **Utilities exist**. The choice of an option involves another set of numbers, called *utilities*, which are defined to multiply by probabilities. Each of these numbers represents the utility, u, or in everyday language, the worth or desirability of a consequence.

These two theorems are called 'existence theorems' for they prove that two sets of numbers underlie coherent preferences. We will see in Chapters 4 and 5 how a simple reference gamble provides a practical measuring device for probabilities and utilities, as well as showing the constructive proof of the two theorems.

Multiplying a utility by a probability creates a probability-weighted utility that represents the worth of a consequence reduced by its probability of occurring. Repeat this calculation for each of the consequences, j, of each option, i, and sum those expected utilities:

$$EU_i = \sum_j p_i u_{ij}$$

3. **Choose the option with the higher expected utility**. After making the expected utility computation for each option, select the option with the highest expected utility.

$$\max_i EU_i$$

As Simon French pointed out in 1994,[17] the above three steps constitute a model that describes the rational decision maker, not necessarily how people actually decide, which has been studied extensively since 1954.[18] The expected utility model is often referred to as a *normative* model because it describes how people *should* decide. But any model is only an approximation, like an architect's model for a proposed building, which leaves out many features of the building to be constructed. At best, decision models only suggest to decision makers what they *could* decide, so I and other decision analysts describe them as *prescriptive*.

As I've already mentioned, some critics have suggested that people don't always obey these principles, so that invalidates decision theory, but that view ignores the two-way logic of the system. Yes, the three principles imply the existence of probabilities and utilities, and they specify how those ingredients should be combined. But it's also true that those three features imply the principles, not uniquely, for there are other sets of principles that logically imply the same three features. Indeed, many others have elegantly elaborated the theory[19] while the applied discipline of decision analysis has remained relatively unchanged. We decision analysts start with the theorems, helping our client to build a model using the three features, and if this is successful, the client's preferences will end up being coherent – at least within the small world of the problem. Inconsistencies between small and grand worlds will be explored at the end of Chapter 4 (and elsewhere).

Now you can see Spinoza's point. Insofar as we wish to help people make coherent decisions, we are compelled by logic to use probabilities, preference values and trade-off weights (described in the next section) as the key elements of any quantitative model for making a choice. You can proceed as an analyst with the confidence that these quantities in modelling decisions to create a better future will be useful.

From Decision Theory to Decision Analysis

Surprisingly, it was a classical historian and Greek scholar who first published decision theory as an applied discipline for business decisions, although he did not know about the works of de Finetti and Savage. Robert Schlaifer (Figure 2.5), a Professor at Harvard University, bridged the gap between theory and practice in his 1959 book, *Probability and Statistics for Business Decisions*.[20] He learned the mathematics needed for a deep understanding of the theory from a Harvard colleague, Howard Raiffa (Figure 2.6), the Professor of Managerial Economics, who with Duncan Luce, had published in 1957 *Games and Decisions*, which explored decision theory concepts and their relevance to conflicts of interest.

Figure 2.5

Figure 2.6

Raiffa and Schlaifer worked together in writing *Applied Statistical Decision Theory*,[21] which was published in 1961, shortly after I had started my post-graduate work at the University of Michigan. It is a formidable read, because most of it is about Bayesian statistics, which was then new to me, and it included only a couple of case studies with their associated decision trees.

In the 1960s, Raiffa, Schlaifer and other staff, along with many post-graduate students, created an impressive array of textbooks, case studies and computer programs.[22] Two books stand out for me: Raiffa's 1968 *Decision Analysis*, and Schlaifer's 1969 *Analysis of Decisions under Uncertainty*.[23] I first found and read the latter book, cover to cover, captivated by the way Schlaifer had turned a rather mathematical and abstract theory into something that could be practical, which appealed to my undergraduate study of electrical engineering. My hunch was confirmed on reading Raiffa's more digestible book, which I only discovered shortly after I had devoured Schlaifer's.[24]

Figure 2.7

One effect of Raiffa's book was the widespread adoption of 'decision analysis' as the name for the applied use of decision theory. Many decision analysts point to Professor Ron Howard's (Figure 2.7) earlier 1966 paper, 'Decision analysis: applied decision theory',[25] which applied a systems analysis approach to decision theory, as the person who introduced the term, although he confirmed at the 50th Anniversary Meeting of the Decision Analysis Society that he and Howard Raiffa had jointly agreed the new name.[26]

Apparently, neither had been aware of Kepner and Tregoe's 1965 book, *The Rational Manager*,[27] whose chapter 10, entitled 'Decision Analysis', set out seven 'basic concepts of decision making', similar to the 10 ingredients I introduced in Table 1.1. Their focus was on multiple objectives, including 10-point scoring of consequences, 10-point weighting of objectives and sums of weighted scores as guides to action. Probabilities were used as a risk analysis of potential problems to stimulate thought about contingent actions or multiplied by the scores of possible adverse consequences and summed to provide a risk index of overall seriousness for each course of action. Not quite a full Raiffa decision analysis, but moderately close.

There are no references to decision theory, not even in their 1981 book, *The New Rational Manager*,[28] which again used the term decision analysis for the process of reaching a decision. Nor do any decision analysts reference Kepner-Tregoe. Perhaps the zeitgeist of the 1960s stimulated them, Kepner, a social psychologist, and Tregoe, a sociologist, as it did Raiffa, a mathematician, Schlaifer, a historian, and Howard, an electrical engineer. Decisions are ubiquitous, whatever your discipline. Thus, Kepner-Tregoe training courses continue worldwide, while Raiffa-Schlaifer decision analysis is taught in colleges and universities, where it is positioned as a social science or as a technical approach like engineering, or a combination of both, a socio-technical discipline, which is the stance of the book you are holding.

In the 1960s and 1970s, the focus in decision analysis was on uncertain, financial consequences, with decision trees inhabited by probabilities and partial cash flows on its branches, and sums of the cash flows as terminal values at the end consequences. Decision trees began with decisions, defined as irrevocable commitments to spend

Figure 2.8

money, irrevocable in the sense that if you changed your mind, you would have to spend more money to change direction, another decision. Initially, it was the business community that found decision analysis useful, as Rex Brown (who gained his PhD at the Harvard Business School during the heady years of the 1960s), reported in 1970 and again, with Jake Ulvila in 1982, in two Harvard Business Review articles.[29]

Although the initial positioning of decision analysis by Raiffa and Schlaifer focused on managing uncertainty, Raiffa acknowledged in his 1968 book that multiple attributes could also be accommodated in decision theory, although he devoted only nine pages of the book to give an impression of how this could be done. In the summer of 1968, he was invited to collaborate with the Rand Corporation, where he wrote a new report, *Preferences for Multi-Attributed Alternatives*.[30] He later worked with his PhD student, Ralph Keeney (Figure 2.8), in writing the definitive 1976 book, *Decisions with Multiple Objectives: Preferences and Value Tradeoffs*.[31]

The 1993 Cambridge edition added additional material for modelling values based on strength of preferences between consequences, including the logical system of axioms and proofs that defined a fourth equation that describes coherence:

4. **Calculate weighted utility**. The utility for every option-consequence under a given criterion, u_{ijk}, is multiplied by a weight for each criterion, k, and summed over all the criteria:

$$u_{ij} = \sum_k w_k u_{ijk}$$

The 1993 edition effectively completed the theory underlying decision analysis and includes many examples of applications. Uncertainty and multiple criteria both reside under the heading of decision analysis, as the authors stated in the Preface:

When a decision involves multiple objectives – and this is almost always the case with important problems – multiattribute utility theory forms the basic foundation for applying decision analysis.

The definition of utility as the strength of preference for one consequence over another consequence helpfully distinguishes it from beliefs based on probabilities. Thus, from this point onwards, I'll refer to the strength-of-preference number as a preference value. The basis for judging the strength of preference could be data or it could be a judgement about the extent to which the consequence achieves an objective, as I did in the table of 10 ingredients. That definition is valid provided some reasonable conditions of independence, explained in 1979 by Dyer and Sarin,[32] are met.

The historical separation of decision analysis for modelling uncertainty (Raiffa and Schlaifer) from modelling multiple objectives (Keeney and Raiffa) has created two schools of the same discipline. I belong to a broad church that believes in exploring my client's perception of a gap between where they are now and where they would like to be, so I can see whether modelling preference value or modelling uncertainty, or a bit of both, would be the best path towards reducing or eliminating the gap.

Requisite Decision Models

Once a model is created, its function is to provide the decision maker with the means for exploring possible scenarios about the future. The Latin root of 'model' as a noun means 'small measure', so a model is simpler than the to-be-created reality, usually in any or all of three ways: (1) less important features are omitted; (2) complex relationships are approximated; and (3) some distinctions are blurred. The model should be sufficient in structure and content to resolve the issues that motivated the model's construction; that is, the definition of a *requisite* model.[33] And the criterion for recognising that a model has become requisite is this: the original sense of unease expressed by the problem owners has dissipated, and no new intuitions have arisen after the model's results have been explored. This notion of a requisite decision model is used throughout the book. For more detail, see the section 'Requisite Decision Models' in Chapter 7.

Today, there are many approaches claimed by their proponents to be decision analysis, often developed out of experience with poor decision making, as was the case for Kepner-Tregoe. As useful as some have proved to be, they are based on ad hoc methods that are not grounded in decision theory. As a result, they can give results that violate the principles of consistency and could give misleading results,[34] without anyone realising. I feel more comfortable knowing that whatever help I give my client is sufficiently robust and valid that it would stand up in a court of enquiry, as has been demonstrated in both the US and UK.[35]

Summary

The history of decision theory and decision analysis showed that the three key ingredients, preference values, trade-off weights and probabilities, are the logical consequences of coherent preferences, so a decision analyst can feel confident that those are the right ingredients for helping a decision maker whose preferences are not yet well formed, labile or even contradictory. The modelling process stimulates deeper thought about the problem, helps to direct the search for data, and makes explicit the decision maker's intuition and gut feelings. Different assumptions and points of view can be explored to the point where the decision maker's preferences are sufficiently clear and coherent that the sense of unease has evaporated. At that point, a requisite model has been created, providing clarity for the decision maker and commitment of the key players to the way forward.

3   The Language of Numbers

> When you can measure what you are speaking about, and express it in numbers, you know
> something about it; but when you cannot measure it, when you cannot express it in numbers,
> your knowledge is of a meagre and unsatisfactory kind.
>
> Lord Kelvin (William Thompson), 1883[36]

We learned in the last chapter that three numbers are required for a model based on decision theory. They are most usefully thought of as applying to the consequences of decisions: *preference values*, the extent to which consequences realise your objectives; *trade-offs*, the extent to which more on one value can be balanced by less on another; and *probabilities*, your degrees of belief about the likelihoods of the consequences, calculated by multiplying individual event probabilities along each path of a decision tree. Before those key ingredients are discussed in the next three chapters, it will be important to consider what the numbers represent, for not all characteristics of numbers are also true of the things they represent. If four tennis professionals are to play a doubles match and their relative ranks are 1, 2, 3 and 4, the team of players 1 and 4 isn't necessarily an even match against the team of 2 and 3, even though each team's average rank is the same, 2.5.

Occasionally, a newspaper will report that the day's temperature is twice that of the same day in the previous year. Does that ratio of two numbers, each representing the day's maximum temperature, also correspond to something real about temperature? Here's a simple way to find out. Suppose the temperatures today and a year ago today were 30 and 15 degrees Celsius. Now convert them to Fahrenheit (you can do it with this simple algorithm: double the temperature, subtract 10 per cent of that number from the doubled temperature, and add 32): 86°F and 59°F. Ah, those are not in a ratio of 2 to 1. Why? Because their zero points of the two systems are different, further complicated because their units are unequal; it takes 9 Fahrenheit units to equal 5 Celsius units. So, ratios of the numbers representing temperatures taken from either of those scales don't represent ratios of temperature.

Furthermore, because the units are not equal, decisions taken assuming the wrong scale could have unforeseen consequences, as a friend who lives in Nevada visiting me one September in London discovered after he arrived, with a suitcase full of winter clothes, that the average temperature of 20° he had been told by his travel agent represented Celsius not Fahrenheit temperature, which is 68°. On a more serious note, NASA estimated that the loss of the Mars climate orbiter in 1998, at an estimated cost of $125 million, was caused by a confusion of mathematical units in teams working on the orbiter. One used imperial units, inches and feet, while another team used metric units, and nobody noticed that different scales were being applied.

We need to be consistent in decision analysis models and be clear about the extent to which we can sensibly interpret the results of combing numerical measurements of preference value, trade-offs and probabilities. This chapter clarifies the features of numbers that act as measures of these three key ingredients, thereby ensuring that the interpretations of model results are meaningful.

As the tennis teams example illustrates, averaging ranks can be misleading. Ratios of temperature measured on Celsius or Fahrenheit scales don't make sense. Combining scales with different units is bad practice. Not everything we can say about numbers is also true of what the numbers represent. As Magritte's subtitle on his painting of a pipe says, *Ceci n'est pas une pipe*. And Figure 3.1 shows a photograph I took many years ago of a sign identifying a former gold mining town in the US state of Colorado. The town was established in 1859, its elevation is 8,463 feet above sea level, and its population then was 118. The total doesn't mean anything at all!

In general, measurement is not just a process of attaching numbers to whatever we are measuring: it is also the process of establishing the correspondence between a property of the world and a number system. Let's now consider how that correspondence can be established, and see how it is applied in decision modelling, so it is possible to ensure that numbers are interpreted and used meaningfully.

Figure 3.1

Establishing Meaningful Measurements

To establish the correspondence between properties and numbers, four questions require answers.[37]

1. *Representation*: Can the property be represented by some system of numbers?
2. *Uniqueness*: How free are we in assigning numbers?
3. *Scaling*: What scale will make it possible to take measurements?
4. *Meaningfulness*: What statements about the numbers are also true of the properties?

The axiom systems in decision theory are based on judgements of preference, which is, of course, a subjective concept. Thus, the three quantities that are logically implied by the axioms represent an ideal state of mind, not necessarily how real people think about decisions. Those three quantities represent the properties of an ideal decision maker's preferences, so let's see how the properties stack up to the above four requirements.

Representation

A necessary condition for the three key ingredients is the transitivity relationship for preferences we met in Chapter 2: if A is preferred to B, and B is preferred to C, then A must be preferred to C. Failure of transitivity indicates that there is no system of numbers for the property. A moment's thought shows that transitivity also holds for probabilities (if A is more probable than B, and B is more probable than C, then A must be more probable than C). The same is true for preference values (if C is more valued than B, and B is more valued than A, then C must be more valued than A). Note that the above sentences about A, B and C can all be true, which would imply that it must be the combination of values weighted with probabilities that makes the first sentence true.

Finally, larger trade-off weights always represent greater differences in relative importance. So, a tick for all three. (Consider the relationship 'loves': If A loves B, and B loves C, A doesn't necessarily love C. Love isn't transitive. Thought for the day.)

Uniqueness

Probabilities must obey the laws of probability, basically the multiplication and addition laws presented in Chapter 6. Preference values can take on any values, negative and/or positive, with larger numbers representing more desirability and negative numbers for undesirability, although there are practical limitations, as described next. Trade-off weights uniquely express the magnitude of differences that matter, so they are always positive numbers. Another tick for the three.

Scaling

Probabilities are numbers between 0 and 1.0, inclusive, with zero meaning 'no way' and 1 indicating 'for sure'; numbers less than 0 or greater than 1 are not allowed.

Preference values may also range from 0 to 1, but could take on any values, as in a Celsius scale. Sometimes zero is defined as 'least preferred' and 100 as 'most preferred', as I did for the blind problem. Other approaches are also possible depending on the context. For example, the lowest point on a scale might be defined as 'least acceptable', which would lead the decision maker to reject any option that fell below on that criterion because no trade-off could be made. The highest point might then be described as 'most technically feasible' to represent an option not yet considered but at least in theory possible. Regardless of how the two points are chosen for preference values, the reference points should be close enough to include all existing and feasible options, for if they are unrealistically too far apart, it will be impossible to judge trade-off weights because the assessors will be confronted with ranges that are unimaginable.

Weights for the scales are eventually expressed as decimal numbers that sum to one across all the scales for a particular model, whatever method is used for assessing them.

Meaningfulness

In decision theory, probability is considered as a measure of a person's degrees of belief. The belief could be about facts or events from the past, present or imagined future. Turning that sense of uncertainty into a probability is an act of creation, aided by effective methods for eliciting the numbers, as discussed in Chapter 6.

What do the numbers say about your experience of uncertainty? We can agree that larger numbers mean less uncertainty; 0.8 represents twice the certainty of 0.4, but being twice as certain as 0.8 is impossible. Or is it? Instead of numbers between 0 and 1, let's translate the probabilities into mathematical odds (which are different from betting odds) by calculating the ratio, $p/(1 - p)$, $0.8/0.2 = 4$. If you now learned something that led you to increase your probability from 0.8 to 0.9, the odds would become $0.9/0.1 = 9$. The odds have more than doubled.

Here's another way to think about probability, often mentioned by the founders of decision theory. A probability of 0.8 means you should be willing to bet 0.8 to receive a unit in return; for example, bet $8 to receive $10, if the uncertain event occurs (or $80 to receive $100, and so forth for any amounts).

Which set of numbers, probabilities, odds or bets makes more sense to you as representing your uncertainty about something? Chapter 6 explains a method for assessing a probability that applies to both repeated or unique events and requires only judgements of preference.

Next, consider the meaning of preference values, defined as the strength of preference for one consequence over another. PV scales are defined uniquely for each criterion. Two types of scales are typically used for scaling preference values, ratio and interval, and the relationship between preference values and the numbers representing them is different.

You encountered interval scales in the blind problem. The best and worst consequences on each criterion defined the 100 and 0 positions. Thus, each scale consisted of 100 units, and each unit represented the same strength-of-preference value, so the difference in value from 0 to 10 was the same as 90 to 100. Whatever the size of the interval, the equality of the intervals along the scale is a defining characteristic of this type of scale, which is often referred to as an 'equal-interval scale'.

In practice, differences between the preferences values of any two consequences can meaningfully be compared to the difference between any other two consequences. Thus, if consequences A, B and C are scored at 0, 80 and 100, respectively, then the difference in preference values between A and B is four times as great as the difference between B and C. But it would be incorrect to claim that B is 80 per cent of the value of C. Ratio statements about interval-scale numbers do not represent ratios of values, as was illustrated above with Celsius and Fahrenheit temperature, both of which are interval scales (economists often call them *cardinal* scales).

However, sometimes the zero point describes a true 'no value' consequence. With 100 assigned to the best consequence, or any other desirable consequence, this scale is referred to as a *ratio scale*. Like the interval scale, all the increments on a ratio scale of preference values are equal, but now it is possible for ratios of numbers to represent ratios of preference values. For example, if options are drugs for pain relief, then the zero point on the criterion 'extent to which pain is reduced in two hours' means the drug didn't have any effect at all. The 100 position might represent complete relief from pain. Then a drug scoring 80 indicates that its pain relief is experienced as 80 per cent as good as no pain at all.

Finally, we turn to the meaning of trade-off weights. We saw in the blind problem that swing weights were assessed by asking the question, 'How big is the difference between worst and best positions on this scale, and how much do you care about it?' as compared to the same question about another scale. The first part of the question focused on the real-world difference, the second part on the importance of the difference. Thus, a swing weight meaningfully captures both an objective difference and a subjective judgement about the importance of that difference.

Note that a swing weight does not mean just the importance of the criterion. If all the options realise nearly the same preference values on an important criterion, then that small difference requires a small swing weight. It's also possible for a very large swing on a less important criterion to receive a large swing weight.

The most important point about swing weights is that they are scale constants: they equate the units of measurement from one scale to the next, making it possible to add weighted averages and provide an overall weighted preference value index for each option. The logic is a variation on Savage's sure-thing principle. If on one criterion, all options have identical scores, then the weight is zero, so the scores would be multiplied by zero and thus make no contribution to the final weighted scores for the options. That's OK because whichever option you choose, you will obtain the value from the zero-weighed criterion; giving a criterion in a model no weight doesn't mean you will fail to receive the value on that criterion. The model's purpose is to discriminate the options, and differences between the options' indexes allow you to see the *relative* values of the options, not the actual values you will eventually realise by choosing one option.

This variation of the sure-thing principle shows that simply assessing the 'importance' of each criterion does not provide a proper scale constant. Swing-weighting does. Relying simply on importance without taking account of the differences between reference points could easily result in a model whose final results are like mixing Fahrenheit and Celsius measurements within a single project.

This last feature of numbers, meaningfulness, is the most important characteristic of a numbering system. It is a wise decision analyst who keeps that in mind when interpreting the outputs of a model.

Validity, Reliability and Precision

Throughout the rest of the book, I will periodically invoke the three characteristics of all numbers if they are to be used to assist decision making. As an experimental psychologist, I am aware that any characteristics we measure must be valid and reliable, and as a discipline we have developed many approaches to testing the degree of validity and reliability. A valid measure is one that actually measures what it is purported to measure, which can be established by correlating a new measure with others that claim the same for their measure. Reliability is the consistency with which the same number appears on retesting. A measure can be reliable even if it isn't valid, but it would be difficult or impossible to establish validity if the measure was unreliable. Finally, as an engineer, I am concerned to establish the precision of any measurements.

To illustrate these concepts, imagine stepping on a scale to see how much you weigh. My bathroom scale is the old type with a pointer that only displays my weight to the nearest pound, but the scale at my gym is electronic and displays the weight to one-tenth of a pound. That's precision. When I step off either scale, then back on again, my bathroom scale might give me a reading that is one pound more or less than the previous result, but the gym scale will only vary by about a tenth of a pound. That's reliability. Every now and then after dusting my bathroom scale, it gives me an entirely different weight because I accidentally moved the reset dial away from zero when the scale was just sitting on the floor. Its precision and reliability were unaffected, but its results were not valid because it wasn't calibrated properly.

In summary, it's important to understand what the numbers can and can't tell us about the properties being measured. For interval scales, ratios of differences in preference values are meaningful, while for ratio scales, ratios of differences *and* of preference values are properly interpretable about the property being measured. Swing-weighting ensures the comparability of units across all criteria, thereby legitimising any model in which weighted preference values are summed. And we need sufficient validity, reliability and precision in all inputs to ensure we're entering meaningful numbers in our decision models. Good enough quality in, good decision quality out.

Figure 3.2

Interpreting Numbers

What do quantitative models based on expected utility represent? Economists have constructed economic theories based on the presumption that we as consumers make choices that are consistent with expected utility, or that collectively we act as expected utility maximisers. This positions expected utility as a *normative* model, a standard describing how choices are made with full and perfect information, and reasoning that is rational in putting the information together to find the optimal choice, the one with the highest expected utility.[38]

In 1954, Ward Edwards (Figure 3.2), fresh from Harvard with a PhD in psychology, published a seminal paper in the journal *Psychological Bulletin*, that asked whether in their day-to-day choices people actually do maximise expected utility.[39] That paper, the first to review the psychology literature on decision making, stimulated so many studies that in 1961 Edwards, then a professor at the University of Michigan, proposed a new discipline, which he named Behavioral Decision Theory,[40] the study of how people *actually* make decisions. In 1967, Edwards and Amos Tversky, who had received his PhD at the University of Michigan in 1965, co-edited a Penguin Modern Psychology book, *Decision Making*,[41] which included Edwards' 1954 paper along with 14 key research papers describing different aspects of real-world decision making from 1951 to 1967.

Descriptive Models

Models that describe, explain and predict human choice behaviour emerged over the ensuing years, now known as *descriptive* models, and they were often formulated in terms of deviations from the normative model. Daniel Kahneman came to the University of Michigan in 1965 – he had known Tversky at Israel's Hebrew University – and their subsequent collaboration resulted in many papers on human

Table 3.1 Three heuristics and their biases in judging outcomes of uncertain events

Heuristic	Definition	Bias
Representativeness	The degree to which one event resembles another.	Ignores the difference in the likelihoods of the outcomes.
Availability	The ease of recalling instances of similar or identical outcomes.	Ignores the relative frequencies of the outcomes.
Anchoring	Making an estimate by adjusting a starting value.	The judgement up or down is insufficient.

judgement and decision making. Their earliest oft-cited paper appeared in 1974, 'Judgement under uncertainty: heuristics and biases',[42] published by the prestigious journal *Science*. This article described three heuristics (rules-of-thumb), representativeness, availability, and adjustment from an anchor, which people apply when confronted with decisions about an uncertain future, and how these can introduce systematic errors or biases into their judgements (see Table 3.1).

In collaboration with Paul Slovic, who studied under Edwards from 1960, Tversky and Kahneman edited a book (with the same title as the *Science* article; clearly a winning area of cognitive research at the time) published in 1984, whose 35 chapters explored many more heuristics and biases and their effects on decisions in real-world situations.[43] Edwards recounted to me that at a meeting in the early 1980s of 30 behavioural decision analysts, he asked the question, 'How many of you believe that the expected utility model satisfactorily describes actual choice behaviour?' Not a single hand was raised. When he then asked, 'How many of you believe that the expected utility model should be considered as a guiding, normative model?' All the hands went up.

In the meantime, Tversky and Kahneman had begun to publish their research outside psychology, with a focus on economics journals, which brought their research to the attention of economists, one of whom, Richard Thaler, became an early contributor to the emerging field of behavioural economics. He has become a prolific contributor of papers, many co-authored with Tversky or Kahneman.

Sadly, in June 1996, Tversky died of metastatic melanoma, at the age of only 59. Had he lived another six years, he could have become a Nobel laureate in Economic Sciences along with Kahneman, who was awarded the honour in 2002. In his acceptance speech, Kahneman was visibly moved and made clear that his friend and colleague should be standing at the lectern with him. In 2011, he reluctantly wrote a book, *Thinking, Fast and Slow*, concerned that few would read it, but it became a best seller, and remains in print, well worth a read.[44] In 2015, *The Economist* rated Kahneman as the seventh most influential economist in the world, not bad for a psychologist (there is no Nobel prize for psychological science). Thaler described his journey in behavioural economics in his 2015 book, *Misbehaving*, and two years later, he was awarded the Nobel prize in Economics. So, behavioural decision theory and behavioural economics received a stamp of approval, and their message of cognitive deficiencies is now widespread.

But how then does that square with a 1967 paper in the *Psychological Bulletin* by Cameron Peterson and Lee Roy Beach[45] who reviewed experimental research that, like Kahneman and Tversky, compared how people make inferences about uncertain quantities when presented with information about proportions, means, variances and correlations, in both populations and samples? They found that people respond in the direction probability theory and statistics would predict, although not always as radically, and 'that probability theory and statistics can be used as the basis for psychological models that integrate and account for human performance in a wide range of inferential tasks'.[46]

Six years later, Cameron Peterson edited an entire issue of *Organizational Behavior and Human Performance*, which consisted of papers about hierarchical or multi-stage inference. For example, my probability for rain tomorrow depends not just on the probability given by the app on my mobile (cell phone), but also on my experience of the forecast's credibility. That is, two uncertainties are involved: *p(rain|forecast of rain)* and *p(forecast of rain|rain)*, two conditional probabilities, the first a probabilistic prediction, and the second the credibility, expressed as a probability of the prediction, a two-stage inference. Most of us learn from an early age not to believe everything we are told, hear or see, that some sources of data are more credible than others. One finding of these studies was that when the credibility of the source data was taken into account, the observed behaviour of participants came even closer to the normative statistical models than had been found in the Peterson and Beach paper, which were mostly one-stage inference experiments.

The heuristics and biases research relies heavily on descriptive scenarios requiring participants to make probability estimates, statements of preference between uncertain outcomes or choices between alternatives, all single-stage inference problems. I have not read every paper published by Tversky and Kahneman, but of the many I have, there was no reference to the positive view of human performance that emerges from the studies by Peterson, Beach and their colleagues. Further doubt about the cognitive deficit generalisation appears in a recent *Psychological Bulletin* paper, where the authors, Tomás Lejarraga and Ralph Hertwig, distinguish between research using descriptive scenarios as stimuli from situations in which participants engage their learning and experience. They argue that 'the focus on description at the expense of learning has profoundly shaped the influential view of the error-proneness of human cognition'.[47]

Several authors have gone some way towards integrating descriptive and normative models in a way that could help people make better decisions.[48] Somewhere between descriptive models about how people actually decide and normative models of how they should decide, lie *prescriptive* models about how people *could* decide. These models are intended as intellectual tools that enable people to realise their full capability for making requisite decisions, that is, they resolve issues of uncertainty and multiple objectives so the decision maker can see a clear way forward.

The main characteristic of prescriptive and requisite models is that although they include characteristics of the real world as it is now, they also look forward to the future, which Lee Roy Beach suggests is the way decision makers engage their memories,

Figure 3.3

reasoning and imagination, stimulating them to recall relevant past events, focus on the present, and create expectations about the future.[49] It should then be possible to turn the numerical results of the modelling into a coherent narrative about the future that will guide subsequent decisions. The Roman god Janus, one face looking backwards and the other forward, is a convenient metaphor (Figure 3.3). In building a decision model, we look backwards to find relevant data and we look forward using our human ability to express numerically our preference values, uncertainty and trade-offs.

In decision analysis, we are careful to use numbers as a language that will help us to look at our preferences in a way that can't easily be done using words alone. We can put the numbers together and see logical consequences that might not have been obvious just from words alone, a process that helps us to construct coherent preferences. For example, ask a friend who follows tennis to tell you who might win the men's singles at the next Wimbledon, and each time a name is given ask for an assessment of a probability that that person will win. If you write down the probabilities, and your friend can't think of anyone else, ask for a probability that someone not named will win. If you now add all the probabilities, their sum will almost certainly be greater than 100 per cent. Subsequent revisions by your friend may well change the relative ordering of the potential winners, suggesting that your friend's preferences are changing and being updated as new numbers that sum properly are constructed.

Summary

The important take-away from this chapter is that measurement isn't just a process of attaching numbers to our feelings of uncertainty and value: it is ensuring that whatever we say about the numbers is aligned to our feelings. The heuristics and biases research showed that our feelings fell short of the numbers, with the result that some people rejected decision analysis as not doable. However, the experimenters used the numbers properly for the problems they presented to the participants in their research, so it is they, the experimenters, who demonstrated human capability for using numbers well. I recall Professor Dennis Lindley's exasperation, in a meeting of statisticians, economists and psychologists, when he asked why psychologists continue to study biases in people's probability assessments instead of just teaching them to use numbers properly. Our knowing about the world is indeed limited to what we have been taught and learned from experience, and decision analysis modelling extends our abilities to make coherent choices about the future.

Perhaps Lord Kelvin's provocative statement, quoted at the beginning of this chapter, is too strong. Most certainly we know some things, like love, hope, happiness, grief and despair, that are profound. Perhaps if he were with us today, he would agree, but I suggest that what he meant was that numbers are another language that can help us to deepen our understanding of whatever the numbers represent. This is the point of view of the book you are holding. The next three chapters show how our human capability to look forward, imagining, anticipating and planning, by being explicit with probabilities, preference values and trade-offs, can extend our mental capabilities.

4 Preference Values

The determination of the value of an item must not be based on its price, but rather on the utility it yields. The price of the item is dependent only on the thing itself and is equal for everyone; the utility, however, is dependent on the particular circumstances of the person making the estimate. Thus, there is no doubt that a gain of one thousand ducats is more significant to a pauper than to a rich man though both gain the same amount.

Daniel Bernoulli, Swiss mathematician and physicist, 1738

Chapter 2 defined preference value as the extent to which the consequences of a decision maker's actions achieve his or her objectives. In the blind problem, we saw differences in the assessed preference values for the two criteria, personal and family well-being. In a sense, 'well-being' stands for the fundamental objective of staying as healthy as possible.

Fundamental Objectives

Underlying most decision problems is a fundamental objective whose clarification is crucial to building a successful decision model.[50] For example, discussion by a group of UK military officers evaluating the capability of new equipment often centred on the performance characteristics or measurable effectiveness of the equipment as they attempted to judge its military capability. When considering a particular system, one officer asked, 'What if this system provides more capability than I need?' I suggested that it would therefore provide less military value than the full performance characteristics for which it was designed.

That shifted the group's discussion to what was meant by military value, and participants soon agreed it was the extent to which the equipment could help to achieve a mission's objectives. This in turn led to a discussion about the last UK's Strategic Defence and Security Review, which includes the types of missions, worldwide, that may well engage the UK military in the future. Where are the threats to the UK's security and what capabilities will be needed to meet those threats? The UK considers itself a global player, so needs flexibility in responding to a variety of threats, which informs what capabilities it will need. Missions differ between the army, navy and air force, so their mission values will also differ. This is a clear example of how value is affected by context.

In another project, a three-star NATO general was finding it difficult to see the difference between capability and military value. But eventually he realised that his family owned three cars, identical in make, model and year, not different in capability but with substantial differences in the value they provided for the family. His was in constant use ferrying him around to various meetings, his wife's car helped to keep the family home operating well, and the third car for his two adult children enabled them to lead busy lives. Same capability, different value for each member of the family.

Pharmaceutical companies provide a further example. They share the fundamental objective of improving and extending people's lives, but this is interpreted differently by each company's divisions. The research division discovers new compounds, and their fundamental objective might be to maximise the number of new compounds. The development division conducts research to establish the drug's safety and efficacy, and the fundamental objective is to maximise its chances of approval by regulatory authorities. The marketing division's fundamental objective is to maximise revenues from sales of the drug. Each of these divisions will use different criteria to define the way in which they will meet their fundamental objective. The development division, for example, might consider the extent to which the drug meets unmet medical need as one criterion, and the extent to which it complements or replaces other similar drugs already marketed by the company as another criterion.

Once an approved drug is available, the fundamental objective of the prescriber is the drug's clinical value to the patient. And clinical value depends on the extent to which the patient will respond favourably. This means that the prescriber must know something about the patient's medical history, other drugs he or she may be taking, possible co-morbidities and other relevant context issues that might affect the extent to which the patient will respond well to the drug's benefits while minimising risks from unwanted side effects, the two key criteria that constitute clinical value. The prescriber might even engage the patient in a discussion about the trade-off between favourable and unfavourable effects of the drug, the subject of Chapter 5.

These examples exemplify an important characteristic of preference value: it is contingent on context; there is no such thing as absolute value. Note, too, that each objective is best described by the combination of a verb and noun: provide sufficient military capability, improve people's lives, ensure clinical value for a patient.

Means and End Objectives

Fundamental objectives provide direction but are not necessarily helpful in resolving today's decisions. In 1990, I facilitated a decision conference for Sequent Computer Systems, which specialised in high-end computer hardware and software that enabled simultaneous computations to take place in parallel. Although the focus of the meeting was to decide on a new organisational structure that would enable the company to grow, at one point I asked about the group's views on the future for computing, which then was not clear as main-frame and scientific computers were dominant, with desktop computers just becoming more accessible. They explained their '2020

Vision', that by the year 2020, computers would be 'facilitating human interaction'. Of course, in 1990, there were no personal computers, no laptops, no tablets and no smart phones. Facebook and other social media didn't exist. Then, nobody in the group could explain how the vision would be realised, but they agreed that Sequent's choices in the future would be guided by the path more likely to facilitate human interaction.

However, their immediate need was for a new organisational structure that could grow flexibly as they responded to the many opportunities for faster computing. The vision would be retained but was of little relevance to the choice of a new structure for the organisation. This example illustrates a fundamental objective that is the end objective, but that means objectives might be more useful in making a choice now. Achieving an end objective is then easier because it relates directly to the levers, the means objectives, that are under the control of the decision maker. And the consequences of realising means objectives bring forward a changed context that is ready for the creation of a new set of means objectives, still with an eye on the fundamental objective. Yes, winning the game is the fundamental objective, but that is done by scoring more immediate goals (or whatever sports analogy you prefer).

How can a fundamental objective be identified? Here is a conversation I had with a UK politician, who had heard me speak about decision analysis.

> 'That's all very well, but your decision-making ideas aren't going to help me win the next election,' she said.
> I asked, 'Why do you care about winning the election?'
> 'So, I can gain power.'
> 'Why do you care about power?'
> 'To make things better for the people.'
> 'Why do you care about making things better for the people?'
> 'Well ... it's because ... because ... that's what's important, it's what politicians do!'

Her fundamental objective was finally revealed by answering my repeated question, *'Why do you care about ...?'* But the means objective of winning an election was uppermost in her mind.

Many people believe that the fundamental objective of a commercial organisation is to make a profit. When I ask, 'Why does your company care about profit?', the answer is usually along the lines of 'So we can do what we are in business to do', and enquiring about the purpose of the business can elicit fundamental objectives like those in the previous section. In commercial organisations that are in business for the long-haul, profit is the *means* for achieving their fundamental objective.[51] Profit requires looking backward; it is a measure of achievement, enabling an organisation to make realistic plans for moving forward. And profit is, of course, required if a company wishes to continue realising its fundamental objective.

So, if profit isn't the fundamental objective, then surely creating shareholder value is. After all, shareholders want a return on their investment, so money must be the fundamental objective. However, reality is more complex. To move forward, companies owe obligations to their customers, employees, suppliers and communities, and if they do these well, they can provide a fair return to their shareholders. Maximising shareholder value became a sacred mantra in the 1980s and 1990s but is now recognised as unrealistic and unbalanced.[52] Indeed, of all the many commercial companies I've worked for, none has applied only a financial criterion in evaluating the consequences of their decisions.

This doesn't mean that looking forward ignores financial criteria. Many commercial companies use net present value (NPV) as one of their objectives. Briefly, NPV is the sum of cash flows (money in minus money out) over any time-period, with cash flows over the time-periods discounted because money is desired earlier rather than later: the higher the discount rate, the more the organisation values positive cash flows now.

For example, if the discount factor is 6 per cent, then a £1,000 positive cash flow in 12 years would be valued today at £500. A simple rule of thumb: divide 72 by the discount rate to find the number of years it would take to halve the same cash flow received then. The rule also shows the number of years at a given interest rate that it would take for an investment to double in value. Most clients have never heard of this rule, and it's a handy way to explain why the accounting department and senior management in their organisation are always harping on about speeding up receipt of positive cash flows. In short, positive cash flows received today are valued today as more than the same amount received later.

Like any forward-looking model, assumptions must be made about the many factors and uncertain events that can influence the positive and negative cash flows, and finance departments help to ensure that the assumptions are consistent across projects in different parts of the organisation. This is crucially important for senior executives who must compare these projects to ensure an appropriate allocation of resources across all of them. But the required information is often simply not there because there are no systems to record expenditure on a project-by-project basis, or no manager is held accountable for obtaining the information, or the organisation lacks the competence to calculate NPVs.

Some organisations outsource these calculations to one of the big consultancy firms, who then send in teams of people who are authorised to monitor and record expenditure and make the necessary computations. Some university business schools require that NPV calculations should be repeated under different assumptions so that decision makers are provided with a range of NPVs rather than just one for a given project. Decision makers who insist on only a single NPV are ignoring uncertainty and at worst encouraging only substantial, positive NPVs. Indeed, I once met a person who had just quit her job at a large consultancy firm because she admitted she had wasted the last six years of her life creating favourable NPVs by lying.

Equally inadequate is to turn the NPV calculation on its head by asking what discount factor would cause the cash flows coming in to be exactly balanced by cash flows out. The answer is known as the internal rate of return (IRR), and I know of one oil and gas company that required an IRR of 8 per cent for all its projects. The managers I was lecturing to at the time admitted they worked hard at finding just the right assumptions to satisfy the 8 per cent, but not so extreme that it would be deemed unrealistic. Occasionally, someone will argue that IRR should be the measure of a project's value. 'So, if project A's IRR is 10 per cent and project B's is 8 per cent, would you prefer A to B?' I ask. The answer is usually yes, with no more questions.

'But A requires an investment of $10 million, whereas B needs only $5 million. Do you still prefer A?' That ends the discussion. As percentages require both a numerator and a denominator, one must be a constant in any model that uses a percentage as a criterion. As argued in Chapter 3, numbers must be meaningful.

Finishing this critique, I would like to point out that I have never been able to find a single paper published in a peer-reviewed journal that establishes the validity of these discounted cash flow (DCF) models. Such a study should track NPVs of all their projects over many periods of time and then calculate an average of any single measure of financial gain they wish to use and look at the correlations with the original NPVs. Several organisations told me they keep track, but they add that it's never really been properly written down.

From a decision-analytic point of view, single financial figures don't adequately represent the values of future consequences. In the blind problem of Chapter 2, it would be unrealistic to assume that the operation would be a success as a basis for choosing. For more complex decisions, a decision tree that includes uncertain events and subsequent actions would lead to many possible consequences, each with its own NPV that is conditional on the outcomes shown on the branches of the tree. Risks would be represented by the probabilities of event outcomes, and the discount factor would be chosen based solely on preferring positive cash flows earlier than later.

In summary, when making decisions about the future, we are not comparing apples with oranges, we are comparing their preference values, but those values are influenced by the context of the decision. As I said in Chapter 1, a Waldorf salad requires apples, not oranges, so only the apples add value to the salad. The fundamental objective describes the aims or purpose to be achieved, whereas the means objectives are associated with the enablers for achieving the fundamental objective. Some combination of means and end objectives are represented in the decision problem by criteria, often referred to as *attributes*, which we turn to next.

Identifying Criteria

Chapter 1 defined criteria as the standards by which achievement of the objectives are assessed. Let's now see how the criteria are identified. Once the fundamental objective is clear, the facilitator might ask, 'What could be measured to show that the fundamental objective has been achieved?' Invite your client to construct a list, although it is likely to be rather short,[53] so follow by asking if they have thought of everything, which helps them to dig deeper.

Prompts

One of my colleagues, Stuart Wooler, who used decision-analytic modelling to help middle-level managers choose new careers, found that just asking them for their career objectives often resulted in a shorter list than if he first provided *prompts* of fundamental objectives that he derived from his research, as shown in Figure 4.1.

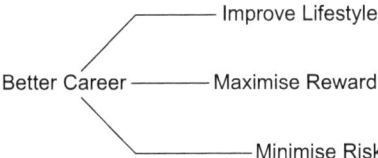

Figure 4.1

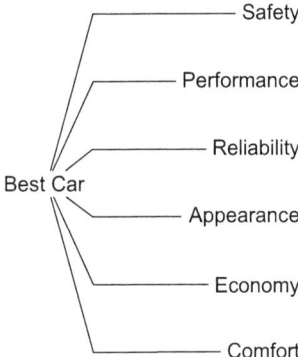

Figure 4.2

He asked each manager what those objectives meant for them, what their goals were and what they wished to achieve, helping them to formulate criteria containing both a verb and a noun, along with a clear definition for each.

Participants in this research found that the *prompts* led them to think more deeply about what they wished to achieve, which enabled them to develop two or more measurable criteria for each of the three objectives.

Sometimes you already know from experience what the criteria are, as for choosing a car. Figure 4.2 shows six characteristics of cars that one major company taught to all its salespersons, represented as a *value tree*.

The six criteria serve as *prompts* for the salesperson who attends to what the customer might want or could be suggested as worthy of consideration. A car dealer's salesperson will first ask what sort of car the buyer is seeking – size, SUV, sports car, people-mover, type of engine, etc. This editing phase reduces the number of options by eliminating the obvious non-runners; in behavioural decision theory, this initial process in decision making is called 'elimination by aspects', or EBA, and is something we may do as consumers before making an important purchase.

However, as a decision analyst you might start by asking questions about your client's fundamental objectives, which could begin with a question, 'What makes it difficult to take a decision?' 'Why are you feeling uneasy about this problem?' Or even, 'Tell me more about why you want a car.' Anything to explore your client's sense of inner conflict, for it can reveal a key trade-off between opposing 'wants', such as for a commercial company, more benefit and less cost for developing innovative products, or for a government, less environmental impact and less cost for managing radioactive waste, or for a health-care provider, more benefit and less risk in approving and prescribing new drugs.

In considering what car to purchase, applying EBA may reveal the trade-off. We start by thinking about what we can afford and eliminate anything above a certain upper limit, so the implied trade-off is between maximising benefit while minimising cost. And cost might be just the purchase price, leaving the definition of economy, shown in Figure 4.2, as 'running costs'.

The Kepner-Tregoe approach to decision making distinguishes between *want* and *need* objectives, which separates what one would like to achieve from what is absolutely required, a useful distinction to be kept in mind when a client insists that a particular achievement level must be obtained on an objective, which may unrealistically restrict any trade-off with other objectives.

Maslow's hierarchy of *psychological needs* shows the variety of objectives that motivate humans to pursue their objectives, from basic physical needs like satisfying hunger and safety, to more subjective personal needs such as aesthetic needs and self-actualisation. That hierarchy might provide prompts when working with an individual client. If working with clients from an organisation, exploring the meaning of their vision or mission statements may serve as prompts that will call to mind objectives that participants have taken for granted and not yet expressed.

Figure 4.3 shows part of a more complex value tree for comparing the benefit-safety balance of pain-killer drugs that can be purchased without a prescription. This model was created by a team of experts and pain clinicians to compare different analgesics.[54] Of course, the purpose of such drugs is to reduce or minimise pain, but as all drugs exhibit both favourable and unfavourable effects, it would be prudent to look at all the effects before taking the medicine (especially the side effects, which we will look at when we further explore this study shortly and again in Chapter 5). In Figure 4.3, we see two other benefits: how long the pain-killing effect lasts and how quickly it will start to work.

Defining the criteria ensures clarity about what the numbers represent. A definition you might expect as a user of a drug isn't necessarily the way the medical profession defines it for the purposes of research. You can see this in the definitions given by the experts:

- **Pain relief**: Proportion of patients suffering moderate to severe pain who individually report pain intensity reduction by 50 per cent or more.
- **Duration of action**: Average time to re-medication for 50 per cent of patients.
- **Speed of onset**: Average time to perceptible pain relief.

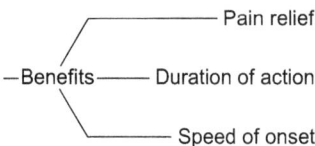

Figure 4.3

These definitions are appropriate for the population of users, and medical professionals are particularly enamoured of medians for measures of effectiveness.

Whatever the discipline, the objective for defining criteria is to establish *operational measures*, namely, clear, verifiable, empirical methods for obtaining numbers representing a phenomenon which often can't be measured directly. An example is temperature; when we measure it using a thermometer, we are actually measuring the length of a liquid in a glass tube.

Method of Triads

This approach is useful when options are available, perhaps after an EBA process has eliminated the unacceptable options but many remain, and your client is wondering how to proceed. The method is based on personal construct theory, which is about an individual's way of understanding the world, created by the psychologist George A. Kelly.[55] He developed a method for eliciting the key dimensions, or *constructs*, that are the basis for a person's impressions of other people. His method for finding those constructs is to ask the person to write down names of different people, like father, mother, best friend, boss, neighbour, etc. He would then invite the person to find a way in which two people on the list are different from a third person in a way that matters, then ask how it mattered A response might be that two were more friendly, in contrast to the third who is rather unfriendly, or that two are very intelligent, while the other was less so.

In the late 1970s, my colleagues Patrick Humphreys and Ayleen Wisudha applied this approach when programming what I believe was the first computer-based model for interactively creating a multi-criteria decision analysis (MCDA) model, MAUD (Multi Attribute Utility Decomposition).[56] The program asked the user to type in at least four options, then engaged in an interaction which ensured the homogeneity of the options (the option 'take a year off work' can't be compared with new-job options because the criteria are of different sorts). From a list of the same kinds of options, the computer then randomly selected and displayed three of them and asked, 'Are two of these similar to each other but different from the third in a way that matters?' If so, the computer invited the user to provide a description of the difference, which at least gave a name that could be developed as a criterion for an MCDA model. Repeating the process with different triads sometimes led the user to think of a new option. It didn't take long to identify a complete set of criteria. This is especially useful when you are working with a single client, but I've also used it in a group setting.

Comparing Options

If a group has first identified several options, then the following approach, which I learned from Cam Peterson, quickly enables a group to formulate criteria. On a flipchart, white board or projected Excel sheet, make a vertical list of options. Label the heads of columns to the right with the names or initials of the participants, as shown in Figure 4.4, for any number of participants.

	Options	Joe	Mary	Helen	Matt	etc.
1	[Short name]					
2	[Short name]					
:	[Short name]					
:	[Short name]					
N	[Short name]					

Figure 4.4

Now proceed as follows:

1. Ask the participants to write a column of numbers from 1 to N on a piece of paper.
2. Next, instruct each person to individually think about all the options, without discussion, and decide for themselves which one they feel is best and which is worst.
3. Then, instruct them to write 100 on their own list next to the best option and 0 next to the worst option.
4. Now, write numbers between 0 and 100 (ties are OK) for each of the remaining options, such that differences between numbers make sense in terms of how close or far away they are from the 0 and 100 and each other. Doing this individually engages everyone, whereas collectively often favours the extroverts in the group.
5. When everyone has finished, ask each person for their numbers, and record them on the display. That will create a buzz as participants discover how different or similar their numbers are, which will be useful in the next step.
6. With the whole group attending, scan each row noting the extent of differences between the numbers. Ask individuals for reasons associated with the lowest and highest numbers. Record those differences, using green for positive and red for negative reasons.
7. Once all the rows have been scanned and differences discussed, work with the group to convert the positive and negative reasons into criteria.

A major advantage of this approach in a group is that it prevents any one person from dominating the discussion, and everyone gets a chance to contribute. At the end of the decision conference, I often ask participants to compare their initial ordering of the options with the ordering now agreed in light of the modelling and discussion. Without this initial expression, it sometimes happens that at the end of the meeting one or more people might say it was all obvious from the start, which for some participants is a way for them to deny they have learned from the whole process.

Other Approaches

Most facilitators try out different methods for eliciting objectives and criteria and choose what they feel is most likely to work with the individual or group. Some use large Post-It notes written by individuals and stuck on a whiteboard or flipcharts. Rearranging the notes into clusters of similar criteria around individual objectives is useful for creating MCDA models like those presented in Chapter 13. Sometimes, break-out groups can be given the same or different tasks, then reassembled to report their agreed objectives or criteria. The revealed diversity of opinions and judgements feeds the group's deliberative discourse, creating new insights which move the group towards agreement as the feedback from sensitivity analyses in the model show that many disagreements don't matter to the form and content of a final model to which all could subscribe.

Structuring Criteria

Once the objectives and criteria have been identified and defined with verbs and nouns, it is useful to structure these as a hierarchal *value tree* which shows the criteria conditional on the objectives. Figure 4.5 shows the full model that compared over-the-counter pain-killer drugs.

This value tree represents the benefit-safety balance for each of six drugs, ibuprofen (fast-acting), naproxen, ibuprofen, diclofenac, paracetamol and aspirin (those are the

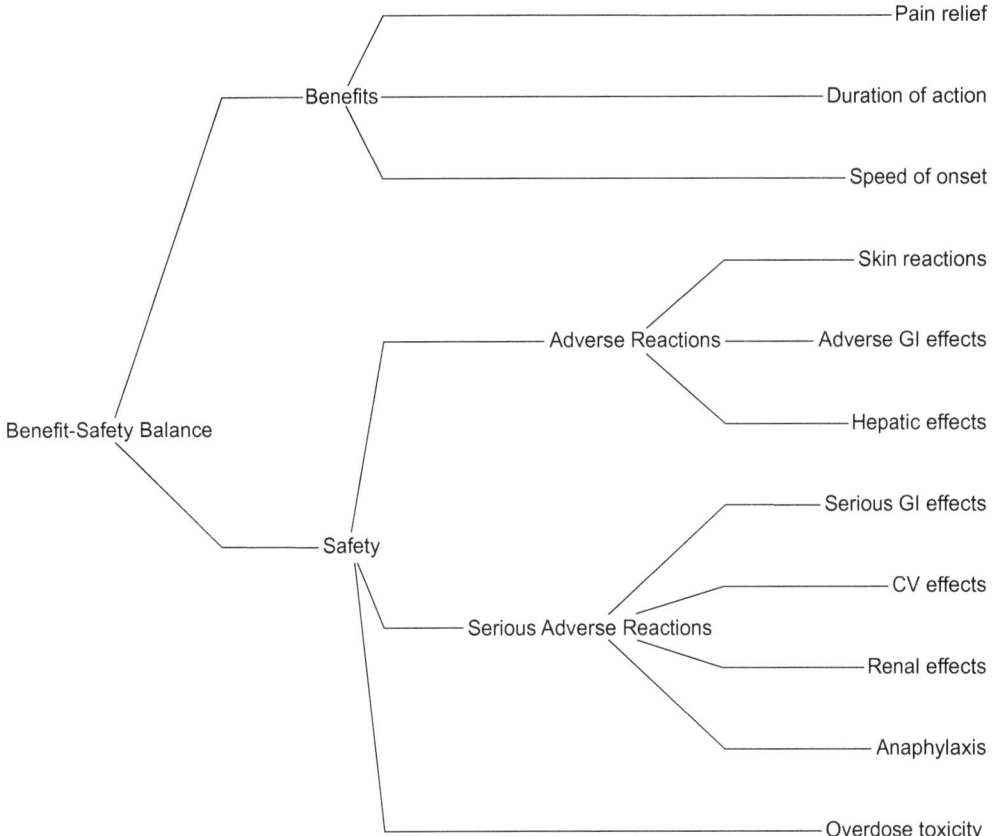

Figure 4.5

generic names; the trade names are often different from one country to the next). The fundamental objective is to provide benefits safely, which invokes two sub-objectives, maximising benefits and safety (usually defined as minimising side effects). Three criteria define the benefits, the extent of pain relief, how long the pain will be relieved and how quickly the drug will start to work. Possible side effects, typically considered as risks, are divided into those creating mild adverse reactions that can be managed, and serious ones requiring hospitalisation. Overdose toxicity (the potential for accidental or deliberate overdose) is a final risk criterion. (CV and GI stand for cardiovascular and gastro-intestinal. Short names and abbreviations, well known to the experts, enhance readability of the value tree.)

For drugs, favourable effects provide benefit value, while unfavourable effects create dis-value. Converting the latter to safety is simply a matter of applying an inverse preference function to the input (easily done with software such as Hiview3, p. 227), so lower levels of unfavourable effects are associated with more safety. Weighting the criteria ensures that the units of benefit and safety are equivalent so they can be added.

Note that the value tree, unlike a decision tree, doesn't show any options. These are at some point asked for by the software so it can receive input evaluations associated with the options for each of the 11 criteria.

As criteria are created, the facilitator keeps in mind the following five conditions of a good set of criteria and how you might help the group to ensure these requirements are met:

1. **Comprehensive**: Do the definitions of the criteria capture all the main reasons for differences that matter among the consequences? First impressions about the advantages and disadvantages of the consequences often lead to a short list of criteria. Help your client to expand the list and increase the depth and breadth of the criteria.[57]

2. **Communicable**: Are the definitions stated in clear, non-technical language, sufficient for any interested person to understand the concerns represented by each criterion? If your client says that the proffered definition will be understood by everyone in their discipline, ask them for a non-technical definition. This will likely lead to disagreements, further discussion and an attempt to formulate a definition that can be agreed.

3. **Non-redundant**: Are the concerns unique to each criterion, namely, they don't overlap with other criteria, or say the same thing in two different ways, or in any way double-count concerns expressed in other criteria?

4. **Requisite in number**: Are criteria sufficient in number (no more and no less to make a difference to the decision) for expressing all the key concerns about the consequences? At the start of modelling, it may be necessary to be over-inclusive, with later discussion and sensitivity analyses showing which criteria don't have any important effect on the final results of the model. Even so, it may be necessary to include irrelevant criteria to show that they were considered and don't matter to the decision.

5. **Mutual preference independence**: Is the preference order of consequences on one criterion unaffected by the order on any other criterion, and vice versa? *Any* summing of weighted preference values requires this condition, which is weaker than statistical independence. It is common for statistical correlations to occur among the preference values, but if a statistical correlation between two criteria appears to be very high, then either the criteria must be redefined to satisfy this condition, or a more complex decision theory model adopted. You may discover a violation of this condition if, when participants are scoring the options on one criterion, they ask to see the scores that were given on a different criterion. That makes clear that scores on the current criterion being considered would be different if the scores on the related criterion were high than if they were low. You might then ask if these two criteria are truly preference independent. Ask, 'How might your preferences on this criterion be affected by either high or low scores on the other criterion?' If they say it wouldn't make any difference at all, then you can safely conclude that preference independence holds. Otherwise, it fails, and you would then redefine either or both criteria to ensure preference independence. If that proves impossible, then the more complex equations of multi-attribute decision theory could be applied, but that usually ends in tears because it's too difficult to apply.

Assessing Value Functions

Pain relief requires individual patients to report about their experience, so they are the measuring instrument for experienced pain, as a thermometer measures length to determine temperature. The elapsed time in hours when they take the drug again, and how many minutes pass before they report that the pain begins to subside, would be recorded in a log, either self-reported or by an observer. Similarly, how long the drug continues to work before another one is taken and how quickly the drug starts to work would be self-reported. Studies on these features vary in their degree of objectivity accompanying the measures, but they all require some subjective judgements by patients (or for other medical conditions, the views of a physician).

For the pain-relief study, data from many patients were statistically summarised and reported as proportions of patients satisfying the pain relief criterion or as averages for the other two benefit criteria. When many studies about the same topic are reported, the data across all studies are amalgamated in different ways. Ideally, it would be done by a meta-analysis that deploys statistical methods to combine the research data into a single number. In medicine, random controlled trials (RCTs) measure *efficacy*, how well a drug works under controlled conditions, with patients who have qualified to be included in the trials. RCTs are usually necessary for a drug to be approved.

How well a drug works once it has been approved and used on a variety of patients, as established in further research or assessed by clinicians, is considered a measure of *effectiveness*. In other words, RCTs establish how drugs should work, while real-world experience establishes how medicines actually work. This distinction can be seen in many disciplines, often signalled by an expert who says, 'Well, this is how it is supposed to work in theory, but actually it's like this.' Thus, the data constitute a mixture of research data and experience, sometimes 100 per cent data, sometimes 100 per cent judgement from experience, or more typically, data massaged by experience, especially when numbers represent the future and past experience is judged to be a fallible guide to the future.

For the pain-killer drugs, a combination of these two approaches established the numbers. The experts and clinicians discussed the available data and agreed among themselves what they considered to be representative numbers. Another way to characterise their approach is that they relied on their mental models of how pain drugs work in the human body (which requires knowledge of the drug's chemistry or biology and how the body absorbs, uses and metabolises the drug), the efficacy/effectiveness distinction and the quality of research that provided the data, to arrive at an agreement about numbers that represent today how we think a drug's effects will be realised in the future. In short, data doesn't speak for itself: it must be interpreted to create valid preference values.

But who is to do the interpreting? My experience with experts, whatever their specialty knowledge, is that they always disagree. That's why I prefer to work with teams of experts, who can represent the diversity of opinion in their specialty area, to build models that will be helpful for decision makers. I subscribe to the aphorism that many heads can be better than one, rather than the one that says too many cooks spoil the broth (although I'll admit it can apply to cooking). It is possible for a group of experts to out-perform even their best member through a process of deliberation with one another as they share their expertise and knowledge, creating consensus preference values by discussing their experience and knowledge, and making persuasive arguments, constructing narratives about the future, a process I'll describe in more detail in Chapter 7.

The remainder of this chapter focuses on the technology of scaling preference values, a process known as *scoring*, which applies whether a single individual or a group is doing the scoring. I've based most of the following on decades of research by psychologists who have developed techniques for measuring subjective constructs, or as statisticians call them, latent variables, to ensure that the measuring instrument actually measures what it claims to measure (validity) and does so in a way that can be replicated (reliability). In this chapter, the psychological construct is preference value.

Whatever method is used, the assessed values will depend on the context and be conditional on assumptions about the future. Asking directly for values may elicit the response, 'Well it all depends.' Enquiring about what the value depends on will help to identify both context and conditioning. In some cases, the answer will reveal that two people are thinking about the criterion in two different ways, which could lead to teasing out two new criteria. For example, the objective of reducing risk, followed by the question, 'What do you mean by risk?', usually elicits many different and conflicting criteria, as can be seen in Chapter 17.

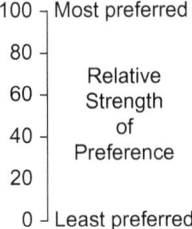

Figure 4.6

Interval Scaling

The blind problem demonstrated a straightforward way to assess preference value: just ask for the numbers. Here are the steps, generalised for any number of consequences:

1. **Establish scale range.** For each criterion, identify the options associated with the most and least preferred consequences.
2. **Define the scale.** Assign 100 to the most preferred option and 0 to the least preferred. If someone says, 'But there is still value in the least preferred option', explain that the zero point is like a temperature of zero; it's only a reference point. Draw the scale shown in Figure 4.6 on a flipchart. Explain that the consequences of the remaining options are to be scaled relative to those two points (ties are permissible), and that it is differences in value that are to be compared to see if the numbers make sense.
3. **Score the options.** Assign numbers to the remaining options according to their relative strength of preference. First, point to the 50 position on the figure and explain that a consequence given a score of 50 means that the 100-rated consequence must be as much better as the 0-rated consequence is worse. Next, choose one of the consequences and ask if its value is closer to 100 or closer to 0 and invite the assessor to provide a value. Then, compare the difference between the assessed number and 100, with the difference between 0 and the assessed number. Point out that the scores create ratios of differences that must make sense. Continue scoring all the consequences under that criterion. You may need to remind the assessor that the 0 and 100 are unique to each scale, that those numbers for the previous scale may represent values that are different from the current scale, and that a weighting process after the present scoring will ensure comparability of units across all scales.
4. **Check consistency.** Compare differences in pairs of assessments. For example, in the blind problem, I asked if the 80-point added value from Dead to Blind was four times the 20-point added value from Blind to Fully sighted (Figure 4.7). You may have to remind the assessor, 'Of course, the ratio of the differences in the numbers is 4 to 1 but is that ratio about the same as how you feel about the differences?' If not, invite a revision of the blind score. While scaling many consequences, it isn't

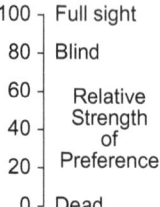

Figure 4.7

necessary to look at all the differences, but when the scaling is complete, ask if the differences on the scale look about right, especially when some options cluster around one number and other options cluster elsewhere.

The last step helps to ensure that the numbers describe an interval scale of preference value. If during the scoring process with a group, someone holds out for a very different score, make a note of the alternative point-of-view and promise to run the finished model again with that number in a sensitivity analysis to see if it makes a difference to the overall result.

If several people disagree, then facilitate the discussion of the reasons for the differences of opinion. This usually creates a narrowing of the range of numbers, so suggest using the median of participants' assessments. Explain that the model is usually not sensitive to differences of opinion within plus-or-minus five points; the median will most likely be acceptable to everyone. In general, the more complex the model, the more imprecision in a single part can be tolerated. Fortunately, even modest decision analysis models are generally tolerant of imprecision.[58]

Ratio Scaling

So far, we've looked at interval scales in which favourable effects, like being fully sighted or reducing pain, gain higher preference values, with zero associated with the least preferred effects. However, it's also possible to look solely at undesirable effects with zero meaning no undesirable effect and 100 assigned to the most harmful effect. Because zero is defined as 'no harm', the absence of the effect, the scores define a ratio scale; ratios of scores represent ratios of experienced harm. The potential harm of drugs provides an example.

In one study, a group of experts scored the harm from 20 psychoactive, recreational drugs on 16 criteria of harm, which covered physical, psychological and social harm. Harm was defined as a combination of seriousness and number of people experiencing the effect. Figure 4.8 shows a scale for the criterion Drug-Related Mortality, defined as: 'The extent to which life is shortened by the use of this drug, e.g. road traffic accidents, lung cancers, HIV, suicide'. Drug Specific Mortality, which is its intrinsic lethality (you could die from taking too much), was the subject of another criterion.

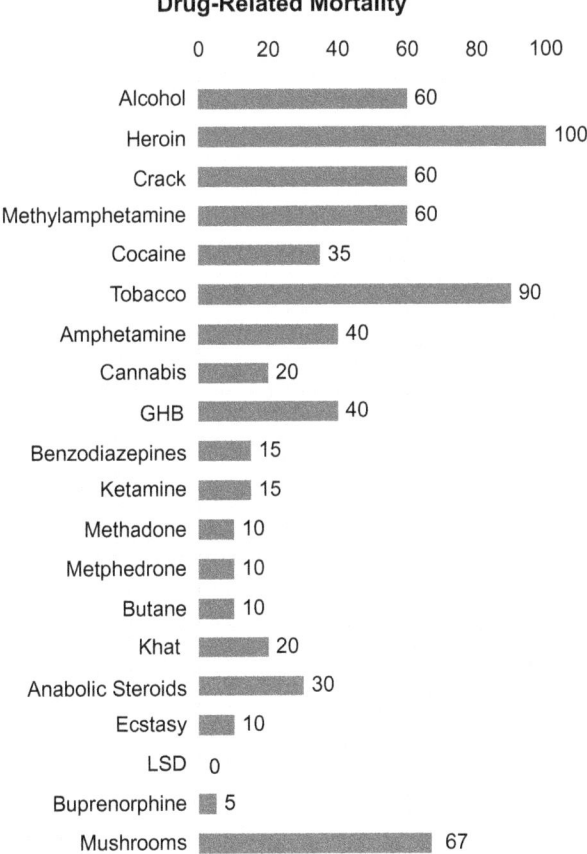

Figure 4.8

For each criterion, the facilitator asked the group to judge which of the 20 drugs was the most harmful. Here, the group agreed heroin, so it was assigned a harm score of 100. The group then went down the list comparing each drug to heroin and agreeing a harm score as a percentage. Thus, alcohol was judged to be 60 per cent as harmful as heroin for drug-related mortality. As the scoring continued, the group ensured the consistency of the scores, first by deciding whether an option's harm was more or less than one already scored, then assigning a number derived from discussion among the experts with experience and knowledge about the criterion.

At the completion of these 20 scores, the facilitator asked participants to reflect on the numbers to see if they were about right, and any final adjustments were made (that's why mushrooms scored 67, more than alcohol, but less than 70 so there would be a big gap to tobacco's 90).

Directly assessed preference values were required for the harm of drugs study because research data was lacking for most of the drugs on most of the criteria, in particular for the proscribed drugs. We turn now to see how measurable data can be transformed into preference values via value functions.

Value Functions

Value functions are a conversion of metrics, measurable data, into preference values. Figure 4.9 shows for the analgesics case study a linear relationship between preference values and the duration of action, as judged by the panel of experts. All six drugs lasted for at least four hours, and none went beyond nine, so those two positions defined the least and most preferred positions on the preference scale.

The experts had in mind an average patient, so the left chart shows that each additional hour adds as much more value as any other. However, patients experiencing chronic pain might prefer an analgesic that is sufficiently long-lasting that they don't take too much and thus exceed the recommended dose in one day. For them, the value function might look something like the right chart, an S shape. This clearly shows that shorter durations of action are of low value and longer durations are of higher value. It could be argued that the left, linear value function is a fairly good approximation to the S-shaped value function. Both show that the curve continues upward as the hours increase; each is an increasing function. Convention refers to these scales as 'direct' in the sense that the graph shows the numbers on both axes always increase.

Of course, some value functions go in the other direction, from 100 to 0 as the measured quantity increases. For example, most people would think that the sooner a pain-killer drug starts to work, the better – a decreasing function as fewer minutes are most preferred, with the value decreasing for drugs that take longer times to start working, an inverse S, something like the left graph in Figure 4.10. The first 15 minutes drops the value from 100 (most preferred) by 15 points, 100 to 85, but an additional 15 minutes sheds the preference value by 85 points to 0 (least preferred). For speed of onset, a linear function isn't an acceptable approximation for the average patient looking for pain relief reasonably soon. Convention refers to these scales as 'indirect' because as numbers on the horizontal axis increase, the numbers on the vertical axis decrease.

The right chart, with two functions, came about in a workshop to model the benefit-safety balance of two drugs compared to a placebo, a case study based on real

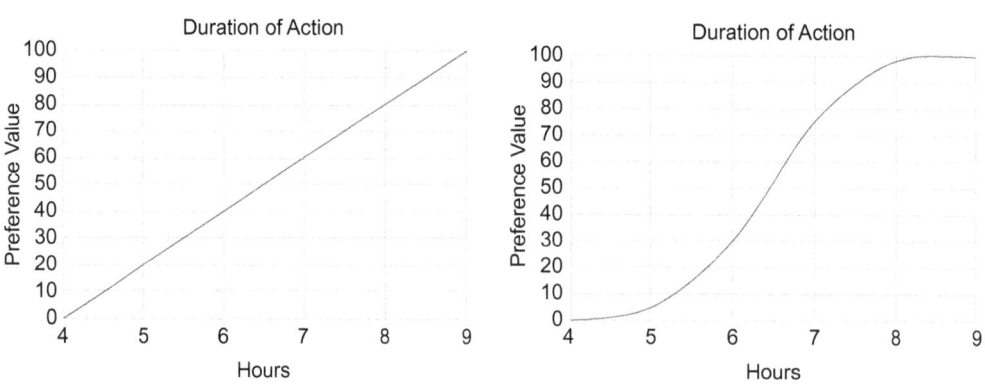

Figure 4.9

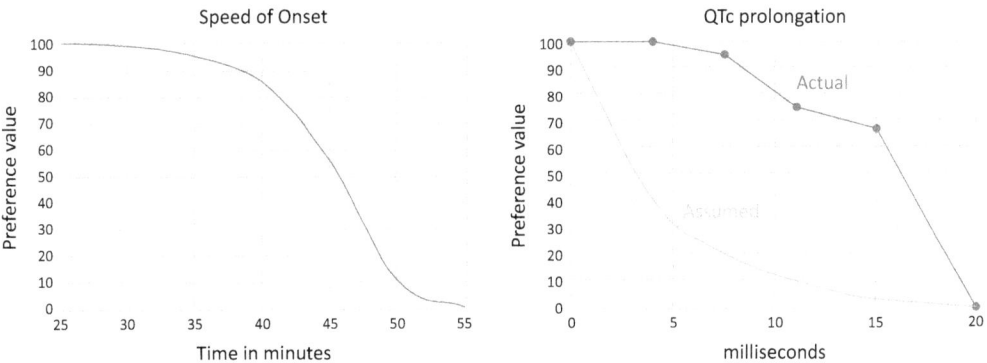

Figure 4.10

experience invented by a pharmaceutical company scientist. It was the topic for an MCDA modelling workshop attended by experts from academia, consultancies, drug regulators and the pharmaceutical industry. Discussion by the group revealed that one of the criteria, QTc prolongation, the time it takes the heart to recover from its last beat, is not a linear function, so I invited a senior regulator to allow me to elicit his preference values for the range of effects he judged to be possible.

It took a little less than 10 minutes to achieve the upper curve with the computer program I was using to model the drugs.[59] I didn't bother to spend a little more time to iron out the slight kink in the curve, as this meeting's purpose was to demonstrate the scope and desirability for decision-analytic modelling to support regulatory decisions about new drugs. Computer software enabled on-the-spot construction of the graph, which was projected for everyone to see. As soon as it was completed, the scientist who had constructed this case study stood up and gasped, 'But that isn't at all how we thought the regulator would think about this effect.' He explained that he and his colleagues assumed the curve would be convex, and he traced out in the air what is shown here as the lower curve.

I took the opportunity to suggest that we had just experienced a historical moment: how different value functions, now made explicit, could lead to different decisions about a drug! At that time (2005), no regulator in the world had used any quantitative model to support decisions about new drugs.

There are many ways to construct value functions, but let me show you a method that minimises bias. It is based on methods used in research on psychophysics, the discipline in psychology that studies the relationship between the magnitude of a presented stimulus and its experienced sensation (like the measured volume of a sound at a given frequency and the perception of the sound's loudness – which is concave looking upward).[60]

Steps for assessing a value function, illustrated for the duration of action of pain-killer drugs:

1. Begin by establishing whose values are to be represented. I assumed it was for someone with an inflamed muscle that could last for a few days and who doesn't want to exceed the daily dose.

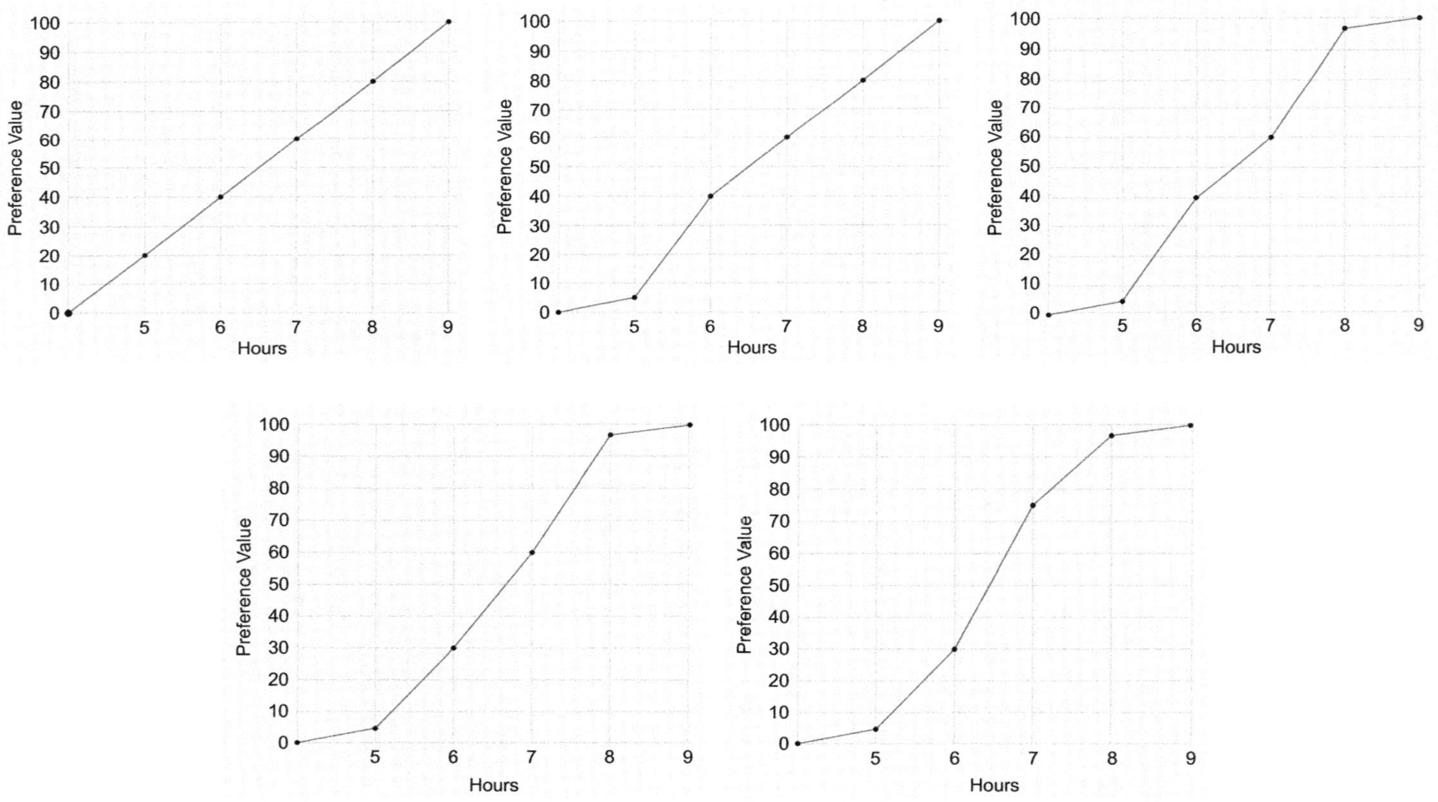

Preference Value
100
90
80
70
60
50
40
30
20
10
0
5
6
7
8
9
Hours
Preference Value
100
90
80
70
60
50
40
30
20
10
0
5
6
7
8
9
Hours
Preference Value
100
90
80
70
60
50
40
30
20
10
0
5
6
7
8
9
Hours
Preference Value
100
90
80
70
60
50
40
30
20
10
0
5
6
7
8
9
Hours
Preference Value
100
90
80
70
60
50
40
30
20
10
0
5
6
7
8
9
Hours

Figure 4.11

2. Consider only the consequences to be scored and establish the most and least preferred consequences. For duration of action, the shortest is paracetamol at four hours and the longest is naproxen at nine hours, a range of five hours, an odd number that is desirable because it avoids a central point. In the upper-left chart in Figure 4.11, 4 to 9 gives five one-hour intervals. Show the six points as increasing in a straight line.
3. Adjust each of the four in-between points up or down to create a preference value curve that feels about right, but always check ratios of increments on the preference value axis to ensure they, too, feel right.
4. Start at the extreme values of the metric and work inward, alternating between left and right. Here, I started with the (5, 20) point and adjusted it down to (5, 5), as shown in the upper-middle chart. Then, I moved to the (8, 80) point and adjusted it upward to (8, 97) – eight hours is nearly as good as nine (upper-right chart).
5. Returning to the lower left, I moved the (6, 40) point downward to (6, 30) because I felt the increase of 25 points from the (5, 5) point was indeed about five times as good (lower left). Looking at the remaining point at (7, 60), I felt that an increase of just 30 points from (6, 30) was big enough; so, I moved it to (7, 75); that increase of 45 points for seven hours from six was appropriately a little less than twice the increase of 25 points for the increase of six hours over five.
6. Check to see if the overall shape adequately represents your preference values. I thought the resulting curve felt about right.

Anchoring Bias

Why, you may well ask, didn't I just start at the lower left and move upward, comparing increments as I went, or start at the upper right and work downward? The answer is that because the desired curve didn't reside in my head ready to be plucked out, it had to be constructed, on-the-spot, when it was needed for the model. My general approach was to use the endpoints as anchors for judging the increments for points 5 and 8, which then served as anchors in adjusting points 6 and 7. I alternated between the two anchors to reduce bias in the curve.

Cognitive psychologists have known since 1937 that a starting point can create an *anchoring bias* for value judgements,[61] and physical scientists have known since the late nineteenth century about this 'lagging-behind' behaviour in physical systems, calling it *hysteresis*. If I had started my assessment at the upper-right point and worked all the way downward to the lower left, or started at the lower left and worked upward, I might well have defined the two different curves shown in Figure 4.12, which are like those on the Wikipedia page for hysteresis. The starting point causes subsequent points to lag behind.

The research on anchoring in human judgement consistently finds that all sorts of relevant and irrelevant features can 'bias' a person's judgement.[62] For example, ask a group of people to write on a slip of paper the last two digits from any of their credit cards. Then ask them to write 'yes' or 'no' if they think the tallest tree in the world is

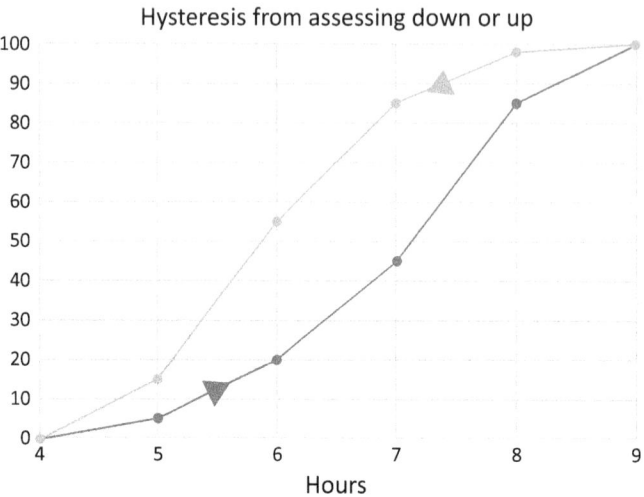

Figure 4.12

taller than the number they wrote down (no looking it up!). Finally, ask them to write an estimate, in metres, of the height of that tree. All without talking to one another.

If you now analyse the data, you will find that people who chose lower credit card numbers gave, on average, lower estimates for the tree height than those whose credit card numbers were higher. (As I write, the tallest tree is in California, a Coast Redwood, 115.92 metres or 380.3 feet tall.) Many experiments show an anchoring effect, so it seems inappropriate to call it a 'bias' if most of us are affected so strongly about a starting point for our judgements. Perhaps evolution has wired our brains to take care when our values are challenged. You will meet the anchoring phenomenon again in Chapter 6 when I suggest ways to minimise it when working with a group.

Anchoring exerts a powerful effect. To deal with it in assessing value functions, we need to apply two approaches: (1) exploit the opposing effects of two anchors by alternating between the extreme left and right positions and work towards the middle; and (2) make consistency checks of paired comparisons of intervals. This latter method, first introduced in the mid-1800s, formed the basis for the scaling methodologies developed by the psychometrician Louis L. Thurstone in 1927, whose later work described the measurement of attitudes and values.[63] For our purposes, we compare only two intervals of value at a time, but increasing the number of pairs as more points on the value function are assessed as the ascending and descending alteration proceeds. In particular, it is important to compare intervals at both ends of the curve against each other.

Comparing ratios of differences in values is, of course, crucial to ensuring that the final preference value scale is a meaningful interval scale. You will find many opportunities to make these paired comparison checks of intervals, and it won't take long for your clients to catch on. Their discussions will eventually include ratio comparisons of intervals as they become accustomed to the process and are able to create interval scales by intuitively comparing the differences. Scoring will then proceed apace. Patience on the part of the facilitator at the start of scoring, with a comment that the process will speed up as it becomes more familiar, will not go amiss.

Bisection Method

One method for assessing a value curve that is mentioned in the decision-analytic literature is the bisection method. First, define the (0, 100) endpoints and then determine what value of the measured data metric should be associated with a preference value of 50. The next steps would be to define the metrics for 75 and 25. In other words, you keep bisecting the preference value intervals and assess what metrics should be associated with them. You now have defined a five-point scale at metric values of x_0, x_{25}, x_{50}, x_{75} and x_{100}.

I don't recommend using this approach. The problem is that it establishes an anchor at a preference value of 50, and the 25 and 75 metrics are likely to be too close to the 50 metric, resulting in a steep middle portion of the preference value function. This can be overcome. The central anchor acts much more powerfully than the end anchors, and that's why I suggested above that you divide the metric into an even number of intervals, thus avoiding a middle anchor point. You could also try trisecting the finished curve, because x_0, x_{33}, x_{67} and x_{100} should define three equal intervals of value.

Single-Peaked Preference Functions

So far, I've mentioned only direct (0–100) or inverse (100–0) relationships for the preference scales; the peak is at one end or the other. However, it is possible for the peak to appear between the ends as a *single-peaked preference function*. Imagine that you are selecting a bottle of white wine for a meal, a wine that is neither too sweet nor too dry. Your preference value function might look something like the chart shown in Figure 4.13.

I've only once encountered a single-peaked value function in working with commercial organisations. Surprisingly, it was for profit. The company was the UK branch of Mars Confectionery, a global private business that remains owned by the Mars family, so there are no quarterly public financial reports prompting short-term reactions by senior executives. During a decision conference in which a value function for profit about their confectionery products was considered, I assumed they would prefer more profit to less, but was told that would be true only up to a point at which their preference would decline. When I asked why, they explained, 'It would show we weren't giving our customers value-for-money.'

When I asked what they would do if they were earning too much profit, they said they would either lower the price or increase the size of the candy bar. When I mentioned this to Ralph Keeney, he suggested there might be two fundamental

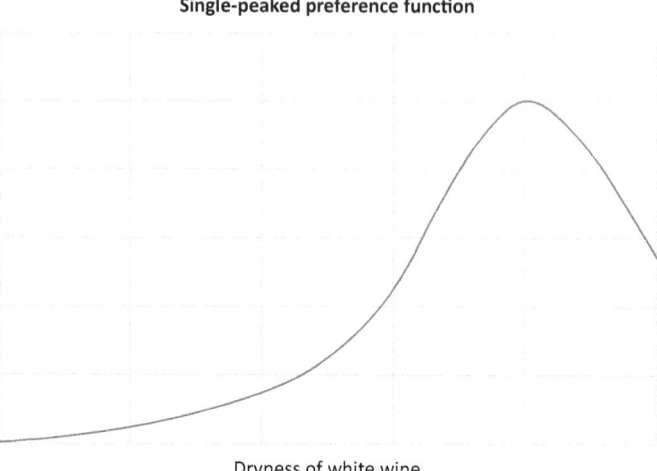

Single-peaked preference function

Dryness of white wine

Figure 4.13

objectives that are competing here. I knew that Mars's core values included quality and value-for-money (which today are among their five guiding principles), so perhaps keeping the price down and the quality up were the determinants of a profit function that is part of the Mars DNA.

In Chapter 2, I mentioned Jimmie Savage's distinction between small and grand worlds, and that decision theory is only applicable to small worlds; there is no theory of coherent action for grand worlds because many features interact, are reflexive (A affects B, and B affects A), and are dependent in different ways on context. The value function for the small world of a department's budget will not be a subset of the value function for the larger world of the whole organisation (unless they are both linear). It's best to treat any value function as conditional on the small world issues and context for which the model was created, as well as the risk attitude of the individual or group that assessed the function.

Higher-Ordered Preference Value Scales

For some people, assessing numerical scores is a task to be avoided. I've found this is more of a problem for university arts graduates than those who studied science. My colleague Carlos Bana e Costa, who works mainly with politicians, developed a methodology that is entirely qualitative, and works well with those who are phobic of numbers.[64] I've also found it useful in groups when participants can't agree about numbers. The method goes by the name of MACBETH, which stands for **M**easuring **A**ttractiveness by a **C**ategorical **B**ased **E**valuation **T**echnique.[65] Carlos is a professor at the University of Lisbon and his approach leads to quantitative scales that provide more information than a simple rank ordering, but less than an interval scale, so that's why it qualifies for the name of higher-ordered preference value scale.[66]

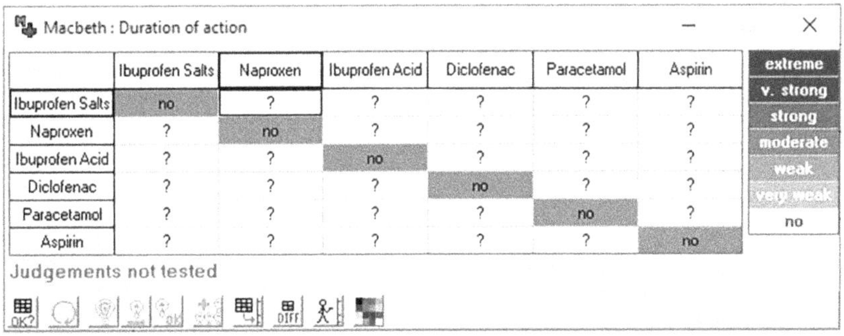

Macbeth : Duration of action							—	×
	Ibuprofen Salts	Naproxen	Ibuprofen Acid	Diclofenac	Paracetamol	Aspirin	**extreme**	
Ibuprofen Salts	no	?	?	?	?	?	**v. strong**	
Naproxen	?	no	?	?	?	?	**strong**	
							moderate	
Ibuprofen Acid	?	?	no	?	?	?	**weak**	
Diclofenac	?	?	?	no	?	?	**very weak**	
Paracetamol	?	?	?	?	no	?	**no**	
Aspirin	?	?	?	?	?	no		

Judgements not tested

Figure 4.14

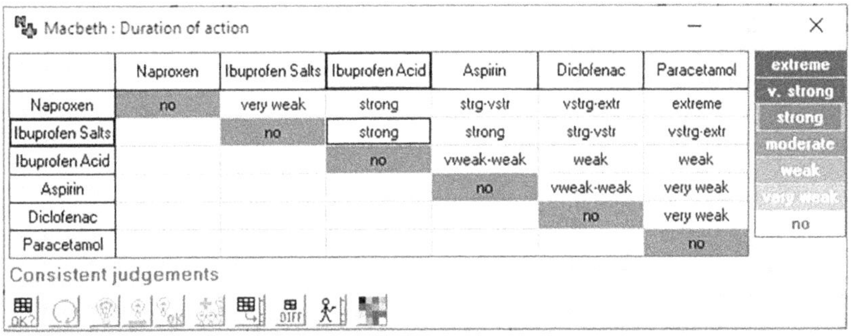

Macbeth : Duration of action							—	×
	Naproxen	Ibuprofen Salts	Ibuprofen Acid	Aspirin	Diclofenac	Paracetamol	**extreme**	
Naproxen	no	very weak	strong	strg-vstr	vstrg-extr	extreme	**v. strong**	
Ibuprofen Salts		no	strong	strong	strg-vstr	vstrg-extr	**strong**	
							moderate	
Ibuprofen Acid			no	vweak-weak	weak	weak	**weak**	
Aspirin				no	vweak-weak	very weak	**very weak**	
Diclofenac					no	very weak	**no**	
Paracetamol						no		

Consistent judgements

Figure 4.15

Let's use MACBETH for the analgesic drug case to determine the values for the criterion Duration of action (Figure 4.14). (I have here used a simpler version of the program that is no longer available.) The process starts by typing the names of the drugs as they appeared in the research paper, in either the top row or the first column.

The next step is to rank order the drugs, which I've done in Figure 4.15 by dragging the names of the drugs in either the top row or left column (whichever you choose, the program automatically reorders the other list).

The next task is to replace all the question marks above the grey cells by selecting a cell, then clicking on any of the seven words on the right that correspond to my judgement about how much more the row drug is preferred for its duration of action (or more desirable or better than) compared to the column drug. I started with the upper-right-most cell and judged that naproxen relieves pain for very much longer than paracetamol, so I clicked on 'extreme'. I then moved to the left, intending to complete the naproxen row, but found that difficult, so I went back to the paracetamol column and filled in the entire column, making weaker and weaker difference judgements as I moved to the bottom. After that, I moved down the diclofenac column, and so forth on to the final judgement of very weak in comparing naproxen to ibuprofen salts.

Notice that moving from the top of each column to the bottom and from the right of each row to the left, the preference assessments either decline or are tied. As you

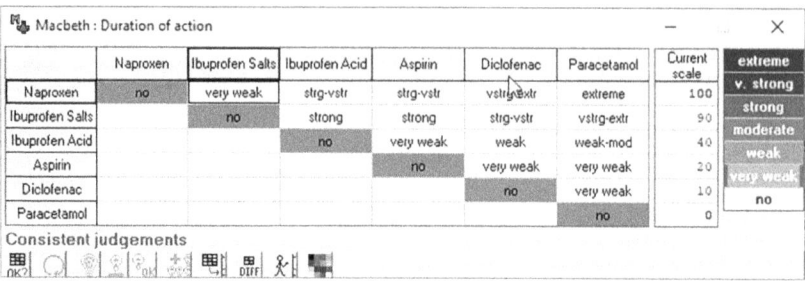

Figure 4.16

enter your preferences, MACBETH will detect any inconsistencies in your judge-ments with an information box that suggests what needs to be changed to ensure consistency.

It isn't always necessary to complete the entire matrix, so when using MACBETH with other people, I usually ask them to complete the top row, the right column, and the remaining empty cells on the diagonal cells just above the 'no' ones. You can see that throughout I was comparing one difference with another difference, which was exactly the kind of judgement required for an interval scale.

When MACBETH signals 'Consistent judgements', it is ready to calculate numbers that preserve all the qualitative judgments of preference. I clicked on the matrix-to-scale icon and a scale appeared at the right of the matrix (Figure 4.16).

A further click on the 'Show thresholds' icon (the stick figure pointing to the scale) inserts vertical red lines for the scores between 0 and 100. These indicate the range over which the scores could be changed without violating any of the qualitative judgements in the matrix. Click and drag any option, moving it up or down until the scores feel about right. For my use of a drug to reduce inflamma-tion, I would move the bottom three a little closer to one another, and perhaps slightly raise ibuprofen acid. The final scale can then be considered as meaningful and considered as an interval scale (Figure 4.17).

For this example, the lengths of the red bars range from 15 to 20 points, rather more than my earlier suggestion that the precision of directly assessed preference values is about plus-or-minus 5 points. But then, this is by definition a methodology that is qualitative, so less precision is to be expected. Even though I illustrated here the non-linear function for duration of action, the final rank order of the analgesics did not change from the ordering in the published paper that used a linear scale for duration of action.

Because the preference values can be changed within the constraints of the red lines, there is no single unique interval scale that is defined by the MACBETH method. Nor are there fixed numbers associated from the start with any of the words from 'no' to 'extreme'. When MACBETH determines that the inputs are consistent, it applies a mathematical method called linear programming to determine a set of scores that are consistent with the input orderings of differences.

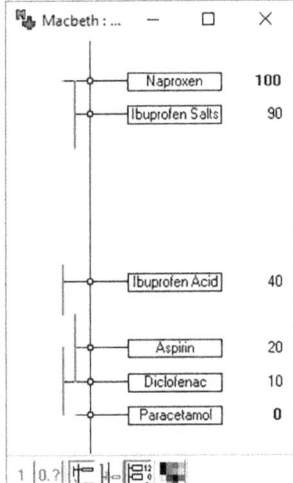

Figure 4.17

Here is my experience about how and why MACBETH has been helpful in my consultancy work:

- The ability to put more than one expression in a cell, which enables differences of opinion to be accommodated.
- The checking of consistency during the process with suggestions of what could be changed to ensure that the inputs are consistent.
- The ability to change numerical results in the final scale which preserves the ordering, as that helps a group to agree results without becoming bogged down in discussions of details.
- Scoring, as above, and weighting are separated into different processes whose results are combined as weighted averages to give final results.
- It is easy to interpret the meaning of what the final numbers mean and what they represent (for the analgesics, it is how much I value the objective duration of action compared to the most and least preferred drugs).
- The system is consistent with the axioms of decision theory, so can easily be defended.

If you are acquainted with the Analytic Hierarchy Process (AHP), you will see that the above six characteristics of MACBETH are very different from the AHP in their way of helping an individual or group to gain clarity about the problem they face. In addition, the AHP process is the subject of published debate,[67] so I don't use it.

Reference Gamble Methods

Another method for eliciting a preference value is to use a reference gamble. Let's see how that works for determining the preference value for being permanently blind

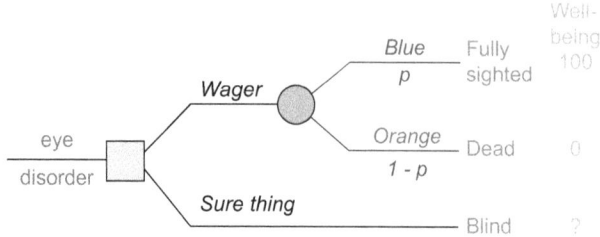

Figure 4.18

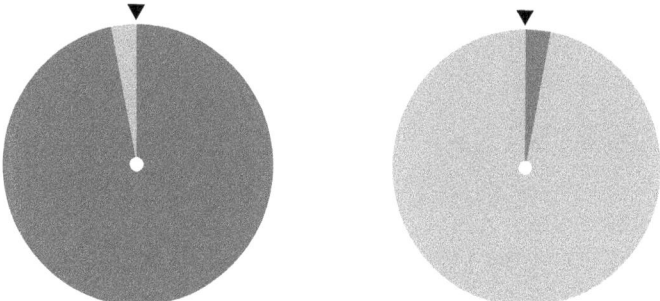

Figure 4.19

(Chapter 1). This is a choice between a sure thing or an uncertain event, with the same consequences as before (Figure 4.18). Note that 'Blue' is darker shaded than 'Orange'.

Now, imagine you have the eye disorder, but instead of choosing an operation or not, suppose you were offered this wager: spin the left wheel shown in Figure 4.19, and if the wheel final stops with the black triangle at the top pointing to the large darker shaded area, you will become fully sighted, but if it points to the lighter shaded area, you will die. As the wheel is mostly dark, I assume you would accept the wager.

Suppose, however, the wheel was changed to look like the right wheel: I expect you would reject that one; the dark slice is too small, suggesting that the probability of being fully sighted isn't large enough. In fact, each of the small slices was 3 per cent, so there must be a position between these two extremes that would leave you with a difficult decision – the point at which you are indifferent between choosing the wager or the sure thing. Experience suggests this 'point' is actually a range, usually less that plus-or-minus 5 per cent.

To find that range, I would again use the theory of limits, rocking back and forth, successively increasing the size of the small slices, noting how you slow down in choosing as you are confronted with less and less extreme slices and getting closer to your range of indifference. A possible sequence is shown in Figure 4.20.

The 'Ahhs and Mmms' suggested 'getting close' to the indifference point, with the dark area at 60 per cent for the third wager and 80 per cent for the last one. I split the difference and set the dark slice at 70 per cent. That elicited, 'A little more', so I set it to 75 per cent, which resulted in 'Either way'. That point of indifference for the sure thing

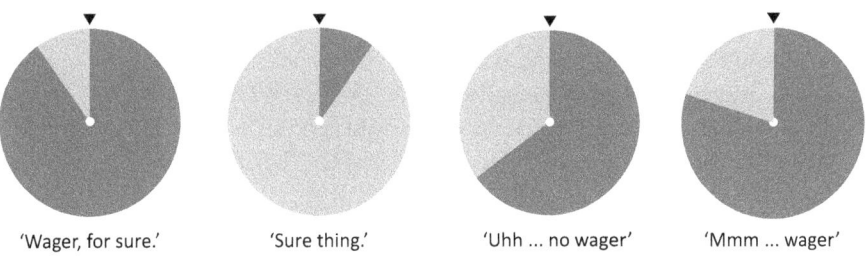

'Wager, for sure.'   'Sure thing.'   'Uhh ... no wager'   'Mmm ... wager'

Figure 4.20

or a wager showed a 75 per cent chance of 100 and a 0 per cent chance of zero, giving an expected value for the wager of $(100 \times 0.75) + (0 \times 0.25) = 75$. This means that on the 0–100 value scale, the wager is worth 75. At that point, the assessor is indifferent between the wager and being blind, so Blind's preference value must be 75.[68] By only asking questions of preference, the value for being blind is established. Recall that in Chapter 1 the result of a direct assessment was 80, not 75. I'll explain in a moment why reference gambles can result in different numbers.

If you have a more complex model with many consequences for a given criterion, then you would first identify the best and worst consequences to establish the 100 and 0 points of a value scale, then apply the reference gamble's sure-thing consequence individually to each of the other consequences. Thus, if you have N consequences, you must find the indifference value for $N - 2$ reference gambles, which can be rather tedious if N is large.

If the assessor(s) finds direct numerical assessments to be too difficult, or too subjective, or too imprecise, I start with one reference gamble using an important sure-thing consequence. By the end of the process, the assessor learns that he or she actually knew more about the value of a consequence than they thought. The wager grounds the assessment, making the value judgement more concrete. After applying the reference gamble approach two or three times more, usually numerate assessors suggest shifting to direct value assessment rather than the preference gamble.

You have also now seen the 'constructive proof' that utilities exist, which I first mentioned in 'The Axioms and Theorems of Decision Theory' section in Chapter 2. The reference gamble requires only a statement of preference (a choice, not a decision) between an uncertain event and a sure thing. A series of choices as the relative sizes of the light and dark sectors are changed leads to an indifference point that is defined by a single number. See the link at the end of this chapter which gives instructions on how to construct a reference gamble. It can also be used to assess a probability, as we'll see in Chapter 6.

After the assessment of a value function, ask your client or group of experts if the resulting value function feels about right, especially after you've shown how the differences in the options on the metric have changed the differences in preference values. After some experts expressed concern about long QtC intervals, I showed the default linear function in Hiview, which the regulators immediately rejected, saying they could certainly tolerate some interval created by a new drug. That led to the concave QTc prolongation function shown previously. The group had considered two drug options, X and Y, as compared to the placebo. For QtC prolongation, the placebo scored 0, drug Y, 7.5 ms and drug X, 15 ms, that is, equal spacing. But their preference scores were 100, 96 and 66, a relatively large difference between drugs Y and X. That felt about right to the regulators; Y was OK, but X was worrisome.

Value or Utility?

Strictly speaking, the single number at the indifference point of a reference gamble is a utility, not a value. Why? Because in judging the indifference point, the assessor is comparing a two-outcome uncertain event against a sure thing, so his or her feelings about accepting a gamble against the certainty of the sure thing may itself bias the judgement towards the sure thing. In other words, the assessor may adjust the feeling of value downward, making the sure thing relatively more attractive than it would otherwise have been with direct assessment.

Does this difference between utility and values matter in practice? Very often it doesn't, as utility and value curves can be fairly similar, and if a model includes many criteria, then small differences on a single criterion will make little difference to the final results. Also, utility curves are often linear, although of course you only discover that if you've taken the trouble to apply a reference gamble. Instead, I rely on the discussion during the assessment of a value function.

For example, in the workshop developing a model of the benefit-risk balance of two drugs and a placebo, the regulator made an off-hand comment that he wasn't worried about short QtC intervals. That suggested to me it would be worth exploring his value function and, sure enough, it turned out to be quite concave, especially compared to the convex function of the pharmaceutical company. At other times, if the assessor is worried about something but can't explain why, they may well be experiencing aversion to the uncertain event itself, which could be picked up in a utility function.

Fixed Scales

All the scales discussed so far are relative scales, whose 0 and 100 points on the value preference scale are associated with the least- and most-preferred points on the metric scale. However, sometimes you might like to widen the scale, because the options have not yet been fully identified or you would like some wiggle room to do sensitivity analyses that might increase the range of the consequences beyond the limits of the preference scale. Fixed scales give that additional flexibility.

For example, the scale in Figure 4.21 provides a realisable range of consequences. Whatever defines the top and bottom of the scale, the limits must be achievable, otherwise swing weighting will prove to be difficult because that process requires judgements about differences between endpoints, which must be imaginable.

This scale allows a person's strength of preference to be expressed as any number between 0 and 100, inclusive, which satisfies two requirements for a useful scale. The

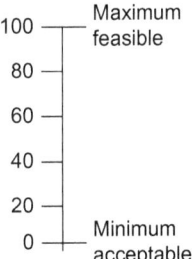

Figure 4.21

first is to provide sufficient precision, and the second is to accommodate diversity in a group setting. As a group of experts who are unaccustomed to scoring start to use the scale, they usually provide scores in 'tens', namely, 10, 20, 30, . . . and so on. As they begin to become accustomed to translating their experience into a number, their thinking and debate become more nuanced and 'fives' begin to appear, 5, 10, 15, 20, 25, etc., as more precision is required for each participant to express his or her judgements. Eventually, a consequence might be scored at a 5 by one participant with another saying, 'It can't possibly be better than a 1!' Thereafter, the group makes use of units on the 0–100 scale, enabling them to express the diversity of the group's judgements.

Another type of fixed scale is defined by categories, as applied in 2005–06 by the UK's Committee on Radioactive Waste Management (CoRWM), a project to determine the best strategy for managing the UK's accumulation of high- and medium-level radioactive waste.

Committee members accepted early in the project that although much of the waste would remain radioactive for thousands or even hundreds of thousands of years, there was no point in developing a model with those very long timeframes. Instead, they agreed that the country could do no more than build today the best that would be technically feasible and operate safely over the next 300 years, satisfying their overriding objective of minimising impacts, as measured on 25 criteria.

Construction of the scales for every criterion by a team of experts began by defining points 1 and 9 as maximum feasible and minimum acceptable, respectively, with the latter meaning that a score below 1 would result in discarding the option because performance on all or even one other criterion couldn't compensate for the poor performance. The team were then asked to define point five so that the added value in moving from 1 to 5 would be the same as from 5 to 9. Then, point 3 and 7 were similarly defined as halving the values between 1 and 5, and between 5 and 9, respectively. This created a 9-point scale of equal intervals.

The example in Table 4.1 shows the agreed definition of one criterion, Flexibility, along with definitions of five points on the scale.

The levels are combinations of three design features, monitoring, adaptability and retrievability. They could be considered as sub-criteria, but it is easy to see they're not preference independent, so combining them in definitions that successively weaken

Table 4.1

Flexibility	
Extent to which the disposal option is expected to allow for future choice and respond to unforeseen or changed circumstances over the 300-year time span.	
9	System is fully monitored and adaptable, and the waste is easily retrievable using the existing system
8	
7	Key system elements can be monitored and are moderately adaptable, and the waste retrieval requires some modification of the system
6	
5	Some system elements can be monitored, adaptability is limited, and waste retrieval is moderately difficult
4	
3	Few system elements are monitored, little adaptability in the system, and it is difficult to retrieve the waste
2	
1	Monitoring options is severely restricted, the system is not adaptable, and waste retrieval is very difficult

each feature worked well for the expert scorers. In general, even if sub-criteria are preference independent, experts may be able to score at the aggregated level, which saves time and helps to keep the model as simple as possible. However, if experts cannot agree about scores at a given level, then further decomposition may reveal why the disagreements arose and allow agreement at the decomposed level.

An advantage of fixed scales is that they can reduce scoring and weighting bias. In relative scaling, because the worst and best performing options define the range, it is possible for the endpoints to repel or attract scores of the other options, depending on whether a scorer wishes their favoured option to be distanced from the scale's least preferred option or closer to the most preferred one. With no options defining the endpoints, scorers are encouraged to focus on the endpoint values, not on the options.

Another advantage is that swing weighting can be easier if it isn't necessary to know what the options are. For example, the criteria for many personal purchases, such as a car or house, might be established before or during the search for options. In organisations, scoring might be accomplished by those who are in direct contact with the outputs of the organisation, with weighting done by those at higher levels, especially if the weights represent trade-offs between parts of the model that have been scored by different organisational units. Fixed scales can also be used to assess public views about the relative importance of criteria, as CoRWM members did in eliciting weights from different public constituencies, which is discussed further in Chapter 7.

Summary

The sense of unease many clients feel about the gap between where they are now and where they would like to be often relates to a fundamental objective that is not being adequately achieved. We saw this when members of the UK's Ministry of Defence felt that current equipment was not providing the capability needed to meet future threats; current capabilities in some areas were not achieving sufficient military value, while other capabilities were providing more value than needed. The fundamental objective was military value, not capability, not performance, not effectiveness.

We saw that value is contingent on context. Improving and extending human life, a fundamental objective of many pharmaceutical companies, is interpreted differently by each company's divisions in a way that is consistent with the fundamental objective, which provides direction, and is the desired future end position (as was Sequent's 'facilitating human interaction') but needs to be relevant to actions that can be taken today, that is, the means to the ends (as CoRWM's criteria levels are today's characteristics of a policy option that are the means for realising value in the future). Winning an election is a politician's means objective for achieving sufficient power to be able to make things better in the future. Profit is the means objective that enables commercial organisations to do what they are in business to do.

Meaningful preference values require that criteria relate to the client's sense of unease. But criteria must be constructed in a way that makes them comprehensive, communicable, non-redundant, requisite in number and mutually preference independent. If these requirements are met, then it will be possible to combine preferences across different criteria, provided they are properly weighted, the subject of the next chapter.

Preference values of an option's consequences can be directly assessed or, if measured data are available, a value function can be constructed to convert the metrics into preference values. If any increment of value on one part of the preference scale is equal to the same increment of value anywhere else on the scale, then a linear conversion is appropriate. The 100 and 0 endpoints on a criterion's preference value scale might be defined by the most and least preferred consequences, respectively, which establishes a relative scale, or by any realisable range of the metric, which defines a fixed scale.

Fixed scales are commonly used when measured data is available. The value function can take any form, but proper psychophysical techniques applied during the assessment help to minimise or eliminate anchoring bias, which is likely to occur if the bisection method is applied. Most value functions are direct when both the metric and preference values increase, or indirect when they go in opposite directions. A single-peaked preference function is possible, but rarely encountered in practice.

Usually, preference values are expressed on interval scales, whose arbitrary zero point prohibits any sensible interpretation of a ratio of the numbers, as a temperature of 100 degrees (Celsius or Fahrenheit) is not twice the temperature of 50 degrees. However, ratios of differences in preference value are properly interpretable.

If the zero point on a preference scale corresponds to an absence of the characteristic being assessed, then a ratio scale of preference allows ratios of the numbers to be interpreted properly, as we saw in the drug harm example. Higher-ordered preference value scales, like MACBETH, are assessed by asking the assessor to compare pairs of options, which provide more information than a simple ranking of the options but less than a directly assessed preference scale. With slight adjustments to the final scales, they can legitimately be considered as interval scales.

Reference gamble methods have frequently been used in assessing preference values and have the advantage of requiring the assessor to state only a preference between a single gamble of a best or worst consequence on the one hand, or an intermediate consequence expressed as a sure thing on the other. The probability of the best consequence is varied until the assessor declares a state of indifference between the gamble and the sure thing. The success probability is then taken as the utility of the intermediate consequence.

The preference value of a consequence is not an absolute number; it is always conditional on the small-world context of the issues being considered, as Daniel Bernoulli anticipated in 1738.

A spinner wheel can be created by downloading files from https://www.cambridge .org/gb/universitypress/subjects/management/strategic-management/decision-ana lysis-creating-future?format=HB#resources.

5 Trade-Off Weights

The philosopher Isaiah Berlin's central thesis was 'that ultimate human values are objective but irreducibly diverse, that they are conflicting and often uncombinable, and that sometimes when they come into conflict with one another they are incommensurable; that is, they are not comparable by any rational measure'.

John Grey, 1996[69]

Or more prosaically, 'You can't compare apples with oranges.' So I've been told on many occasions by participants in workshops during the weighting phase of modelling options with multiple objectives. I briefly mentioned the resolution of this apparent dilemma at the beginning of Chapter 4, but now it's time to think more deeply about Isaiah Berlin's thesis and what it implies for decision modelling.

Perhaps Berlin was thinking of core values, the principles that guide one's behaviour, as distinct from the value created by the consequences of decisions. I value helping other people; that's what decision analysis means to me, so my work with others creates value for them and so for me. I'm also slightly more introverted than extroverted, so I also value time by myself to think about things that are important. In Berlin's sense, these values are conflicting; the more I devote to helping others, the less I have for myself. But not comparable by any rational measure? My original thought in writing that last sentence was to use time as a measure, but time is the resource I give to create the value that matters to me personally. Resource is the input, the output is value, the extent to which my objective of helping is achieved.

In 2007, I participated in five BBC Radio 4 programmes entitled National Treasures. In each of the first four programmes, the moderator presented two different national treasures to determine which one of them should receive a (hypothetical) grant of £500,000. I fondly remember the first programme as Germaine Greer spoke for the Thames-river gateway, from the river's mouth on the east coast of England back up to Tower Bridge in London, and then Tristram Hunt, now the Director of the Victoria and Albert Museum in London, championed Stonehenge. Robert Hewson, an expert in cultural values, assigned points out of 10 to each treasure on four dimensions of value: historic, emotional, social and existence (bequest value, what heritage is all about). After Deborah Meaden, an entrepreneur from the BBC's Dragon's Den (still there as I write this) gave her view from a business perspective, I was asked as a decision analyst to pull the threads together and make a recommendation to the politician on the panel, MP Edwina Currie, as the final decision maker.

I agreed with the higher total cultural value score for Stonehenge, but an audible gasp by the moderator and other panellists could be heard when I said I would recommend investing in the Thames Gateway. 'Why?', the moderator asked. 'The cultural value,' I explained, 'of Stonehenge was already so high that an additional £500,000 would not add as much value as would be realised by spending it on the Thames Gateway.'

It is this notion of *added* value that lies at the heart of swing weighting, and shows why Berlin's view was incorrect. You don't compare apples with oranges; you compare the added value of each, which depends on the context.

What Is Swing Weighting?

It is a process for assigning numerical weights that represent the *relative* importance of the criteria on which the consequences of the alternatives are assessed. And the purpose of the weights is to provide a common unit of preference value across all criteria. Important decisions usually involve multiple objectives and decision analysts apply multi-criteria decision analysis (MCDA) in constructing a model that can accommodate the many criteria that characterise the issues facing the decision maker. Based on multi-attribute utility theory, MCDA models combine preference values across all the criteria to provide a single weighted preference value for each option. But to do this, swing weights must be assessed to provide that common unit.

To illustrate the process of establishing the common unit of preference, let's start with the pain-killer drug example introduced in the Structuring Criteria section of Chapter 4. Recall that a group of medical doctors and pain experts met to assess the benefit-safety balance of pain-killer drugs that anyone can purchase without a prescription, known as over-the-counter (OTC) drugs. The alternatives considered were:

1. Ibuprofen FA (fast-acting, soluble)
2. Naproxen
3. Ibuprofen tablet (acid)
4. Diclofenac
5. Paracetamol (acetaminophen)
6. Aspirin

The group identified three favourable effects and eight unfavourable effects (possible side effects). Let's consider just the three favourable effects, whose definitions and metrics are repeated here:

- **Pain relief**: Proportion of patients suffering moderate to severe pain who individually report pain intensity reduction by 50 per cent or more.
- **Duration of action**: Average time in hours to re-medication for 50 per cent of patients.
- **Speed of onset**: Average time in minutes to perceptible pain relief.

For participants who are new to the MCDA process, I like to start the swing weighting process right after the options have been scored on the criteria for one node with two to four criteria, at least one of which participants mentioned was important. This enables the group to see the overall result for that node, which gives participants confidence in the modelling process and helps to maintain motivation for completing the model. Figure 5.1 shows the three scales under the Benefits node, with the left scales showing the input measures and the right scales their linear conversion into preference values on relative scales.

Pain relief

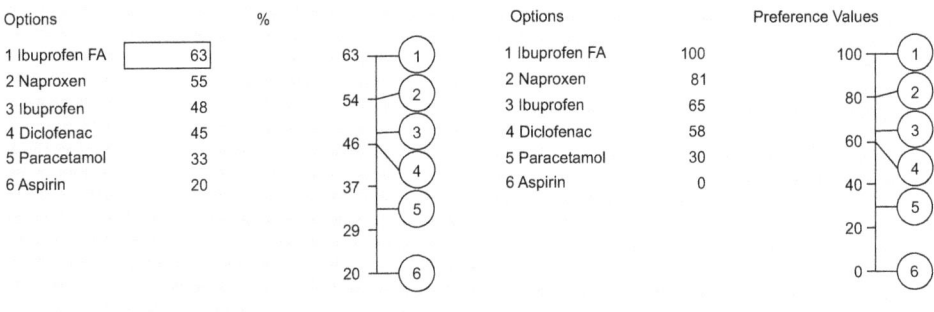

Duration of action

Speed of onset

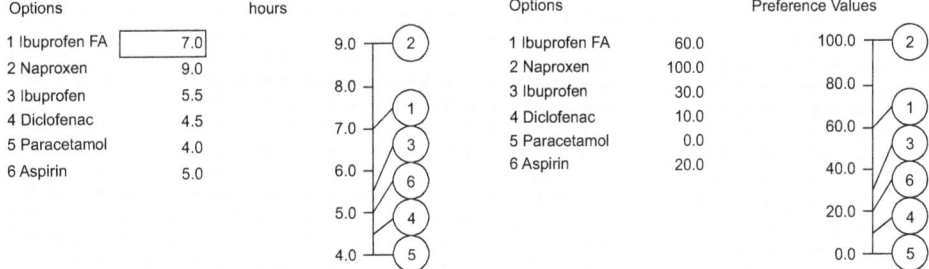

Figure 5.1

Recall that for these relative preference values, zero represents the least-preferred value and 100 the most-preferred. Thus, for pain relief, higher proportions of people are more preferred. Same for duration of action. But for speed of onset, shorter times are preferred to longer ones. During the scoring, it's important to point out that 100 on one scale can represent a different level of strength of preference than on another scale, and the same is true of the zeros. These are interval scales.

With scoring completed on these three scales, I said something like this. 'I'm sure you recognise that the 0–100 difference on some scales is larger than on others. For example, both Fahrenheit and Celsius scales include 0-to-100 portions, but the difference between 0 and 100 is a larger range of temperature on the Celsius scale; it takes nine Fahrenheit units to equal five Celsius units. So, our next step is to weight the scales to provide a common unit of preference value across all three scales.'

Swing Weighting Methods

The first step provided a graphical representation of those three criteria using vertical 'thermometers' with tops and bottoms defined by the options. These can be created on a white board, flip chart or computer program specifically designed for MCDA modelling. Figure 5.2 shows Hiview3's default display of the best and worst options for the three benefit criteria:

'What you have said is that for pain relief, ibuprofen fast-acting is best and aspirin is worst.' After a moment's pause so the experts could digest this new display, I repeated the summary for the other two criteria. I then switched the display to show the input data for the options (Figure 5.3).

I'm working with smart medical practitioners, and they do understand what is meant by the generic question that I have in mind for comparing the worst–best differences on each scale, which is this: '*How big is the difference and how much do you care about it?*' I explain to the group that I want them to consider the added value in moving from the bottom of each scale to the top, and this requires two considerations. First is the actual measured values at the top and bottom, which in this case is

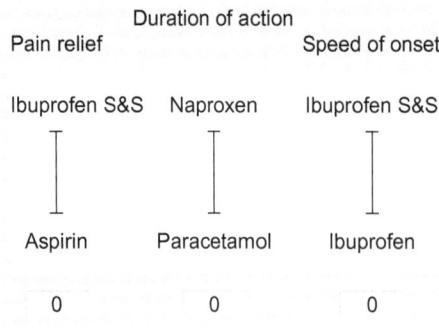

Figure 5.2

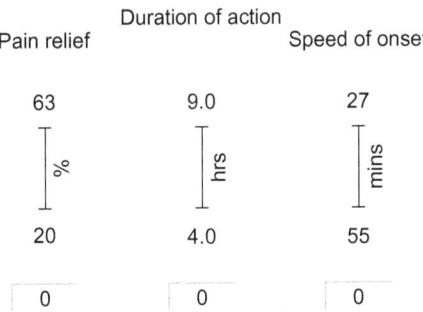

Figure 5.3

shown in the percentages, hours and minutes, respectively. Second is how much the differences in the worst–best pairs of numbers will matter from a clinical point of view.

Going slowly at this first stage, I elaborate: 'Think about the improvement from 20 to 63 per cent, 43 percentage points, for pain relief, compared to the additional 5 hours for duration of action, compared to the reduction from 55 to 27 minutes, a 28-minute improvement, for speed of action. Which one is the most clinically relevant improvement?' If they ask, 'For whom?' I answer, 'That depends on who is taking a decision and its context. Tell me more about both.' In this case, the decision maker was agreed to be an average customer in a pharmacy and the context was to purchase an analgesic to reduce or eliminate pain. It's up to the group, not the facilitator, to establish who the decision maker might be and the context of the decision.

In comparing the swings on the three criteria, some participants argued for pain relief while others favoured speed of onset, and they agreed it would depend on an individual patient's situation. I suggested they think about the average patient, and the group agreed it would marginally favour pain relief. 'Let's assign an arbitrary weight of 100 to that improvement; we can change it later if a new insight emerges', and I replaced the zero under pain relief with 100.

I went on by asking which difference was next best, and all agreed speed of onset. I asked if they could give a weight, 100 or less, such that the ratio to 100 could represent their ratio in strength of preference. They agreed and I asked participants to think of a number, but not to say it as I want to give everyone time to formulate their own view. I mentioned the anchoring heuristic in which the first person to speak can anchor everyone else, so from now on we will apply the 'think – discuss – agree' process to ensure the best possible assessment from the group.[70]

After a brief pause for thinking, I asked everyone to say the number they have in mind so I could identify those holding the most extreme views. I asked the person who gave the highest number to explain why they assigned that number. Allowing no discussion of their reasons, I asked the person who gave the lowest number to justify their assessment. Only after that person finished did I open discussion of the numbers to the group and ask if they could agree a new number. Applying this process quickly resulted in a weight of 90 for speed of onset, followed by a weight of 40 for duration of action. Entering those weights gave the display shown in Figure 5.4.

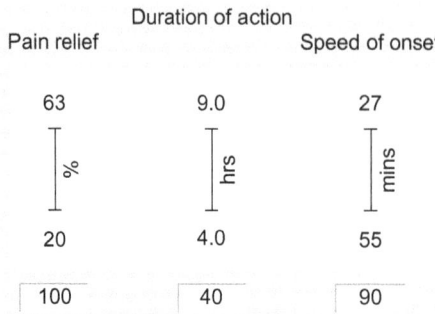

Figure 5.4

A new group usually finds weighting to be difficult – at first. Once they have done it and seen how it produces sensible results, they feel more comfortable in making the subjective judgements required. At some point you may find it helpful to explain (especially to medical practitioners, who have had drilled into them the importance of evidence-based medicine) that the data is only half the story. All data must be interpreted for its relevance in decision making (for example, some side effects of taking a drug are more clinically relevant than others, whereas a notable or valuable change in benefits might be considered more clinically meaningful[71] than others).

Consistency Check

This step is crucial! I pointed out to the group that increments of preference value can be added. I asked the group, 'Is your preference for a 5-hour increment in duration of action along with the 28-minute improvement in speed of onset, a preference value total of 40 + 90 = 130, 30 per cent more than your 100-point preference value for an improvement of 43 percentage points for pain relief?'

Most of the group looked surprised and agreed that was about right. I, too, was surprised because usually a group disagrees, largely because they are thinking about the importance of the criteria, not criteria increments. Participants often feel that all criteria are important, otherwise they wouldn't have included them in the model, so they tend to overweight the criteria. I may remind them that we are modelling differences among the options, and if all options provide the same level of performance on a specific criterion, then that criterion doesn't differentiate the options,[i] so it would receive a weight of zero whatever its importance. 'Of course,' I add, 'even small differences *could* be important.'

When a consistency check fails, I ask participants what they would like to change. Usually, they reduce some of the weights, but that can disrupt the ratios of the changed weights. For example, the above weights of 90 and 40 might be reduced to 80 and 20, making the latter sum the same as for pain relief. But now the initial 90:40 ratio, a little

---

[i] This is, of course, an instance of Jimmie Savage's 'Sure-thing' axiom in his landmark 1954 book *The Foundations of Statistics*.

bigger than 2:1, has changed to 80:20, or 4:1. The group usually makes several changes until all the ratios seem about right. They also learn the constraints imposed by requiring consistency in weights.

Reality Check

The computer normalises the weights so they sum to 100, multiplies their decimal versions by the preference values associated with each option and adds the products, then displays a bar graph of the results for the Benefits node (Figure 5.5).

I asked 'What do you think of that? How does it look? Does it make sense? Does it seem reasonable or not?' Most participants agreed it was OK, clearly to their surprise and relief that this rather unfamiliar task had provided a result that corresponded to their experience.

Then, someone said 'Why is there no pain relief bar for aspirin? It does give pain relief; it can't be zero.' I reminded the group that zero doesn't mean no pain relief, rather it shows that aspirin is the worst of the six drugs for pain relief. Similarly, paracetamol and ibuprofen are worst for duration of action and speed of onset, respectively, so each of their bar graphs is missing the corresponding slices.

This process of showing a result early helps the group to understand that the MCDA modelling process is able to capture the group's experience and so provides reassurance that this new process may indeed be valid. I reminded them that we haven't yet scored and weighted the side effects, which could change the results shown just for benefits.

Difficulty Thinking about Differences

If participants are new to the weighting approach and at least some participants are finding it difficult to think in terms of differences, I have two other ways of thinking

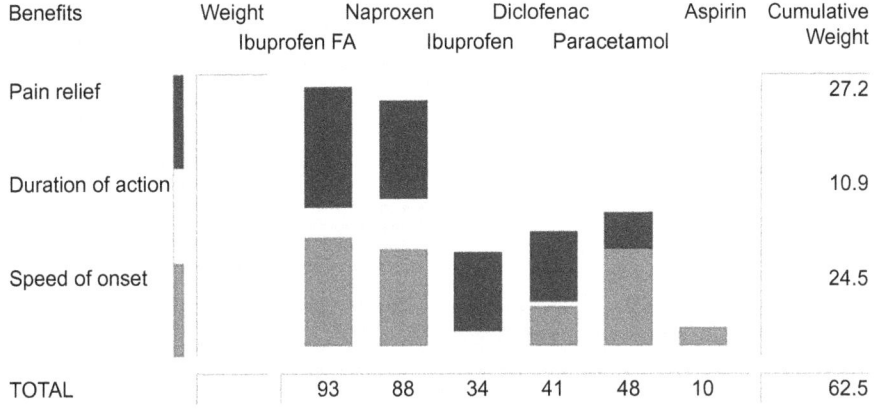

Figure 5.5

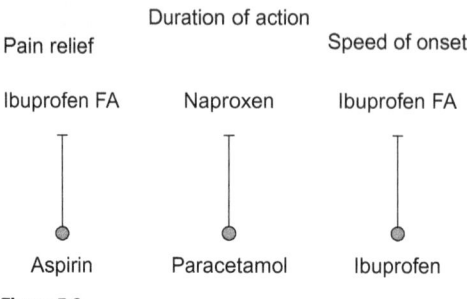

Figure 5.6

about swing weighting that can enable the group to better understand the approach. The answers here are based on what a panel of experts agreed were the final weights.

First, I try what might be called the *ground-zero* approach. I start by asking the group to imagine a hypothetical drug that scores at the bottom of the three benefit scales, as shown in Figure 5.6 by the dark circles.

I'll refer to those circles as defining a hypothetical 'dark drug' option. I ask, 'If you could make the benefits of the dark drug as good as the best drug but on only one of the three scales, which one would you move to the top? As good as ibuprofen FA for pain relief, or naproxen for duration of action, or ibuprofen FA for speed of onset?' Usually, that question, which although introducing a hypothetical option, helps a group to agree the criterion with the biggest difference that matters, in this case, the one that would be the best added clinical value. Here, they would have agreed it was pain relief, so I move the dark dot for pain relief to the top and ask, 'What's the next most important improvement?' Speed of action would have been the reply. The ranges of improvement have now been rank ordered, so you assign 100 arbitrary points to the first one and carry on with direct assessment of weights.

If there had been more criteria, you might have continued with the paired comparisons, always comparing each remaining criterion to the 100 criterion, until the group can agree on the rank ordering of the trade-offs. Most groups will initiate giving numbers before all comparisons are complete.

The second approach exploits the *trade-off* feature of weights. This approach works best if you have already drawn the three numbered scales on a flip chart, with dark and light sticky circles as shown in Figure 5.7. Ask the group to consider a hypothetical **light** drug that is as good as ibuprofen FA for pain relief but as poor as paracetamol for duration of action. In terms of the input data, the light drug has a 63 per cent chance of pain relief but lasts only four hours. Now consider a **dark** drug that is as poor as aspirin for pain relief but as good as naproxen for duration of action; only 20 per cent chance of pain relief but lasting for nine hours. Which drug do you prefer, the light or the dark one, whatever its speed of onset?

I would expect the group to have chosen the light drug. Now imagine moving the light spot on pain relief down next to the dark spot, making it as poor as aspirin for pain relief; the group should prefer the dark drug. You point out that this change in

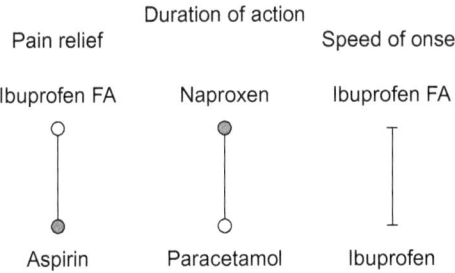

Figure 5.7

preference implies there is a location for the light pain relief circle that would result in a judgement that the light and dark drugs are about equal in strength of preference, a point of indifference, which I expect would have been located at the 40 per cent point on the pain relief scale. Thus, the weight on duration of action would be 40, namely, a 40-point increment on the pain relief scale is equivalent to all 100 points on duration of action.

Restore the light spot to the top of the pain relief scale, move the dark and light spots on duration of action to the speed of onset scale, enabling you to compare it to the pain relief scale as before. This time, indifference between the light and dark drugs would occur by lowering the light spot on pain relief to 90 per cent.

The advantage of this approach is that you don't have to ask for direct assessment of numbers. It is only necessary to move a single spot to find an indifference point. That could be a helpful way to explain trade-offs at the start of the weighting process.

However, there are two disadvantages to this approach. The first is that a best-worst combination might be impossible. Even though the criteria are judged to be mutually preference independent, they might not be statistically independent, so some best-worst combinations are unimaginable. The second is that although the scales are defined by input metrics at the extremes of the scales at the start, but at the indifference point the range of one of the scales has shortened into a region of preference that doesn't necessarily correspond to any option's input metric, so it is difficult for assessors to think about (and also may be associated with a non-linear value function).

These two disadvantages are sufficiently problematical that I will only occasionally ask for best–worst and worst–best preferences for all pairs of criteria to establish the rank orders of the weights, then move to direct assessments of weights.

Paired Comparisons

You'll notice that the three methods rely heavily on paired comparisons, the method introduced in the previous chapter for eliciting people's ordinal preferences that can be turned into interval-scale metrics. Comparing the swings on just two criteria at a time reduces the cognitive load in thinking about many criteria all at once (as is required in conjoint analysis[72]), and its simplicity helps participants in a decision conference to formulate and then discuss reasons for their preferences, as well as learn from others. Once the group becomes accustomed to judging paired comparisons, participants speed up and quickly develop their ability to scan the other criteria to anticipate which pair they want to consider next.

Problems

Let's turn now to resolving difficulties and questions that might arise during the swing weighting process.

Failure to Agree

The final weighted preference values of an MCDA model usually exhibit a property known as the 'flat maximum', which means that modest changes in a single weight typically won't affect the final rank ordering of the options very much at all. I explain to the group that a swing weight within ±10 percentage points is good enough, so consensus isn't necessary. If the range of disagreement in a group about weights is much more than that, it may be worthwhile to explore why this is so. Perhaps the opposing participants are interpreting the criterion differently, in which case further discussion and clarification might lead to two sub-criteria, which could be added to the value tree or, software allowing, added, scored and weighted to give the single set of values required by the original criterion.

If just one expert persists in holding an extreme weight, write it on a flipchart and use the median value given by the other members of the group, with a promise to the outlier expert that his or her view will be tested in a sensitivity analysis of the final model. If that presents no resolution, then it may be necessary to report two results to the accountable decision maker along with the reasons for the differing weights. Methods for achieving a degree of consensus in groups of experts are elaborated in Chapter 7.

Misunderstanding What a Weight Represents

Despite your explanations that the weight refers to the importance of a bottom-to-top range on a criterion, not the importance of the criterion itself, the latter may stick in the mind because that does accurately describe a 0-to-100 range on a ratio scale, for which zero means absence of the characteristic, as in zero weight or length. Then, the swing from nothing to something is thought of as the importance of the something compared to its absence. Let me unpack that sentence.

I can illustrate what that means by using my work with Professor David Nutt in modelling the harms of 20 psychoactive drugs.[73] All the criteria were harms, and every scale was anchored at zero, representing no harm, therefore most preferred. The top of each scale was the most harmful drug on that criterion, the least preferred, so when I elicited weights it was just a matter of comparing the most harmful drugs on two

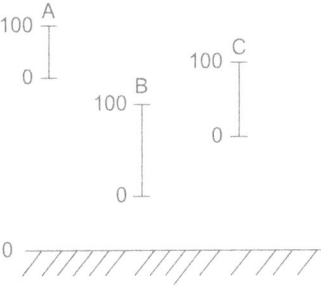

Figure 5.8

scales compared to no harm on each, so participants effectively compared the relative harms of the most harmful drugs at the top of each scale.

The main reason we usually use interval scales in MCDA is that for many collections of options, the zero point doesn't exist, or all the options are already achieving sufficient values that it is only their differences that will inform the decision, especially if even the worst values are all very high, so compared to zero they wouldn't easily be discriminated. I generally try not to use the word 'importance' when assessing weights for interval scales, but if someone asks if really we are simply comparing the importance of the criteria, I say, 'No, you are assessing importance of the difference between top and bottom.' To show what that means, I sketch this on a flip-chart (Figure 5.8).

The bottom is ground-zero, no value. Here are three 0–100 Best–Worst scales for criteria A, B and C. Although the values are higher in some absolute value sense for A, the weight for B would be higher than for A because the difference is larger. Those two scales characterise the Stonehenge versus Thames Gateway comparison. Scale C overlaps bits of A and B, but its length is shorter than B, but longer than A, so its weight would be between the other two. This helps to make clear that it is differences in importance, B > C > A, not criteria differences, A > C > B, that are captured in swing weighting.

Participants acquainted with other multi-criteria approaches or disciplines, such as the analytic hierarchy process (AHP), or statistical regression analysis, may find it difficult to understand that a weight in MCDA represents both an objective difference and a subjective judgement about the relevance of the difference for making a decision, in short, a value difference. And value is necessarily subjective, so is always dependent on context. I've never been clear about what a weight in AHP represents, and, indeed, Jim Dyer in his critique of AHP says the weights are 'arbitrary'.[74] As for beta weights in statistical regression, they represent the objective strength for predicting one uncertain quantity from another, with no concern for the value of the prediction.

Objection to the Subjectivity of Weights

This view is often held by participants who believe that decisions should be objective, which requires reliance on empirical evidence. I remind the group that all evidence has to be interpreted for its relevance, and this requires an understanding of the context for the decision. A weight represents both how big the worst–best difference is and how much you care about that difference, with the word 'care' replaced by an equivalent verb or verb phrase that is specific to the context. For example, 'clinically relevant' in a medical context, or 'mission effective' in a military context, 'socially desirable' in a government policy context, or 'strategically important' in a business context.

There is no objective theory of decision making. Indeed, decision theory, which is the basis for MCDA, contains only three quantities, and they are all subjective. Values multiplied by probabilities are guides to decisions: the very, very small probability of winning the lottery multiplied by the huge win is actually smaller than the cost of a lottery ticket, and that's why I don't buy lottery tickets. But some people consider the fun of engaging in anticipating a win or even the good that is done by the UK's National Lottery as worth the small cost. They have effectively given more weight to those non-monetary consequences to justify their purchase.

Weighting in Hierarchical Models

Left-to-right or right-to-left? Or for value trees that are vertical, bottom-up or top-down? In this section, I argue for right-to-left (or bottom-up). Left-to-right (or top-down) is only a consistency check about the consequences of collections of bottom-up weights.

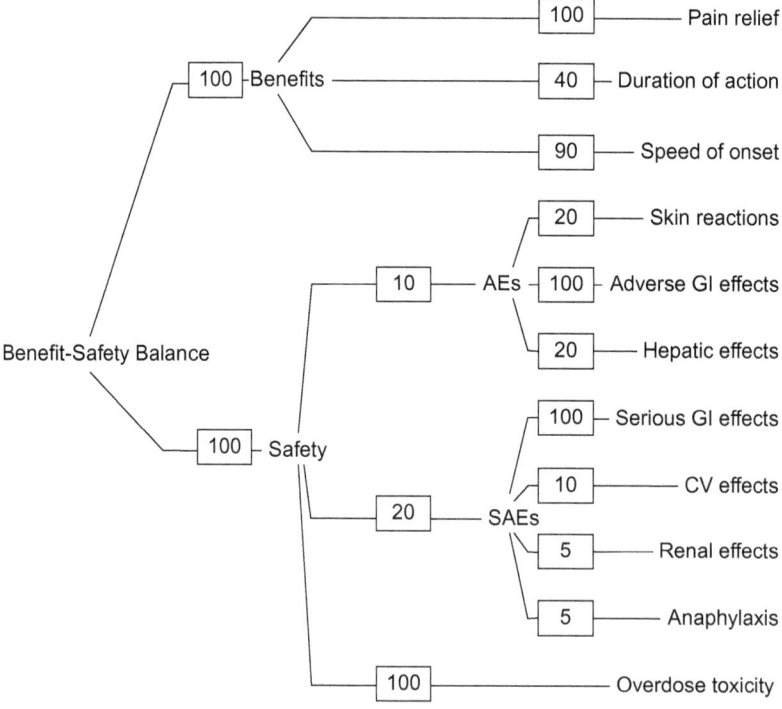

Figure 5.9

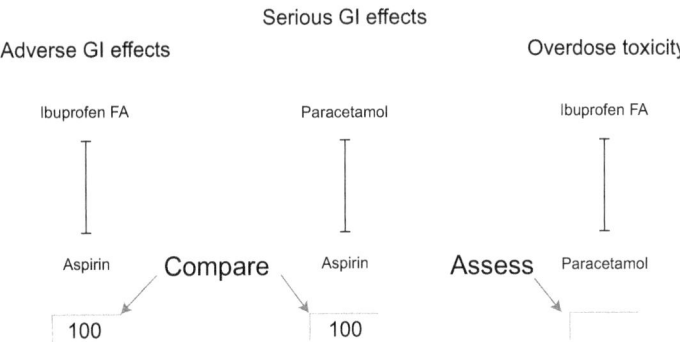

Figure 5.10

The weights of 100–40–90 assessed by the experts are shown in Figure 5.9 on the upper-right branches of the complete value tree. Next, I helped the experts assess swing weights for the three Adverse Events (AEs) criteria, 20–100–20, then swing weights for the four Serious Adverse Events (SAEs) criteria, 100–10–5–5. I emphasised that 100 was to be assigned to the largest difference in added clinical value for the criteria under each individual node, but that the 100s might be different from one node to the next; equating them to a common unit is the next step.

On completion of the weighting for the SAE criteria, I asked the group to move left to the Safety node so we could compare the weight of 100 for Adverse GI effects with the 100 for Serious GI effects, as we hadn't yet made any comparisons between nodes, and those two 100s might not be equal to each other (Figure 5.10). We also needed to assess the swing weight for Overdose Toxicity.

Participants quickly agreed that neither 100 should be retained because the difference on Overdose Toxicity was much more clinically relevant, meriting a swing weight of 100. They also said that the swings on the GI effects were in a ratio of about 2:1 and much lower than 100. After a short discussion, they arrived at weights of 10–20–100. The computer duly multiplied all the weights on the AEs by 0.20 and on the SAEs by 0.40. This effectively provided a common unit of preference value across all the safety criteria.

That left equating the units for the 100-weighted benefit criterion with the 100-weighted safety criterion, the crucial trade-off. After much debate, the group agreed that the increased chances of pain relief afforded by ibuprofen FA over aspirin, 63 compared to 20 per cent, provided about as much added clinical value as the difference in overdose toxicity between paracetamol and ibuprofen FA, resulting in equal weights of 100–100,[ii] so a unit of benefit equalled a unit of safety. The weighted scores share a common unit, so they can be combined after the weights have been normalised by the computer so they sum to 100, while preserving their original ratios.

[ii] Paracetamol is the only drug of the six for which an overdose can be fatal. Its pain-killing effects wear off sooner (4 hours, on average) than for the other drugs, so many people take another pill after the pain starts to return, made worse if they've forgotten when they took the last pill. Each year, 150 to 250 people die of an overdose in the UK.

	Units	Weight	Ibuprofen Fast Acting	Naproxen Fast Acting	Ibuprofen	Diclofenac	Paracetamol	Aspirin
BENEFITS								
Pain relief	%	27.2	63	55	48	45	33	20
Duration of action	hours	10.9	7.0	9.0	5.5	4.5	4.0	5.0
Speed of onset	minutes	25.5	27	30	55	45	30	50
SAFETY								
Skin reactions	number	0.5	24	26	24	41	77	124
GI effects	Preference	2.7	100	100	100	100	90	0
Hepatic effects	Preference	0.5	100	50	100	100	0	30
Serious GI effects	Preference	5.4	75	50	75	70	100	0
CV effects	Preference	0.5	75	80	75	0	75	100
Renal effects	Preference	0.3	100	0	100	100	100	100
Anaphylaxis	Preference	0.3	50	50	50	50	100	0
Overdose toxicity	Preference	27.2	100	80	100	75	0	20

Figure 5.11

You might try doing that calculation in Excel or on a calculator to gain a feeling for how simple the mathematics is. Multiply the weights along each branch of the tree, sum the 11 products, then divide each product by the sum to give the final criteria weights. I displayed the computer calculations of the normalised weights to the expert group as a final consistency check and they agreed the weights looked about right as capturing the differences among the drugs.

I like to create an *Effects Table* that shows all the input data and the final normalised weights, which enables your client to see that some rows of data weigh more heavily in the final overall results (Figure 5.11). I include this table in the report to the client. You can see that those results are most heavily influenced by Pain relief, Speed of onset, and Overdose toxicity.

The light grey benefit cells identify the drug providing the best benefits for each effect, while the dark grey safety cells show the worst drug for side effects. Note that hard data was available for the three benefits, but only for one side effect, skin reactions.

The right-to-left process of swing weighting in a hierarchical model requires good visual displays for your group. I used to do it on a large whiteboard after drawing the value tree, followed by drawing a thermometer scale for each criterion. But that can become tedious for a large value tree, so it's best to use the help of MCDA software. For example, in Hiview 3, select a node and the computer can display the appropriate scales to be compared, as shown in Figure 5.12 for the Safety node (left) and the Benefit-Safety Balance node (right).

A Last Consistency Check

Show the bar graphs of the final result and ask the group if it looks about right. This Hiview3 graph in Figure 5.13 shows the separate contributions of benefits and safety to the final totals. The longer each portion of a bar is, the more clinically relevant the benefit and the safer it is.

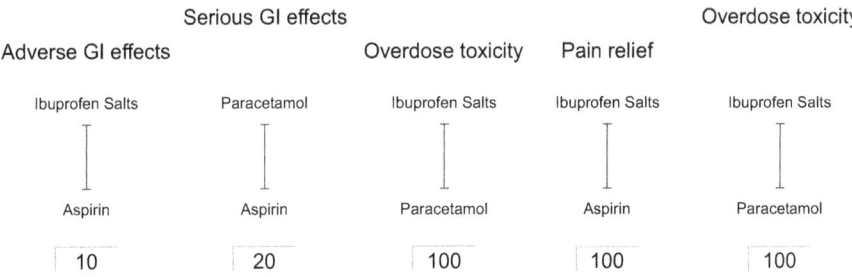

Figure 5.12

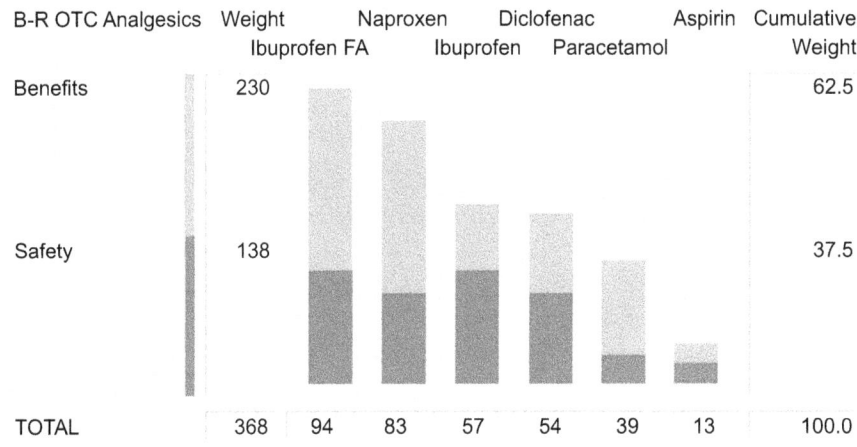

Figure 5.13

The cumulative weight of 62.5 is the sum of the weights in the previous table of the three benefits, so 37.5 is the sum for safety. As a consistency check, I asked the group if the ratio of the clinically relevant differences among the drugs is 63:37, about 2:1. They agreed that was about right.

The graph in Figure 5.14 shows the contribution to the totals of the individual criteria.

It's clear that three criteria dominate the final results: pain relief, speed of onset and overdose toxicity. The group agreed that was so.

Next, we explored sensitivity and scenario analyses, which can stimulate new ideas, identify errors in logic and generally improve the model, helping to resolve any remaining sense of unease. More will be said about that for different model types in Part III.

Some Final Words of Advice

When I started to write this chapter, I thought it would be at most four pages long because swing weighting is so easy. Clearly, I was wrong. As I reflected on my

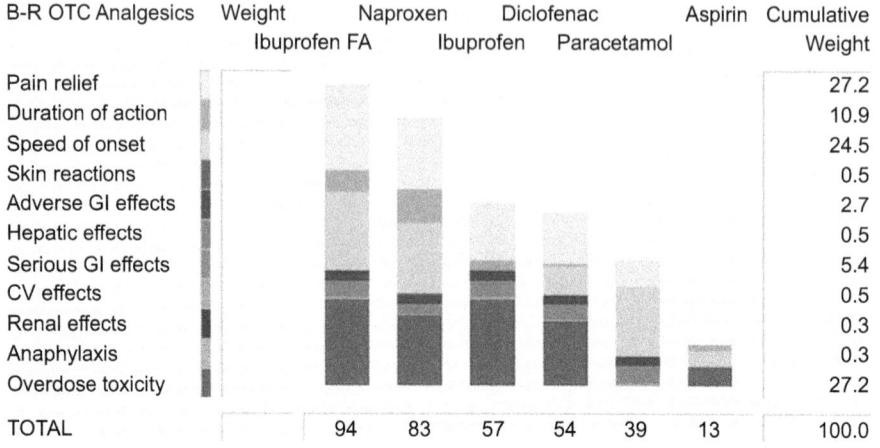

Figure 5.14

experience when I first started MCDA modelling, I remember finding it difficult, as do many participants new to decision conferences (and not just a few decision analysts as well!).

An initial clarification for me many years ago was when Dr Scott Barclay, the designer of the first version of Hiview, suggested the phrase 'How big is the difference and how much do you care about it?' That was a key step, later reinforced by Ralph Keeney in his important paper on value trade-offs,[75] which makes clear that weighted values of different measures can only be combined if they are using a common unit of measure. You wouldn't add inches to centimetres without first converting one metric to the other via a scale constant. Quite clearly, when weights are assessed as simply the importance of the criteria, as many methods that claim to be MCDA models do, this is an error. As we've seen, importance is indeed part of Scott's question – it's the 'how much do you care about it' part, but the 'caring' refers to a range of numbers on a criterion, not just the criterion itself. That's why we can say that swing weights represent *relative* importance, always relative to the ranges of numbers, but never solely the importance of the criteria.

Summary

This chapter introduced swing weighting as a necessary step in building a decision analysis model to create a common unit of measurement for the performance of all options on all criteria, assuming that any input data have been converted either linearly or non-linearly into preference values on 0–100 scales. The weights act as scale constants for combining and comparing preference values. The weights are elicited by asking assessors to compare the largest ranges of performance of the options on two criteria and judge how much they care about those differences. That is the basic task, repeatedly comparing differences in added value for pairs of criteria until every criterion has been considered.

The process starts with the criteria, not with their parent node, by scanning the criteria to establish which shows the largest difference in added value and assigning that criterion a weight of 100. Using paired comparisons, the value-added differences on each of the remaining criteria under the same node are compared to the 100-weighted criterion. Consistency checks follow: compare sums of weights to one another, which often results in a lowering of some weights to correct for the initial bias of thinking that all criteria are important.

Once weights have been assigned to all criteria under the right-most parent nodes, then paired comparisons are made of the 100-weighted criteria under each node. This process is repeated moving further to the left until all comparisons of the 100-weighted criteria have been exhausted. Multiplying weights (as decimals less than or equal to 1) along each path in the tree gives a product for each criterion and these are normalised, so they sum to 1 (and are expressed as a percentage). Assessors are invited to judge whether the resulting weights make sense as capturing the relative value added of the options on the criteria.

If assessors find it difficult to assess weights, two variations on swing weighting might help to clarify the concept of value added. In the *ground-zero* approach, assessors are asked to imagine a hypothetical option whose performance scores at the bottom of all the criteria under a parent node, and are then invited to make that option better by moving to the top of each scale in order of the most value added. In the *trade-off* method, two hypothetical options are compared, one best on criterion A and worst on B, the other worst on A and best on B. Successive paired comparisons will identify the one criterion that always comes out top, giving it a weight of 100. Pairing that criterion successively to the other criteria and adjusting it downward to find an indifference point will determine the weights for the remaining criteria.

Just as non-linear value functions provide an opportunity for clients to interpret the data, so swing weighting can be positioned as an opportunity for making judgements about the *relative* importance of the criteria. Communicating what the swing weights represent is easier if you use the language of your client. For example, they can be positioned to represent differences in *clinical relevance* for a medical context, *mission effectiveness* for a military context, *social desirability* for a government policy context or *strategic importance* for a business context. The sooner you are able to use language that is familiar to your client, the quicker you can drop the jargon of decision analysis, while retaining the rigour of our discipline. It is clarity about the meaning of value that enables us to resolve Isaiah Berlin's problem and proceed with confidence in helping our clients with comparing what may initially seem to them to be incommensurable.

6   Uncertainty and Probability

> If a man will begin with certainties, he shall end in doubts; but if he will be content to begin with doubts, he shall end in certainties.
>
> Sir Francis Bacon, 1605[76]

It's time to move on from values, which we saw can include dis-values such as harm, and address how to express our doubts as probabilities about future events and consequences. Recall that I rather skipped over the source of the probability of a successful operation in the blind problem of Chapter 1. We'll now see how that could have been determined, but first let's be clear about what is a probability.

The Meaning of Probability

In the twenty-first century, two different meanings of probability are in wide use: relative frequency and degree of belief. Frequency refers to collections of things, with the probability of selecting a red card from a well-shuffled deck of 52 playing cards, or the probability that two dice rolled simultaneously will show 'snake eyes', two ones. In these cases, probabilities are a characteristic of the deck of cards or the dice. In short, probabilities are characteristics of things, the external world.

The degree of belief interpretation is that probabilities are measures of an individual's beliefs about something that is uncertain, which might be related to collections of things, but can also apply to unique events, like the probability that a person will set foot on Mars before 2050, or that your favourite tennis star will win the singles match at the next Wimbledon. It applies to the outcome of uncertain events and to the consequences of the outcomes, which can be uncertain quantities. And it is used scientifically to express uncertainty about hypotheses. Under this interpretation, probabilities are characteristics of people's thinking, the internal world.

Some have argued that probabilities based on relative frequencies are objective, and therefore more scientific, while those based on degrees of belief are subjective and, many scientists believe, are not to be applied in scientific statistical analysis of objective data. On the other hand, many people find the subjective interpretation to be useful, as probability theory allows expert judgement about probabilities to be modified with objective data by applying Bayes' rule. That was proposed in 1961 by Robert Schlaifer[77] and has been taken up by the business community, as well as by many scientists whose purpose is to reduce uncertainty by conducting experiments.

Decision analysts also find it attractive in helping clients who frequently deal with situations in which it is difficult or impossible to define the collections of things to which 'objective' probabilities could apply. In particular, decisions about the future that involve unique events require consideration of similar though not identical events, as has been characteristic of oil and gas exploration, and in developing new drugs. As data is received, probabilities are revised, and at any stage it is possible to report the probability that there is oil or gas in a given location, or that a new drug will be approved by a regulator. I'll expand on this theme in Chapter 18.

More generally, the degrees of belief definition of probability can apply to any uncertain events, uncertain quantities, or hypotheses, and it is these probabilities, sometimes revised with data, which are used in decision models. That can't be said of the significance levels of traditional statistical methods: a hypothesis is either true or not under a relative frequency view of probability, so the probability is either one or zero. Significance levels and confidence intervals are probability statements about data, not about hypotheses, although they are often misinterpreted as though they prove or disprove a hypothesis. Probabilities can apply to both favourable and unfavourable outcomes, unlike the term *risk*, which is usually associated with the probability of an unfavourable effect. For example, possible side effects of taking a drug are often described as risks, and their probabilities are reported in patient leaflets using ranges of relative frequencies – for example, less than 1 in 10, 1 in 100, 1 in 1,000 or 1 in 10,000. Nothing more in this chapter will be said about risk, which is the topic of Chapter 17.

Defining a Degree of Belief Probability

If relative frequencies define 'objective' probabilities, what defines a probability that expresses a degree of belief? One definition is that it is the amount you consider would be a fair amount to bet for a unit return if the outcome you are betting on occurs. If you believe there is a 0.70 chance your favourite for the Wimbledon singles will win, you should be willing to place 70 pence on a bet that pays £1 if your favourite wins. Or £7 to win £10, or £70 to win £100, etc. Here, probabilities are interpreted as betting amounts, and this simple interpretation usually works for clients who are sceptical about subjective judgements. But, as you can see, your willingness to bet might also be influenced by your utility for money – you might accept the lower amounts where your utility for money is linear, but not for larger amounts if your utility function is concave, as Daniel Bernoulli suggested in 1738.

Here is a nearly fool-proof interpretation – a choice between two gambles. Consider your uncertainty about whether person X (you choose a named person) will win the men's singles at the next Wimbledon. The left gamble in Figure 6.1 shows you would win the car of your dreams if your named person were to win; if he didn't win, you would get nothing. We want to assess your current probability of his winning, so we

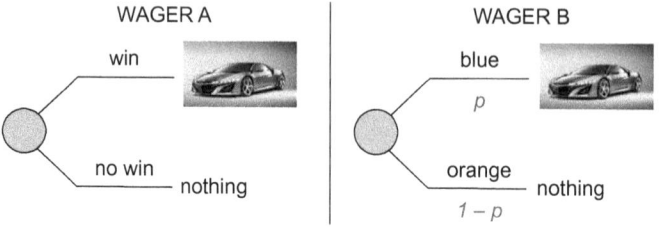

Figure 6.1

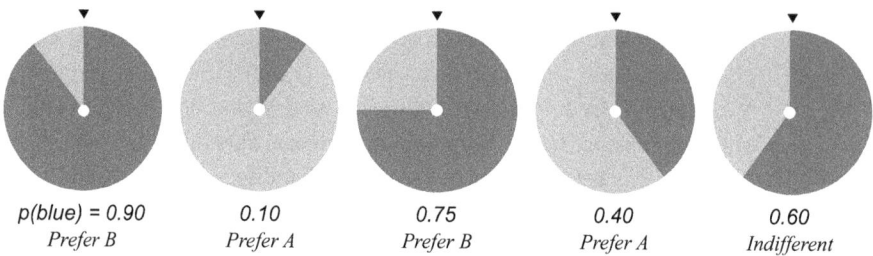

$p(blue) = 0.90$	0.10	0.75	0.40	0.60
Prefer B	*Prefer A*	*Prefer B*	*Prefer A*	*Indifferent*

Figure 6.2

deploy the right gamble and the spinner wheel we encountered in Chapter 4 for assessing your uncertainty as a probability. Now we use the same technique of changing the relative size of the blue sector, raising or lowering the relative size of the blue portion, until you are indifferent between the two gambles. In either wager, you might win an expensive car, so the consequences are identical.

Well, almost. Since you must wait to see if you've won wager A, you might prefer wager B for a win today, so to make the two wagers identical, choosing wager B today means you must wait until the day of the Wimbledon singles to actually spin the wheel for wager B, no matter who wins. Now the two wagers are identical. (If the car doesn't interest you, then replace it with something you would value a lot, sufficiently for you to take the two wagers seriously.)

As the two wagers are identical in their consequences, they engage your risk attitude equally, and their consequences will become known on the same day, so none of those factors should affect your preference for one wager over the other at the indifference point. It's only the value of p that matters. Figure 6.2 shows a sequence of spinner changes that led to a probability of 0.6.

This process of finding an indifference point between a wager on an uncertain event compared to a wager on a reference gamble is a constructive demonstration of the proof that probabilities, defined as degrees of belief, exist. It is rare for a person to keep insisting they can't make a choice, particularly when the uncertain quantity or event in question is something they care about. Of course, that depends on interpreting the angle of the darker (blue) sector as a proportion of 360 degrees. That is reasonable because we can interpret the angles shown on a clock with two hands down to the minute, even without markings of the minutes on the clock's face.

As an aside, I often met up at noontime in the early 1970s with Professor Dennis Lindley, then the head of the statistics department at University College London, and we took lunch together at the University's staff dining room. On one occasion, as we entered, he spotted an elderly man at one table and went over to him, asking if we could join him. He graciously agreed and I was then introduced to Professor Egon Pearson, the developer with Jerzy Neyman of statistical significance testing, which remains in widespread use to this day.

In conversation with him, I asked why the two of them did not take a Bayesian approach to their work (as Jimmie Savage did in 1952). He replied that although they both knew about Bayes' rule, they couldn't see how the required prior probabilities (discussed below and in Chapter 18) could be determined. I said that I had never had any trouble eliciting probability judgements from scientists, who always had some ideas about the hypotheses they were testing in their research, otherwise they wouldn't be conducting the research. He was surprised, and I conceded that in the late 1920s, when their approach was developed, nobody knew then what we know now about assessing personal probabilities. After all, that was before Ramsey's important 1931 paper.

In summary, the meaning of a personal probability is that it is a number between 0 and 1.0, p, which makes the assessor indifferent between a wager for the outcome of an event, uncertain quantity or hypothesis in question, as compared to a two-outcome reference gamble one of whose sectors displays *p per cent* and the other *(1−p)per cent* of the whole circle. No relative frequencies required, just a preference between two wagers. No need, even, to play the gamble.

Probability Rules

Both the classical and Bayesian schools of statistics agree about the rules of probability, which are essentially the grammar for how probabilities can be combined. Any decision model that includes probabilities must obey those rules, for they are considered as a normative standard. Practically speaking, an event (like flipping a coin) leads to an outcome (heads or tails), and each of those is followed by a consequence (winning or losing). On a decision tree, the probabilities are associated with the event's outcome branches, assuming the event E has occurred. The rules of probability refer to the outcomes as subscripts of E, for example, E_1 and E_2 for the flip of a coin, which I use here, although the same rules would apply if the probabilities were associated with consequences.

Rule 1: For any event E_i, the probability for the assessor with knowledge K is any number between 0 and 1. In mathematical terms:

$$0 < p(E_i|K) < 1.$$

The probability is 1 if, and only if, K logically implies the truth of E. Now let's assume K so the equations are easier.

Rule 2: If only two outcomes are possible for an event and they are *mutually exclusive* (whichever one occurs, the other can't), then the sum of their individual probabilities must be 1.

$$p(E_1 \text{ or } E_2) = p(E_1) + p(E_2)$$

The probability of realising either a heads or a tails from the toss of a fair coin is 0.5 + 0.5 = 1. You are certain to get one or the other. This can be extended to any number of outcomes, provided they are mutually exclusive. And if the list of outcomes is *exhaustive* (the list is complete), then the sum of the probabilities must obey rule 1 because one of the outcomes on the list is certain to occur.

Rule 3: If two events, E and F, are not mutually exclusive, so that F's outcomes are relevant to assessing the probability of E's outcomes, then the probability of both outcomes occurring is equal to the probability of E given F times the probability of F.

$$p(E \text{ and } F) = p(E|F) \times p(F)$$

Should I carry an umbrella this afternoon (of concern for those of us who live in London)? That depends on whether the forecast is for rain where I live, outcome E, and whether the forecast is accurate, F. The probability it will rain this afternoon depends, then, on both the forecast and its accuracy. So, for me, the probability it will rain *and* be accurate is the forecast for rain *given* that it is accurate multiplied by the probability of the forecast's accuracy.

The term $p(E|F)$ is called a conditional probability, but in fact all probabilities are conditional, for they depend on who is assessing the probability (K) and the information available at the time. For weather forecasts, that includes the general area to which the forecasts apply. Weather forecasters depend in part on relative frequencies, but also on current meteorological conditions, which they combine in their heads to create a forecast. Interest in other outcomes, F, G, H, etc., related to E, is called '*extending the conversation*' about E to include both causes and relevance, as explained later in Chapter 16.

These rules constitute the grammar of probabilities, often referred to as the *probability calculus*, so related personal probabilities must be *coherent*, or consistent with the rules, just as words in a sentence are constrained by the rules of grammar. As we must learn the rules of grammar to speak so others can understand us, so we can learn the rules of probability to ensure that our probability assessments are coherent. We will see how this applies in more detail for models that contain many events in Chapter 18.

Assessing Personal Probabilities

Let's return now to the eye problem of Chapter 2 and ask where the 0.70 probability of the operation's success came from. Success rates are often recorded for medical procedures, but you might think differently if the history had been 7 out of 10 rather than 70 out of 100. Even if it was 70 out of 100, further questioning of the ophthalmologist about the characteristics of their patients might have revealed that success rates were lower for the sex opposite to yours, for ages different from your age, and so on and so forth, until the record shows one person who matched all your characteristics, but that person died! Also, the ophthalmologist's skills might have improved, making the earlier data less valuable.

Sometimes we overestimate probabilities for favourable outcomes and underestimate them for unfavourable outcomes. Here, only two outcomes are possible, and if only the success rate had been mentioned, the unfavourable event's outcome probability of 0.30 (required by rule 2, above) might be mentioned by the patient to see if it is as realistic as the 0.70 for the favourable outcome. It is that sort of questioning that can provide a good assessment, sometimes aided by use of the spinner wheel.

Occasionally, I have encountered an expert who refused to give any probabilities at all. For example, when in the late 1970s I asked an expert who was knowledgeable about oil and gas fields in the North Sea (between the UK and Norway) what the total volume of gas would be for one named field, he gave a low and high estimate, explaining that you can never be sure until the field is finally exhausted. I asked him for a probability that the final value would be between the high and the low and he replied, 'It will be either between or outside.'

I needed a probability distribution for a project I was working on, so I showed him the probability wheel, set to 50–50, and asked him would he rather bet on a spin of the wheel or that the final volume would lie between the limits. He became quite red in the face and rather angry, saying that he wasn't a betting man, and only after much discussion would he agree that the probability was more than 80 per cent. I asked about another oil field, for which only a single estimate was given, and said that I assumed he was more certain of that field's reserves. 'Not at all,' he said. 'That was a field about which we were even more uncertain.' I concluded he was not a probabilistic thinker, and I managed to elicit probability assessments from other experts.

Experts who won't quantify their current level of uncertainty as a probability may be thinking of probability as a characteristic of things, for which repeated similar random events are the only valid measure of probability, and there is not yet sufficient data to turn a relative frequency into a probability. Explaining that the degree of belief interpretation is valid usually helps groups of experts to quantify their collective uncertainty, because that represents a better summary of the current state of knowledge about a topic than could be provided by any individual expert.

The above discussion raises the question, how good are people at assessing personal probabilities? But first, what do I mean by 'good'? We met the three components of quality back in Chapter 3: validity, reliability and precision.

It is, of course, impossible to establish the *validity* of a single probability assessment. Even if I judged the probability of rain this afternoon to be 95 per cent and it didn't rain, I had admitted there would be a 5 per cent chance of no rain. However, if I kept a large collection of my weather forecasts, it's reasonable to expect that on all occasions when I predicted 95 per cent rain, it should have rained on 95 per cent of them. Research of that sort is extensive, and it began with general-knowledge

Table 6.1

Tick the correct answer	Write your probability of being correct: 50–100%

1. A group of kangaroos is called
    a. a troop
    b. a pack
	_____

2. The capital of New York State is
    a. New York City
    b. Albany
	_____

3. In surface area, the larger ocean is
    a. Atlantic
    b. Indian
	_____

4. Which city is farther north?
    a. Rome
    b. New York City
	_____

questions like the those shown in Table 6.1. Try it yourself (and if you give less than 50 per cent to any question, you ticked the wrong alternative).

Imagine that you have answered many of these questions, each one printed on a separate card.[i] Once you have finished, sort the cards into separate piles, making as many piles as you gave different probabilities. So, there may be a pile of 50s, 55s, 60s and so forth. Now, for each pile, count the number of cards on which you ticked the right answer. If you are an accurate assessor of probability, you should have ticked the right answer 50 per cent of the time for the 50s pile, 60 per cent of the time for the 60s pile, etc. You could also plot a graph of your 'calibration', as it is called in the literature, like the ones shown in Figure 6.3.

Notice that when these people said they were 80 per cent sure they had ticked the right answer only about 65 per cent of the time; they were over-confident. And when they said 50 per cent, they were correct about 55 per cent of the time. Over-confident for high probabilities and under-confident for low ones, which has also been found when the probabilities range from 0 to 100 per cent. This finding, replicated numerous times for general knowledge questions, has led many investigators, me included, to conclude that people are generally over-confident when expressing their uncertainty as probabilities.[78]

---

[i] Spoiler alert! Answers to four questions: troop, Albany, Atlantic, Rome.

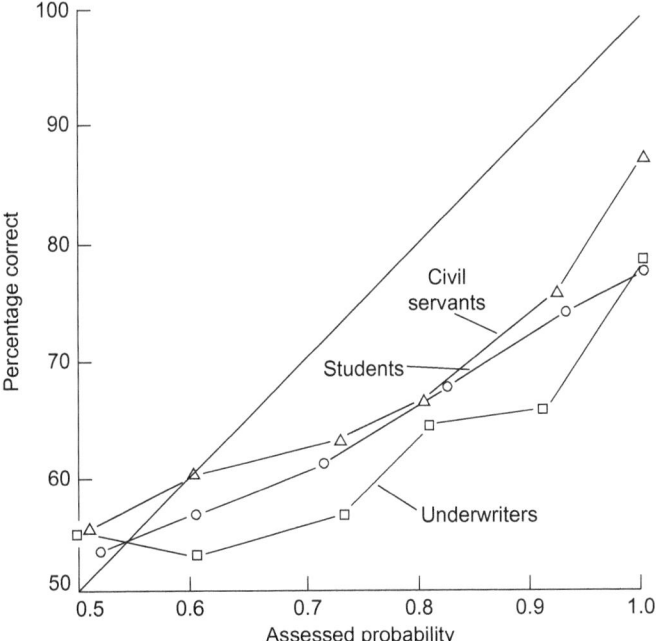

Figure 6.3

But we were over-generalising, as I first learned from a former colleague, Jack Dowie, then a lecturer at the UK's Open University. He created in the late 1980s a course called 'Professional Judgement', which among other topics introduced the students to the concepts of uncertainty and probability. To help students improve their ability to reflect on their feelings of uncertainty and express it as probabilities, he set 'prober' exercises during the course and required probability assessments for the multiple-choice questions on the final exam. Lo and behold, those probabilities were well calibrated. Since then, psychologists have managed to account for the variability of human judgement by differences in the demands of the task, such as the familiarity of the topic, experience with the task requirements and the extent of feedback about the event outcomes (which, for example, helps meteorologists to become better calibrated with probability forecasts).[79] In short, assessing probabilities that are well calibrated is a skill that can be learned. (But I continued to be over-confident in judging the probability that writing a chapter in this book will be complete in the time I had planned, especially this chapter!)

Research now suggests that although over-confidence is the most common finding, people *can* make well-calibrated probability judgements.[80] But here is a health warning: I don't think good calibration is possible if the resolution time horizons are beyond two years, at most, for events or uncertain quantities that are influenced by human activity.[81] The evidence for calibration for longer-term events is lacking. Good calibration depends on receiving feedback about perhaps at least 200 outcomes fairly quickly. Perhaps that's why the underwriters in Figure 6.3 were excessively over-confident, as their knowledge of outcomes was incomplete.

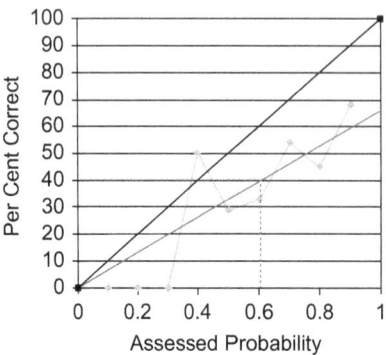

Figure 6.4

Some years ago, I attempted to close this gap by referring back to probabilities that I had helped developers of drugs at a major pharmaceutical company to assess 10 years earlier. The drugs were in late-stage development, so it would be many years before they were approved, or not; that's why I had to wait so long to see if they had been approved. The resulting calibration curve in Figure 6.4 is based on only about 60 assessments, so there is considerable variability in the calibration curve – the (0.4, 50) point is based on only two projects. The lower solid dark grey (red) line is a 'best fit' to the data points and shows clear evidence of over-confidence: assessments of 0.6 were correct only 40 per cent of the time. I had spent only about 10 minutes training the developers in assessing probabilities, including using the spinner wheel, so although they were experts in drug development, the training was not sufficient to create good calibration. And they didn't get feedback soon enough to improve their ability to assess probabilities. Even if they thought they remembered their original assessments, their remembering of them might well have been subject to hindsight bias, as Baruch Fischhoff found in remembered probabilities about the outcomes of President Nixon's visit to China in 1972.[82]

The Process of Eliciting Good Probabilities

Facilitators assist people in assessing probabilities of *event outcomes* (the winner of the next Wimbledon singles; tomorrow's weather; which horse will win a race; an operation's outcomes; which of several hypotheses is true) and of *uncertain quantities* (the number of people who will be hospitalised for influenza in my country next month; the amount of oil left in a particular well; the market share that a new product will achieve by the end of the next financial year; the cost of building a repository for nuclear waste deep underground). First, let's define the characteristics of 'good' probability judgements, and then it will be possible to understand the process of eliciting them.

Like any aspect of a decision model, probability judgements need only be as good as required to help the decision maker resolve the issues at hand. In other words, the assessed probabilities should be requisite. It requires some practice and experience for even the most capable expert to translate their feeling of uncertainty into a number, but this process of construction and refinement occurs in the process of building and exploring a decision model. In some cases, experts are convened separately, just to construct probabilities that others will use in modelling. As for eliciting value preferences, I prefer to work with groups so that differences in perspectives and experience can be shared in the group, enabling the group to arrive at consensus probabilities that are in some ways better, and can be uniquely different from any individual assessment or the average of several assessments.[83]

The following five-stage protocol includes items whose relevance is to be determined by the facilitator. I am pleased to acknowledge that the items are largely based on *A Manual for Encoding Probability Distributions*, written by Carl-Axel Staël von Holstein and James E. Matheson, and published in 1979, by the USA's Defense Advanced Research Projects Agency, so it is in the public domain. Its 201 pages include a 30-page appendix, 'Intuitive judgment: biases and corrective procedures', written by Amos Tversky and Daniel Kahneman, a little-known early work of those two outstanding contributors to the field of behavioural decision making. I have modified and added to the items, reflecting my experience of eliciting probabilities from a variety of clients in very different fields. My revised protocol now includes 30 items, shown in the appendix to this chapter. Other investigators continue to write about probability assessment, particularly in how it has been applied to areas such as policy analysis, health care, environmental decisions, and other topic areas.[84]

The comment I made in Chapter 4, in the section on Assessing Value Functions, that experts always disagree, holds as well for probabilities. Like judgements of preference value, people might be biased, as when they appear to be over-confident of desired outcomes and under-confident about undesirable ones. However, there is inevitably some data or information that is relevant to every assessment, and disagreements benefit from making explicit the underlying implicit assumptions. The following protocol attempts to minimise bias and to encourage discussion about many of the assumptions that have been found in elicitation sessions with groups of experts. I'm assuming that all participants have received an email about administrative details, the purpose of the meeting and how they could prepare for it. Names and organisational affiliations of all participants as well as any relevant background information would be included as an attachment.

1.   Introduction

The facilitator and participants introduce themselves, give their institutional affiliations, roles in their organisations and professional backgrounds. This is followed by a reminder by the leader of the group or the facilitator of the meeting's primary task: to construct probability distributions for the event outcomes or uncertain quantities that are needed for the project under consideration. A brief mention of the potential for 'many heads to be better than one' leads to a warning that people often are over-confident about good outcomes and under-confident about undesirable outcomes.

To illustrate, ask the participants to think, but not speak, about the number of bones they have in their body. I suggest we all have some idea, holding up one hand and pointing to its separate bones. I ask everyone to think of their uncertainty about the answer, and to decide on a low and a high number such that they are 100 per cent sure the true number falls within those limits. Also, I want the *shortest* range of numbers within which they are 100 per cent sure; zero to infinity isn't allowed!

After a short pause for thinking, I tell the group the answer: 206 in an adult, more in children as some bones become fused during growth. 'OK, confession time. Hands raised if 206 fell outside your range, either below the low or above the high.' Several hands always go up, and I comment on the undeniable over-confidence, and I ask why they thought this came about, which can be revealing of either institutional or personal biases. Of course, you might use a different uncertain quantity to suit your clients, but the bones-in-the-body question works for everyone, even medically trained participants (who often shame-facedly admit they should have known the answer). It is appropriate even if the group's task is to assess probabilities only for discrete event outcomes, like Chapter 1's blind problem, or the four questions in Table 6.1.

2.   Motivation

In this stage, participants reveal their expertise about the topic, which shows the diversity within the group. The facilitator's role is explained as guiding the process of achieving the primary task, but not contributing to the content of the discussion. Participants are also asked if they are in any way stakeholders in the project and if they are aware of any potential actual or perceived motivational biases.

3.   Structuring

This stage begins with a definition of the quantity as it was presented in the before-meeting email. Some participants might already have raised issues about this in the introduction. Often, the original definition sails through and is accepted by the group, but later turns out to be insufficient once the facilitator asks about how the quantity is usually assessed. For example, when working with geologists and chemists in a project to assess a probability distribution for the horizontal permeability for water through rock at a particular location in the UK, I soon discovered that disagreements in the group arose because some experts thought of 'permeability' as 'hydraulic conductivity', and discussion revealed that hydraulic conductivity metrics are approximately 10^7 times larger than permeability measurements. There were differences in the way their disciplines modelled horizontal permeability (which neither had previously known, to their surprise), so they revised the definition to one that was agreed.

The main requirement for a good definition is that it passes the '*clairvoyant test*'. This means that if the event were asked of an infallible clairvoyant, that person would not have to ask more questions before giving the answer. For example, in the rock permeability example, it was necessary to define permeability with an equation, specify the units, the type of rock and its location. It was the diversity of the experts that enabled them to quickly drill down to an agreed definition.

Once agreement is reached about the definition of the quantity and its metric, the group is asked to explain the factors that influence the quantity and what information is available about the quantity. Even if a single expert is assessing a single uncertain event, like the outcome of the blind operation, it's worth asking if all influencing factors and all information have been considered.

The next step is crucial: what assumptions are to be accepted as fixed, and which sources of uncertainty are to be treated as the major determinants of the elicited probabilities? It is not requisite to treat everything as uncertain. If a model has already been built based on best estimates, then sensitivity analyses, which wiggle each fixed estimate between a low and a high, can identify those outcomes which hardly change the model's outputs, so can be treated as fixed, from those that matter, so are retained as the main sources of uncertainty. At this stage, as clarity builds, it is sometimes necessary to redefine the problem.

4.   Conditioning

At this stage, the group defines a reference class which provides a body of data that is relevant to today's specific task. For example, in the blind problem, it might be all worldwide data, or the country data, or the data from an organisation specialising in the operation, about the proportion of successful operations for this medical condition. The group is then asked to provide their assessment of an average probability, along with upper and lower limits, of the available studies, or if there is no reference class, then a less-informed estimate.

The group is then asked to give an intuitive estimate of today's uncertain quantity and to evaluate the precision of their estimate. For the blind problem, the ophthalmologist might have suggested that their prediction for this patient of 70 per cent might be within plus or minus 10 percentage points. An evaluation of predictability at this stage can be provoked by the facilitator suggesting that when predictability is limited, things are rarely as good as one hopes, nor as bad as one fears (which suggests regression towards the mean of the reference class). A short discussion of anchoring may also be worth mentioning. This step will reduce anchoring on the average and prepare the assessors for dealing with today's uncertain quantity.

The next step is to discuss scenarios for extreme outcomes of the uncertain quantity (like the number of bones in the body). This is an important step as it helps to overcome the narrowness of the range of values. Ask the group what a very high probability would be, followed by how such a probability could occur, which might be a short list of possibilities. After that discussion, ask for an agreed high probability. Next, repeat this step for a very low probability, how it could occur, and agree a low probability.

5.   Encoding

For the discrete outcomes of an uncertain event, which should be mutually exclusive (only one person can win a Wimbledon singles event), list the outcomes and judge the probability of each, ensuring they sum to 1.0, or 100. If the outcomes of many events are to be assessed, ensure that the probabilities are consistent with the second probability law, especially if the uncertainty about some later events depend on earlier outcomes, or even on the decisions to be taken. A decision tree helps to visualise these comparisons and their conditionality (see Chapter 16).

The process for an uncertain quantity begins by taking participants through seven steps for assessing a graphic of the *cumulative probability distribution* for the defined quantity. The quantity I'll use here is the tallest tree in the world, which I once knew, but have now forgotten. The sequoias in California are my reference class, as I've seen them, and I'm pretty sure the tallest isn't more than 500 feet, nor shorter than 250 feet. I'll write as if you were now assessing your uncertainty for this quantity. Graphics will assist the process, so you might use a computer spreadsheet program, or one specifically designed for creating probability distributions, projected onto a screen for all participants to see the construction of a table and its probability distribution. This will engage all participants. Here, I used Excel.

1. Divide the low–high range agreed at the end of the previous stage into five equal intervals and type them into a column. Type the values of a linear function in the right column (see Table 6.2).
2. Select the two columns of numbers (not the titles) and select Insert, Charts, Scatter (X, Y), and choose straight lines with circular dots. Right click on the horizontal axis and reset the limits. Do the same for the vertical axis. You can enter labels for the axes and a chart title later. The chart should look like the one shown in Figure 6.5.
3. In the table, lower the point (300, 20) to better reflect your probability that the true height is less than 300 feet. Then, raise the (450, 80) to express your uncertainty that the true height is less than 450 feet.
4. Repeat step 3 for the remaining two points. You may find it necessary to adjust the points from the previous step. I had to further lower the left one and considerably raise the upper-right one.

Table 6.2

Possible value of x	Probability of x or less
500	100
450	80
400	60
350	40
300	20
250	0

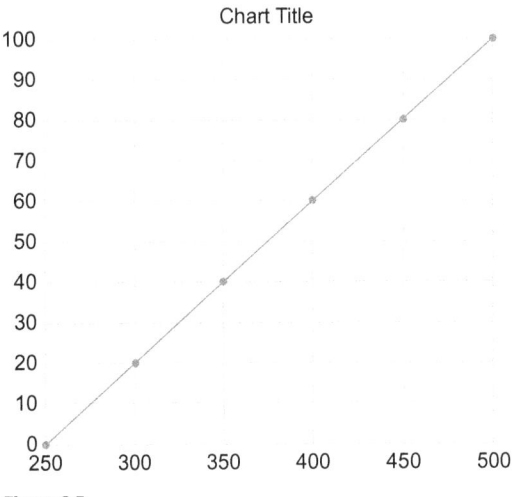

Figure 6.5

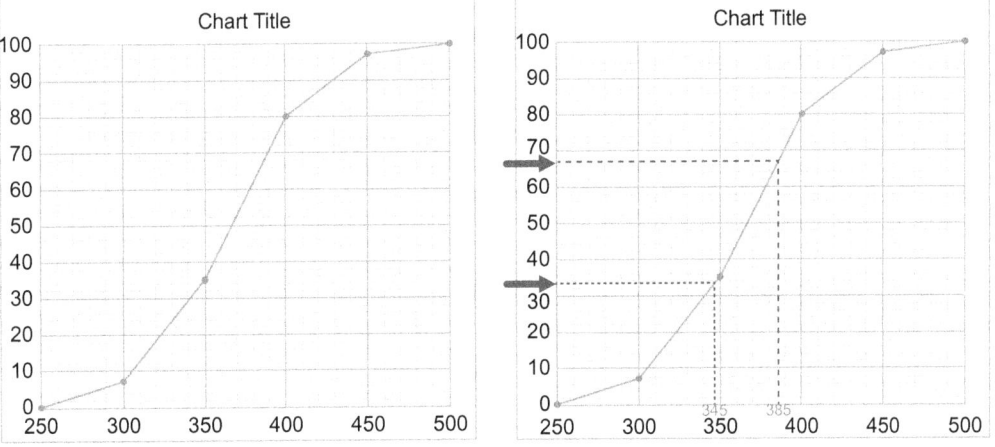

Figure 6.6

5. Look at the whole curve to see if it reasonably represents your uncertainty. For example, I had a little wobble in mine, but I know that my uncertainty steadily increases up to a point when it then steadily decreases. So, no wobbles. Revise as necessary. I finally arrived at the left curve in Figure 6.6, with major and minor gridlines added to facilitate the next step. The resulting curve now shows my uncertainty increasing as I move along the horizontal axis until I am 100 per cent sure the tree is less than 500 feet.

6. This is a consistency check. Enter the curve on the vertical axis at the 0.33 and 0.67 points. Move horizontally across the curve, then down and read off the values on the horizontal axis. Here, that's about 345 and 385. Check to see that the three resulting intervals form equally good bets as to where the truth lies. For me, I think the

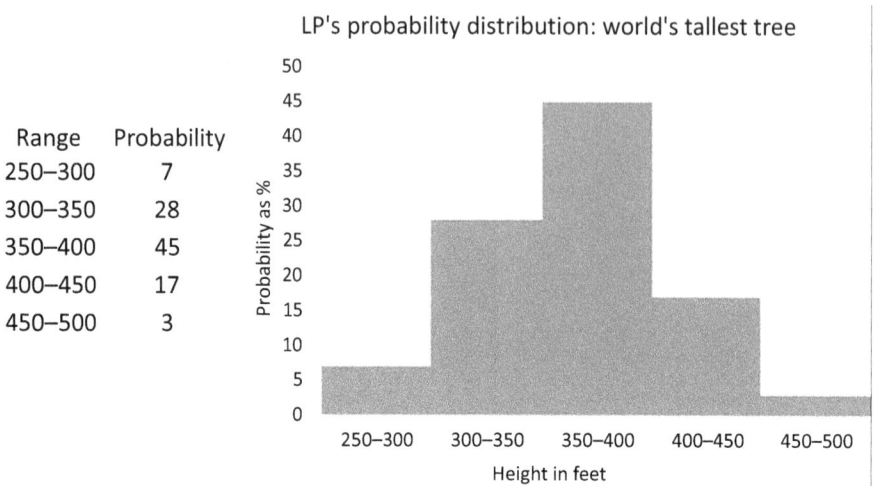

Range	Probability
250–300	7
300–350	28
350–400	45
400–450	17
450–500	3

Figure 6.7

interval from 345 to 385 is the least good bet. It's too narrow, so I might move the 400 point down to about 70. But its close enough at 80. If you are working with a group and a majority of participants choose the same interval, then it is too wide. It may be necessary to repeat some of the above steps to revise the distribution. The 33 and 67 per cent values on the horizontal axis are referred to by statisticians as *tertiles*. Getting the tertiles right is a powerful aid to preventing the cumulative curve from being too steep, a consequence of over-confidence.

An optional, but often informative, step is to translate the cumulative probability distribution into a *mass*, or *density function*. This shows how your uncertainty is allocated across the five intervals. The following steps are an approximation.

On the Excel spreadsheet, make a new column of the five intervals, type in their ranges and the associated additional probability at the end of the interval minus the probability at the end of the previous interval, as read off the cumulative function. For example, the first row is 7 – 0 = 7, the next row is 35 – 7 = 28, and so forth, as in the table shown in Figure 6.7.

Select the 10 cells of numbers in the table and plot them as a bar graph. To do this, select Chart, Chart Design on the ribbon, Quick Layout and select the design with all bars together. It should look like the graph in Figure 6.7 (and I added the titles).

Consider the shape as a further consistency check. The right tail is lower than the left and there is more probability to the left of the central region than to the right. I'm more sure about the 300–350 interval than the 400–450 one, and I'm most sure of the central interval. Yes, that looks good to me and reasonably reflects the uncertainty I now feel at the end of the exercise. So, now I look up the answer, and it is … 381 feet or 116 metres. I'm surprised! My memory wasn't too bad, but my best guess from the start was about 360 feet. No, sequoias grow too slowly for it to have increased by 20 feet since I last used this example in the classroom about 10 years ago.

Notice that the method for encoding the cumulative distribution asks for cumulative probabilities given the measures on the horizontal axis. An alternative method is to start with cumulative probabilities and ask for the corresponding measure. For example, after the assessor has given you a range of possible measures from 250 to 500 feet, you might ask the assessor, 'At which height might you be just as sure that the true value is above or below that height?' Whatever the person says, call that X_{50}. That gives two equally good bets, 250 to X_{50}, and X_{50} to 500. Next, ask the assessor to split the 250 to X_{50} bet into two equally good bets; that gives X_{25}. Repeat that for the X_{50} to 500 bet; that gives X_{75}. Now you have four equally good bets, 250 to X_{25} to X_{50} to X_{75} to 500. Easy, wasn't it?

But there's a problem. That method has long been known to create cumulative functions that are too steep, resulting in density functions with too much probability in the central region.[85] The 50–50 cumulative probability has created an anchor at X_{50}, so the assessor doesn't move the X_{25} and X_{75} measures far enough away from X_{50}. You could confirm this if you do the tertile consistency check: the assessor will choose the central X_{33} to X_{67} range as the best bet. Although this method continues to be taught, largely because it is so easy, it is to be avoided. Start with measures on the horizontal axis and ask for cumulative probabilities, not the other way around.

The next step for the Encoding stage is to ask how the probability distribution will be used in assessing performance of a system, perhaps with concern for which tail is adverse to ensure its probability is reasonable. It would obviously be the left tail for profit and the right tail for the number of people experiencing an adverse reaction to a drug. If several probability distributions are assessed for a project, it may be helpful to compare them to ensure they are consistent with one another.

At this point in the assessment process, the participants have arrived at a consensus distribution. So, my final question to the group is this. 'Could you defend this distribution in a public enquiry or court of law?' I added that question after giving a presentation in 2002 at a meeting of the International Atomic Energy Agency about groups of experts assessing probabilities of uncertain quantities in systems for the long-term storage of radioactive waste. An American lawyer commented that a group approach could not be used in the USA because as juries don't allow presentations by groups, only a single expert could take the stand. That prompted me to add my question to the protocol, which I then used for all subsequent probability assessments. I'm pleased to say all participants gave an answer that is some version of, 'Yes, given the assumptions.'

Participants are then asked for their comments on the elicitation process, which are used to improve the process and are often quoted in reports to the sponsor.

I've listed the above steps in the Appendix at the end of this chapter, which you can copy and convert to editable text so you can record your client's responses if an audit trail is required. A typical observation is that for a project requiring many probability distributions, the process can be shortened by leaving out some steps as participants learn how to translate their uncertainty into probabilities and as they become more adept at working collaboratively. In the UK, the Nuclear Decommissioning Agency has implemented this protocol, building on the experience of over 100 probability elicitation sessions since 1991 of uncertain quantities involved in modelling the geological disposal of nuclear waste. Their 2017 report is well worth reading for its thorough, up-to-date, practical guidance.[86] It's also a good example of how to make a protocol live.

Making Uncertainty Explicit

If at this point you have attempted to express your uncertainty about an event or uncertain quantity and found it difficult or are worried about the lack of precision in your estimate, you might well ask why bother? Use words instead: not at all likely, unlikely, likely, possible, probable, very sure, highly likely, and so forth. English is rich in words and phrases to express one's uncertainty. Isn't that good enough? Didn't the words and phrases I just used suggest increasing certainty? Research suggests that the answer is a clear 'No' for two major reasons.

The first is that words are even more imprecise than probabilities. Here's an early example, drawn from the 1977 *Handbook for Decision Analysis*:[87]

For example, an intelligence analyst, a professional in the art of reasoning about the plausible, was asked to substitute probability estimates for some of the verbal qualifiers in an article he had written. The first statement was 'The cease-fire is holding but it could be broken within a week.' The analyst said that he meant there was a 30 per cent chance the cease-fire would be broken within a week. Later, an analyst who had helped the original analyst prepare the statement said she thought that there was an 80 per cent chance that the cease-fire would be broken. Yet, both analysts had previously believed that they were in agreement about what could happen.

The *Handbook* also reports an attempt by a US intelligence agency to specify the acceptable range of probabilities associated with 16 statements about uncertainty, but the 22 analysts who were familiar with the specification continued to use probabilities outside the specified ranges. For example, their probabilities for 'probable', 'likely', 'probably' and 'we believe' ranged from about 20 to 90 per cent, both sides of 50–50! Subsequent systematic research confirmed these findings.[88] Using words to express one's uncertainty can seriously mislead.

The second reason for preferring probabilities to words is that uncertainty about event E is often decomposed by *extending the conversation* into its constituent events, so these individual probabilities need to be combined to yield the uncertainty for E, the *compound event*. It's not clear how to do this with words, but with probabilities it is done by applying the probability laws. For example, suppose that for you to be assured of adequate supply of electricity in your region of the country in three months' time, it is necessary for five power stations to be online. Imagine that each of the five has reported they are 90 per cent sure they will be fully online by then. Each of the five is independent of the others, so by the second law of probability, the probability of all five being ready is $0.9^5 = 0.59$, little better than flipping a fair coin. If 0.9 is best described by the phrase 'highly likely', and each station reported they were 'highly likely' to be ready, the regional manager might well think that all five together might be 'highly likely', or perhaps 'a very good chance'. That's certainly not the right phrase to describe a probability of 0.59.

This oversimplified example, which is based on the real experience in the 1980s of the UK's Central Electricity Generating Board (CEGB), illustrates a serious problem: passing verbal statements of uncertainty up the managerial hierarchy, from those working on the generators, to the foreman, to the head of the maintenance department, to the director of the station, and so on to the top of the region, converted a 'probably' to a 'likely' to a 'probable' to a 'good chance' to a 'highly likely' as it passed from one person to the next in the reporting chain. When studies revealed this distortion in the CEGB, they changed the reporting system: probabilities went straight from the repair people directly to a central regional group where they could then combine the probabilities properly. Problem solved. It's also one way to avoid uncertainty about a favourable uncertain event becoming more certain as it travels up the reporting chain, and about an unfavourable event getting less certain as it travels upward. Eliminate the bias by changing the system.

Decision analysts define probability as a degree of belief and in practice I find it useful to distinguish uncertainty from probability: uncertainty is a feeling and probability is a measure of the felt degree of uncertainty. We don't naturally think of uncertainty as numbers, so they're not waiting to be plucked fully formed, obeying the laws of probability. That must be learned. Our feelings of uncertainty might arise from something we've forgotten and wish to recall, from either insufficient or too much information, from actual or perceived variability in some external stimulus, or simply from ignorance.

But as I mentioned earlier, some people are what I call 'non-probabilistic thinkers', that is, they tend to see the world as black and white, either something is or it isn't, rather like Hamlet's 'To be, or not to be, that is the question', although he does get to worrying about the in-between sleep, which puts him in a state of uncertainty with tragic consequences. I first encountered people who did not seem to understand probabilities when I was a graduate student studying the psychology of people's understanding of probability, when two participants in my experiments, one an Indian and the other Chinese, gave personal probabilities that were very nearly random responses to the stimuli they were shown. I wondered then if there were cultural differences in how people deal with uncertainty, and it was nearly 10 years later that I formally tested that hypothesis, greatly helped by George Wright, at the time of writing a professor at the University of Strathclyde and a founding editor of the *Journal of Behavioral Decision Making*.

Our initial study discovered over-confidence for almanac questions in English students, but much more for Chinese students, nurses and businessmen living and working in London, as you can see in the graph in Figure 6.8.[89] The surprise was to find that Chinese assessments from 0.5 to 0.9 hover around a horizontal line, suggesting that for these participants the probability is either about 50–50 or 100 per cent.

In a second task, we asked participants to sort 29 cards, each containing a word or phrase like 'Highly likely' or 'Very improbably' into groups that have the same

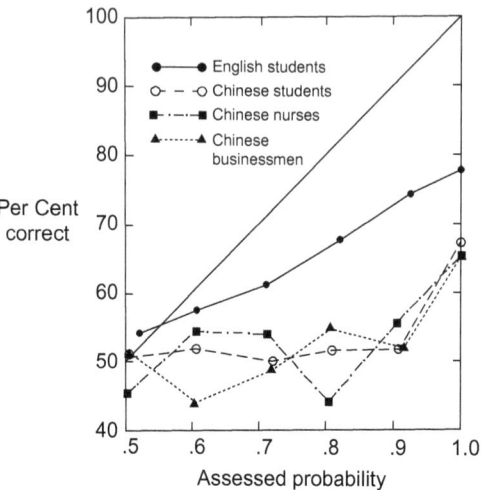

Figure 6.8

meaning. Consistent with their apparent over-confidence, the Chinese students created very few piles, while the English students created many more. In a third, task participants were given a paper questionnaire and asked to provide a 'reasonable response' to 45 questions about events that had not yet happened (Will you catch a head cold in the next month?) and others about factual matters that most people aren't sure about (Is the Suez Canal over 100 miles long?). The Chinese participants used on average more Yes/No responses than the English students, who used appreciably more words about uncertainty than the Chinese groups.

We were worried that these stark differences might be a result of the relative unfamiliarity of English for the Chinese participants. So, over a series of subsequent studies we studied how students living in India, China and Malaysia would respond to the three tasks when written in their native language, with the questionnaires administered by native speakers. We again found more over-confidence and less discrimination of uncertainty in the Asian student participants compared to British students.[90] Later research established that over-confidence in American students is similar to their British counterparts, and that Japanese students respond more like Westerners than the Chinese.[91]

I asked a Chinese PhD student at the London School of Economics, whose research found good calibration for probabilities assessed about outcomes of the card game bridge played by middle-class Chinese people in Beijing, what character represents probability in Mandarin. He said there wasn't one, and the closest he could come was three characters, which he translated as 'the may happen possibility'. Although we Westerners think of probability as a characteristic of a future outcome, that phrase seems to locate uncertainty as a characteristic of the present, a kind of propensity now for a future event outcome to occur.

What has this discussion of cultural differences about probability to do with decision analysis? In my view, it has the potential to help us understand better why people might disagree about how to approach a problem. Here's an example of an exchange, reported in *The New York Times*, about an exchange in October 1975 between Cyrus Vance, then the USA's Secretary of State under Gerald Ford, and Deng Xiaoping, then the First Vice-Premier under Mao Zedong. Vance is trying to persuade Deng that China should sign the Nuclear Non-Proliferation Treaty.

Vance: The hazards of accidental launch are real and could have devastating effects if one didn't know where the weapon was launched from.
   Deng: Only two countries could launch an attack, your country and the Soviet Union. Meanwhile, nuclear development just cuts down the amount of food available for the people of India.
   Vance: Accidental launching will become more likely with the indiscriminate spread of nuclear weapons.
   Deng (waving finger): It won't be so easy. If India, or other countries, does it, it could signify its defeat and even destruction. As for other things, the US and the USSR think they are in a position to prevent other countries from developing weapons. Our position is they have a right: France, China, India and so on. The most important thing is to encourage yourselves and the Soviet Union that you would not be the first to use nuclear weapons; second, to reduce the number; and third, to do away with them all.

The Cold War was then on between the USA and the Soviet Union, so when I read this then it seemed to me that these two men were not communicating with each other, each was making a claim that the other couldn't hear. Vance starts by establishing the serious consequences 'if one didn't know'; he establishes uncertainty. Deng counters with certainty that only two countries, the USA and the Soviet Union, could launch nuclear weapons. Then, Vance introduces uncertainty again: 'will become more likely'. But that just angers Deng, so he resorts to telling what three things must be done now. It seems to me that Vance is a probabilistic thinker, while Deng is a strict determinist in his thinking: do this and do that, end of story. Their different world-views don't connect usefully.

It's not just an East–West difference. My experience in modelling uncertainty suggests than 1 in 10 or 20 people I've worked with don't feel comfortable with any elicitation approach, as I earlier explained in my interactions with an oil-well expert and a laboratory chemist on the permeability of rock. Now, combine this understanding that some people are non-probabilistic thinkers and that assessing probabilities about anything that can be influenced by human activities is not valid for outcomes that are two or more years away, and you are faced with a dilemma: what sorts of decision models can be developed for these complex, serious situations.

I had no answer until the day I was in Seattle to give a lecture about the cross-cultural research my colleagues and I were conducting, and read in *The Seattle Times* for 23 April 1977, an article entitled 'Arms race makes war inevitable – China'. Vice Premier Li Hsien-nien, speaking at an industrial conference of more than 7,000 attendees, said, 'We must race against time and quicken the pace of industrial development, build the national economy and strengthen our socialist state', to protect China against the threat of the Soviet Union. In other words, assume World War III is inevitable and do all that is possible now to delay the inevitable.

That was my answer to the modelling question. Assume that an undesired future state is inevitable, model options that can today contribute to delaying the impact of the consequences, and define criteria as how well the options will perform in delaying the inevitable. This was applied by the Committee on Radioactive Waste Management, in which all 24 of the impact criteria described what can be done now to delay the leakage of radioactive radiation into humans, and to minimise the undesirable outcomes of the decisions that will be taken, such as effects on the environment. That is a very different framing of the problem from the early attempts to model uncertainties in decision trees about the transmission of radionuclides from disposal in steel canisters deep underground, into the geosphere, then to the biosphere, and eventually into people, as compared to a multi-criteria decision analysis (MCDA) model whose criteria expressed how well the extent to which each option's design features would allow for any remediation needed in the next 300 years.

The next section explains another way to quantify uncertainty that can be used in portfolio analysis, or at any time when your clients feel that probability isn't quite the right way to characterise the uncertainty they are feeling. If you appreciate the beauty of mathematics (or are in touch with your inner geekiness), you may enjoy the next section.

Proper Scoring Rules, or the Utility of a Probability (Optional Topic)

One approach is to include a 'confidence' criterion in a decision model and provide a special scale that is similar to a two-outcome bet, which requires a person to choose the best bet that is similar to the uncertainty they feel. This scale, which is called a 'proper scoring rule', enables the bet to be turned into probability. Any rule that converts scores to probabilities is considered 'proper' only if it encourages an assessor to choose a bet that is an accurate representation of the assessor's state of uncertainty.[92] How can this be possible when the person's state of uncertainty is known only to that person? Let me demonstrate this seemingly impossible claim by showing how the bets and probabilities are connected.

Table 6.3 shows one such proper scoring rule; it is a logarithmic rule (namely, the score for probability p is proportional to $\log_{10}p$). Because the logarithm of any number less than one is negative, we call the resulting numbers 'penalty scores'. For example, if you judge there is an 80 per cent chance of rain tomorrow and therefore a 20 per cent chance it won't rain, then if it does rain, your penalty score is only −9, but if it doesn't rain your score will be −70! The object, over many probability assessments, is to achieve a total sum of your scores as close to zero as possible. One way to do this is to be very knowledgeable. If you judge the probability to be high and you turn out to be correct, then you are given a low penalty score. Just looking at the scoring system isn't sufficient to see how these scores can minimise your penalty score by expressing your uncertainty accurately as a probability. So, a little arithmetic will clarify this claim.

Suppose you decide to cheat a little and say you are 90 per cent sure, hoping for a score of only −4. Of course, if it doesn't rain, then you will get a score of −100. Since

Table 6.3

	Score if outcome	
Probability of outcome	does occur	doesn't occur
0	$-\infty$	0
0.10	-100	-4
0.20	-70	-9
0.30	-52	-15
0.40	-40	-22
0.50	-30	-30
0.60	-22	-40
0.70	-15	-52
0.80	-9	-70
0.90	-4	-100
1.00	0	$-\infty$

your true belief is 80 per cent, you must think there is an 80 per cent chance of earning that score of –4, and a 20 per cent chance of receiving –100. That gives an expected score of

$$0.80 \times (-4) + 0.20 \times (-100) = -23.2.$$

But your expected score would be closer to zero if you were to report accurately:

$$0.80 \times (-9) + 0.20 \times (-70) = -21.2$$

The expected score associated with an inaccurate report of your uncertainty is *always* worse than the expected score for your real belief. Surprisingly, this statement is true whatever your real belief! (Try it yourself for any other combination of a real belief and a cheat.) So, in the long run, your score will be minimised by reporting your uncertainty accurately.

Close examination of the scoring system shows that while you might minimise your score by giving a high probability if the outcome occurs, you could receive a disproportionately large negative score if the event does not occur. And notice that being absolutely sure brings a penalty of minus infinity if you are wrong (as the New York City author Damon Runyon once said, when betting on a sure thing, always save the cab fare home)! So, you will have to balance your confidence that the outcome will occur against your uncertainty that it won't. The scoring system helps to show what that balancing act means. It also provides an audit trail enabling different assessors to be compared after many assessments have been made. That's how meteorologists became good at probabilistic weather forecasts. The person with the lowest total score is both knowledgeable about the events in question and is good at reporting their uncertainty accurately.

Because this scoring system is logarithmic, it ensures that the score for a compound event can be derived by summing the scores associated with the component events. For example, if probabilities of 0.6 and 0.5 are assigned to two events, giving scores of –22 and –30, respectively, the probability of both events is 0.6 × 0.5 = 0.3, which is associated with a score of –52, the sum of the two component scores.

Notice that I have positioned proper scoring rules as aides to learning how to translate one's uncertainty into a probability. However, the more usual presentation is for using scoring rules to motivate assessors to express their 'true' probability, which assumes there is such a thing. As I've already said, I don't believe there is. We human beings feel at times uncertain and expressing that uncertainty in the form of a probability must be learned for the simple reason that there isn't a probability generator in the brain. So, I position proper scoring rules as one way for comparing your feeling of uncertainty about, say, the outcomes of an event, to the uncertainty generated by a pair of scores in a proper scoring rule. We don't start with expressing a probability, as is suggested in Table 6.2, instead we look first at each pair of penalty scores to find left and right penalty scores that create a feeling of uncertainty similar to that of the outcomes of the real-world event you are facing. The result over many assessments of this matching process of adding your penalty scores would be a sum as close to zero as could be expected given the levels of uncertainty you are encountering.

Practically speaking, you might begin by looking at the second row, –100 and –4, and ask yourself if those penalty scores reflect your uncertainty about the real-world event's occurring or not. You might well say you are more certain than suggested by the –100, so then move down to the –4 and –100 row and ask if you are so sure you are willing to lose 100 points if you are wrong. If not, then move up to the third row, –70 and –9, and repeat this process of swinging between extremes (yes, to avoid a 50–50 anchor) until a specific probability emerges from your thinking. You are in effect training yourself in assessing probabilities, especially if you do it for events that are soon to occur, which give you feedback about which score was realised for each event. Eventually, you will feel more confidence in assessing probabilities directly.[93]

Much more could be said about proper scoring systems for there is a considerable theoretical and empirical literature devoted to the topic, mostly aimed at finding ways of helping people to learn how to assess unbiased probabilities.[94] Rather than extend this brief introduction, here are some common questions about scoring systems and answers to them.

1. Why not use a linear rule, which is simpler and doesn't provide such a big penalty for low probabilities?
There are three reasons, one theoretical, one empirical and one practical. First, a linear rule, which gives a score for p proportional to $1 - p$, isn't a proper scoring rule. To take the previous example, if you really are 80 per cent sure, then under a linear rule you will receive a penalty of only –20 if you turn out to be right and a penalty of –80 if you are wrong. That gives an expected penalty of

$$0.80 \times (-20) + 0.20 \times (-80) = -32.$$

Now consider your expected score if you give a more extreme probability, 1.0 (which gives a linear penalty of 0 if you are correct, and −100 if you are wrong):

$$0.80 \times (0) + 0.20 \times (-100) = -20.$$

Obviously, your expected penalty is less for reporting a more extreme probability than you believe. Under a linear scoring system, the expected score is always lowest by reporting 1.0 when you are more than 50 per cent sure and 0 when you are less than 50 per cent sure. The linear score is improper because it does not encourage accurate reporting of uncertainty. And that is exactly what has happened in empirical tests of the linear rule; people in the experiments gradually drifted in their probability assessments to 0 and 1.0. The practical reason against the linear rule is that most people do not feel the same increase in preference in moving from a probability of 0.1 to 0.2 as from 0.8 to 0.9. The former is usually seen as a bigger difference in preference, and that larger difference is captured in the logarithmic rule.

2. Are there other proper scoring rules that use positive rather than negative scores and which wouldn't be so severe for small probability outcomes that occurred?

Yes, the quadratic rule, in which the score associated with p is a function of $(1-p)^2$, but it is even more penalising of small probabilities than the logarithmic rule. In addition, the score for a compound event is not the sum of the scores for the component events. Probabilities must multiply, so the corresponding penalty scores must add. For this property to hold, the logarithmic score is needed.

3. Why use the penalty score associated with the probability of the outcome's success; why not use the expected penalty score?

Because the scores each side of 50–50 are symmetrical, namely, the outcome scores for p are the same, but interchanged, for 1 − p, so the expected value for probabilities above 50–50 will always be lower than the expected values for probabilities below 50–50. Take the example again. We saw above that the expected penalty score for being 80 per cent sure is −21.2:

$$0.80 \times (-9) + 0.20 \times (-70) = -21.2.$$

Here is the expected penalty score for 20 per cent:

$$0.20 \times (-9) + 0.80 \times (-70) = -57.8.$$

That's not a proper scoring rule result. On the contrary, it encourages you always to give probabilities of zero if you think it more likely the outcome won't occur, and 1.0 if you think it more likely it will occur, with only 50–50, whose expected value is 30, as a safe haven in between. At least it's better than the linear rule!

Summary

This chapter began with the two current definitions of probabilities: relative frequencies and degrees of belief. Decision analysts find the latter more useful because it can accommodate relative frequencies, unique events and the truth of hypotheses. The operational definition of probabilities as degrees of belief is found in a preference judgement comparing two win-lose gambles with identical consequences. One is a gamble about the outcome of the event whose probability is to be assessed, and the other is a spinner wheel with two moveable, coloured sectors representing the relative chances of winning or losing the spin. Adjusting the sizes of the sectors until the assessor feels indifferent between winning a big prize from the event or from a spin of the wheel establishes the probability of the event's outcome as identical to the relative size of the coloured sectors on the wheel.

We saw that probabilities are constrained by three rules, which come into play when assessing probabilities for outcomes, and when an outcome of one event is relevant in assessing outcomes from a related event. We explored the question of how good people are at assessing personal probabilities, and invoked three criteria of goodness: accuracy, or calibration of the assessor, reliability or repeatability of an individual assessment, and precision, or narrowness of the assessment. Much research suggests that people are often over-confident in assessing higher probabilities and under-confident for lower ones, but we also found that people within their own area of expertise can learn to be well-calibrated if they are given feedback about the outcomes.

As an aid for assessing probabilities, I explained a five-stage process beginning with an introduction to the process of assessing a probability, then exploring participants' expertise about the topic and any potential real or perceived motivational biases, structuring the assessment, conditioning it on similar events, and finally encoding the probabilities in seven steps and agreeing a consensus distribution (if a group of experts is being consulted).

Although personal probabilities are rarely established with high precision, research shows that words expressing uncertainty are even less precise, so when communicating uncertainty, probabilities are less likely to be misinterpreted than words. However, not everyone in the West, and fewer in many Eastern countries, are inclined to think in terms of probabilities, although they are capable of it. One way to become capable in expressing uncertainty as probabilities is to train using proper scoring rules.

Although the research on people's behaviour in assessing probabilities suggests that people are often biased, they say nothing about what people are capable of doing with training and experience. This distinction between actual behaviour and capability is well-understood in sports, where training and practice are the keys to effective performance. So it is with assessing probabilities.

In summary, people can make precise, reliable and accurate assessments of probability if:

- the assessor is inclined to think probabilistically;
- the assessor is knowledgeable about the substantive area;

- complex events are broken down into simple events;
- proper assessment techniques are applied;
- coherence is exploited during the assessment;
- the assessment process is iterative;
- the problem is restructured when assessment becomes difficult; and
- assessments are generated by groups of experts (see Chapter 7).

Appendix: Probability Assessment Form

Introduction

1.1 The project and its purpose
1.2 Today's tasks
1.3 Reason for probability distributions rather than best estimates
1.4 Interviewer and his/her background
1.5 Participants and their backgrounds
1.6 Background to the study
1.7 Assessing probabilities

    Background in behavioural decision theory and decision analysis
    The meaning and interpretation of probability
    Assessing probability
    Precision, reliability and accuracy
    Experimental research showing over-confidence
    Design of the process
    Calibration – an exercise (e.g. number of bones in the adult body)

2. Motivation

2.1 Participants' expertise regarding the uncertain quantity
2.2 Are participants stakeholders in the project?
2.3 Potential motivational biases

3. Structuring

3.1 Definition of the uncertain quantity
3.2 Approaches to assessing the quantity
3.3 List of relevant factors and information

'When people say that they have considered everything they could think of, they usually haven't.'

3.4 List of assumptions

3.5 Sources of uncertainty

3.6 Redefinition of the problem

3.7 Choice of scale (i.e. units)

4.   Conditioning

4.1 Definition of a reference class

4.2 Assessment of the average and the range for the reference class

Average_____

Upper limit_____

Lower limit_____

OR, if no reference class. Less informed estimate _____

4.3 Intuitive estimate of the quantity_____

4.4 Evaluation of predictability

4.5 Discussion of extremeness of the intuitive estimate

When predictability is limited, things are rarely as good as one hopes, nor as bad as one fears.

4.6 Discussion of anchoring

When you adjust a value, you rarely adjust enough.

4.7 Discussion of a scenario for extreme outcomes

What would be a very high value? _____

How could such a value occur?_____

What is the probability of such a high value? _____

What would be a very low value?_____

How could such a value occur?_____

What is the probability of such a low value? _____

5.   Encoding

5.1 Construct the cumulative probability distribution by converting from a linear function

5.2 Check tertiles and revise distribution

5.3 Which tail is adverse?

5.4 Construct the probability mass (density) function

5.4 Compare this distribution with others generated during this session

5.5 Could all participants defend this distribution (e.g. in a public enquiry)?

5.6 Comments by participants on the process

Epilogue to Part I

In the 1970s, two senior underwriters from a major UK insurance company attended an executive course on decision analysis I had been teaching at Brunel University. At the end of the course, they told me that decision analysis makes explicit all the things an underwriter does implicitly when assessing a risk. Since then, I've heard the same thing from experts in many areas, which reinforces my view that the 10 ingredients of good decisions make intuitive sense as well as being derived from a theoretical analysis of coherent preferences. Thus, they provide the elements of a framework for helping a decision maker in almost any field do a better job of creating the future.

Experience teaches decision analysts about action in an uncertain world with its conflicting objectives, so our mental models of what we've learned utilise those 10 ingredients. Recall that the Preface started with this quote from Voltaire: 'It is said that the present is pregnant with the future.' The 10 ingredients can be organised into a decision model that will stimulate new perspectives and insights, clarify possible futures, ease your client's sense of unease, and enable them to take a good decision with confidence. Your client will be better helped if you assist them in creating a decision model that takes advantage of their own experience and mental models, challenging them to think afresh, so let's explore further the nature of our mental models.

To begin, consider the quote from François de La Rochefoucauld shown at the start of the Preface: 'Badness of memory everyone complains of, but nobody of the want of judgement.'[95] Our active, working memories are limited in the number of items they can retain while working on a problem. One of the most cited papers in psychology, published in 1956, 'The magical number seven, plus or minus two', was written by George A. Miller,[96] one of the founders of cognitive science. He suggested that most people can keep in their short-term memory at most seven chunks of information, give or take two, although later studies argued that the number depends on the material, and the limit is closer to four.[97] When I first came to London in the late 1960s, the telephone numbers consisted of three letters followed by four digits, XYZ-1234. The London area known as Hampstead gave its first three letters HAM to the telephone numbers, one chunk of information, followed by the four digits, another chunk, thus two chunks that are easy to remember. But demand for telephone numbers grew, and now all telephone numbers, mobiles included, are 11 digits long, usually grouped into three chunks of three or four digits. A bit more challenging for the memory.

Hierarchical ordering of the material eases its retention from long-term memory, and that is how most of us organise the information stored on our computers, with files in folders stored in higher-level folders, and those in even higher-level folders. One of the major advantages of decision models is that they are always hierarchical, so we are at any one time required to attend to about four, plus-or-minus, chunks of information, which research since Miller's paper suggests is more realistic. Our mental models are also organised hierarchically, with those of experts able to remember more information in their area of expertise than non-experts about the same topics.

And so it is with the ingredients of decision models, 10 items divided into two parts, five about structure, the other five covering content, plus five process steps for creating any decision model. Decision analysis is most effective when each step in the process of building a model stays within the 4 ± 2 chunks of information. That's important because by understanding the parts, your client will become confident in the overall results when the parts are put together with Raiffa's 'logical glue', the probabilities that multiply by preference values, and the weights that multiply by preference values on different scales, so that a common unit of preference enables the weighted preference values to be added. In practice, that job of aggregation is left to computers, which are capable of handling far more than the human mind can manage.

You may have noticed that the process of assessing any of the three quantities, preference values, trade-off weights or probabilities requires comparing differences, preferably just two differences at a time, paired comparisons, long preferred for scaling many psychological properties. And it helps to keep the cognitive burden tolerable, thus avoiding inappropriate oversimplification of the problem by the assessor – for example, that only one or two criteria are needed, when more characterise the problem at hand.

Another good reason for engaging computers is that for models larger than the blind problem, too may chunks of information exist for the human brain to keep them all in mind to reassemble them. The classic birthday problem illustrates our inability to aggregate information. When I give a lecture about probability, I ask, 'What are the chances that two people in this room will share the same day of birth, any day out of 365, although not necessarily the same year?' The surprising answer is that the probability is slightly better than 50 per cent with only 24 people in the room. If the lecture is attended by more than 24 people, I suggest we do an experiment to test the validity of that result. I start by telling my birthday and ask if anyone shares it. If not, the next person tells theirs, and so on until we hear a coincidence.

How is the probability of a coincidence calculated for any given number of people? By applying the multiplication law: multiply the probabilities of no coincidence as each person reveals their birthday. After I say my birthday, what is the probability of the next person's probability being different? It's 364/365. Multiply that by the probability of no coincidence when the third person speaks, 363/365, times the next, 362/365, and so forth, a series of numbers each only a little smaller than 1.0, but reducing. Then, subtract the product from 1.0 to get the probability of a coincidence at any stage in the multiplications. The graph in Figure EP.1 shows the result for up to 60 people in the room. It's almost a sure thing with only 50 people.

Curiously, our inability to aggregate multiple chunks of information is hardly mentioned in the heuristics and biases research, yet it is one reason why wholly

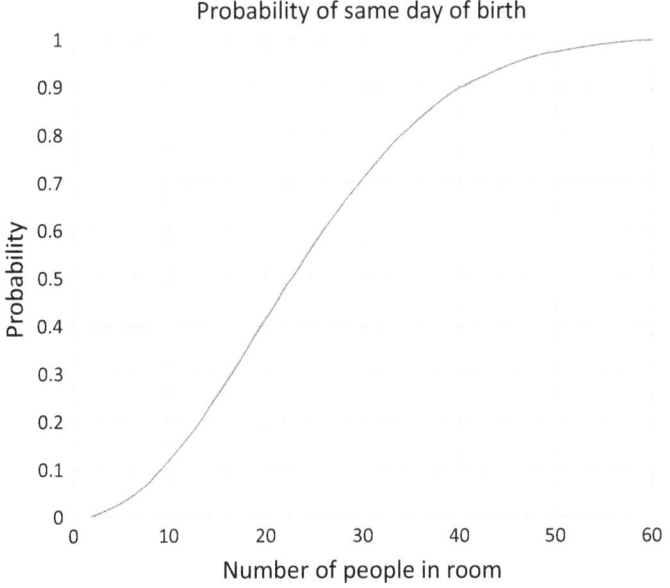

Figure EP.1

intuitive decision making can fail. It is the disaggregation of a complex problem, making judgements about the pieces, then turning over the task of aggregating to a computer, that is better able to serve as a guide to the accountable decision maker. Many disciplines, from insurance underwriting to medical diagnosis, to approving new drugs, which often present many more chunks of information than the human mind can encompass, are learning how decision models can utilise expertise about the parts and use a computer to aggregate them into an overall view that reveals new features, which is a characteristic of all hierarchical models, as shown in Part III. You can study the properties of hydrogen and oxygen separately, but when they act together as water, we see new properties.

Training and experience with the 10 ingredients as applied to the seven problem types in Part III will engage the technical skills covered in the chapters so far. Eventually, it will be clear that it is possible to compare the seemingly incomparable if consequences represent added value and probabilities accurately reflect our uncertainties. Then when the ingredients are combined, we may find that doubts have been turned into certainties, in the style suggested by the quote from Sir Francis Bacon at the start of Chapter 6.

Finally, keep in mind that decision modelling is fundamentally a subjective process: framing the problem, choosing relevant data, assessing values, probabilities and trade-offs, and interpreting the results. Some clients wish for an objective way to decide. They argue that with sufficient data a choice will become clear. That is often the claim of 'Big Data'. But data and evidence do not automatically translate into decisions. Data may well be relevant, but insofar as decisions are about the future, data must always be interpreted for its relevance, and assumptions are inevitably required. There is no such thing as an objective decision about the future.

To some extent, English speakers implicitly learn that 'objective' is better than 'subjective' because of its application in using adjectives to describe a noun. For example, as I write on a cold day, I am wearing a warm, woollen shirt. If I had written 'woollen, warm shirt,' that doesn't seem quite right. The reason is that in English, the more subjective the adjective, the further from the noun it is placed. In speaking and writing English, we implicitly learn to communicate what we feel as distinct from what is objectively real, and perhaps that objectivity is to be preferred. Decision modelling requires a mixture of both.

Part II

The Social Principles

The next five chapters show how to work as a consultant deploying your decision-analytic technical skills. Although the necessary social skills are gained through experience, and painfully learned by one's mistakes, there are nevertheless guiding principles that provide frameworks for the decisions you must make in helping your client.

7 Decision Conferences

8 Behaviour in Organisations	9 Process Consultancy	10 Facilitation Skills	11 Group Processes
Organisation types	Consultancy types	Works groups	When participants disagree
Organisation strata	Schein's 10 process consultancy skills applied to decision conferencing	Facilitator's tasks	What defines an expert?
Task complexity		Dealing with conflict	Choosing experts
Individual capability	Trust	The computer model as a transitional object	Group research
Accountability and authority			Observational research
Business functions			
Leadership			

Theory, Research and Experience

Figure 7.0

7   Decision Conferences

[Might it] be possible for a rather small, intimate group to establish a problem-solving process that capitalizes upon the total pool of information and provides for great inter-stimulation of ideas without any loss of innovative creativity due to social restraints?

J. W. Thibaut and H. H. Kelley, 1959[98]

Early in 1978, I applied decision analysis to evaluate the feasibility of a gas-gathering pipeline system in the North Sea. Tony Benn, then the Secretary of State for Energy in the Labour Government, was concerned about the flaring of gas that would occur if decisions about linking oil fields being developed in the vicinity of the Brent field were not taken before 1980, when gas would start to flow. He established a company, Gas Gathering Pipelines (North Sea) Limited (GGPL), to examine the feasibility of constructing such a system.

The GGPL built a deterministic model that included many assumptions about outcomes of the modelled events, nearly all of which were uncertain, so was built on 'best guess' assumptions about the outcomes. Sensitivity analyses showed that with favourable assumptions about the seven key uncertainties, the landed price of gas would justify building the pipeline, but under unfavourable assumptions, it would not. And the 'best guess' model left no trace of the possible risks. It was at this point that I was asked by an organisation of oil-and-gas consulting engineers to apply decision analysis to the problem.

After asking many questions of the experts, I learned that the whole pipeline system was too large to be built in one season. Rather, it would take two or three successive years as spring was the only time when weather was sufficiently favourable for ships in the North Sea to undertake the necessary construction. I wondered if the reduction in uncertainty from the first stages of construction could inform probability assessments for later stages, so I asked what the first-stage decision would be and was told it would be a choice between a northerly or westerly first leg from Brent. Those alternatives became the initial choice node in a decision tree, followed by event nodes with their outcomes and uncertainties, then decisions conditional on those outcomes followed by more outcomes and their uncertainties, and finally a third year's decisions and their outcomes, altogether a tree of 512 branches, each ending with two consequences: the landed price of gas and the energy lost through flaring by fields not connected to the system (a surrogate for the political consequences as the public became aware of wasting energy).

To my surprise, and that of my sponsors, this analysis showed a smaller range for the landed price of gas than for the deterministic model, but either model could justify a 'no build' decision. However, by incorporating the political consequences of flaring and assigning a modest weight, of at least 10 per cent, the decision model favoured building the gas-gathering system, beginning in 1979.

Whether that model came to the attention of the decision makers, I don't know; I can find no trace of GGPL. But I do know that the oil and gas companies subsequently banded together to build it themselves. What I learned at the time was the importance of properly framing the problem. The deterministic model was the result of an 'optimisation' mindset: find a configuration for the pipeline that minimises the landed price of gas. But that failed to take account of the many uncertainties in the project. Indeed, at that time, it wasn't even known how much gas could flow through a pipeline of a given diameter; only the insurance costs of the rig at each field could be foreseen with confidence. The deterministic model was a good example of starting with certainties and ending with doubts, while the probabilistic model showed that enough was already known to justify taking the first steps, particularly as uncertainty would be reduced at the later stages in the model, and that decision was bolstered by incorporating the political consequences of flaring; a decision tree with multi-attributed consequences.

A major difficulty I encountered in the GGPL project concerned the diversity of opinion and judgements held by the many experts from whom I elicited probability distributions. The experts frequently disagreed, and I relied on discussions among small teams of experts to provide their appraisals.

This same problem arose in my next assignment, with Maritime Engines and Motors, a medium-sized, British manufacturing company considering in 1979 the redesign of their major product, which provided 70 per cent of their annual revenue.

The Operations Manager asked if I could help break this deadlock, so I interviewed the MD, Marketing Manager, Finance Director and many others as I successively developed and revised a decision tree. At each stage, the interviewee suggested changes to the model; there seemed to be no 'right' representation of the problem. After the MD approved the final version, which recommended the redesign, he invited me to the next meeting of the company's Board, and I suggested we bring my research unit's computer[i] along so we could make changes if any were suggested by Board members. At the meeting he explained the decision tree, the outcome probabilities and the multi-attributed consequences to the members and asked for their views. They accepted the structure, but, in turn, three board members made changes to probabilities or weights, which were tested, cumulatively, for their effects on the results. Only after the third change did the model reject the redesign, and no Board member was willing to accept all three changes. Consequently, the Board recommended the redesign, and it was implemented within a month.[99]

---

[i] That was a luggable, 25kg IBM 5110 computer, with oscilloscope display, detachable keyboard, large magnetic tape drive, two programming languages, APL and Basic, with ... wait for it ... a whopping 64K of RAM!

This project not only broke the stalemate in taking a decision, but also showed that agreement among key players about the details of a decision wasn't necessary for them to agree what to do next. An optimal model wasn't necessary, just one that was good enough to resolve the Board's sense of unease about modernising the company's most popular product. It was not necessary for the key players to achieve consensus about all the details, particularly if their different views did not make a difference to the decision. I suggested in the published paper of the project that the model was 'requisite': good enough to resolve the sense of unease about what to do, which I explore later in this chapter. This case study is further developed in Chapter 16.

Working with Groups of Experts

At the time of this consultancy work, I was employed full-time at Brunel University, a former UK Technical College that had been upgraded to a university in 1966. The newly formed School of Social Sciences included the Department of Psychology, where I was located, along with new departments of economics and sociology. The Head of the School, Dr Elliott Jaques, wanted a new course for our first-year students to develop their skills in observing and interviewing people engaged in everyday activities. None of us who agreed to teach the course had been taught such skills, so Dr Jaques arranged for our team to learn those skills in a series of meetings he arranged for us at the Tavistock Institute of Human Relations in London.

We were ushered into a room with a circle of chairs and invited to sit down along with the leader, Isobel Menzies. She explained that as a group we would observe our own group as we worked on our task of learning about observation. Then she fell silent. We all looked at each other – long pause – then someone suggested we introduce ourselves, which we did. She thanked us and again fell silent. I don't now recall much of what happened next, other than to say it was totally unexpected for all of us. Being academics, we had brought our notepads and pencils and were ready to be 'taught', but it soon became clear that we would be learning through experience, with no lectures, no required reading and no homework. Everything that was happening in the 'here-and-now' of the group could be observed, and Ms Menzies, who was a psychoanalyst, would occasionally offer an observation of what she saw was happening in the group, often helpful and occasionally challenging, especially when none of us had seen an event that she did, and we could all recall had actually happened, followed by a discussion of why we had not seen or remembered it. We were learning how our minds were recreating and constructing our own versions of our immediate social world, sometimes distorting, or even denying what others were able to see, and frequently disagreeing with one another.

I became sufficiently interested in learning more about group processes to sign on to several subsequent courses, including one at the Tavistock that engaged 24 of their students in a weekend Group Conference of plenary sessions, with the consultants guiding the conference. We often broke into three groups of eight participants, each with a consultant, enabling the groups to explore small-group relationships in their own way. We occasionally engaged in inter-group exercises, appointing someone in each group to visit one of the other two groups, specifying their degree of authority, which could be simply to observe and report back (if the observed group agreed), all the way to full authority as an ambassador to negotiate between our groups. Exploring how inter-group relationships affected each of the groups was discussed in the plenary meetings, along with issues concerning the limits imposed by the consultants who organised the conference. I found the safety of this temporary community to be an excellent way to learn about the dynamics of within-group and between-group relationships,[100] and I began to think about how an understanding of group processes could help me to facilitate working with groups of experts. More about this in Chapter 11.

Then, in 1980, I learned about a new development in the USA called a *decision conference*.

The First Decision Conference

In May 1979, Westinghouse Elevator Company had arranged to attend a 'Contact Meeting' with a decision-analytic consulting company, Decisions and Designs Incorporated (DDI), one of the 'Beltway Bandits' located outside Washington, DC, that were funded by the US Government in exchange for a great variety of services to various government departments. DDI had received a large contract from the Advanced Research Projects Agency of the Department of Defense,[101] but were now branching out to more commercial work. I had visited DDI on several occasions in the 1970s, and it was one of the founders of the company, Cameron Peterson, to whom this book is dedicated, who had invited Jerry Brown, the General Manager of the Westinghouse Elevator Company, and a few of Brown's close colleagues, to the meeting. This was an unusual arrangement for a management consulting company, which usually visits the client to gather information, goes back to their offices to model the problem, then returns to the client with their PowerPoint presentation explaining the problem and showing the solution.

To Cam's surprise, a busload of participants showed up, the manager and his entire project team. They were designing a new factory that would include a tower to test the design of a new elevator ('lift' in UK English), plus five other function areas, each described by several options that provided more benefits at more costs. For example, a 1-storey, 7-storey, and 20-storey tower defined the options for the testing function. Scoring and weighting by the group provided Cam's assistants, particularly Ken Kuskey and Scott Barclay, with sufficient information to develop an efficient portfolio of options[ii] for any budget (as explained more fully in Chapter 14).

By the end of the second day, after much debate and discussion, they had agreed an affordable design for the new factory. To obtain alignment of team members on a best

---

[ii] Using the IBM 5100 and Design software, which later became Equity for PCs.

design in such a short time was so unusual that DDI decided to call this facilitated, on-the-spot, modelling process a 'decision conference'. Westinghouse commissioned many more in the years that followed.

When I heard about this first decision conference soon afterward, it was a head-smacking moment for me, as the group dynamics and decision-analytic parts of my brain started communicating with each other. I needed to experience one, so a director of DDI, Clint Kelly, flew to London in the spring of 1980 to facilitate a decision conference for the UK's Post Office (now, Royal Mail). As I sat in as an observer, I felt sure I could do this, and in January 1981 I facilitated my first decision conference. Interestingly, it was for a company that had previously hired a management consultancy company to help them decide whether or not to build a new factory, but they applied the usual process of visiting their client, interviewing and gathering data, doing the backroom modelling, then presenting the client with their findings.

When the company contacted me, they explained that the consultancy organisation hadn't adequately addressed their problem, and they agreed to a decision conference because it would only take two days and not cost much, in either time or money. Fortunately, DDI had completed the development of their Hival computer program for the IBM 5110, which enabled the rapid construction of a multi-criteria model that incorporated three major scenarios about future demand for the company's major product, and made possible many instant sensitivity analyses, all in real-time with the client. By the end of the decision conference, the best option was to upgrade an existing factory, not to build any new ones. And that's what they did.

Over the next few years, I had the good fortune to facilitate a great many decision conferences for International Computers Limited (ICL), at that time the UK's biggest computer company, and for Mars Confectionery UK, giving ample opportunities to change and refine the decision conference process. Helped by decision analyst Scott Barclay, who entered the elements of the decision model into the computer as the group created them, I learned to guide a group in *how* to think anew about a problem, but not *what* to think. My primary task was to mobilise their expertise, ensure the model accommodated their different viewpoints, encourage them to explore the reasons for their differences and treat information as a neutral commodity. I asked them to think broadly in developing alternatives and establishing criteria against which the alternatives were to be evaluated, but I refrained from contributing to discussions of the content other than to ask for explanations and point out possible inconsistencies. I found that my neutrality about the content ensured the client's continued ownership of their problem and its solution, and improved implementation as all the key players had been heard in the decision conference.

But when I reported this new development in professional meetings, two questions arose: how can the facilitator know when the model is good enough; and is it valid? Let me digress to answer those questions before describing decision conferences in some detail.

Requisite Decision Models

Let's start with the second question. Is a model developed in a decision conference valid? That is, does the model accurately reflect the real world? No, these are models of the future, not the world as it is now, although they always contain some elements of the current situation. Did they turn out to be valid descriptions of what actually happened? Well, not always. For example, one ICL manager was concerned about the flat revenues of the seven European countries for which he was responsible, so he convened a decision conference to see if they could devise better sales strategies. The model tested their current strategies against possible new ones that participants developed in the decision conference. The model revealed they were following the wrong strategies in all seven countries, but showed how a portfolio of new strategies could improve revenues.[102]

Three months later, I asked the ICL manager if those countries had implemented the new strategies. He said they hadn't, but he went on to explain that releasing the country managers from their original strategies had led them to think of even better strategies, and these were now being implemented. Within 18 months, revenues, orders and profits doubled and continued to climb for three more years.

I apologised to the ICL manager for providing help that was rejected, but he quickly said that without the decision conference there would have been no change. He explained that the model provided a new way to talk about the business and enabled the country managers to see they were wrongly positioned, but it also served as a guide to action by displaying alternative strategies whose collective impact could increase revenues and profits.

That observation by the ICL manager answers the first question. Yes, the model accurately described the current reality of the seven countries as profits and revenues formed two of the four benefit criteria along with relevant costs. But the other two criteria, participants' confidence of success and future potential for each strategy, stimulated the creation of new strategies, some requiring cutbacks to mere 'holding' strategies, while others were more vigorous. Thus, the model included both current and new strategies, enabling the computer to find combinations of strategies that would be better than those currently operating.

All the country managers agreed at the end of the decision conference about new country strategies, and the ICL manager's sense of unease about revenues and profits had been resolved, awaiting confirmation from the results of the new strategies. The subsequent improvement in performance did not validate the model because good consequences don't always follow from good decisions. But the ICL model was good enough to reveal a serious problem in the seven territories and to point to better alternatives. It also resolved the ICL Manager's sense of unease about the poor performance of the seven sales outlets. The model was fit for purpose – *sufficient in structure and content to resolve the issues of concern*. That is the definition of a *requisite model*.[103]

And how much effort is required for a model to become requisite? Dr Elliott Jaques, who had participated with me in one of the Mars decision conferences, gave me the answer: it is *when no new intuitions arise*. The closest analogy is to an architect's model, such as a small physical model of a to-be-built structure or a 3D computer representation of it, which helps the client to visualise and understand how the structure will look and fit into its surroundings. This prompts questions, such as 'what-if' changes, possible improvements or new features that might otherwise not have been appreciated without the physical model. It was Robin Gregory, and his co-authors Sarah Lichtenstein and Paul Slovic who first used the analogy of an architect's model to describe a decision model as representing a to-be-created future.[104] Such a model always includes options that describe new ways of achieving desired objectives and foresees possible consequences, both good and bad. And it allows for the testing of assumptions, uncertainties and differences of opinion among the key players.[105]

The following are the five characteristics of a requisite decision model:

1. **Definition**: The form and content are sufficient to resolve the issues of concern.
2. **Generation**: Through an iterative and consultative interaction among specialists and key players, facilitated by an impartial decision analyst.
3. **Process**: Driven by the sense of unease arising from discrepancies between participants' feelings and model results.
4. **Criterion**: When no new intuitions arise.
5. **Represents**: A shared understanding among participants of an agreed way forward; shows what *could* (not *should*) be done.

This last feature was often mentioned in interviews of participants about what they felt about decision conferences compared to typical meetings in their organisations.[106] Managers commented that at last everyone is now pulling in the same direction. Alignment was a key advantage, helped by a computer model that doesn't talk back, whereas in ordinary meetings, disagreements often escalate at the expense of issues on which participants agree. If the results are considered as unacceptable, I remind the group that it is only 'reflecting back in changed form'[iii] what you told it, and I suggest we dig into those results to see why this result was obtained. Sometimes we find a mistake, a wrong input, but more often the result is found to be logically sound. Further reflection may develop new insights, such as that an important consideration is not reflected in the model, so it needs revision. Whatever the reasons, participants soon discover that any attempt to game the model, so it gives the results they want, simply doesn't work because the gaming usually creates unexpected consequences in other parts of the model, making the results even less acceptable.

This short description is very different from the way many people think about models, which is that they reflect an existing reality or that they predict the future. Both might be included in any requisite model, but the above five characteristics go further by providing support for thinking about troublesome issues, particularly when the decision maker faces an uncertain future. As for the question of validity, in fact the model reflects the social reality of the group; it describes that existing reality, which is

---

[iii] A useful phrase I learned in the group conference work, when a consultant made clear that his intervention was a description of what had just happened in the group but expressed from a different angle.

a separate issue from what decisions will subsequently be taken and whether they are valid. Requisite models will continue to be mentioned throughout this book, so this sub-section needs to be digested thoroughly!

Decision Conference Stages

Further exploration of the decision conferencing process was instigated in September 1989, when Peter Hall from ICL and I formed the International Decision Conferencing Forum (IDCF), which has met every year or two in England, Scotland, the USA, Australia, Germany, Portugal and Spain. The 21st and last conference was held in London on 5–6 October 2019. The main purposes of the meetings were to exchange experiences of facilitating decision conferences, to resolve social and technical issues we encountered, and to establish principles of best practice.

Thousands of decision conferences have now been held in at least 15 countries, facilitated by members of the IDCF and others, and it's clear that as facilitators we have much in common, while delivering decision conferences in different ways. In particular, some clients required several decision conferences to resolve the issues they were struggling with, while other organisations took to using decision conferences for many of the important issues that required resolution as quickly and efficiently as possible. One IDCF member, Tim Morgan, an ICL employee who had developed a multi-criteria decision analysis (MCDA) template from his extensive budget prioritisation work with local government authorities,[107] changed the noun phrase into an adjectival one, *decision conferencing*, which is commonly used today for sustained working with an organisation. Let me turn now to a description of the features shared by decision conference facilitators.

In 2007, I wrote about the definitive characteristics of decision conferencing.[108] There are five:

1. **'Hot' issues**: Decision conferences work best when the issues faced by an organisation are live and in need of resolution, which can include crisis resolution.
2. **Attended by key players**: Participants are chosen to ensure they collectively represent all the main perspectives on the issues that are the subject of the decision conference.
3. **Impartial facilitation**: The facilitator attends to the process of building a decision-analytic model, engaging participants in identifying options, objectives and criteria, namely, the structure of the model, then in eliciting probabilities, values and trade-offs, without contributing to the content of the discussion, which is the job of the participants as they are the experts about the issues. The facilitator maintains a stance of impartiality.
4. **On-the-spot modelling**: This includes continuous display of the developing model so participants can monitor the structure, text and numerical inputs. This supports peer review operating to correct mistakes and identify disagreements that need further discussion.

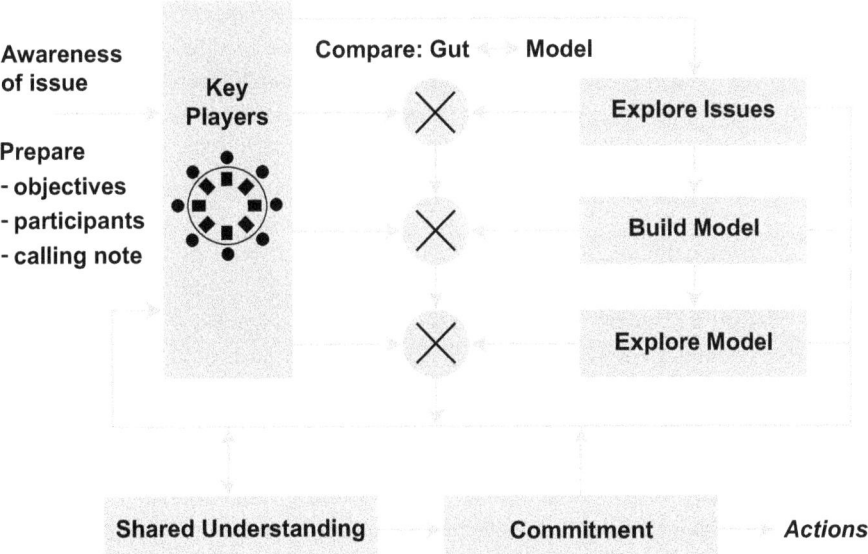

Figure 7.1

5. **Interactive and iterative group process**: Participants are encouraged to contribute to the developing understanding of the model as it is constructed and to report any sense of unease when that arises in any individual. Dissatisfaction about inputs or results drives the dialectic in the group, which can lead to improvements in the model to the point that it becomes requisite.

The block diagram in Figure 7.1 provides an overview of the main stages.

Initial Meetings

You receive an email or telephone call. Someone who has heard about decision conferencing is seeking help for their organisation. My first question often is, 'How do you think I could help?'

For example, a member of the UK's newly formed Committee on Radioactive Waste Management (CoRWM) called me, explained why the committee existed, what its primary task was, and said the group was now floundering. She knew about my decision-analytic modelling of possible sites in the UK for depositing radioactive waste deep underground and wanted to explore the possibility of my helping CoRWM. We agreed a meeting date.

More generally, the answer will have something to do with their sense of unease, which they will explain. Here are some real examples. 'Our health-insurance company is losing a million each week, and we need to stop the outflow within the next three months.' 'We need to create a strategy for our newly formed group.' 'We have more opportunities than we can afford to explore, so need to prioritise our activities.'

'A foreign journal has criticised our product as dangerous, which is inconsistent with our extensive data about its performance, so we need to forestall a possible ban by the government.' Better decisions are implied, though rarely mentioned, so you continue the conversation, only asking questions to understand their problem or the issues that are giving difficulty.

This is the moment of danger when budding decision analysts move into selling mode, suggesting how they might help the client with some form of decision analysis. Wrong move. You can't possibly know enough about the issues they are facing to even begin to suggest a solution, and even if you did, they will not be ready to hear you, so they will thank you, and you will never again hear from them. Instead, it's better to continue exploring the client's sense of unease until you feel you might be able to apply your decision-analytic skills in working with the client.

If you agree to help, then throughout the entire process you apply the principles of a process consultant, which are explained in Chapter 9. The key stance of the process consultant is to work *with* the client, applying your skills to help the client resolve the issues he or she is facing, but never suggesting a solution, for you don't own the problem, the client does, and it is the client who is accountable for their decisions, not you. Sometimes the potential client wants a face-to-face meeting, which I prefer because much useful information can be obtained about the context of the problem, especially if you visit the client's organisation.

First Meeting

The building, its location and environment, the way visitors are greeted and managed, all begin to provide an impression of the organisation's culture. For example, in my first meeting with the European Medicines Agency (EMA) in 2008 to discuss a possible research project, I soon realised that everyone was wearing a badge hung around the neck with a coloured ribbon. Mine was red, but most were blue, and I soon discovered that opening doors throughout the building required a blue badge, with other colours giving only restricted access. Blue gave full access everywhere, whereas my red one required a blue-badge escort at all times. Other colours gave access to only those parts of the building that required their holder's services. Such strict security was required to ensure that only authorised persons could access the confidential information provided to them by pharmaceutical companies about new medical products for approval in European Union countries. This culture of security required that releasing any written product to the public first had to be vetted by an internal committee to ensure that the content precisely represented the impartial recommendations agreed by the organisation's committees, thereby maintaining the public's trust in the EMA. At the first meeting, it also became clear to me that the organisation valued openness and transparency.

Those values also characterised the work of CoRWM, as I discovered at my first meeting, which was with Fiona Wathall, a retired UK colonel, who explained that the UK Government established CoRWM in 2003 to make recommendations for the long-term management of radioactive waste. The review of options was to be open, transparent and inclusive, and the work of the committee was to 'inspire public confidence', as anything associated with nuclear energy and waste disposal often generated public opposition. Members of the committee had been chosen to represent very different viewpoints, from an advocate and expert in nuclear power, to a former president of Greenpeace UK, to a professor of social science at a UK university. The committee had commissioned a public survey of attitudes and issues about nuclear waste, and had devised a list of concerns, but were now finding it difficult to agree on next steps. One member had been dismissed for his overly critical attitude of the committee's work, and another had resigned in protest at the dismissal.

I expressed my concern that if the committee continued as now, they would likely fail in the government's charge to them. I suggested that the history of nuclear waste disposal in other countries such as the USA and Canada had considered many options, both above-ground and below-ground storage, and considered competing objectives such as safety, security, harm to the environment and cost, all of which could be brought together in a decision analysis model. I suggested meeting with the committee to explore possible ways forward.

Second Meeting

This may be desirable if your client wishes first to explore with key players the suitability of a decision conference for their problem. Following my first meeting with Colonel Wathall, I was invited to attend the nine-member CoRWM committee to discuss with them the potential suitability of a decision analysis model to facilitate the current state of their work. I explained what MCDA was and can do, and it seemed to fit with their elimination of some options (like dumping the waste in the ocean, which would be illegal, or firing it in rockets to the sun, which was unacceptable because sometimes rockets fail and fall back to earth – and . . . they are very expensive).

The discussion was long and at times heated, with a variety of objections, such as how could ethical concerns be accommodated in a quantitative model, and that CoRWM's job was to synthesise the many elements of the waste management problem, whereas MCDA was a reductionist approach, which could miss the big picture. I responded by saying that if some solutions (options) would be more ethical than others by leaving a final solution to future generations, then a 'Yes, later' would score zero and 'No, now' would score 100. As for the reductionist objection, I agreed that MCDA starts by dividing the big problem into smaller problems of option-consequence combinations, but that it also logically reassembles the pieces to give an overall ordering of the options. And I emphasised that as the MCDA model is hierarchical, new features typically emerge in this constructivist stage, as the properties of water are not evident from independent study of hydrogen and oxygen.

As this large problem would require several workshops to work on the smaller problems, I suggested that my colleagues at Catalyze, an off-shoot consultancy company of the LSE that I helped to form along with a former HP Manager, Bob Kitchen, could work over the following months to develop the MCDA model. I suggested it might take many months of workshops and meetings with the whole committee, with a final decision conference to reassemble the small problems in early 2006, well before the committee were required to report their recommendations by July. The Chair of the committee thanked me for my help and said it would now be discussed by the group, and they would get back to me. Within a few weeks, a contract was signed with Catalyze.

Preparation

Decision conferences and facilitated workshops require careful preparation, usually at a short meeting with the decision maker who will be held accountable for the recommendations of the group. Four items are agreed at that meeting:

1. **Objectives**: The purpose of the meeting. One short sentence should be sufficient.
2. **Participants**: Who is to be invited? These are key players chosen to provide a diversity of knowledge and experience in applying the knowledge, which will help to resolve the issues, and can include people from outside the originating group, department or even the organisation. In considering who to include, ask if anyone not on the list will read the final report and dispute the conclusions by showing that an important aspect had been neglected. If so, they, or a representative of their view, should be included.
3. **Administrative arrangements**: Date, time, location and any other particulars so each participant can make their own plans without asking further questions (although there almost always will be one or two who will ask).
4. **Calling note**: A letter of invitation to the meeting addressed to each participant or an email written as one would to an individual, not a group, that sets out the following, a paragraph for each:

   a. Administrative arrangements.
   b. The purpose of the meeting.
   c. That it will be conducted as a workshop/decision conference facilitated by [name of facilitator]. A brief description of a decision conference might be attached. Although many clients ask for an agenda, explain that decision conferences have no fixed agenda, but you can then include a sentence describing the stages that are typical of most decision conferences, as described here in the next sub-section.
   d. How the participant could prepare for the workshop. This could be as simple as reflecting on the expertise they could bring to the meeting, to asking them to read relevant attachments, or anything else. Preferably, as little as possible, because the information needed during the meeting is most likely already in their heads, and busy people won't have much time to prepare.
   e. A final paragraph asking for their full participation throughout this important meeting without interruption. A final invitation to get in touch if further information is needed.

The calling note is intended to make sure all participants understand what the meeting is about, why they are being asked to attend, and that it is important. We normally do not allow observers, as their presence can negatively affect the group process, particularly if they never speak. If they are invited, there must be a good reason for their presence that would be acceptable to the group. For example, in CoRWM, an independent outside observer appointed by the commissioning UK Department for Environment, Food & Rural Affairs (Defra), along with a Defra member, attended each public meeting to ensure transparency and impartiality in the discussions.

Interviews?

Sometimes, an in-house team wants to gather information from interviews and from journals and other public sources considered relevant to the topic of the decision conference before the decision conference, but I usually discourage this as inevitably far more information will be collected than is actually needed. Anyway, the experts will already know this information and they can report it when it is needed, or instantly find it on the internet. That has become a standard mode of operation in a decision conference: *only report data when it is needed.*

Although it may be possible to shorten the time for the decision conference by interviewing participants before the meeting to gain their views about one or more of the issues, objectives, criteria or options relevant to the purpose of the meeting, I usually discourage this. The reason is that interviews can create commitment on the part of the interviewee to their expressed viewpoint, making it more difficult for them to change or broaden their thinking during group discussion. Most participants won't have fully formed preferences about the many issues an interviewer will ask about; their thinking has not yet coalesced. As I have repeatedly stressed throughout this book, preferences are constructed by the mind, and most of us, including experts, prefer to live with relatively open minds until we must decide. Judgements about values, trade-offs and probabilities are malleable, and sharing our collective experience and knowledge enables us to make an informed judgement when it is needed.

Occasionally, a team builds a straw-man model that is displayed at the start of the meeting, but beware, because it can take more time to explain and justify that model than would have been the case if it had been constructed from scratch in the decision conference.

At some point, explain to your client that a decision conference has no fixed agenda because issues are discussed when they arise in the process of building the model. Some clients insist on an initial PowerPoint presentation at the decision conference to provide context, information about the issues and data that sets the scene for why change is needed. You might agree that a short slide show about context can be helpful, but that the first item to be discussed will be the issues, and data will be accessed later when it is required for the modelling. Suggest that the presentation should be no longer than 10 minutes, with 10 or fewer slides.

You will also need to decide who will run the computer during the decision conference as it is difficult to listen while typing, unless you can do both simultaneously. Also, if you are not familiar with the client's topic, you don't want to hold the process up by asking how to spell unfamiliar technical terms group members are accustomed to using. As the computer output is continually projected, your assistant must be able to tolerate others watching while he or she types. Sometimes a new assistant can be quickly trained before the meeting if the software is user-friendly, and best of all is someone from the client's organisation who is experienced with the software. I sometimes include an experienced decision-analytic colleague to co-facilitate and include their fee in the charge to the client.

Remember to arrange for refreshments, ideally at the back of the room so they can be accessed during the meeting, and include short refreshment breaks. Warn participants that the meeting will resume only when everyone is back in the room; that should minimise being captured by their phones.

Meeting Room

Before the meeting, the facilitator (often with the help of the client) ensures that the meeting environment will be conducive to the decision conferencing process of interactively building a model and engaging in peer review during the process. Two features of the meeting room are crucial:

1. Everyone should be able to see everyone else.
2. Everyone should be able to see the visual aids, usually a flip chart and the screen onto which the computer model is continuously projected.

Long, rectangular tables are to be avoided because everyone on one side can see those on the opposite side, but they can only see the two people next to them on their own side, without bending forward or backward. And the most senior participants often assert their authority by sitting at one of the table's narrow ends, a head-of-the-table effect that attracts dominant personalities who talk more frequently and exercise greater interpersonal influence.[109] In a decision conference, everyone is expected to contribute, and all are treated equally, which is emphasised by seating at round tables. Strange that we often eat at round tables but meet around rectangular ones. When heads of nations get together, it is usually at round tables. Social psychologists have long known that more cooperative behaviour is exhibited around round than rectangular tables. (UK House of Commons take note: your seating exacerbates conflict.)

Figure 7.2 shows how you might arrange a room for six or 24 participants, depending on the availability of small rectangular or circular tables. In the larger group, participants can see one another quite easily with just a slight movement of the head or body when a direct view is obstructed. Experiment a bit and you will find that most rooms can be adapted satisfactorily.

Be sure to provide power cabling so participants can plug in their laptops (and remember to bring a multi-plug adapter if you are travelling to a different country). Participants bringing laptops enables easy access to data when it's needed.

The rooms I dread most are those with either a singular rectangular table or individual end-to-end rectangular tables that can't be moved because they are physically attached and wired up with places to plug in laptops. Avoid these. Instead, keep in mind the huge round table that hangs in the Great Hall of the UK's Winchester Castle

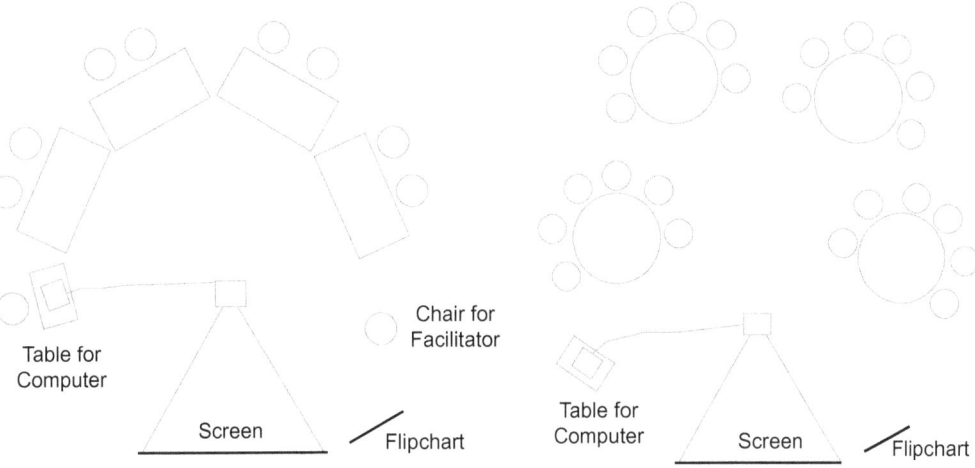

Figure 7.2

Figure 7.3 Photo courtesy of Christophe Finot on Wikimedia

(Figure 7.3), once thought to be that of the legendary King Arthur, although radiocarbon dating in 1976 revealed that its timber was cut between 1250 and 1280, so it is actually of medieval origin. Later, King Henry VIII ordered its repainting, adding his likeness at the centre, including the Tudor Rose. But it is 5.5 metres (18 feet) in diameter and weighs 1.2 tonnes (2,600lb), so think of it only as a reminder that problem solving is more likely to be effective if participants are seated in a way which signals that everyone is of equal status; thereby minimising or eliminating head-table biases.[110]

The Decision Conference

As the facilitator, you should arrive at least an hour or two early to ensure that the meeting room is properly arranged, or to arrange it. As participants arrive, introduce yourself as the facilitator and welcome them to the meeting. When the leader arrives, suggest that introductions should start the meeting: name, area of expertise, organisational affiliation and what outcomes they hope for the meeting – the latter enabling you to understand their expectations for the decision conference. When everyone has assembled, ask the leader if they are ready to begin, thus making clear you are not the leader. That's the first step in ensuring the group owns the problem, and they will subsequently own the solution.

To Start

Introduce yourself, along with a short history, establishing your credentials for facilitating the group. Consult the list of participants you were sent before the meeting, and make a map of seating with first names, which you repeat back so you can quickly learn who is who. With introductions complete, reiterate the purpose of the meeting that was explained in the calling note and ask if that is clear and acceptable to the group. Some discussion might be necessary to agree the fundamental objective of the meeting (which I sometimes write on a flip chart), and you then explain that the objective will be achieved by satisfying the three generic purposes of decision conferences:

- to generate shared understanding of the issues (not necessarily consensus);
- to develop a sense of common purpose (allowing individual differences of opinion);
- to agree about the way forward (commitment to the direction, not the individual paths).

Explain that these objectives can be realised because in decision conferences information is treated as a neutral commodity. Whoever has it, we need it.

For example, in a decision conference I facilitated for a NATO three-star general, which was attended by representatives of all the NATO countries, participants were of various military ranks, so the general made clear that rank was irrelevant in expressing information, expected or unexpected, good or bad news, whoever holds it, don't hesitate to tell the group.

Finally, explain the loose agenda you have in mind:

- establish context and explore the issues;
- create the structure of a model that will aid thinking;
- input data and judgements;
- explore the model, do sensitivity analyses;
- agree the way forward.

Explain that most decision conferences find this is an iterative process, so progress sometimes requires returning to a previous stage for revision, which may then necessitate changes in later stages. Also, it is typical of decision conferences for any organisations with vertical accountability structures defining relationships among employees to point out that the group is not to make or approve decisions, rather it is to provide recommendations that will enable the boss to take decisions, for it is only that person who is accountable for the consequences. Answer questions as they arise.

Now, let's consider each of the five following sub-headings, which develop what happens in the horizontal rectangles of the block diagram at the start of this section.

Exploring the Issues

This stage generates a shared understanding of the issues that are to be addressed in the decision conference and which issues should find some sort of representation in the model. I often start by asking the group to state the issues that must be considered if we are to achieve the objectives of the meeting. Then invite discussion about the issues. Ask questions to clarify the current situation and why it is felt a change is needed. Watch body language and invite comments or questions from anyone who you sense might have reservations about speaking so early. Discuss and revise the original objective of the meeting as necessary and emphasise that making recommendations for this desired change is the group's *primary task*.

It is during this discussion that you will become surer about the type of decision model to be developed. In my early years, I often dreaded this beginning because I wasn't sure I could think of any way to deal with the complexity I was hearing. But I soon learned to ask more questions so I could understand how they think about the problem, a process of *appreciative inquiry*[111] that never gives solutions, but seeks to understand the problem better. Eventually, something would click in my head, and I could begin to explore how best to construct a model that would address the issues and perhaps go some way to resolving the expressed sense of unease.

In hindsight, I now see that the click would occur as the group's discussion connected in my thinking to one or more of the five structural ingredients of good decisions, objectives, criteria, options, events, and outcomes, as they are defined in decision theory, but not necessarily the terms used by the participants. (As an example, even after attending several decision conferences, one of my present-day clients still refers to criteria as *parameters*.) The client always has some sort of framework for expressing their sense of unease, and it is the facilitator's job to see how that can be represented more precisely in the language of decision theory's 10 ingredients, as we saw in Chapter 1. In general, conflicting objectives favour multi-criteria value models and value-tree representations, while uncertainties about future events favour probability models and decision-tree representations, with or without multiple criteria. More distinctions are given in Part III.

This introductory process might be different for groups whose participants are acquainted with one another, familiar groups, compared to those who aren't, unfamiliar groups. Especially in the initial stage of exploring the issues, some participants in unfamiliar groups may attempt to establish a leadership position in the group, arguing with one another about what the 'real' issues are, making clear they are personally well informed, and that they can be the 'saviour' of the group. In 1965, Bruce Tuckman suggested that groups go through four stages, *forming, storming, norming* and *performing*.[112] After participants have been brought together, the forming stage, differences in their knowledge, lived experience and work preferences may give rise to anxiety and conflict, the storming stage. As they work together under effective leadership, resolving their differences and using their individual strengths as needed, norms of behaviour develop, which contribute to accomplishing the primary task, the norming stage, and the group then enters the performing stage, working cooperatively and effectively. This framework isn't always realised in a linear fashion, one stage after the previous one, but it can provide a useful starting point for the facilitator's appreciation of the feelings and behaviour of unfamiliar groups.[113] My experience with familiar groups is that as they are accustomed to working with one another, they start 'performing' quickly, focusing on the primary task. More elaborated approaches are described in Chapter 11.

Building the Model

We start with structure. Did the discussion of issues focus more on uncertainty or multiple objectives, or a mixture of both? Which of the five structural ingredients of a decision model seem to you might begin the process of making explicit the structure of a decision model? If multiple objectives dominate, then start by helping the group to identify and define the objectives and criteria, as described in Chapter 4, and build a value tree as the immediate goal. If uncertainty about future events is more prominent, then move towards defining the first set of decisions and uncertain events with their plausible outcomes and subsequent decisions, the beginnings of a decision tree representation of the problem. Sometimes, the group may find it difficult to distinguish the differences between the five ingredients, so your assistance in helping them to define them as consistent with decision theory will clarify the differences. Indeed, much of what you do as a decision-analysis facilitator is help the group to develop a consistent, well-defined language that unpacks what they consider as 'too many parameters'.

Once the structural ingredients have been identified and defined, putting them together is best done with the help of a computer program. The case studies in Part III show how different combinations of the ingredients serve different needs and how software programs can facilitate structuring.

The next stage in modelling is entering data, values, trade-offs and/or probabilities under the guidance of the facilitator, using any of the methods from Part I. As I mentioned just before the end of Chapter 3, invoking the Roman god Janus, we often look backwards to see if any data might be relevant to moving forward. That's particularly true if the goal is to improve something; we gather data about how it is currently operating, then use some of that data in modelling how it could be improved. You might start by asking if the assessment of preference values or probabilities might be informed by available data. If so, these could be entered directly into the computer followed by the assessment of linear or non-linear value functions. If not, then direct numerical assessments will be required. And, of course, assessments of trade-off weights always require subjective judgements, even though they are partly based on differences in the performance of the options, for which data might be available.

Throughout the process of eliciting judgements, making *consistency checks* is crucial to ensure that preference values, trade-offs and probabilities are realistic. Probabilities must obey the laws of probability, differences in preference value must be compared, and ratios of sums of weights must be checked to ensure they represent relative importance. Failure to make consistency checks runs the risk that probabilities for favourable outcomes will be over-rated and unfavourable ones under-rated, that preference values will be too similar, and weights too high.

If participants are new to decision analysis modelling, eliciting the inputs for only a part of the model shows how the pieces fit together, and they don't then have to wait to see how all the numbers combine to provide a result. This also keeps motivation high even for those who know what's coming.

For example, after completing the value tree for evaluating pain-killer drugs, introduced in Chapter 4, I asked the group to provide the inputs for just the three benefit criteria. Participants provided published data summaries, and these were input to the computer, which transformed them into 0–100 preference scores, as you might recall from the discussion at the start of Chapter 5. I then engaged the experts in eliciting swing weights for the three benefit criteria, as shown in the section on swing weighting methods. The computer then displayed the bar graphs for the six drugs, and I asked the group if this felt right. They could see the relative contribution of each criterion to the total and agreed it did indeed represent their view about the relative benefits of these drugs. Scoring and weighting of the safety criteria then proceeded apace. For an unfamiliar group, that first stage of scoring, weighting, assessing probabilities and seeing the results for part of the model takes time, but that is well spent as it maintains the group's energy and speeds up the remaining tasks.

In making any subjective assessments, it's useful to adopt a *think, report, discuss, decide* technique, which the facilitator explains is an approach that minimises bias introduced by the first person to express their judgement and encourages focused debate about a number. The group is asked first to think of a number, then when everyone in the group has done so, they are asked to report it. The facilitator listens for the highest and lowest numbers and asks those participants to explain their reasons for the low or high number. Alternatively, I might construct a frequency distribution of the reported numbers on a flipchart.

Then the entire group is invited to discuss and debate their reasons for their numbers to see if they can agree, such that everyone's judgement is within plus-or-minus 5 points (on a 0–100 scale); the median (middle) number is then entered into the computer. If one or two people hold out for a very different number, I ask them to record their disagreement until after the model is complete and we can then try their numbers to see if they make a difference to the final result.

This simple *think, report, discuss, decide* technique takes advantage of a decision model's insensitivity to the precision of its input preference scores and probabilities.[114] And I can report that in all the hundreds of decision conferences I have facilitated, it has never been necessary to write both an agreed and dissenting report of a decision conference. The closest I have come is when two different groups tackled exactly the same problem and came out with very different results, but it was possible to account for the differences by tracing back to different assumptions about the context that had been adopted by the groups.

The lack of a need for precision in the inputs to a decision model helps to support the three purposes of a decision conference: shared understanding, sense of common purpose, agreement about the way forward. A model that is relatively insensitive to some imprecision of its input probabilities or preference values can gain the approval of all participants sufficiently to agree about recommendations.

However, the trade-off weights in MCDA models are another matter, for they can change the results, as we see next.

Exploring the Model

This stage in the decision conference builds on the shared understanding that has begun to develop among participants as they discussed and debated the numerical inputs to the model. In this stage, participants can conduct 'What If?' analyses, changing scores, weights or probabilities to see if different judgements and disagreements among participants will change the results. Usually, only a few changes will make an appreciable difference to the results, so participants can home in on only the important differences and then decide how to deal with them.

First, the facilitator shows the overall results as graphical representations, zoomed so all participants can see the results clearly. Ask the group if these results feel about right. Follow through any disagreement by digging deeper into the model to see why or how that result occurred. This is a good time to explore alternative preference values or probabilities from individuals who disagreed with the group's assessments. Usually, these won't have much of any effect on the final results, but if they do, ask the group how this difference in judgement should be handled. They might make some concessions and change their agreement slightly, but more likely they will stick to their original number, at which point the individual who disagreed typically gives way, saying they can still support the final results. Only on one occasion did that person, who had made valuable contributions to the discussion, say he could not sign up to the final report (and the leader of that decision conference later told me that the participant had a vested financial interest in an alternative outcome).

As participants often feel more unsure in their elicitation of weights than of preference values or probabilities, it's very important to explore how changes in the weights might affect the final result. Refer back to the pain-killer drugs case study of Chapter 5 to be reminded of the steps in assessing criteria trade-off weights. The next step in a decision conference is to conduct *sensitivity analyses*, changing the weight on a criterion or node in a value tree over its entire 0–100 range to see the effects on the

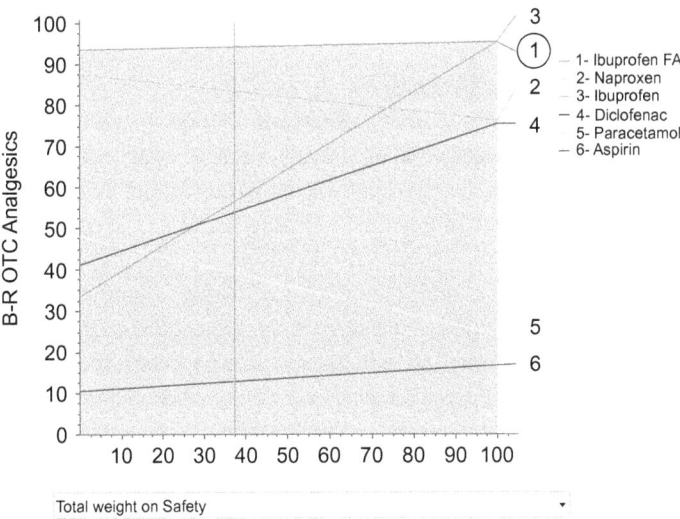

Figure 7.4

overall results (which is quick and easy with specialised computer programs). I usually start with the weight on the node associated with dis-value, in this case the safety node, whose lack pulls down a drug's safety score.

The graph in Figure 7.4 shows the overall weighted preference score on the vertical axis while the horizontal axis gives the sum of the normalised weights on the criteria under the safety node. The vertical line is located at the sum of those weights, here at 37.5, the cumulative weight on safety in Figure 5.13. Remember that these weights are normalised, the input weights divided by their sum and displayed as percentages. The six sloping lines show how each option's final weighted preference score would change if the weight on the node were decreased or increased. Here, it can be seen that ibuprofen FA remains most preferred over the entire range from 0 to 100, while aspirin remains least preferred. More typically of MCDA models, two upper lines cross, with one dominant for lower weights, but overtaken by the other at higher weights. The instructive aspect of this display is that when participants begin to understand it, they see how it confirms their experience; some options become more preferred as the weight increases, while others become less preferred. Here, for example, paracetamol becomes less preferred at higher weights because its potential toxicity becomes more dominant.

Many prescribing physicians are surprised by this result because although in the UK they routinely prescribe paracetamol (acetaminophen), it is never the most preferred painkiller at any weight. One of the experts in this decision conference pointed out that paracetamol is the only one of these six painkillers that can be fatal in overdose.[115] As mentioned briefly earlier, two sorts of people might overdose: those who pop another pill as the pain returns, thinking they are like M&M candies, so neglecting the warning on the maximum number to be taken each day; and those who can't remember when they took the last pill, especially the elderly, so take another too soon. Of course, only paracetamol should be prescribed for patients who are taking medicines to reduce blood clots, as the others are all NSAIDs (non-steroidal anti-inflammatory drugs), which can raise the risk of bleeding.

These kinds of insight inevitably arise from exploring the model. Yes, the risk from paracetamol was represented by its input preference score of zero for overdose toxicity, but the full impact of that single score became more evident when put in the context of the other drugs along with all the other criteria. The context made this one feature more salient.

But context can have the opposite effect, too. CoRWM provides an example. One member of the team explained to me early in the project that only over his dead body would he approve deep storage of radioactive waste because all rock is fissured and in many thousands of years the radioactivity would be conducted by the groundwater to the land above and thereby into plants eaten by animals and humans. In the final three-day decision conference, in which an entire day was devoted to sensitivity analyses, trying different scores from committee members and from different constituencies of the public, along with sensitivity analyses on weights, the final result showed that the waste should be buried deep underground. When I later asked the member who would not accept deep disposal why he now supported it, he said, 'Because all the other options were even worse!'

It was a day of sensitivity analyses that led him to this conclusion. My colleague, Mara Airoldi, wrote on a flip chart every disagreement that remained unresolved during the first two days of refining the model and we then tested the sensitivity of the model to every disagreement. None changed the preference for deep disposal over storage. So, it's important to ensure that someone makes a note of the disagreements as they arise. They will serve as an aide-mémoire when you write the report of the meeting.

Exploration inevitably involves making changes to the model as new insights are generated, participants consider neglected issues and implement further changes, all the while comparing the status of the model at each stage of its construction with their intuitions. Sensitivity analyses will reveal the weaknesses and strengths of the model, in particular how robust it is to changes in the inputs. The analgesics model is very robust; nothing can knock ibuprofen off its top spot. More typically, the most preferred option remains best over ranges of inputs that have been agreed by the group, the result of a robust model.

For example, when the CoRWM expert groups scored the options on their criteria, we kept a record of the ranges of any disagreement. When the modelling finally showed the three deep disposal options were most preferred over all the shallow options, we then biased the model by replacing all disputed scores for the shallow options with the most favourable scores and for the disposal scores with the least favourable scores. To everyone's surprise, the difference between the two sets of options decreased only slightly and the deep disposal options remained most preferred. That finding characterises a robust, requisite model.

When all inputs have been agreed, and a base-case model has been agreed, the group might recognise that some of the assumptions made along the way might not hold for the future. In that case, you might suggest trying out combinations of assumptions so they can use the model to 'try out the future before having to live it', as Rob Wilmot said to me in the early 1980s. This usually involves changing many inputs at one go, creating a *scenario* that describes a possible future.

Here is an example. A group of experts created an MCDA model of the benefit-safety balance for drugs used to treat rapid remitting multiple sclerosis (RRMS). When they saw the results, they realised that the model didn't work so well for the less common high disease activity (HDA) version of MS, so they set about changing many of the inputs, new scores informed by data and weights appropriate for patients with the HDA. That model placed the second most preferred drug for RRMS in first place for the HDA scenarios.[116] It was the earlier sensitivity analyses that suggested what to change in the RRMS model to create the HDA model. The structure remained unchanged as the content was changed.

Developing Shared Understanding

A UK manufacturing company had been developing a new technical product for two years, but now needed more investment to continue. But team members could not agree on the best business strategy to raise capital investment for the new product. Technical members of the team argued for completing the current strategy as agreed at the start, which would maintain ownership and control, with a partial sell-off of rights to provide the required funding. The marketers believed a joint venture would bring in sufficient capital to complete the development. Arguments for and against these two strategies covered *financial objectives*, including criteria of short-term and long-term profits and revenues, and capital costs; along with *non-financial objectives*, defined by criteria of pull-through, image consistency with group and division strategy, market dominance and the probability of achieving the strategy, all future-oriented.

An MCDA model effectively traded-off the financial and non-financial objectives, which showed very similar poor overall results for both strategies, but for different reasons. As the group explored those differences, they thought of new strategies, which were successively added to the model and evaluated. Each new addition improved either the overall financial or non-financial results. Learning from each addition, the group then added a combined strategy, a sell-off of one-half plus a joint venture, which met both objectives better than any before.

Peter Hall, a colleague who helped to develop decision conferences, facilitated that group, and he reported, 'It was a turning point for our group. It changed the mindset of our management team in a very constructive way and we are now following the new strategy very closely.' It was the ability of the computer to compare the weighted differences on the criteria that identified the meaningful advantages and disadvantages of the strategic options, enabling participants to focus on them, think creatively about what to improve, and develop a shared understanding of an effective strategy.

Making important differences more salient is an effective way of handing back in changed form the inputs participants had given to the computer. If the experts don't like the results, it's up to them to find out why and you can help them uncover the reasons.

Explore the inputs to spot possible errors in entering the data, show how the pieces have been calculated, make suggested changes, ensure consistency of the inputs, identify possible missing criteria and so forth.

The decision conference block diagram suggests periodic checking of outputs at each of the stages against participants' intuitions. I ask, 'Does that feel about right?', a question that is intended to help each participant consider their lived experience, which may be more felt than thought. Exploring these discrepancies may require iterating back to previous stages of model-building to build the sense of common purpose. When no intuitions arise from exploring the results, then the model can be considered requisite. It is through deliberative discourse and persuasive arguments on the one hand, and modelling of key issues on the other, that participants have been guided to find common ground. The many ways in which the facilitator can support this iterative process are discussed in Chapter 10.

Agree the Way Forward

With a sense of common purpose established, and at least a half hour before the stop time, the facilitator asks participants to discuss and agree a way forward. If the decision maker is present, he or she might summarise what needs to be done next, asking others for their opinions. At this point, it should be possible to construct a brief narrative derived from exploring the model, thereby translating the quantitative findings into words, what Friend and Hickling call a *commitment package*.[117] In the above case of the manufacturing company requiring more investment, the team agreed that the new mixed strategy should be recommended, so they created an action plan on the spot, and this was approved after the decision conference by the senior decision maker.

We've already seen in the CoRWM example how modelling and sensitivity analyses, coupled with serious discourse, enabled even the most sceptical member to agree that deep disposal of radioactive waste was better than storing it. The next example is how a regulatory organisation faced with a crisis was divided on what to do next, but quickly achieved agreement in a decision conference followed by gathering up-to-date information, enabling them to make an important decision that prevented many deaths.

In July 2009, the World Health Organization (WHO) decreed that swine flu (the H1N1 virus) had reached pandemic status in Europe. This presented the European Medicines Agency (EMA) with a rock-and-a-hard-place dilemma because research about the vaccines had not yet been completed. Should the Agency approve the two vaccines right away, even though safety and efficacy had yet to be fully proven, or wait for another month? A hasty approval could lead to criticism if the vaccines were found to be unsafe or not efficacious, but if they waited, and the vaccines turned out to be satisfactory, they could be criticised for the sickness and lives lost that could have been prevented.

At that time, I was in charge of a small research team at the EMA studying how the organisation could be more transparent and clearer about their process for approving drugs. The director of the EMA, Dr Thomas Lönngren, asked me if decision analysis could help with this problem and my positive response led to an afternoon internal decision conference, attended by EMA experts on infectious diseases and vaccines. With the help of my colleague, Dr Barbara Fasolo, we facilitated the group in constructing a decision tree whose initial alternatives were to approve in late September or late October. Uncertainties included severity of the disease, efficacy and safety of the new vaccines, with the 24 paths of the decision tree showing various combinations of the outcomes of the three uncertain events, each path representing a possible scenario for the future, 12 paths representing the consequences associated with each of the two decisions.

Sensitivity analyses on the probabilities showed that judgements about the uncertainty of disease severity had far more influence on the decision than considerations of efficacy and safety. Thus, the decision conference ended with the group agreeing to a subsequent two-hour meeting of internal experts about the epidemiology of the H1N1 disease, and that led to a one-hour telephone conversation with specialists from the European Centre for Disease Prevention and Control, which brought the model up to date. This search for more and/or better information agreed at the end of a decision conference is a typical subsequent action.

The final model showed that a weighted average of the 12 European deaths and serious diseases (DSD) for the September decision were 216,500, and 291,547 for the October decision, a difference of 75,047 DSDs, which made clear that an early decision would be best. Approval of the vaccines occurred on 29 September. Despite scepticism by a few participants at the start of the decision conferences, enough present-day data, along with knowledge and experience about previous pandemics going back to the last century, enabled the experts to formulate agreed probabilities for the outcomes of all uncertain future events, and the likely relative consequences for every scenario. As one person said, 'The greatest value of the exercise was that it was group-based. It brought into the same room different people, with different views, expertise, and seniority.'[118]

This example well illustrates how meaningful assessments about the future can inform a decision model. As Beach and Wise explain in the *Theory of Narrative Thought*[119](TNT):

... the brain structures experience as a narrative in which the past and present imply the future, allowing identification of potential threats in that future, and guiding action to prevent, avoid, or diminish them before they occur. In other words, cognition is primarily about what happens next and how to avoid or take advantage of it.

Ending the Decision Conference

Many decision conferences concern sensitive topics that need to be resolved. When agreement is reached at the end about next steps, it isn't always best to subsequently advertise the results because senior management may need time to consider how to move forward. Colleagues of the decision conference participants will ask their colleagues, 'How did it go? Did you resolve the problem?' Issues about future investments are often sensitive, for example, as are mergers and acquisitions. In particular, issues about strategy, namely, what the organisation should do, will require concrete tactics and plans, and these need to be worked through to ensure the change strategy is feasible.

This is the moment for the facilitator to work with the group, especially the leader, to agree what can be reported back. Best to write these on a flip chart or project onto a screen so everyone can see exactly what is agreed. It might be: 'The group discussed the issues openly and rationally, constructed a quantitative model in which all the issues were represented, then considered relevant data and judgements about the future to provide preliminary results, with these subjected to sensitivity analyses on the uncertainties and differences of opinion. We've now agreed what needs to be done next, and everyone will be informed soon about what this implies.'

Written here in generalisations, this sounds rather wishy-washy, but it's always possible to say it in terms of the purpose of the decision conference and it will be reassuring to outsiders that everyone had a fair hearing, maybe even discovered some things that hadn't before been considered, and that the group was enabled to take forward the need for change in a constructive manner.

Some decision conferences about prioritisation agree to redistribute resource to areas of greater opportunity, which means that the areas of lesser opportunity may lose funding, and that will make staff anxious about their jobs. If this is agreed, it is important to make subsequent decisions quickly to reduce anxiety levels, and this can often be done by reassigning people to areas that are new to them. Best not to leave employees worried, for that can exacerbate unhelpful rumours, assumptions and unwarranted accusations. In short, address at the end of the decision conference how to respond to colleagues who asked you what happened.

Finally, ask participants to spend the next few minutes recalling their expectations for the decision conference, reflecting on what transpired, and how they felt about the whole process. After a few silent minutes, invite them to respond, then be silent yourself. Someone will break the silence with their views, encouraging others. You might also ask what they liked and didn't like about the two days, and what they felt could be improved. Not only do you learn from this, but participants realise they are now thinking differently from how they did at the start. This helps them to acknowledge their learning, which is important as it forestalls attempts to sabotage the result by claiming the results were known right from the start.

Early in my career, a senior manager said he was always impatient about the first stage, exploring the issues, but I later learned that's typical of those whose work preferences are to get on with things, whereas strategists often wish we had spent *more* time exploring and thinking of alternatives and criteria. These two critiques often reflect different work preferences, but these aren't the only two. An effective team includes a variety of work preferences,[120] so whatever participants report at the end may be a reflection on their own work preferences, not just the decision conference process. But I did shorten the initial phase of exploring the issues by providing summaries at various points in the discussion, pointing out that nothing is set in concrete, and we can at any time go back to make changes. 'Is that OK?' If you have done this prematurely, the group will say so and continue exploring.

A final point about ending the meeting. In the calling note, the start and end times for each day are given. It's important for the facilitator to stick to those times. Doing so helps participants to express any sense of unease during the meeting rather than storing it up hoping to raise it later, only to realise the meeting is ending. If they detect that the facilitator is not going to end on time, they may well continue to wait until it is too late, and it never gets expressed.

After the meeting has ended, three more activities remain for the facilitator: (1) writing a report; (2) participating, if asked by the client, in briefing decision makers about the decision conference and its results; and (3) checking back later to receive feedback.

Follow-Through

Sometimes a group agrees that further work is required, often to find 'better data', which can happen if some participants aren't satisfied with the results. Indeed, their sense of unease may have increased, especially if changes to the structure of the model introduced events or criteria that hadn't been thought of. I recall one case in which the first and second most senior person in the decision conference couldn't reach agreement about some elements in the model, so the group suggested the two of them work with me later to see if they could resolve their differences. At that meeting, sensitivity analyses explored reasons for why the most senior person couldn't agree to the result even though he did agree with the other participant's judgements. In the end, the senior manager simply decided that his intuition was correct, and the model was wrong, with the result that the organisation ceased to use decision conferencing.

Fortunately, that is a rare occurrence. More typically, the purpose for the subgroup's follow-through is to gain the approval of a senior person who didn't attend the decision conference. One of the group members sets the scene, followed by the facilitator displaying the model projected onto a screen, introducing the main elements of the model and the processes of scoring and weighting, then showing the main results. Depending on the reaction of the senior person, sensitivity and scenario analyses will help to show how the model can be used.

Sometimes a follow-through reveals that implementation has partly or completely failed, even when the decision maker was present at the decision conference and participants agreed to the next steps. At this point, the facilitator might be tempted to become engaged in planning processes, like creating a Gant chart to assign actions and their timing for specific individuals. As one facilitator told me, 'Great idea! That prevents the hard work of the decision conference from being lost.' But I disagreed with him, explaining that it subverts the authority of the accountable decision maker. He immediately agreed, saying he hadn't thought of that. As we will see in the next chapter, issues of authority and accountability are crucially important, but are frequently handled badly in many organisations.

Report

Within a week or two, the facilitator writes a report of the event, possibly helped by the co-facilitator or assistant. Its structure depends on the confidentiality agreement you've signed with your client and the extent to which the process of creating the model and its findings are to be shared beyond the participants in the decision conference. Sometimes, just describing the results is all the client wants, but they may want a record of the process and even some tutorial material describing the type of model and its basis. Commercial clients usually consider the results as confidential to them, but even so, they may wish to circulate your report more widely in the organisation. That will require you to include more tutorial explanations, for a report written only for participants is often not understood by non-attendees.

Two topics that give problems for outsiders are probabilities as *degrees of belief* and weights as the *relative importance* of the criteria. Since both are subjective, professionals such as accountants, scientists, engineers and others seeking objective interpretations think of probabilities as relative frequencies, and interpret weights as importance, without regard for ranges of difference. I use the concept of indifference between a real-world event and a reference gamble as defining probabilities, which may relate to relative frequencies, and the 9:5 temperature ranges on Fahrenheit and Celsius thermometers as a metaphor for swing weighting as comparing relative importance, as discussed in Chapters 6 and 5, respectively.

Public sector organisations and charities are often willing for you to publish openly and may require it as part of your contract with them. To make it easy for yourself, you might suggest to the client this structure: Title, Table of Contents, Participants, Executive Summary or Abstract, Introduction, Method, Discussion, Conclusion, Appendices. That structure, rather than one that recounts the stages of the decision conference (which is more like a diary of events), is easily converted to a publishable paper, with perhaps one of the participants, who knows the content better than the facilitator, taking the lead in fleshing out the Introduction, Discussion and Conclusions.

To start, I often use a previous report as a template, first changing the title and the list of participants. I then copy and paste tables and graphs to replace the ones in the template, adding and deleting as necessary to support the new narrative, which forces me to think about what needs to be said. As my background is in engineering and experimental psychology, I'm accustomed to think pictorially, but other facilitators may wish to start with the narrative and complement it with tables and graphics.

While you are writing, you may test further the robustness of the model, especially sensitivity analyses and differences between pairs of options. Include any new important result in your report, but acknowledge these were not validated by the group. Don't overburden the report with graphs; narrative summaries often are sufficient.

Send the first draft to the sponsor, who circulates it to all participants for their views for reporting back to you and the sponsor as tracked changes, which can easily be incorporated into a final version. This process will be repeated if a publishable paper is to be created (and be sure your fee includes your contribution, as it will certainly take at least two days of your time). With your client's permission, assign responsibility to the first author for seeing this through the stages of preparation and submission, responding to referees and other matters.

Brief Widely

As virtual meetings grow in popularity, increasingly clients ask for a short PowerPoint presentation of the decision conference and its results. It's possible to do that with 20 slides or less, with the first four or five introducing decision analysis and decision conferencing, followed by 8–10 slides for the steps in building a model: from establishing the decision context, through building the structure, assessing the quantitative inputs and combining them, to examining the results and conducting sensitivity analyses, and finally drawing conclusions.

My dislike of slides containing paragraphs of text read by the presenter leads me to construct mostly only single phrases and very short sentences that can be read quickly, allowing viewers to attend to what the speaker is saying, so I err in the direction of simplicity. Slides are mostly graphics copied from the decision-analytic software and pasted onto a slide that is blank save for a title, with text being revealed as I speak. Edward Tufte's book, *The Visual Display of Quantitative Information*,[121] encourages cutting, cropping and discarding irrelevancies in a graph. He argues that 'ink should be reserved for data', so, I crop out borders, eliminate unnecessary colouring and remove other fripperies that communicate nothing, although they may look pretty, unless I want to draw attention to something. I'm hoping the slides will ease the viewer into feeling what we did is comprehensible and that they have understood the purpose and findings of the meeting.

Sometimes, I brief directly from the model, enabling viewers to interact with it, but that can be difficult virtually. Face-to-face, it can be very impactful, as I report in Chapter 14 about the design of the Type 45 destroyer.

Checking Back

Contacting your clients some weeks or even months after the event can provide feedback that is helpful in designing future decision conferences and in facilitating new meetings. Also, as you work for other clients in the same area, you learn their jargon and can develop ways to use their language. Of course, it's also helpful to find out what happened, to discover ways in which decision conferencing was helpful – or not, and perhaps to learn more about how context influences judgements about both structure and content.

For a major decision conference preceded by many workshops, each on a smaller part of the problem, it's important to discuss with the client and or/colleagues how to better design the workshops as we do them. Learning as we go can benefit from a shared structure of steps to follow. This ensures that full information is available about each part of the problem when everything is brought together in a final decision conference.

Summary

By now, it should be clear that decision conference modelling isn't about finding the right answer to a problem or an optimal solution, for there are as many solutions as there are combinations of all the objective and subjective inputs. But there are better and worse solutions, and sometimes eliminating the worst solutions is the best that can be done, as for CoRWM. They left open which of the three deep disposal options should be pursued by the government.

Furthermore, let's be clear that the model agreed by the end of a decision conference represents the social reality of that group at that time, conditional on their assumptions and judgements. If participants are well chosen to represent a diversity of skilled knowledge and experience, and data are judged to be relevant for the future, then their collective agreement should not be easily dismissed. The model provides a framework of all the elements deemed to be relevant to reducing the gap between now and a more desirable future, and it enables rational debate and persuasive arguments to resolve differences of opinion about the smaller problems, so they can be reassembled into an overall view. In short, participants move from being implicit and qualitative, to explicit and quantitative, with all assumptions and judgements now made openly.

Research shows that decision conferences are most enthusiastically embraced by organisations that are willing to change, where accountabilities are distributed throughout the organisations, and decisions are made after consulting key players.

This chapter positions decision analysis as a socio-technical discipline in which the social aspects of interactions between participants in a group setting are guided by impartial facilitation in the construction of a model whose elements are drawn from the 10 ingredients of good decisions, all within a well-understood context. This enables a group to formulate solutions that are better than those by any individual and ensures that the client continues to own the problem and the solution.

To summarise the above, *a decision conference is a group of key players, sharing an agreed task, engaged in problem solving through deliberative discourse and the construction of rational preferences, facilitated in the context of decision-analytic modelling*. If I had given that definition at the start of this chapter, it probably wouldn't have made much sense. Admittedly, decision conference facilitators have tried different definitions over many years, and I suspect it will be further refined in the years to come, although the purposes may well stay the same: *to develop a shared understanding of the issues, to achieve a sense of common purpose and to gain agreement about the way forward*. It's neither about 'the right answer' nor even an 'optimal solution'.

I think, though, we can agree that decision conferences achieve the speculation over 60 years ago of Thibault and Kelley about the possibility for small groups to perform constructively and creatively in solving problems.

8   Behaviour in Organisations

> Managerial hierarchy is the most efficient, the hardiest, and in fact the most natural structure
> ever devised for large organizations. Properly structured, hierarchy can release energy and
> creativity, rationalize productivity, and actually improve morale.
>
> Elliott Jaques, 1990[122]

At a decision conference for the UK division of an international company, I helped the
managing director (MD) and his directors to develop a medium-term plan (MTP) for
prioritising strategies over the next seven years to ensure achievement of two objectives: growth and profitability. Plans for the current products along with possible new
ones were included as options, all scored for their contributions to the two objectives
and for their investment costs. As expected, some products contributed more value to
one objective than the other, so their relative weights were explored to find a balance
that seemed about right to the division directors, and the first day ended with substantial agreement about a new MTP, which mainly favoured strategies for the current
portfolio of products.

However, at the start of the second day, when the group reflected on their progress,
the MD pointed out that no new products were included in the proposed portfolio of
affordable options. He suggested that the seven-year timeframe might be too constrict-
ing, so a third objective was included: future potential, defined as the extent to which an
option would contribute to profit and/or growth in 7 to 15 years. After participants
scored the options under this new objective and assigned a swing weight to this new
criterion, which was slightly less than the sum of the weights on growth and profit, the
results showed an MTP similar to the first day's MTP, although some strategies had
been eliminated or modified to provide funding for new products. This immediately
pleased the MD, while some directors were less pleased with the loss or reduction in
support of the current products.

What was preventing alignment between the directors and the MD? And why does
this matter to decision analysis modelling? Indeed, what is the point of this chapter?
The answer to this latter question is that knowing where your client is located in their
organisation's hierarchy can seriously impact your choices at nearly every step in
selecting and implementing the 10 ingredients for a decision model that will meet the
needs of your client. You can benefit from an understanding of how decisions differ at
each level in the organisation and how these differences can be considered in applying
decision analysis.

In addition, sometimes a decision conference shows that the sense of unease is the result of an outdated business model, and the facilitator may be asked to help construct a new one. For example, the finance division of a UK charity found it difficult to raise sufficient funds for its operations division, but a decision conference showed that options for improving current fundraising only made a marginal difference, and the new director of the finance division decided it was time to appoint a marketing manager who could coordinate their many separate fundraising activities, databases and strategies. I helped the finance director create a new set of roles, defining role relationships and accountabilities in the last few hours of the decision conference. This was subsequently adopted by the Chief Executive Officer (CEO) of the charity, resulting in a few resignations of fundraising staff and appointments of new staff. As a result, income more than doubled within a year and it continued to rise, enabling the charity to help more people in need.

The answers to the other two questions about the non-alignment of directors are more complex, so let me start with a touch of my professional history. For many years at the start of my career, I would return from a client engagement feeling frustrated that I just didn't understand what was going on in their organisation. I realised I simply didn't know much about how organisations were structured nor about how relationships between employees and managers operate. I read widely about organisation theory, Weberian bureaucracy, Taylor's scientific management, group dynamics, management by objectives, matrix organisations and so forth, but didn't find many answers to explain my observations. However, I soon discovered that the long-term research of Dr Elliott Jaques, then the head of the School of Social Sciences, at Brunel University, where I worked in the 1970s, might resolve my own sense of unease. And indeed, it did, as I learned more about his theory of requisite organisations and saw the data supporting his theory.

First, I'll summarise the main points in his book, *Requisite Organisation*.[123] This is an engaging book of 137 page-pairs, a topic and explanation on the left page and an illustration of the topic via a drawing on the facing page. For a more narrative style, I recommend his more narrative book, *Social Power and the CEO*.[124] Although both books are focused on enterprise systems, most of the concepts apply to any kind of organisation, including the civil service, military, partnerships and voluntary organisations. This is a system that explains and predicts human behaviour in organisations, and whose application can improve an organisation's functioning.

Organisation Types

Most employed people in the West work in organisations that are managerial hierarchies. If you ask your client where they are located in their organisation, they might produce an organisation chart, which, they explain, 'shows the reporting relationships'. The boxes display titles of roles, and sometimes the names of people filling the roles, with collections of lower boxes connected to someone higher in the hierarchy, 'the boss'. It may also contain some dotted lines and those are said to represent relationships to other bosses.

I don't see these today as often as I used to, perhaps because email is so widespread that anyone can communicate in an organisation with anyone else: 'To' the boss, and 'Cc' to others, just to keep them informed. Jaques is clear that reporting relationships are not the same as an accountability hierarchy, in which managers hold their subordinates accountable for doing their best, and for the outputs their subordinates produce. Although not every organisation is a managerial accountability hierarchy (MAH), such as university academic departments, church clergy and partnerships, which are associations where the relationships are collegiate, many of the principles of MAHs are still relevant to them.

To understand what goes on in an organisation, it is helpful to distinguish between the *manifest* organisation (how it is supposed to work, as represented by the official organisation chart), the *assumed* organisation (how people think it works) and the *extant* organisation (how it actually works, revealed by systematic study). Jaques introduced the notion of a *requisite* organisation (how it ought to be), the organisation that is required to get work done in the managerial hierarchy by employees who work together harmoniously, effectively and creatively. The concepts below help to understand requisite organisations.

Organisation Strata

Most organisations have too many levels. In part, this is because organisational strata are confused with pay-grade systems, which establish pay and status brackets. A few organisations are too flat, largely because email has made it possible for anyone to talk to anyone, although this confuses communication with accountability relationships. Most large corporations need no more than seven strata, as Jaques discovered in his research.

The descriptions in Table 8.1 of each level use role titles that are typical for commercial companies, but different titles are appropriate for other kinds of organisations, such as numerical grades for the civil service and ranks for the military. The decision-making limits for a person occupying a role are here made explicit in the middle column of text, with the right column defining the primary tasks that define the role. The times in small boxes will be explained shortly.

Strata 1–3 describe the direct output of the organisation. The stratum 1 employee is in direct contact with the outside world, making available the outputs, usually services or products, required by their first-line manager. They decide how to produce their outputs to the required standards of quality and in time. Stratum 2 managers (for example, Supervisor) work within the systems and procedures devised by the departmental manager and make decisions about what must be done to ensure that the stratum 1 employee can produce the required output. They are often problem-solvers as they respond to the practical constraints of the operating environment. The stratum 3 role (for example, Department Manager) works across several organisational units

Table 8.1

Stratum	Organisation level	Prescribed limits of role	Description of role
7	Corporation	Society.	Provide overall strategic direction.
6 `20`	Corporate Group of Subsidiaries	Strategic direction.	Establish mission and field of operations for each corporate subsidiary.
5 `10`	Corporate Subsidiary; Operating Company	Primary task & field of operations.	Decide products and services, and prioritise financial and human resources.
4 `5 yrs`	Division General Management	Products, services, market sectors.	Organise supply of goods and services, allocate resources, and determine work programmes.
3 `2 yrs`	Department Management	Resource and work programmes.	Organise systems and procedures to keep the work flowing.
2 `1 yr`	First-Line Management	Systems, procedures, standards.	Respond to situation and decide what output is required.
1 `3 mts`	Shop & Office floor	Required outputs.	How to achieve the output.

deciding how best to keep the work flowing by devising systems and procedures to be followed at the first two strata.

Strata 1 through 3 define the direct output nature of the organisation. These three levels may be sufficient for the operation of small businesses, charities, franchises and other organisations, like the franchises of larger organisations (for example, McDonald's local restaurants). Mom-and-pop shops may exist simply as stratum 2 or 3 organisations.

Strata 4 and 5 describe general management of the organisation's business functions. Stratum 4 division managers (for example, Vice Presidents, Executive Directors) organise the supply of goods and services, decide allocation of financial and human resources, and determine work programmes for the departments under their control. They tend to be inward looking, whereas the Stratum 5 managers (for example, Presidents, MDs) are more outward looking as they ensure that the organisation's mission is realised, and they work with their stratum 4 managers as colleagues, prioritising financial and human resources.

Above the double horizontal line are the Stratum 6 corporate directors of large organisations, who work collaboratively with stratum 5 MDs in scanning the societal context and its changes to define and establish the mission for each operating company and how they are to operate. Overall strategic direction is provided by the stratum 7 head of the corporation, the CEO. Some organisations are so large, and are composed of so many types of corporate subsidiaries, that they can be considered stratum 8 companies (for example, Apple, Walmart, Amazon, Royal Dutch Shell and CVS Healthcare).

It's clear that the strata depict the increasing complexity of the roles and the difficulty of work experienced by those filling the role. Is there a single, measurable characteristic of the difficulty of work? Jaques found that there is, but first we must be clear about the meaning of *work*.

'Today at work my boss gave me some work to do that was really hard work.' It is that last sense of 'work', the difficulty of the tasks assigned, which Jaques focuses on in his definition of work: 'the exercise of discretion within established limits'. For our purposes, the exercise of discretion is the process of making judgements, forming preferences and creating choices. And he measures that process with *time-span*, a quantity which characterises the difficulty of work at every level and defines the boundaries between the strata.

Task Complexity

Each role is made up of many tasks, which together define the role-occupier's job. Associated with every task is an explicit or implied date by which the task must be completed, otherwise there would be no need to carry out the task. In short, a task is a 'what-by-when'. As a young lecturer, I once asked the departmental secretary to type up a memorandum. She asked me how urgent it was, and I replied that it was not at all urgent, she could do it at any time. 'How about in two months', she said, and I ashamedly said, 'No, I definitely need it within two weeks.'

Early in his career, Jaques developed the concept of *time-span*, defined as the target completion time of the *longest* task in the role. It represents the level of work associated with a role. It is not necessarily the time at which the consequences of the task will become known. For example, the task of creating a training programme might take six months, whereas the training itself may extend over several years; the target completion date would be six months. Time-span is established simply by asking the employee's manager to identify tasks with long targeted completion times that define the employee's role; the *longest* targeted completion time is the measure of the size of the role.[125]

Jaques and his colleagues discovered that when they asked an individual at any stratum to name the person who they considered to be their 'real boss', they always named someone at the next higher stratum: people in jobs with time-spans up to three months always named someone in a job with a time-span from 3 months to 1 year, and so on up the strata. Thus, the boundaries emerged from the research. It also became evident that promotion within a stratum was experienced as 'more of the same', whereas promotion across a boundary felt 'more and different'.

Independent research by Roy Richardson carried out at the Honeywell Corporation in Minnesota showed that work associated with each stratum is qualitatively different from all the lower strata, with complexity and abstractness increasing at higher levels in the hierarchy.[126] The study confirmed that time-span is a measure of the complexity of work at each stratum, even if the actual work within a stratum is very different from one role to the next. In short, time-span is a single quantitative measure of the size of a role, and it correlates in the high 80s or 90s with the actual pay for the role, or the judgement of felt-fair pay by the employee. It was Richardson's work that persuaded me to accept that this hierarchical structure might well be common to all organisations.

But what does this common structure imply about the ability of individuals to carry out the requirements of their roles? Are they capable of handling the level of complexity the role demands? We turn next to consider the relationship between an individual's capability and the requirements of the role.

Individual Capability

People differ in their ability to deal with task complexity, depending on their knowledge, skill, temperament, values and wisdom. Those five characteristics of any individual Jaques defines as 'cognitive power', the *capacity* to see patterns in complexity, to see the woods despite the trees, to find meaning in apparent noise. Cognitive power is a broader concept than IQ or school performance and it develops as the individual matures, depending on experience and opportunities. Slower-developing capacity usually peaks at a particular age, while faster-developing capacity continues to develop throughout a person's life.

Although these are the findings of the research by Jaques and his colleagues, especially Kathryn Cason, they paint a picture of capacity that some find unacceptable because it claims to show that the potential for growth in capacity is not equal among people. Or that the aspirations of some people to better themselves cannot be met because of the limitations in their genes. We may be equal in the eyes of the law, but we are not equal in what we could be. We have all experienced growth of our own capacity, and we empathise with young people in poor countries whose parents cannot afford to send them to school. It is heartbreaking to hear from these children how much they want to go to school; capacity is locked away in them and cannot be released other than in limited ways. That is why Jaques saw that capacity is conditional on experience and opportunities.

On the other hand, even for those of us who feel our capacities have steadily grown throughout our lives, there remain many things we wish we could do, but can't and never will. We may sing or play a musical instrument well, but we'll never be a virtuoso. I will never be able to write a novel, become even an adequate sportsman or develop acting as a profession. Try as I might, I know my capacities are limited, however caused. So, why do we object to Jaques' claim?

My view is that we confuse cognitive power, or capacity, with capability. The following definitions appear to be consistent with most dictionaries.

Human capacity: The skills and knowledge required for a particular task.
Human capability: The ability to do something because you have the required capacities.

It strikes me that when Jaques uses the term 'capacity', critics think he actually means 'capability'. The examples above about my limitations are not about capacity: they are simply things of which I am incapable. If he had used the term 'capability' rather than 'capacity', I think most objections to his theory about the growth in capacity would dissolve. I have the capacity, skills and knowledge to play the bassoon, but not the capability to play professionally. So, skills and knowledge are associated with capacity, as Jaques confirms, but temperament, values and wisdom should be associated with capability. I do not have the disciplined temperament to play my bassoon well, I don't value playing professionally and I have the wisdom not to try. And, yes, any of these five features can grow or change over time. Henceforth, I will refer to 'capability' in preference to 'capacity'.

Can human capability be measured? Jaques defines it as the time-span of 'the largest role that a person could have the potential to carry, in work that the person valued doing, and for which he or she has gained the necessary skilled knowledge and experience'. Thus, that person's time-horizon for successfully meeting the demands of such a role is a measure of one's potential capability. I find it helpful when interacting with my clients to observe how they deal with this concept of forward time in describing the tasks associated with their role.

For example, in a decision conference about developing new strategies for a stratum 5 business, the stratum 4 director of one of the three divisions complained to the MD that a seven-year time-horizon for strategy was impossible as nobody could see what would happen beyond two years in her part of the business. When I heard this, I thought that the two-to-five-year time-span defining stratum 4 suggested that the role was feeling too big for her. That was confirmed when, a few months later, she resigned and became the MD of a stratum 3 organisation.

Jaques summarised his research of many decades in an article written for the *Harvard Business Review*, explaining that hierarchy emerges in all organisations, worldwide, because of the size of a role and the size of the person filling that role.[127] And this is true of all organisations, not just MAHs. It should now be evident why the directors of the international company referred to at the start of this chapter were satisfied with the first day of their decision conference when a seven-year strategy emerged from the modelling, distributing resources to all the current products, but were not so pleased when a 15-year time-horizon was added, which diverted some resources to new products. It wasn't just that some directors emerged with less resource on the second day than the first, it was because their two-to-five-year time-horizon was more than realised, whereas the MD, who was several years older than the directors, was on the verge of moving to a stratum 6 capability, and the 10-to-20-year time-span of that role meant he was thinking beyond seven years.

You have probably heard of the 'Peter principle', which is that, in a hierarchy, every employee tends to rise to their level of incompetence.[128] This does indeed happen when success at one stratum leads to promotion to the next stratum, but if the growth in a person's capability peaked at the previous level, then they will find it difficult to perform well in the new role, so they attempt to compensate by micromanaging at the level below. A good human relations (HR) department would be monitoring growth in capability, as indicated by periodic reviews of performance in a role, to ensure this doesn't happen. Understanding time-span can help, but applying it for HR departments is beyond the scope here. Chapters 9 and 10 of Jaques' book, *Social Power and the CEO*, show how.

For our purposes, it is sufficient to keep the time-span of your client's role in mind during the early stages of interacting with him or her. After all, creating the future requires holders of organisational roles to exhibit a degree of forward thinking that matches or exceeds the time-span of their role.

Accountability and Authority

This sub-section and the two to follow highlight a core problem behind a manager's sense of unease: the oft-neglected organisational function of accountability allied to authority. Careful analysis of conflict in organisations, clashes of personalities and political manoeuvring may reveal that these are symptoms of confusion about account-abilities and failure to align authority with accountability. To behave with full respon-sibility, managers must:

- be held accountable for determining what outputs their subordinates produce; and
- be given minimum managerial authority in relation to their accountabilities, be taught that they have the authority, and been instructed in how to use it.

Here is an example that prompted a senior International Computers Ltd (ICL) manager to arrange a decision conference for two managers in his division who continued to argue about profits in each of their separate units. The model developed on the first day of a decision conference seemed to achieve some measure of agreement between these two managers. But on the morning of the second day, when I asked how they felt about the previous day's results, the manager of the software unit said it hadn't really solved his problem. He explained that his group developed software products that were then bundled into the computers that were sold by the other manager's marketing unit. 'Why does that matter?' I asked, and he explained that all internal units in ICL were organised as profit-and-loss (P&L) centres, with transfer prices established between centres. 'The problem,' he said, 'is that the software is given away free at the point of sale, as that helps to make the sale, but my unit then receives a zero transfer-price. I simply can't control my group's profits if this continues.'

Nothing had been said on the first day about ICL's new P&L organisational structure, which was very popular in the 1980s to increase competition within the organisation and thus stimulate better outcomes. It soon disappeared, worldwide, as what it actually created was internal discord that failed to achieve harmonious and creative collaboration between groups. Indeed, the software manager had been held accountable for his unit's P&L, but was not granted the authority by his manager to control the transfer price. I suggested that the managers of their units should take this problem to their senior manager, for only the person in that role could resolve the issue. And the decision conference was closed. We didn't need a decision analysis model to resolve this.

Accountability

Managers are accountable for their own personal effectiveness and for the outputs of their subordinates. Accountability is often confused with reporting relationships. An individual can report to one or more people in the organisation, and organisation charts often portray the reporting relationships (as in 'my direct reports'). However, only one person can be accountable for an individual's outputs, namely, that person's manager. A manager is 'a person who is held accountable for the outputs of others, for sustaining a team capable of producing those outputs, and for giving effective leadership to that team'.[129] Thus, 'accountable for' is not the same relationship as 'reporting to'. All managers hold their subordinates accountable for doing their best. Clarifying what outputs of his or her subordinates the manager is accountable for is a necessary step in creating effective working relationships and for ensuring that the organisation's work gets done. Accountabilities define the job, and lack of clarity about this is a major source of conflict as people try to work together; they can either arrogate authority to themselves or pass the buck. The resulting conflict and inefficiency are then mistakenly blamed on the motives and personalities of individuals.

Good job descriptions define four to six accountabilities, not the many tasks to be performed for meeting the accountabilities, as that is micromanaging. The 'how' is best left to the holder of the role. Some job descriptions include a list of responsibilities that are expected of the person in a role. However, responsibilities can be delegated, whereas accountabilities cannot.

Authority

Making accountabilities and the required authority explicit establishes a context in which people can get on with their work, in their own styles, with their own idiosyncrasies. Once accountabilities are clear, then the degree of authority must be sufficient for the individual to realise their accountabilities. The minimum authority needed for full managerial authority in the accountability hierarchy is as follows:

1. Veto any new appointment.
2. Decide types of work assignments.
3. Decide personal effectiveness appraisal and any merit review.
4. Decide removal from role, within due process.

Not all these four would be possible in organisations other than MAHs, because authority is often personally earned and hiring is based on qualifications and firing on unacceptable behaviour (think academics, clergy, politicians). Minimum authority applies to an MAH, whereas in *all* organisations there are *lateral* role relationships of authority that vary, whether or not they are made explicit:

- **Prescribing**: directing a person to carry out a task or to stop.
- **Auditing**: assessing performance, stopping it and reporting.
- **Coordinating**: aligning activities of individuals or groups.

- **Monitoring**: observing performance, persuading and reporting.
- **Service giving or getting**: providing or obtaining service.
- **Advising**: giving advice, informing and providing information.

Authority decreases from the top to the bottom of this list and can apply within and across roles at the same or different levels in an organisation. A clear understanding of these six lateral authorities is crucial to cross-functional relationships and is the key to avoiding the complexity of matrix structures, which often don't work because team members are required to maintain communication with both project and functional managers, accountabilities are unclear, authorities rarely made explicit, and allocation of financial resources becomes difficult. Indeed, I was unable to establish decision conferencing in one matrix-organised pharmaceutical company because potential participants spent so much time in meetings communicating with one another, they didn't even have sufficient time to do their work well.

Pharmaceutical companies provide a particularly clear example of the need for some sort of integration between project and functions, as both are needed in developing new drugs. Development is usually carried out by teams whose project managers are held accountable for delivering drugs that are safe and efficacious, while acknowledging it will be science that determines the final outcome. Several function managers are held accountable for providing services as required during the development process, which require testing a drug to ensure it is not toxic, doesn't cause cancer, is absorbed and secreted properly, and is efficacious. Each test requires specialist knowledge and expertise, so performing these functional tasks is what separate units do. In short, developing drugs requires both project and functional management. How is this to be achieved?

In a requisite organisation, this is accomplished by establishing not only vertical accountabilities and authority, manager and subordinate, but also specifying lateral authorities between project and function roles. For example, the lead person in each drug team might be given the authority to ask for and obtain service directly from any of the functions without having to gain authority from the function manager. It is also possible for the function manager to establish a role that is accountable for ensuring the specific function expertise is used well and appropriately, with the authority to monitor the project team's use of the function expertise, including the authority to persuade the team about its use and report this back to the function manager. Any deficiencies would then lead to the function manager to discuss these findings with the project manager, which they would resolve as colleagues. If that failed, then they would refer the problem upward to the head of research and development.

There may also be a need for collaboration between project teams, with a member of each team given coordinating authority, and the same might be required for collaboration among function teams. The projects manager might also establish a senior-level committee with the task of auditing each of the project teams, reporting their findings to the projects manager and possibly with the authority to stop a project.

These examples are intended to illustrate how accountability and authority can be implemented within the constraints of an accountability hierarchy, provided that authority in both vertical and lateral role relationships is made explicit. The reason for including them in this chapter is to provide sufficient information for decision analysts to understand the behaviour they observe in organisations, for otherwise decision-analytic modelling can miss a problem that inevitably arises when accountabilities are not matched with the authority needed to meet those accountabilities.

Managerial vs Technical Roles

In many organisations, the only way to earn a higher salary is to move up in the managerial hierarchy, which means acquiring subordinates as one does so. This creates a problem for more technically minded people, like scientists and engineers, who want to get on with their specialties with few or no subordinates at all. For example, a world-class geologist who specialises in mineral exploration might be assigned to a stratum 6 role, with pay that is equivalent to a stratum 6 corporate director who oversees exploration by several subsidiaries. Lower down, a stand-alone stratum 5 company may depend on an outstanding chief design engineer with lateral auditing authority over stratum 4 designers, who are the subordinates of the stratum 5 MD. Again, we see that an appropriate level of lateral authority can enable individuals in technical roles to exercise their expertise in an MAH even if they do not wish to manage people.

Business Functions

The operational spine of a business is to:

1. develop and improve products and services;
2. provide or produce the goods or services;
3. procure inputs needed for producing the goods or services;
4. deliver the goods or services;
5. maintain effective client or customer relations;
6. market by analysing client needs and devising promotions to encourage clients to seek the goods and services; and
7. develop new types of businesses or transform existing business units.

In addition, staff specialist functions assist managers with:

8. financial policies and priorities;
9. scheduling, resourcing and business analysis;
10. human resourcing; organisational development;
11. compensation and training;
12. working methods technology;
13. legal policies;
14. legislative developments; and
15. public affairs – relations with major organisations other than clients.

This is just Business 101, but I mention it here because in some organisations sight can be lost between the operational spine of the business as contrasted to the staff specialist functions, which are enablers of operations. In decision-analytic modelling that is focused on operations, it is helpful to associate fundamental objectives with the spine functions, but recognise that specialist functions are required to realise those spine functions, and all functions require a mix of resources, human, financial and material. It is easy to become focused on beefing up the staff functions, so when assessing trade-offs, the facilitator may need to remind the group that the point of the organisation is the spine functions, not the specialist functions.

Leadership

'Leadership is that process in which one person sets the purpose or direction for one or more other persons, and gets them to move along together with him or her and with each other in that direction with competence and full commitment.'[130] Jaques and Clement argue that good leadership in MAHs arises from requisite organisation combined with competent hard work rather than from any special personal traits or charisma, which can be beneficial to a leader, but are not sufficient by themselves to maintain effective leadership. Working capacity is a necessary condition; if you are promoted to a job above your working capacity, you cannot be an effective leader.

I discovered an example of poor leadership in an insurance company whose board had just hired a new MD from outside the organisation, prompted by the retirement of the previous MD. The new MD contacted me because he was finding it difficult for his subordinates to exercise their judgement in carrying out their assigned tasks. They frequently referred decisions to him that they should have been taking themselves. In discussing these issues in a decision conference with the new MD and his subordinates, it soon became apparent that the previous MD had required all subordinates to refer important decisions to him. As a result, he had created a dependency culture throughout the organisation, which stifled effective decision making and prevented much-needed change. Although I never met the previous MD, who had spent his entire working life in the company, working his way to the top, I suspected he had been promoted well beyond his capacity to do the top job, so he was micromanaging downward. The decision conference progressed by ensuring that accountabilities and authority were made clear. Subsequently, several managers resigned.

The essential elements of effective leadership are to set a clear context for the work, to value subordinates' views even if the message is unpleasant, to appraise and coach subordinates, to give freedom within limits, to assign tasks in line with your understanding of subordinates' strengths and weaknesses, to take account of individual work preferences in creating teams and to maintain your credibility by being competent yourself.

For more information about requisite organisation, consult the two main websites devoted to the topic, www.requisite.org and www.globalro.org. Nancy Lee's 2017 book, *The Practice of Managerial Leadership*,[131] well describes the principles of requisite organisation with examples drawn from her own experience in applying it. In looking at it again while completing this chapter, I see that she, too, used the term capability rather than capacity, which must have stuck in my memory. Thanks, Nancy.

Summary

The descriptions in this chapter show that the hierarchical structure of all organisations is an inevitable result of task complexity and individual capability, both of which will influence the structure and content of a decision-analytic model. By actively seeking information about these influences, the decision analyst can better ensure that the model addresses the concerns of their client. Decisions differ from one stratum in the hierarchy to the next in three ways. One is the substance of the decision, what it attempts to achieve; the second is the timeframe for completing the tasks associated with the decision; and the third is the time-horizon for the consequences of the decision.

We would expect that the complexity of tasks, their targeted completion time and the time-horizon of consequences to increase for roles higher in the managerial hierarchy, and knowing how these may be different depending on the role of your client provides material for the questions you will ask your client about their sense of unease. If the accountable decision maker does not attend a decision conference whose main task is to make recommendations to a higher level, then it is wise to ensure that that person's longer time-span is represented in the model. In general, you will find that keeping in mind the forward time-horizons of accountable decision makers ensures that recommendations based on a decision model will be accepted.

It behoves the facilitator to keep in mind that some managers will inevitably be performing their jobs by micromanaging their subordinates, a sure sign they have been promoted to a role above their current capability, and if that manager has called for a decision conference to determine how to correct underperforming subordinates, it won't work, as it is the manager, not the subordinates, that is the problem. And managers who have grown in capacity beyond that required for their roles will become increasingly dissatisfied with their job, which should be recognised by HR or the manager's boss, and promoted to a more demanding role, or helped to find a new job.

The overall theme of this chapter is that the behaviour of people occupying roles in all organisations, especially MAHs, will be constructive and creative if accountability and authority are aligned, and if leaders are capable of performing at the level required by the role.

9   Process Consultancy

Process consultation is the key philosophical underpinning to organisational learning and development in that most of what the consultant does in helping organisations is based on the central assumption that *one can only help a human system to help itself.*

Edgar Schein, 1999[132]

People experiencing problems often don't want to be told what they should do. This is a particularly acute problem when a consultant is attempting to persuade a client that decision analysis can help. That pesky word 'decision' can be seen as a threat, eliciting the defensive response, 'Nobody can tell me how to run my business!' It's best avoided in the initial discussion with a potential client, but how can you do that? Spetzler, Winter and Meyer, in their 2016 book, *Decision Quality*,[133] give a positive spin to the title by an informative sub-title: it's about creating value. And Ralph Keeney made value the focus in the title of his 1992 book, *Value-Focused Thinking*,[134] which suggests that the route to value is creativity, which we know is stimulated by decision modelling, but goes beyond its technical aspects. So, early discussions with a prospective client might best be framed around how resolving the client's problem or sense of unease could add value.

Consultancy Types

In addition, much depends on how you work. Clients may seek any one of three types of help from you. The first is as an expert. The client believes you hold expertise of some kind that may help them clarify an issue or solve a problem. Edgar Schein, in his book *Process Consultation Revisited*,[135] calls this the *Expert* model, in which you sell your expertise and tell the client what they want.

A second possibility is the *Doctor–Patient* model, in which the client faces a problem and wants to hire you to diagnose the problem and suggest a solution. That's often how management consultancy organisations work. Their senior people visit the client to learn about the sort of problem that needs solving, as they have an ample store of procedures that can be applied by more junior people who visit the client, gather information and produce solutions that are presented to the client in a PowerPoint presentation and report. The consultant is working *for* the client, and this business model has proved to keep the consulting firms financially viable.

The third is the *Process Consultant* model, in which the consultant works *with* the client, using their skills and knowledge as appropriate to enable the *client* to solve their problem. This approach makes consultancy more like coaching: the expertise and experience of the coach helps the players to realise their capabilities in the sport. Or like teaching or psychotherapy,[136] where the focus is on developing the capabilities of the client.

At this point, it should be obvious that my preference is for the process consultant model when applying decision analysis, particularly when working with the client's key players, as the modelling shows the consequences of the options, provides ways to test the effects of making different judgements about values, trade-offs and uncertainty, all of which enable exploration of different futures. This aligns the key players, so they are pulling in the same direction, which improves implementation. So, what are the skills required of a process consultant?

Process Consultancy Skills

The descriptions here are my attempt to apply the process consultancy skills to decision conferencing, or any type of facilitated workshop. The concepts are those explained in Schein's book, and the italicised first sentences are his, but most of the descriptions are my words.

Principle 1

Always try to be helpful. That starts with the very first contact and is to be maintained throughout your engagement. Treat every contact with the client as an opportunity to provide help. That applies whatever you *feel* about the task, the situation, the client or the participants. There have been times when a particularly annoying participant in a decision conference turned out to have had an insight that was at first ignored by everyone, including the facilitator. But by being impartial in actions, if not feelings, the facilitator can ask questions that enable the participant to be heard, and their view debated by the group. It has been my experience that this 'difficult' participant can shift the direction of the group and may become a staunch supporter of the decision conferencing process.

For example, the civil servants administering the budget of a UK Government subsidiary engaged in scientific work asked my team to conduct a decision conference to prioritise investments in their research projects. We started the decision conference late one afternoon and resumed the middle of the next morning following their meeting about other issues. We arrived at the back of the room about 15 minutes early, and we heard one person say that what had been done in the decision conference the previous day had been discussed over the bar after dinner, and several participants thought the process was a load of nonsense and shouldn't be continued. I and my team were, of course, alarmed to hear this, but after a short debate in the group, I stood up and said, 'I would not like to continue a process that is not seen to be helpful, so

I suggest that the first item we discuss after the decision conference is resumed is whether or not we should continue.'

The participant who wanted to stop stood and said he and others would exit from the room if the decision conference resumed. I suggested that the group might now discuss whether we should be allowed to start. A very brief discussion by the whole group resulted in our being invited to restart the process, so we moved to the front of the room and I said it was now up to the group to decide whether we should continue. In the ensuing debate, the civil servants who organised the meeting said nothing, but the group eventually decided we should continue, and the objectors remained.

At the next break, I asked the civil servants why there was such a strong antipathy towards decision modelling, and they told me they had sent to all participants a list of the projects that were to be considered in the decision conference so they would come prepared with information to assist the prioritisation process. They then explained that the small disruptive group had before the decision conference met to discuss and establish priorities, so probably felt their work was being undermined. When we reconvened, I explained that I had not known so much homework had been done, but that all information, including their work, would be useful in scoring the projects. After that intervention, the work went ahead relatively smoothly. Indeed, the process continued to be used for many years.

What did I learn from this? First, how important it is to contain my defensive emotional reactions and think instead what intervention would most help the group. Second, in discussing arrangements with the client for a decision conference, to ensure that instructions in the calling note don't accidentally encourage participants to over-prepare.

Principle 2

Always stay in touch with the current reality. That begins with what you are currently feeling because it provides data about what is going on in the group and the client's realities. As we will see in the next two chapters, when groups form they develop a personality, a culture and agreed norms, which can powerfully affect group and individual behaviour. You as the facilitator can sense this by observing and attending to your own feelings.

For example, I once facilitated a decision conference for an unfamiliar group whose new manager had asked them to formulate strategy for the group, but was not attending because, he said, he would agree to whatever the group recommended. About an hour into the decision conference, I was feeling very tired and bored. I observed that everyone was leaning back in their chairs and discussion was desultory and unfocused. I wondered if my feeling was also theirs, so asked the group why no one seemed to be very engaged with the purpose of the meeting. After an embarrassing silence, in which I said nothing, one person said they didn't know what strategy was. Then others chimed in and agreed. Their new leader had given them no clue as to what he wanted. Possibly, he had been told by his boss to develop strategy for their newly formed group, but he didn't know what strategy was either.

This was one of the few times when I purposely stepped out of my role as the impartial facilitator, and said I had a view about what strategy is and would explain it to see if that would be helpful. After a 15-minute lecture, including answering questions, I stepped back into my role as facilitator, and asked if this had been useful. Within five minutes, a vigorous discussion began and by the end of two days a set of recommendations had been formulated.

Feelings are important data and maintaining awareness of them is your key to staying in touch with the current reality of the group.

Principle 3

Access your ignorance. In addition to keeping in touch with your feelings, be clear about what you know, what you assume you know and what you don't know. The latter is easiest when your client uses jargon that is unfamiliar to you, so you simply ask, 'What does ... mean?' When I was engaged to conduct research at the European Medicines Agency, they gave me a 22-page document filled with drug and medical acronyms. There was no possibility of learning these, so while facilitating the modelling of a drug's benefit-risk balance, I simply asked participants for the meaning of any acronym. On one occasion, nobody knew what the three letters meant, but assured me they all knew it was an agreed scoring system used to quantify the seriousness of a certain medical condition. A quick look-up on the internet revealed it was more complex than any of the participants had known, and it included a criterion we had already included in our model, which would have double-counted the available data. So, we deleted our separate criterion and kept the acronym score.

At the other extreme, when you are confident of the meaning, but its use by your client isn't the way you would use it, you might ask, 'What do you mean by ...?' It's possible that a meaning has evolved within an organisation that is somewhat different from its normal use or its dictionary definition, or the opposite, when the dictionary definition is precise, but used loosely in conversation.

Between these extremes lie cases when the word has more than one meaning. A common example is the word 'risk'. It is more commonly used as a synonym for uncertainty and is used to describe any outcomes that are uncertain, for example, that all the outcomes, desired or undesired, from taking a drug are risks. More commonly, only uncertain *undesirable* outcomes are considered as risks, or, more precisely, risk is the probability of an unfavourable future occurrence, as in the risks of side effects from taking a drug or, in the insurance industry, the risk of a loss.

However, risk also describes financial investments, with those more variable in performance being described as riskier. Radiation hazards are in the nuclear industry not just the extent of one's exposure to the hazard, but *also* the number of people exposed. And research by Paul Slovic about how ordinary people perceive risk found that three factors are at play: the *dread* one feels about the hazard; the degree to which the hazard is *unknown*; and the *number of people exposed* to the hazard.[137] For example, in the early 1990s, when bovine spongiform encephalopathy (BSE), commonly known as mad cow disease, was rampant in the UK, scientists were quick to say that the probability of humans contracting the human variant from eating diseased meat was negligibly small, but that did little to reassure. Why? Apply Slovic's findings. Would you *dread* your brain turning into a sponge with death certain to follow? Scientists at first were *uncertain* about what caused it or whether it could spread to humans. And, finally, the *number of people exposed* to the hazard was all those who had eaten the meat of cattle. High scores on all three. No wonder the message of low probabilities was seen as irrelevant.

In short, be aware of your own ignorance and don't assume that others all agree about the terms they are using in discussions.

Principle 4

Everything you do is an intervention. This includes what may look to your client as doing nothing, but that is a decision, so accept the consequences and acknowledge you own them, but recognise that the client does, too. There will be times when it is best to intervene, and others when not to. That can be a difficult decision for the facilitator.

In a meeting, I was facilitating for a managing director and his senior executives, one of whom was unable to make the meeting so had sent a junior replacement. The MD was grilling the junior but not receiving the answer he was looking for. As the temperature rose, the junior became more defensive and the MD more aggressive, and I felt it was time to intervene. Suddenly, the MD stood and shouted 'bullshit', and all I could manage was a feeble attempt to cool the interchange. But it was too late, cohesion was destroyed, and the meeting was unable to recover a sense of constructive dialogue.

Many positive interventions are described in the next chapter, but for now the point here is that anything you do or say should be in the service of helping the group to move forward without becoming dependent on you or expecting you to do their work for them. Every interaction with the client, even when you just observe, has consequences for both you and the client, so you must ensure that the consequences contribute to building trust and the helping relationship.

Principle 5

It is the client who owns the problem and the solution. This is perhaps the most important of the 10 principles for a decision analyst working as a process consultant. For any of the three types of models, expert, doctor–patient or process consultant, the recommended solutions can result in undesirable outcomes, which are then blamed on the consultant. But this is least likely to happen with the process consultant model.

For example, a major UK manufacturing company asked me to help them decide whether to build a new factory or refurbish their current ones. They had hired a traditional consultancy company to look at this problem and, operating in doctor–patient mode, the consultants interviewed key players, collected data, modelled the problem and made final recommendations. But the company told me the consultants hadn't really addressed the problem in a helpful way.

I suggested their accountable and key managers attend a decision conference at which we could model the future uncertainty about demand for their product, the many value criteria they faced and the important trade-offs. They went ahead, helped by the information and data provided by the consultancy company, which enabled a rapid construction and exploration of a decision analysis model. By noon on the second day, they said they now knew what to do, and implemented a refurbishment solution within three months.

This example illustrates the importance of acknowledging from the start that you, as a consultant, cannot know enough about the problem, its history or its cultural influences, so must not remove the client's problem onto yourself. It is the client who is accountable for any consequences that result from acting on the solution to the problem. As a process consultant, you are responsible for doing your best in helping the client to a solution, not for removing the client's problem onto yourself. As Schein says, 'You cannot take the monkey off the client's back.'

Principle 6

Go with the flow. This isn't a recipe for passive reaction to events. On the contrary, it is about actively working to understand your client's culture and personal realities, including the culture of the group with which you are working. To start, you won't know much about those personal and social realities, which will influence all their interactions with you. As we will see in Chapter 11, groups quickly form their own cultures, and a group can be every bit as unpredictable as an individual, especially if you unknowingly touch on areas that are particularly sensitive for the client.

The client has come to you with a sense of unease, so an exploration of the areas that he or she has identified as requiring change will provide a starting position. Since you don't know much about the cultures and personal realities, you could spend some time on what Schein calls 'Active inquiry'. He suggests three stages, as described below.

Pure enquiry – wait, prompt and listen. Try asking, 'What is the situation? What is going on? What is happening? Describe the situation. Tell me more. How do you think I could help?' You're interested in collecting objective facts about the current situation, where the organisation is coming from now, and why the client feels uneasy. Actively listen.

Exploratory Diagnostic Inquiry – explore only. As you begin to understand the source of the client's sense of unease, you can gently explore further by asking, 'What do you or others feel or think is the problem? What are you trying to achieve? Are you more concerned about uncertainty or conflicting values? What options have been proposed for resolving the issues? What might be the consequences? Are senior managers aware of the problem and what do they think about it?'

Confrontative Enquiry – share your ideas. At this point, you may have begun to see the situation more clearly as an outsider, and have formed a view that your client's sense of unease arises from a feeling that some options are more of a gamble than others, or the external environment is increasingly turbulent, or different views internally about what should be done preclude agreement about the best way forward, or trade-offs among competing objectives suggest there is no single best solution.

Ask questions relevant to any of 10 ingredients of good decisions, both structure and content elements, as you begin to formulate how you might use decision analysis. But that will only be your interpretation, so preface your questions with 'I wonder if . . .', which makes it easier for the client to accept a suggestion that is somewhat painfully true, or at least to dismiss it with a 'Hmm, I'll think about that.' Other questions might include 'Could you do . . .?' or to a group considering options or criteria, you could ask, 'Can anyone think of any options/criteria we've so far missed?'

Principle 7

Timing is crucial. Consultants who have worked with many organisations in the same field accumulate knowledge that may be useful to the next client. A good example is that objectives and criteria are often similar within pharmaceutical, information technology, or oil and gas companies, and it's tempting to suggest an objective or criterion you have found is commonly used. You might ask, 'Have you thought about . . .?', but if you do that too early, you may inadvertently create a dependency relationship with the clients, who will then expect you to come up with answers instead of thinking things through themselves, or, if the client disagrees with you, they may start to distrust your judgement, impairing your ability to create a helping relationship. However, if you listen carefully to your client and attend to possible moments when the client might be receptive to a suggestion and be able to take it in, then the time is ripe for your intervention. That said, what worked for a previous client might not work for a new one, so you might withdraw gently from a mis-timed intervention.

Principle 8

Be constructively opportunistic with confrontative interventions. This principle follows nicely from the last. The idea is to watch for the moments when the door is partly open. Find and build on the client's motivations and the organisation's cultural strengths, which would enable them to change. Seize opportunities to intervene with new ideas and insights; take some risks. Here is an example.

Head Office of a major international corporation told the MD of a Far Eastern subsidiary company that their proposed spending on TV advertising for a product that was new to the company's country was too high. The MD disagreed, but his arguments about the special status of the product remained unpersuasive to the Head Office. At the suggestion of a different country's MD who had successfully used decision conferencing to resolve several thorny issues, the Far Eastern MD agreed to a two-day decision conference in his country to explore how to overcome Head Office resistance. The group began by explaining the situation and argued that the product was new to the country, so TV advertising would establish a better approach to carrying out a repeated daily home task, as demonstrated in a small test market.

We would, of course, need at least one more option for a proper decision analysis, so I asked the group, 'If you don't allocate resources for TV advertising, do you return those resources to the Head Office, or are they yours to use elsewhere?' 'The resources are ours', was the answer. 'Then, what else could you spend money on to ensure a successful launch?' I asked. 'Ah, I hadn't thought about anything other than TV,' the MD said, looking embarrassed. Within a short time, the group came up with several other options, and we proceeded to create two multi-criteria decision analysis models, discussed in Chapters 13 and 14, which led to a new strategy that included a reduced level of TV advertising along with two other initiatives.

The point here is that my initial question was potentially confrontational, as it revealed that the MD hadn't considered all the options, and I didn't want him to lose status in front of his subordinates, a sensitive issue in many Far Eastern countries. I constructively said, 'Yes, it's often the case that we discover more options in a decision conference, so let's think about whether there are any here.' Everyone participated in the subsequent discussion and the MD worked well with the group to develop and explore other options, eventually developing a new strategy that Head Office accepted.

Principle 9

Everything is data; errors will always occur and are your prime source of learning. As you can't know everything about context in a meeting with the client, you will at some point make an error even if you carefully follow the principles, and this may upset the client. When this happens, use it as an opportunity to learn more about why the error occurred. But Schein advises us to learn from the errors and 'at all costs avoid defensiveness, shame, or guilt', as any of those feelings may evoke a response from you that might cause the client to question your impartiality.

My LSE Master's degree students and I developed in 2010 a decision analysis modelling approach for assessing the benefit-risk balance of drugs, which could be used by regulators as an adjunct to their legal task of approving new drugs only if their benefits outweigh the risks. Although the approach became an example of MCDA, it actually included considerations of value *and* uncertainty, as well as trade-offs among all the criteria. Statistical summaries of the data from clinical trials provided inputs to the model, which meant that the results of the models represented the average patient in the clinical trials. Those statistical summaries play a major role for regulators in approving drugs, which is appropriate because their decisions are for the public good even though some patients may respond differently to both the benefits and side effects.

With that mindset in 2017, I assisted a commercial, health-care company to model the benefit-safety balance of their imaging agent, along with other imaging agents, which can be administered to a patient to enhance the contrast of an MRI scan. That model helped the company to prepare for a meeting with the European Medicines Agency's Committee for Medicinal Products for Human Use (CHMP). Then, in 2020, the company asked me to facilitate a new decision conference as more data was now available in refereed journals about the performance of all other major imaging agents, so a published paper comparing the agents would provide guidance for radiologists. Covid required the decision conference to be virtual, not my first, but I thought it would be manageable.

It was barely so. Serious disagreements arose as participants could not agree about weights on the eight criteria, two favourable and six unfavourable effects, that choosing the right agent for a given patient depended on many factors, such as the age of the patient, their medical condition, which part of the body was to be imaged and so forth. I suggested that they think of a typical patient, which the group defined, and then the weighting process became easier, but still doubts remained.

A Zoom meeting was arranged for me with the expert who had raised the most doubts about the usefulness of this modelling, and he kept insisting that so far, the model would not cover most of his patients, nor did he feel able to lend his authority to a publication of our work. After exploring his reservations, it dawned on me that perhaps the group's wide experience could be applied to describe other types of patients for which criteria weights would be different. This proved to be attractive for the other experts, so alternative MCDA *vignettes* were devised at the next virtual meeting of all the experts. Across these vignettes, the data remained the same and only the weights on the criteria differed. Eventually, all experts agreed to sign on as co-authors of the published paper.[138]

How does this illustrate Principle 9? Quite simply, that the difficulty arose because I imported my assumption that an 'average' patient was to be modelled, as I had learned for approving new drugs. That had served the company in their approach to the CHMP, but was not the case for helping radiologists in choosing the best imaging agent for a given patient. That was my error, but fortunately the experts were patient as I learned that the model should represent a type of patient, not the average patient, and we moved in the right direction.

Principle 10

When in doubt, share the problem. Inevitably, there will be times when you are uncertain about what to do next, and this is true even for the most experienced consultants. If you feel it is appropriate, share your doubt with the client. I have found clients to be supportive and helpful, even relieved, to be asked so you can explore possibilities together. That can be done in a decision conference by calling for a short break, then discussing your doubt with the leader.

Trust

As you can see, so far this chapter has covered the many aspects of developing a helping relationship with your client. But there is one more important feature that Schein says nothing about in *Process Consultation Revisited*, and only slightly develops in his 2009 book, *Helping*.[139] It is that for the helping relationship to develop, you must both trust each other. The Irish philosopher Onora O'Neil explains that trust is a gift from one person to another; you can't build trust, but you can become *trust-worthy*, and that requires you to be competent, honest and reliable.[140]

To trust you, your client will expect you to be competent in your consultancy role, whether it is as an expert, doctor–patient consultant or process consultant, each requiring different competencies. The client will also expect you to be honest, so when you explain that in your role as facilitator, you are impartial, then you must ensure you maintain that position. This can be difficult when modelling reveals truths the client may not wish to accept, although you can usually speak truth to power by pointing out that the model is only reflecting back in changed form the data and judgements that were input to it. Finally, throughout your consultancy, you are expected to be reliable, coming to meetings properly prepared, on time and consistent in your stance as an impartial, independent guide. Remember the phrase, 'A guide on the side, not a sage on the stage'.[141]

Summary

In the 1980s, I met a senior executive of a UK company who went on to be the MD of two subsequent companies and frequently used my services as a process consultant, often in decision conferences. On one of these occasions, as he entered the room with his top team, he asked me, 'Are you going to give me brain ache again today?' His organisation was facing a difficult time, but he was willing to think deeply about how the whole organisation could be turned around and knew his senior staff would need to be engaged with the change. He was not looking for a quick fix that he could impose.

Those are the conditions in which process consultancy is most effective: a shared sense of unease among key players, a hot topic and willingness to consider change. But those conditions also create anxiety throughout the organisation, which might be assuaged by hiring an outside consultant, whose first task will be deciding how best to help the client: as an expert providing advice, or diagnosing the cause of the problem and advising what to do, or working with the client to develop a satisfactory way forward.

Although any of these three approaches, the expert, doctor–patient or process consultant, might by themselves work for the client, the majority of case studies in this book focus on the latter, the process consultant role, but with a healthy dose of expertise from the consultant about decision analysis and in translating model results into action, but never telling the client what to do. This is so particularly for those who already work full or part time as decision analysts in their own organisations because it is more difficult for them to be impartial than an external consultant.

Whether as an external or internal consultant, it is important for you to ensure that the client owns the solution to the problem, which can be realised in three ways. The first is to include a final section of your written report to the client, which gives the results of sensitivity analyses on the key elements that can affect decisions. The second is to provide a 'front-end' dashboard that displays the final results along with scroll bars to enable changes to those probabilities and/or weights that can change a decision, as illustrated by the swine flu example in Chapter 17. Finally, clients who wish to consult additional key players or gather more data before making a decision may obtain the software so they can conduct their own sensitivity analyses easily, or even change the structure of the model.

How will it be possible to maintain a position of impartiality when working as a decision analyst? That depends very much on your skills in facilitating individuals or groups in building a decision model, the subject of the next chapter.

10 Facilitation Skills

A facilitator brings an understanding of human interaction and how to make the most of valuable time spent together.

Viv McWaters and Jonnie Moore, Creative Facilitations, 2021

A member of an operational research team who had attended many decision conferences I had facilitated for his organisation told me he had tried facilitating a recent meeting himself, but was surprised it was so difficult. I reassured him that although it becomes easier as you gain experience, even then it isn't easy, although that's how it can look, as dancers in a ballet can make a *pas de deux* appear effortless.

Why should this be the case? After all, a decision conference is a meeting, and most of us have some experience in leading a meeting, helped by following an agenda. But it's not just the lack of a formal agenda in a decision conference that makes it difficult, for there is an implicit generic agenda that the facilitator keeps in mind. Instead, it is the extra tasks of facilitating a work group in creating a decision-analytic model on the spot that imposes an additional burden compared to an ordinary meeting of a group.

Work Groups

The focus in this chapter is on a work group, a collection of experts whose primary purpose is to achieve an objective. A decision conference is always a work group. A group of people attending a lecture is not a work group, unless the lecturer breaks up the class into small groups to achieve a task assigned by the lecturer. A unit, group or department meeting whose purpose is to report progress is rarely a work group, although individuals may be assigned actions to be carried out before the next meeting. Meetings held to obtain approvals for proposed actions are rarely work groups; the hard work of coming up with feasible actions has already been done. A true work group is given an objective and tasked with achieving it.

As we've already seen, in carrying out that work, the group needs to consider three things: (1) content; (2) process; and (3) structure.

1. **Content**: the data and judgements required to achieve the objective.
2. **Process**: how the data and judgements are to be obtained.
3. **Structure**: how to combine the data and judgements, usually by discussion or modelling, or a mixture of both.

In ordinary working meetings, the leader attends to all three, but in a facilitated work group the leader attends only to content, while keeping an eye on process and structure, which are the responsibilities of the facilitator, who remains neutral about content. The facilitator cares about the content and may feel like contributing to it, but that can be counter-productive. How so? The answer will emerge as we consider the tasks of the facilitator in a decision conference.

Tasks of the Facilitator

What does the facilitator do to help the group achieve its objective, which is the primary task of the participants? The first is to ask questions about the primary task and establish intermediate goals whose achievement will contribute to realising the main objective. That might begin by understanding the context, framing the problem, anticipating the outcomes of plausible future events and their uncertainties, or exploring the multiple value objectives that characterise the problem. Throughout this initial phase, the facilitator seeks to clarify the concepts and terms used by participants, frequently summarising what has been heard, and encouraging participation. At all times, the facilitator maintains a task orientation, judiciously leavened with touches of humour. Understanding what is going on in the group develops as the facilitator observes the group, attends to the overt and symbolic content of the discussion, and maintains awareness of his or her own feelings.

Observing and Understanding the Group

As we will see in the next chapter, every group has a life, like an individual. In a new group, the life forms quickly and the facilitator will feel it from the beginning as participants introduce themselves and say what they would like to gain from the decision conference. Some groups are more serious and solemn, with few questions at the start, while others are more light-hearted and feel free to engage with one another, but the life develops over time as agreement about acceptable and unacceptable behaviour and norms develop, establishing the group's culture. In a familiar group, with culture already established, it will take some time for the facilitator to become sufficiently aware of the group life; first impressions may be misleading.

Whether working with a familiar or unfamiliar group, the facilitator can understand the group life by observing verbal and non-verbal behaviour. At the start of the decision conference, I note each participant's role in their organisation, for that may well affect how they frame the forthcoming issues. In explaining what they want to get out of the meeting, some participants will raise issues about values (optimistically or pessimistically) or uncertainties (sure or unsure), even the importance of some criteria over others, but rarely are trade-offs raised. Indeed, any of the 10 technical ingredients of decisions might be mentioned, and that provides an opportunity for the facilitator to confirm that the issue will be considered during the decision conference. You might even gain a sense during the initial discussion of the group's risk tolerance.

Participants usually talk in ways that are appropriate to their roles, and you can better understand why role relationships can be supportive or dismissive. For example, in a pharmaceutical company, development scientists will emphasise the extent to which a new drug will meet unmet medical need, while the finance specialists will be most concerned with future profits or the point when cash flows become positive. Market share might be stressed by highly competitive participants as of more concern as contrasted to the quality of products sold mentioned by others. The facilitator can reassure the group that all these considerations will be considered and that good decisions flow from a balance among competing objectives.

During the meeting, the facilitator questions and listens carefully, privately making inferences based on the overt and symbolic content of group discussion. The following example illustrates this process:

The new manager of a data processing division brought his department managers together (for the first time) to discuss ways of improving the service. New ideas were slow to come from the group, and were frequently dismissed as impractical or unworkable. As the manager became more concerned at the lack of progress, he made more and more suggestions, and, increasingly, one participant became more agitated and resistant to any suggestions. The facilitator surmised that a pervasive but unexpressed scepticism in the group was being voiced by this one person. Acting on his hunch, the facilitator asked how others felt about the proposed changes, and this helped to legitimize the expression of participants' feelings. As the doubts of other members were voiced, this one person was relieved of his group role as 'sceptic', and the whole group began to discuss more constructive ideas.[142]

Attending to Overt and Symbolic Content

Individuals in a group often experience anxiety as the direction of the group discussion diverges from the way they are thinking and feeling about the issues. Even though the facilitator has encouraged reporting any sense of unease, participants may hesitate to do so, especially if they don't know why they are feeling uneasy, or it is at the start of an unfamiliar group. 'Best to keep still and wait a while', they may be thinking, 'until I get to know the others better, otherwise I might make a fool of myself.' Good advice, especially for the facilitator who is new to an unfamiliar group; all the more reason to stick to observing and asking questions at the start.

Anxiety that is implicitly shared in a group can lead to displacing it to sources outside the group, so it doesn't have to be faced. If the facilitator thinks this may be happening, careful questioning can reveal what is not being said. This case study shows a way in which the overt content of the discussion is hiding the reality that cannot be overtly expressed:

At the start of a decision conference, a facilitator observed that an aggressive deputy managing director 'held court' and demolished the arguments made by some participants. The group persisted in spite of this, and continued its discussion about how their business centre should become less reactive and instead take the initiative to gain control of its own affairs. This overt issue seemed to be a genuine concern, but the facilitator felt that participants were not just talking about the business centre, they were also talking about their own group at that moment. The business centre had been chosen as a symbol for the difficulties they were experiencing in the here-and-now with their own group: they wanted to take control of the meeting themselves and not be dependent on the managing director and his deputy. The facilitator encouraged contributions from all participants, thus helping to legitimize the voicing of dissenting perspectives. Eventually, this enabled the group to become more proactive in its planning.[143]

This is only one example of how groups handle anxiety. There are many more, and many reasons why anxiety is so common in groups, as you will see in the next chapter.

Monitoring Feelings

Throughout the decision conference, facilitators monitor their own feelings, using these as data about what is going on in the group. The facilitator is a self-aware, impartial observer rather than a detached, scientific observer. All social interactions are recursive: what you say and do affects what they say and do, which in turn reflects back on you. That is the nature of social reality, each reflects and influences the other; there is no simple cause and effect. Decision analysts contribute their knowledge and experience in structuring a problem by applying the 10 ingredients of good decisions, and guide the process of constructing the model, while the group contributes the content. Most groups don't argue with me about structure and process (although if they do, I listen, and if I think I'm on the right track, I suggest that we try this and if it doesn't work, we can change tack). But the facilitators who contribute their views on content are courting danger if they abandon their impartiality.

Maintaining impartiality, however you personally feel, is the key to effective facilitation. The problems of contributing to content can have many undesirable consequences. Here are some examples.

- **Facilitating process is difficult**. If participants disagree with your contributions to content, that can weaken your authority as you are judged to be attempting to bias the results of the modelling.
- **Group becomes dependent**. You appear to know best, so participants feel de-skilled.
- **Members don't mobilise their own expertise**. Your engagement with content will encourage 'group loafing' as you shift to a leadership position and take on the task of thinking more deeply about the issues, relieving participants of that task.
- **Hinders ownership by the group of results**. Since you contributed some content, you become a part-owner of the results.
- **Impedes implementation**. Because the group doesn't solely own the inputs, they won't feel they own the results.

However, the facilitator is not a passive onlooker to the group's discussion of content. Indeed, you will intervene in many ways, always maintaining your position of impartiality.

Intervening

All interventions by the facilitator are intended to help the group accomplish the many sub-tasks that are required for achieving the primary task. The main interventions include:

- **Pacing the task**. This includes time spent at each stage of the facilitator's implicit agenda to ensure the primary task is complete when the decision conference is scheduled to end. As the meeting progresses, the facilitator continuously revises the anticipated time for each stage, informing the group about progress (neither praising nor condemning) with a simple 'We're on track', or 'We need to speed up' if time is pressing. For an unfamiliar group, the start of each stage usually takes longer than for a familiar group, especially the first stage of discussing the issues, and the assessment of the first value, trade-off or probability. But groups learn quickly and soon participants become efficient in using time well.
- **Directing**. All groups at some point start down dead-end alleyways. It can be tempting for a participant to allay anxiety by telling a story, opening a new threat-free issue or providing a counter-example about a different issue. Rather than simply dismissing or ignoring the participant's comment, the facilitator might say, 'Sorry, I'm unclear how this is relevant to our current task, which is to [restate it].' Occasionally, you will be told how it is indeed relevant, or the participant will apologise, and the group will thereby be redirected back to the task. More often, you will direct the group by suggesting a change of tack, the beginning of the next stage or giving instructions on next steps.
- **Questioning**. You will, of course, ask many questions in the first, exploratory stage so you and the group can fully understand what brought everyone to the decision conference and confirm the primary task – or change it. You will need to ask about what is meant by the technical terms and jargon used by participants, even when it seems that everyone (except perhaps yourself) knows the meaning. Disagreements may arise even among participants about technical terms, so it is essential for participants to find a mutually agreed definition. Even common terms, like risk, benefit, impact, safety, harm, strategy, vision and mission, can take on different meanings from one discipline to the next, and even within a discipline. Once we agree what we are talking about, the group can move to the next stage of deepening understanding of the problem and issues by tapping into the skilled knowledge of the experts in the room. Many of your questions will be stimulated by your own ignorance. For example, ask 'Why do you say that?', 'Say more', 'What is the evidence?', 'What are the implications?', 'What might the consequences be?', 'Are there any other perspectives?' and so forth. You might use a question to introduce something you think the group might be missing, as you tap into your experience from models developed by similar organisations, or from your reading or general knowledge. To do that and remain impartial, you might ask the group, 'Have you considered . . . as relevant here?', perhaps quoting from your source without revealing anything confidential. If asked in a casual way, the group can decide its relevance, without their thinking you are an expert about content.

- **Summarising**. As your knowledge grows, it is useful to check that you and the participants share the same understanding of the issues. Periodic summaries enable the facilitator to check what has been learned so far. Verbal summaries can maintain flow of the discussion, and written ones, on flip charts for reference, or saved on a computer for later reference in writing the report, will document progress. Some facilitators are good at creating diagrams as summaries. These summaries create 'milestones' and usually don't include the process of getting to that point, in effect allowing participants to ignore the group's history of arriving at that position and focus on important points to be remembered about their now-shared understanding.
- **Reflecting**. As the facilitator's knowledge of the primary task deepens, it is worth checking that your understanding is accurate. By asking a participant who has stated their position on an issue, 'You seem to be saying [restate a summary of what you have heard]. Am I hearing you correctly?' This is an easy way for the facilitator to prompt a correction when you really aren't sure what the person meant. If you are wrong, you will receive a correction, sometimes from a different person who re-words the original statement, or even disagrees with it.
- **Handing back in changed form**. Sometimes you can stimulate deeper thinking about an assertion by rephrasing it from a different perspective. For example, when working with a team to prioritise their existing projects, I often ask them to think of new projects in addition to the current ones. A typical response is, 'Oh, we can't do that as there is no provision in the budget.' My reply is, 'So there is no point in considering new projects that might make better use of the available resource?' This hints at the possibility that existing projects of lesser opportunity could be closed down to make way for new projects of greater opportunity, a different perspective from the group's assumption that all current projects must continue under the current budget.
- **Interpreting**. As facilitators listen to what is being said, observe body language and monitor their own feelings, we try to make sense of what is going on in the group. Our empathic abilities linked to our facility for rational thought and foresight enable us to interpret the social reality we are experiencing and creating in the decision conference. Interpretations lead us to decide whether and how to intervene. Any of the above interventions might follow, helping the group in its work on the primary task. If the interpretation is wrong, the group will most likely ignore the intervention or reject it. I personally do not think it appropriate for the facilitator to share the interpretation itself in a work group, for that can easily be seen as threatening, and dealing with these feelings then distracts from the primary task. Directly expressed interpretations are best left to psychotherapy groups or to group-process training groups.

At this point, it should be clear that if you, as the facilitator of a decision conference, were to contribute actively to content, you might weaken your authority over process and structure, be seen as incompetent or attempting to bias the results, and make the group dependent on you for more than you are competent to contribute. In addition, the group will not fully accept ownership of the results and subsequent implementation will suffer, if it occurs at all.

This is a special problem for resident facilitators, those who already are employees of the organisation, as they may be well informed about the content of the decision conference and feel obliged to contribute information they feel is not being considered. If this is you, then maintain your impartiality by finding a way to introduce new content without lecturing the group (especially difficult if at one time you were a teacher!). You might say that in preparation for the decision conference, you read such-and-such, which suggested whatever, and ask if this might be relevant to the work of the group. I occasionally do that even as an outsider and usually I'm told it isn't relevant and why. You then carry on without regret or shame; usually just a casual 'OK' is sufficient to discard your intervention. Be sure never to argue with participants about any of the content; let participants do that. That's their job, not yours.

Dealing with Conflict

Conflict can arise in a decision conference, especially when a group feels threatened. Roy Gulick, a former marine officer turned decision analyst after his retirement, was hired by a private organisation funded by the US Government to facilitate a decision conference attended by five department heads and other key players. Their primary task was to find a way of accommodating a 40 per cent cutback in their budget, as mandated by their sponsor, the US Navy. Well aware that the attendees would feel seriously threatened by the shortfall, and each department would attempt to protect their patch, Gulick didn't expect facilitating the group would be easy. After exploring the issues and as the creation of the model began, one department head stood up, objected to the modelling as nonsense and declared he was no longer willing to participate. As he started to walk out of the room, Gulick said, 'I'm sure that after a quick phone call to your department, we can find a substitute for your absence.' The man turned back and took his seat.

Under Gulick's facilitation, the group built and explored a model of a new 'Ready-About' strategy, part of which resulted in closing the objector's department, but with his full support about that decision as the modelling process had enabled him to make his case and he could now see that opportunities would be greater in the other revamped departments. Gulick's quick thinking and non-judgemental response enabled the objector to return to the group and be heard.

Very occasionally, I've experienced serious conflict between participants in a decision conference, not physical violence, but verbal conflict. One notable example included members of a well-known pharmaceutical company whose members from different countries attended a decision conference to prioritise development projects across several therapeutic areas. As expected, participants defended their ongoing projects, but at one point I felt the temperature of the discussion shift from debate to heart-felt accusations, with members standing and shaking fingers at one another across the large, immovable, rectangular table.

As anger grew, I told the group I would like to call a halt to the discussion. I reiterated the group's primary task, to prioritise projects, and said, 'I'll call that

Task A, and I would now like you to shift to Task B, which is to discuss how well we are doing on Task A.' After a stunned silence, one person said, softly, 'Not very well', and then others joined in the discussion about why the group had become so heated. As the group explored what had happened, without my saying any more, they realised they had become over-involved in supporting their own projects and were not seeing the big picture of a portfolio of projects. After only about 15 minutes, I interrupted and suggested we return to work on Task A. The group had recognised some give-and-take would be required and participants were then able to engage in constructive work.

This *double-task* approach to group work was developed by the late Harold Bridger,[144] a psychoanalyst and one of the founding members of the Tavistock Institute of Human Relations in London, where I first engaged in experiential learning about group processes. His first degree was in mathematics from University College London, and he became interested in the connection between mathematics and group processes that characterises decision conferences. He once visited an early London meeting of decision conference facilitators, which he mainly observed, occasionally making a brief intervention that substantially helped the group think more deeply about the decision conferencing process.

Many years later, Bridger wrote that the double-task provides the time and space for the group to work on the discrepancies between what must be done to achieve the primary task and how that affects individual roles, responsibilities and interpersonal relationships.[145] Bridger's two requirements for the transitional process of change are: (1) time and space for the meeting; and (2) a form of 'cover' for safely exploring a new relationship with the external world. Both of these are met by the decision conferencing process: time and space are carefully planned with the client, while the facilitator and the computer model provide the safe cover. And if Bridger were with us today, I think he would agree that, uniquely, the decision model acts as a *transitional object*, enabling the group to explore the future by revising the model's inputs and trying out different assumptions sufficiently for participants to agree the way forward.[146] Exploring the future safely, without yet having to live it, as Robb Wilmot suggested.

Computer Models as Transitional Objects

What does that mean? I'm suggesting that the group needs a way of holding the conflict between where they are now and where they would like to be, facing and accepting their uncertainties and anxieties about a new and different future, giving them time to explore how that gap might be closed. Building a computer model does exactly that. As a transitional object, these are the key features of the computer model acting as a cover:

1. Doesn't argue back or disagree. It accepts whatever it is given, although it may detect inconsistencies in the inputs; for example, MACBETH reports back to the

user when it detects inconsistent judgements, and suggests ways to eliminate them. Decision-analytic programs check that probabilities of mutually exclusive events sum to one, or they might detect options whose consequences are dominated by other options, or they might statistically correlate scores between all options and for high correlations ask the user if this means they are not mutually preference independent.

2. Is not limited in the number of decision ingredients it can accommodate.
3. Provides an overall result by applying the logical glue (preference values multiplied by probabilities or weights) to combine the decision ingredients.
4. Provides ways for changing the inputs systematically to understand how sensitive the results are to different data, judgements or assumptions.
5. Displays results in tables and graphs, which enhance understanding, stimulate insights and assist participants in developing higher-level perspectives.

It does all these things as a neutral observer, handing back in changed form what it has been given. The model is helping participants to learn and formulate new considerations about a possible better future, but they can withhold any final judgements during this 'holding' process of exploring the model. This facilitates communication among the participants as they explore their disagreements and uncertainties systematically, which takes the heat out of ordinary verbal discussions. Overall, these features build shared understanding in the group.

After the decision conference, with further reflection on the shared understanding, helped by the facilitator's report of the meeting, the leader will explain the results in narrative form. The model may be discarded as it has served its purpose; the group is no longer in a transitional state. In other cases, especially when transition is gradual, the model might be retained and modified to test the impact on the way forward and to explore new alternatives that arise as the organisation moves ahead. The model becomes a dynamic assistant as the client manages change.

Summary

With its focus on working groups, this chapter makes the case that the facilitator's helping role in a decision conference is to contribute to the process of obtaining data and judgements about the structure of a decision-analytic model relevant to the client's problem and explain how the elements of the structure are to be combined, without contributing to the content of the discourse. It should now be evident that contributing to content can undermine your ability to facilitate impartially as participants may feel you are biasing the model. In addition, the group can become dependent on you as an expert in their field and this may lead members to feel less inclined to think for themselves, which impedes ownership of the final results, thereby hindering implementation.

The facilitator's key functions are to observe the group, attend to the overt and symbolic meaning of the content, maintain awareness of his or her own feelings and use them as data about what is going on in the group, then intervene to help the group achieve its goals without making overt interpretations.

The many ways for the facilitator to intervene include pacing the task to ensure the limited time is spent usefully in the service of the primary task, directing the discussion to remain on topic, clarifying the meaning of jargon and other words and phrases when meanings seem not to be agreed, questioning to go beyond opinions so as to tap into the skilled knowledge of participants, summarising what has been said to ensure everyone is agreed and the discussion can move on to the next topic, reflecting back to the group what you think you heard to ensure if you have understood, handing back what has been said in a different form to provide a new perspective, and throughout encouraging participation of all members.

Why we do all these things is perhaps obvious at this point, but the overt behaviour of a group can often hide what is going on beneath the surface, as the tip of an iceberg hides dangers below the water's surface to a ship. An understanding of group processes can alert the facilitator to the dangers, the subject of the next chapter.

Finally, while the focus so far has been on the facilitation of decision-analytic modelling, many of the principles and methods apply equally well to all forms of modelling, as can be seen in the excellent survey by Franco and Montibeller, which was written for practitioners of operational research.[147]

11 Group Processes

Many heads are better than one.

John Heywood, 1546

Too many cooks spoil the broth.

George Gascoigne, 1575

Which aphorism is correct? Surely it depends on the context, just as values, trade-offs and probabilities do. And why do we work with groups? If we really need input from others, why not just initiate a survey to find out what the key players think and collate the results to see if there might be a way forward that is generally agreeable. Are groups actually capable of outperforming even their best members? How can a facilitator best help a group to achieve its purpose for being? What makes a group become a high-performing team?

Two papers about the harms of recreational drugs, both published in *The Lancet*, one in 2007[148] and the other in 2010,[149] provide a preliminary answer to some of those questions. Both engaged groups of experts in assessing the many harms that can result from misusing the substances. The results for the two studies are shown in Figures 11.1 and 11.2. Explanations will follow, but first just look at the differences and similarities in the results between the two studies. Taller bars mean more harm.

Although not relevant to this chapter, the different colours of bars in the 2007 study represent the classification of the drugs according to the UK's Misuse of Drugs Act 1971 and the Misuse of Drugs Regulations 2001, in which higher letters of the alphabet indicate more harm. For the 2010 study, 9 of the 16 harms were harms to users and the other 7 were harms to others.

Note that in the 2007 study, heroin was rated as most harmful, alcohol as fifth and tobacco ninth, whereas in 2010, alcohol was judged to be most harmful, with heroin in second place and tobacco sixth place. Ecstasy was judged to be about 40 per cent as harmful as heroin in 2007, but a little more than 10 per cent as harmful as alcohol in 2010. Also, you can see there is more differentiation in the 2010 study, namely, bigger differences among the harms than in 2007.

To account for these differences, appreciate that in the 2007 study, experts rated harms on each of nine criteria, using a 4-point scale, over a series of four short meetings to enable all 20 drugs to be included in the study. Ratings were made separately by each of the experts, who represented a diversity of experience, and the individual ratings for each criterion were presented back to group members who discussed them and were

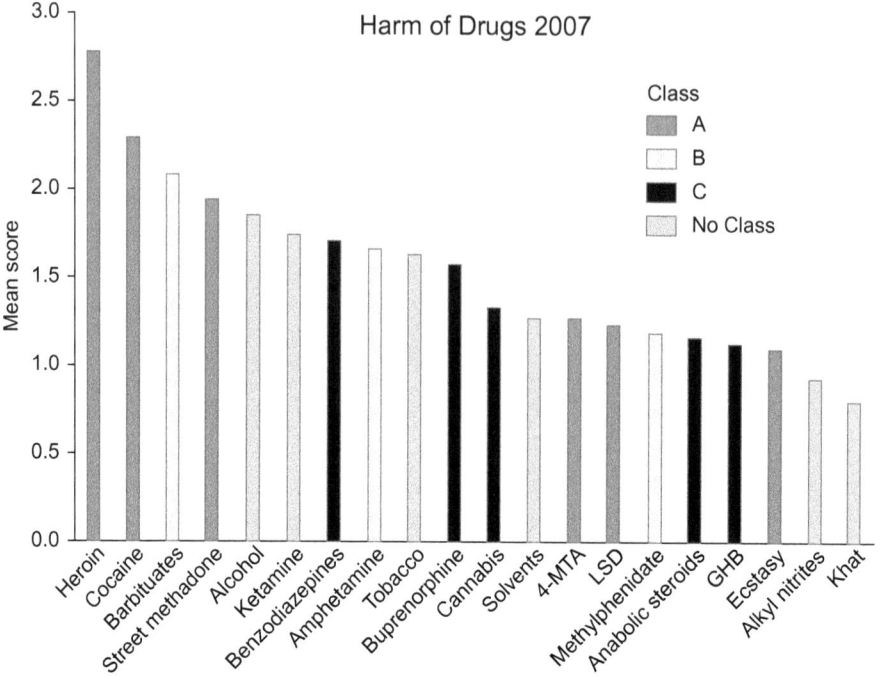

Figure 11.1

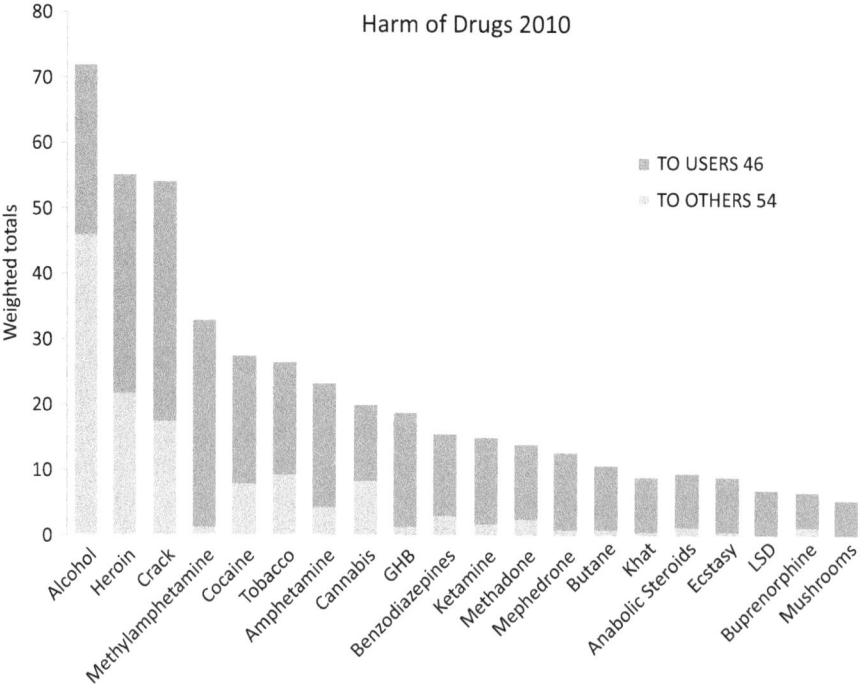

Figure 11.2

invited to change their own scores if they wished, as in a Delphi-process.[150] Ratings were subsequently averaged over all the 16 participants and over the nine criteria, using equal weights in both cases.

In contrast to this ratings-and-averaging approach, the 2010 study applied the scoring-and-weighting-to-consensus methods of MCDA in two decision conferences. First, a meeting of the members of the UK Government's Advisory Committee on the Misuse of Drugs, which developed in 2009 the 16 harm criteria for that study, and the second by 15 members of the International Scientific Committee on Drugs, now known as Drug Science, who engaged in group discussions to collectively judge the scores on 0-to-100 scales and assess relative weights to complete the MCDA model.

In summary, the 2010 paper used more experts and more criteria and applied a longer scale providing judgements about the extent of harm that are more nuanced than is possible with a four-point scale. Deliberative discourse enabled participants to arrive at consensus in scores, while in the 2007 paper, final ranks of each individual were averaged. Differences in harms were assessed in 2010 rather than applying equal weights across the criteria as in 2007. And it would appear that published papers of other experts about the harm of drugs prefer the decision conferencing result, as the 2010 paper has been cited more times than the 2007 paper, even though the former was published three years later. It is now well accepted that the most harmful drug in the UK is alcohol; the 2007 paper missed that because too few harm criteria were considered.

When Participants Disagree

These two studies suggest that when participants disagree and groups are used to elicit expert judgement, a decision-analytic model constructed from the start by a diverse group of experts in a decision conference will do a credible job of representing reality. Surveys don't reconcile differences, even if a Delphi approach is applied. Of course, surveys start the process of challenging participants to think seriously about their knowledge and lived experience, which can be helpful, but it may also begin the process of developing stable and fixed preferences. For a decision conference, I prefer experts whose preferences are still in a labile state, not yet well formed or even articulated precisely. Indeed, many experts can exercise their judgements and form preferences without being entirely aware of how they did it. That has been my experience of working with experts in many different fields. And, as I've said before, experts always disagree.

One source of disagreement is that each expert has accumulated different experience, which induces bias. I once worked with a panel of experts on the topic of how quickly groundwater can pass through rock of a certain type (important topic for modelling the movement of irradiated water from radioactive material encased in steel canisters buried deep underground in rock). In attempting to assess a probability distribution, a laboratory chemist refused on the basis there was too little data, a practical chemist who conducts laboratory experiments would only give lower and upper limits of a distribution, a technician who conducts pump tests on site (by drilling two separated deep holes in the rock of concern and pumping water under pressure into one hole to see how long it takes to be received in the other hole) suggested what the probability density would be between the previous two limits without assessing the function itself, while an expert in erecting many types of structures in rock was willing to assess the whole distribution as the group discussed the issues.

This was a good example of what psychologists have known for several decades: that preferences are not stored fully formed in the head, ready to be plucked out as functions; rather, that preferences are constructed over time, as knowledge and lived experience is accumulated. The numbers are constructed at the point of their elicitation. The decision conferencing process speeds up that process as the facilitator helps the group to focus on one element of the model at a time, and guides participants in reconstructing their individual preferences to the point where, finally, the group can agree to an overall result, conditional on agreed assumptions that heretofore had not been made explicit.

A counter-argument to this position is that the same result could be obtained by averaging the views of the experts, that even if each expert is biased, the biases will balance, and the average will be a satisfactory representation of the truth. That might be the case except for the fact that the biases are often in the same direction, so will enhance one another, as has been shown in the extensive research in cognitive psychology on heuristics and biases.[151]

There is a deeper issue: the notion of 'accessibility', which was elaborated by Professor Daniel Kahneman in his Nobel prize lecture.[152] He argued that reflective thought about a problem depends on the accessibility of cues, factors, criteria and other features that are relevant to the problem at hand. I argued above that my early experience in probability elicitation showed that the subject-matter experts were anchored on their experience. In a study of mild steel corrosion (the rate at which steel canisters containing highly radioactive material corrode), I found that as the experts discussed the issues with one another, the variances of their probability distributions increased, that is, they became *less* sure of themselves, although the means of their probability distributions became more similar.[153] I could hear in their discussions that more factors were brought to bear on the consensus distribution than were evident in their earlier individually assessed distributions. In short, probability distributions are constructed by experts as they interact with one another through the dynamic process of considering data, issues and differing perspective.

Drawing on the experience of decision conferencing, Reagan-Cirincione[154] examined the combined effects of facilitation, modelling and information technology on performance of heterogeneous groups of four to five people in tasks with substantial bias (average teachers' salaries in 25 states predicted from five criteria, and baseball games won by 25 teams predicted from five criteria). She showed that group interaction processes and individual cognitive processing was improved through proper facilitation by an independent person who attends to group interactions and provides a structured process, modelling of a complex task with judgements made about the component parameters, and use of information technology to combine the judgements and give instant feedback of results for group discussion and revision. She found that over 80 per cent of the experimental groups outperformed their most capable member. The study also showed that cognitive feedback alone did not improve individual performance, and group discussion by itself did not improve group performance beyond that of the best individual. Both cognitive feedback to the group and group discussions were needed to improve group performance beyond the most capable individual.

By 2007, a considerable body of research on preference elicitation existed (which covers the elicitation of both preference values and probabilities), and the general finding is that both are constructed in the process of thinking more deeply about the issues, and through interacting with other experts. Indeed, Lichtenstein and Slovic conclude in *The Construction of Preference* that: 'The big picture as documented in this book, is the overwhelming evidence that people often do not have pre-existing preferences but must construct them to fit the situation.'[155] These observations raise the question of what we mean by an expert.

What Defines an Expert?

In 2015, an unsigned editorial in *The Lancet* criticised the basis for the published view of Public Health England (PHE) that e-cigarettes are 95 per cent less harmful than smoking.[156] The data for that figure was based on a decision conference I facilitated for a group of experts led by Professor David Nutt, a neuropsychopharmacologist at Imperial College, London, with the results published by the peer-reviewed journal *European Addiction Research* in 2014.[157] The Lancet editorial criticised the lack of hard evidence, reliance on the opinions of participants, lack of systematic criteria and bias in the selection of experts.

None of this was true, but our 2014 paper had attracted little attention until PHE's use of our data for the 95 per cent claim, which seems to have infuriated many health professionals who believed that e-cigarettes were still harmful, so shouldn't be encouraged. We knew that e-cigarettes were much less harmful than smoking because the main harm in cigarettes is the smoke, and that the editorial had been wrong on many counts, so we formulated a rebuttal that *The Lancet* published in their Correspondence pages several months later. We pointed out there was plenty of evidence of the harms of smoking and that the lack of evidence since e-cigarettes were introduced in 2006 was itself evidence. Our explanation of the decision conferencing process included a description of how peer-review operates during the construction of a model, with sensitivity checking to ensure consistency in the data and judgements. We emphasised that expert 'judgements about scores were based on data along with our own knowledge and experience of the extent of harm and plausible causal mechanisms for harm', and that the 14 criteria were drawn from three previously published studies about the harm of drugs. And we 'selected experts on the basis of their publications, experience, and generally acknowledged professional standing to have diverse perspectives and expertise that could be relevant to assess harms from nicotine products', and who 'collectively have published more than 300 scientific reports relevant to understand nicotine and tobacco harms'.

Sometimes, decision conferences produce results that others don't like, so it's important that experts are chosen to ensure diversity of experience and judgements about the primary task. So, let's be clear about what an expert is expert about. When I worked as a consultant and researcher for Commercial Union (CU), a large UK insurance company, in the 1970s, and with the European Medicines Agency in the 2010s, I first explored how insurance underwriters and drug regulators arrived at their decisions, to insure a potential client's premises or to approve a drug. In both cases, data is available, so I was expecting some sort of modelling was applied. But to my surprise, I discovered that in both cases, decisions were made intuitively. The process of judging the risk of insuring a building by an insurance company, or the benefit-safety balance of a drug by a drug regulator, was entirely implicit and intuitive. (Both are concerned about risk, and more is said in Chapter 18.)

Puzzled about how underwriters did their job, I toured the famous organisation of underwriters, Lloyds of London, where I observed a broker approach an underwriter to engage in discussion about a new risk, followed by the underwriter signing the broker's document. No reference was made to any tables or computers. I subsequently asked the underwriter how he made his decision to sign, and after some thought he said, 'I suppose it's just a matter of several features associated with the risk.' 'How many are there?' I asked. 'I'd say just a few, maybe 7 to 10,' he replied. Later, I told the senior CU underwriter, Roger Miller, who had escorted me at Lloyds, that after asking similar questions of many underwriters, I still didn't see how they assessed risks. 'Oh,' he said, 'there is one thing they all have in common.' 'Really, what is that?' I asked, concerned I had missed the obvious. 'They all mentioned some part of the body,' he explained, quoting my interviewees, 'You get a nose for that sort of thing,' or 'I just play it by ear,' or 'Well, you can only suck it and see,' or 'It's a gut feeling,' even 'We just dip a toe in the water.' 'The one part of the body they never mention,' said Roger, 'is the head.'

At the EMA, it is the Committee for Medicinal Products for Human Use (CHMP) that recommends to the European Commission new drugs or changes for those already marketed. Several times I observed the Committee, composed of one member from each European state and a few co-opted others, and was impressed by how thoroughly they discussed and debated the evidence, usually arriving at a consensus decision, occasionally voting 'Yes' or 'No', with more than a majority required for a positive opinion, otherwise the Chair declaring a negative opinion. Interviews with regulators from six countries revealed no common basis for how the evidence was integrated, although several subjective methods were explained as their personal approach.[158]

So, here are two disciplines that eschew modelling in favour of implicit, qualitative and subjective thinking. This is contrary to research dating back as far as 1954 that compares the accuracy of decisions made intuitively to those that rely on algorithms for combining ratings or scores of an expert, showing that models generally are better than the experts, or are at least as good.[159] That makes sense, particularly for complex problems involving many criteria, for as I explained back in the Epilogue to Part I, we humans are limited in our capacity to keep in mind the many pieces of information we would otherwise have to keep in our short-term memories at the same time. And, of course, there is more than memory involved in dealing with many pieces of information: there is mental processing to be considered. Experts have developed rules for serial processing of information, such as anchoring-and-adjustment or elimination-by-aspects (EBA) heuristics,[160] enabling them to translate their experience and knowledge into larger chunks of information than is characteristic of non-experts.

We take advantage of chunking in structuring a model during a decision conference. For example, in defining the harm criteria in *The Lancet* 2010 study on the harms of recreational drugs, we defined harm as not only a matter of the extent of harm to the individual, but also the number of people experiencing the harm, two quantities that were to be considered together in scoring. Had we not done this, it would have doubled the number of criteria from 16 to 32. For any given criterion, group discussion sometimes focused more on extent, and for other criteria more on the number of people harmed. So, it is important to recognise and use the capability of experts to handle criteria that are complex; that is part of what makes them experts – they can see the forest *and* the trees. I learned back in the 1980s that Shell call this 'helicopter vision', the ability to see the big picture, but also to zoom down to explore the detail.

Another characteristic of experts is that they are continuously learning, gaining more knowledge and experience, capitalising on the brain's ability to reorganise itself, develop insights and create new ways of thinking. The peer review that accompanies the constructive discourse among experts in a decision conference sees the experts learning from one another as they debate the issues. I've observed that their agreement about a preference value, weight or probability is rarely a compromise, but is close enough to what they personally now believe they can agree. And this agreed figure may well have not been in anyone's mind to start with. That's because in listening to others, especially to arguments from the outliers, there is a gradual shift in the group away from an average, and the more they discuss, the more individuals shift their views, to a point where the finally agreed figure might well be more extreme than anyone had considered at the start of the discussion. This open-mindedness of experts enables them to reach sufficient consensus about the inputs that they can then support the model's outputs.

Choosing Experts

An international expert on expertise, James Shanteau, provides this operational definition of experts: 'those who have been recognised within their profession as having the necessary skills and abilities to perform at the highest level'. This means that the facilitator needs only to ask their client how they would identify experts who could attend a decision conference.[161] Commercial companies usually find sufficient expertise in-house, although it might be scattered over several units or departments. Some might work collaboratively alongside external experts, while others will leave the entire exercise to outside experts, merely observing and answering any questions of fact put to them by the experts. Occasionally, I have worked solely with inside participants, who first create a model, then bring in outside experts to validate the structure of a model, review any preference values or probabilities, leaving the task of assessing weights to the outside experts, an approach that helps justify the validity of a model's results if it is to be published in a peer-reviewed journal.

With government agencies, experts are often already in-house, but heavily committed to many projects, and can only spend limited amounts of time in a decision conference, which requires finding ways to engage them for only two to four hours at a time. That's often possible and allows for more reflection between sessions, although it can interrupt the flow of a decision conference, especially if any experts leave and are replaced by new ones. Best to warn your client at the start that dropping in and out of a decision conference is not acceptable.

The number of experts depends on the complexity of the task, which also affects the size of the group, as discussed in the next section. Much depends on how many criteria and how different they are from one another: the more diverse the criteria, the more experts will be needed. For example, just three benefit criteria and eight safety criteria for the OTC pain-killer model was handled easily with just two pain experts during the first two-day decision conference, and was then peer-reviewed by an additional five pain experts in a subsequent half-day session.

However, a larger and more diverse collection of experts was required for the harm-of-drugs decision conferences because there were 20 drugs and 16 criteria, which required expertise about each drug and both the magnitude of harm and how many people experienced it. For the CoRWM study about how to dispose of nuclear waste, a decision conference consisting of the nine Committee members, who themselves represented considerable diversity of opinion, established cost and 10 impact objectives, the latter made operational with 24 criteria, which were so different that they required separate workshops of three to five specialist experts to first define and later score the nine options.

Of course, diversity of experts means that when they all work together, not all participants contribute to scoring. It's usually the experts on a particular option-criterion combination that engage with one another, but it is heartening to see how well they learn from one another to the point where a side-lined expert observing what the specialists are saying might interject with a 'Have you thought about such-and-such?' type of question that can challenge the specialists to change direction or reconsider something they hadn't thought of. It is this process of exploring outliers that can result in revised assessments which are outside the group's original range of thinking, as Reagan-Cirincione found in her research. Averaging experts' first assessments could have given results different from using the final agreement of the experts. That's another reason for the differences between the 2010 and 2007 *Lancet* papers on the harm of drugs.

Group Research

Using the currency of your own country, ask participants in a group of people to solve the following problem without talking to their neighbour:

A man buys a horse for $60 and sells it for $70. Later, he buys the horse back for $80 and sells it for $90. How much money did he make in the horse business?

Once everyone has an answer in mind, ask them to tell and explain it to the person sitting either side of them. You can expect the discussion to become quite raucous as disagreeing neighbours try to defend their answers. Interrupt and ask neighbours to form small groups of three to five people and see if they could agree an answer, then report back to the main group.

It's such a simple problem, yet it's easy to get bogged down by added detail, wondering where he obtained the initial $60 to start, if he borrowed it, or if he invested the $70 and later bought it again, why he bought it back, if he sold it to the same person the second time, why it was the same horse, and so forth, adding complications that weren't in the original statement and are irrelevant. But once group members have discussed the problem, they usually can agree that the correct answer is $20.

Only when researching this chapter did I discover that I once knew the man who invented the Horse Trader problem, as it's now known. His name was Norman R. F. Maier, who worked in the Psychology Department at the University of Michigan, where he taught courses on organisational behaviour and leadership, a topic in which I had no interest at the time, sadly. His research on democratic leadership included a study that examined the effect on group thinking of a leader who refrained from contributing to the content of the problem, and it was this paper that introduced the Horse Trader problem.[162]

In Maier's study of many small groups of five or six students, all groups nominated a representative and were then shown the Horse Trader problem. Each participant was given a card and asked to write their answer in the 'Before' space printed on the card. In half the groups, the representative was given the role of observer, whose job was to listen to the group but refrain from engaging in the discussion; that was the control group. In the other half, the experimental group, the representative was given the role of discussion leader, whose job was to encourage participation of all members and to ask questions that would engage the whole group, but not to express their own views on the problem. They then engaged in an eight-minute discussion and wrote their answer on the card in the 'After' space.

Thus, the answers of the 177 people in the 'leader' experimental groups could be compared to the answers given by the 176 persons in the 'observer' control groups to see if discussions were more effective when led by a democratic leader. And that is what they found. The right answer was given initially by all groups a little less than half the time. But that increased after discussion to about 84 per cent in the leader groups and 72 per cent in the observer groups. This early research established that group discussion not only increases the ability of individuals to solve the problem, but it also shows this increase is heightened by the impartial stance of a facilitator, who does not contribute their views about the subject under discussion, so is an important determinant for group effectiveness. So, yes, many heads can be better than one.

Maier's 1963 book, now out of print, was one of the earliest to report applied research into how problem solving could be improved by groups. Today, a vast literature on group processes and dynamics exists, but the possibilities for using decision support technology to assist problem solving, as Reagan-Cirincione suggested, is barely mentioned. So, what are the enabling conditions for groups to be effective? The following eight sub-sections are based in part on my 2011 review of that literature,[163] but here adapted and described as applied to decision conferences.

Group Size

The key determinant, as discussed above, is the complexity of the problem. The more the numbers of options and criteria, the more participants will be required. Experts tend to live well within their areas of expertise, so their breadth of knowledge and experience relevant to the primary task must be considered, too. Fortunately, the client usually knows the experts or has access to the professional network(s) that can be consulted to find the best people.

That said, for narrow problems, two to four experts should be enough, along with a few other knowledgeable participants. For broad problems, like the harm of drugs, 15 or more participants may be needed. I like the simile of a musical ensemble: how many instruments are required to convey the full colour of the music? Four to six is like a jazz combo, or a string ensemble, which allows for individuals to shine in their brief solos. Six to 15 broadens the scope, while still allowing individual contributions. Beyond 15, individual contributions are limited, so groupings of instruments converse with one another, but require a conductor so that playing together can create a satisfying fullness. Experienced facilitators can manage these larger groups without much difficulty, although it can be demanding and exhausting as you attend to everything, think about what is happening and ask questions. A co-facilitator can lessen the burden for you both.

In creating a list of attendees, remember to ask your client if there is someone else who might read the decision conference report and criticise it for not having considered an issue they consider important. If so, then that person is a key player and should be invited as a participant. They might be from a different part of the organisation and in no sense a problem owner or even a stakeholder, but their ability to make a useful contribution to the primary task makes them a key player. For example, research groups may invite marketing staff to their meetings about prioritising products, which ensures the company focuses on developing products for which there are markets.

Stage of Development

Familiar groups, especially ones you've worked with before, are easier than unfamiliar groups or ones new to you. Although Tuckman and Jensen described the stages for a small group as 'forming, storming, norming, and performing',[164] this is rare in decision conferences. I think this is because the preparation for the event ensures that all participants were sent a calling note setting out clearly the purpose of the meeting and what is expected of them. At the start of the meeting, everyone is asked in the introductions to say what they hope to gain from the session. All this eases the process of 'forming' as everyone knows they can contribute. Because the leader and facilitator fulfil different roles, and there is clear agreement about the primary task, there is no need for aggressive attempts by individuals to establish their credentials, establish their leadership or exercise their grievances; the decision conference looks forward, so the 'storming' stage is seldom seen. Indeed, when the facilitator explains the stages common to all decision conferences, exploring the issues, building a model, exploring it and agreeing recommendations, the process of 'norming' has started, which then begins the process of 'performing'.

Norms

These are the ways of working together. Every group is different, and it occurs quickly in a decision conference as the group implicitly establishes what behaviour is acceptable or unacceptable. These are often imported from participants' previous experience, and they may well include aspects of fairness, equity and respect. I most definitely do not mean procedures like Roberts Rules of Order, which are wholly inappropriate for decision conferences.

Nor do I suggest establishing 'terms of agreement' at the start of a decision conference, for that quickly establishes the facilitator and/or the leader as the 'headmaster' or 'headmistress' of the group, also inappropriate. We assume that everyone present is an adult capable of policing their own behaviour and it is up to group members to admonish if they feel it is needed. I once worked with a co-facilitator who brought 'executive toys', small objects you could squeeze, manipulate into different shapes or roll around, distributed them across the tables, and suggested that interacting with them was a good way to deal with anxieties and let off steam. Again, that is treating adults as children, and I found it a most embarrassing exercise.

That said, I know of one exemplary exception, which was hugely successful. The first Committee on Radioactive Waste Disposal, charged in 2004 with recommending a management strategy for the UK's radioactive waste, began by developing a set of five key principles, the first of which was 'To be open and transparent'. They then conducted themselves in a manner consistent with these principles, to the extent that a retrospective analysis of their successful work revealed an important implicit norm that had guided their work: 'To respect alternative points of view.'[165]

The facilitator helps to establish the implicit norms by listening first then asking questions, by encouraging everyone to join the discussion, by respecting all points of view and by keeping quiet when the group is working well, although the facilitator or outside experts may from time to time challenge a group's norms if they feel they are inhibiting work on the primary task.

Roles

As I've already mentioned, the different roles of participants at their workplace can contribute to identifying criteria. Research staff may focus on innovation, manufacturing staff on some form of do-ability, marketers on market share, finance people on cost and profit, the managing director on future potential, each bringing to the discussion what they know best and often with the different time spans associated with their roles. But the facilitator might find that each of these specialists is ensuring that their patch remains safe and secure. In some organisations, the boundaries between units are relatively permeable, while in others they are very much like independent silos, so bringing people together from different units can be seen as threatening and anxiety-producing.

It is usually the most senior person, the leader, in the group who will decide what to include and exclude. A more permissive leader may try to include all suggestions, which can lead to too many criteria. Sometimes it's best to stay at the higher level of fundamental objectives, and it is the facilitator who will assist in ensuring the model includes the requisite number of criteria, sometimes asking if discussion suggests it is a criterion which doesn't contribute much to discriminating the options, so the effects of the other options will swamp any effect this one could have. I have found that more technically minded participants often over-complicate decision models with detailed criteria that hardly contribute anything to the final result. (If only we could establish that at the start of modelling!) When we find in conducting sensitivity analyses that too many criteria have been included, it may actually be useful to show that eliminating them doesn't change the order of the options.

The main point here is that everyone speaks most confidently from the requirements of their role and their experiences in it. The facilitator assures the group that everyone will be heard and that all criteria of relative importance will be included in the model.

However, participants may also engage in role-like behaviour, which I will discuss in the next section on observational research.

Status

The facilitator emphasises that information is considered a neutral commodity, which is shared at the point in building the model when it is needed, whatever the status of the person who holds it. Seating in the room is arranged so that everyone can easily see one another and the projected output of the computer, with tables arranged in a horseshoe shape or around round tables, all to minimise role status differences. But that doesn't eliminate status differences: it just helps to minimise their effect on the model and to limit bias.

Junior people may be less inclined to share their views to ensure they don't embarrass themselves, so they may need special encouragement by the facilitator. It's also best in some cultures to address questions first to junior participants, because if a senior person provides an answer first, the junior people won't then divulge their views, especially in many Eastern countries, where saving face is of paramount importance. In some of these countries, the senior participant will just listen to the answers and then provide their answer as they make clear the discussion is now ended. Even in Western countries, the facilitator will observe differences in how a group manages a discussion, some waiting patiently to let each person finish, while others will interrupt and talk over one another. That's time for the facilitator to say something like, 'Sorry, I have two ears, but can hear only one conversation at a time, please.'

If participants are drawn from two or three levels (Jaques' strata) in the organisation, discussion by participants at the lowest level may be seen by higher-level participants as 'down in the weeds', paying too much attention to the trees instead of the forest. Or the facilitator may hear weed-like discussion by higher-level participants, and can easily bring them back to the requisite level of discussion by observing that it's not clear how the discussion is contributing to the primary task, which seems to be bogged down in detail.

Overall, observing how status differences may be affecting the discussion is an important implicit task for the facilitator.

Cohesion

Decision conference participants are chosen for their potential contributions to the primary task, so it's no surprise that group members start the meeting with a feeling of cohesion about the task, and they usually bond together within a short time. Research by social psychologists shows that the stronger the feeling of task cohesion by participants in the group, the better the group performance.[166] But this does not require that participants all like one another in a decision conference, although it does in sports and other teams where it can contribute to good performance. In other words, it is task cohesion, not social cohesion, that is associated with good performance.[167] And the facilitator encourages task cohesion by helping the group to stay focused on the primary task, with the assurance that eventually a satisfactory result will be created by the group by the time the model exploration is completed.

However, there is one group activity that can destroy cohesion, and that is anonymous voting. I can well remember one notable occasion when hand-held devices were used to input numbers, which enabled the projected display of a histogram of participants' choices. To start, they clustered sufficiently for the median number to be input to the computer model, which was projected on a separate screen. But suddenly, the clusters were accompanied by a single vote far from the cluster, and that continued to happen several times. I could see the group becoming uneasy, with a few asking for the outlier to reveal themselves, but nobody did. I could feel the cohesiveness of the group slowly being destroyed, so called a break.

A quick check of ranges by inputting various numbers soon revealed that all the hand-held devices had been calibrated incorrectly – all keys were 1 ahead of the number that had been chosen. As the keys ranged from 1 to 9, pressing a 9 showed up as a 1. I abandoned the devices and asked for shows of hands for each number instead. I then recorded the numbers of hands up on a flip-chart, and then input the median of that distribution to the computer, if the group agreed. If there were serious disagreements, I instead asked those participants at the extremes for their reasons, then opened the discussion, followed by a new vote. That usually worked, with exceptions noted for later examining in sensitivity analyses.

I had also tried anonymous voting in training sessions, and as soon as an outlier occurred, I could feel the cohesiveness of the group suffering. I recollect that this effect had been found in research by social psychologists, but despite extensive searches, I can't locate any such reference. Needless to say, anonymous voting is verboten in any decision conference I facilitate. Raised hands are sometimes used to get a sense of how agreed or divided the group is, but never is it used to establish a quantity agreed by the group.

Leadership Styles

We've already said in Chapter 8 that leaders establish direction and motivate others to willingly follow in executing plans. Leadership style is the method for doing this, and decades of research shows there is no one best way. But whatever the method, one crucial factor is the extent to which the followers trust the leader. I mentioned the importance of trustworthiness of the facilitator at the end of Chapter 9, but this also applies to the leader: he or she must be competent, honest and reliable, too.[168]

Fortunately, most of the leaders whose groups I have facilitated did meet those three requirements, but not all. Indeed, occasionally, the leader fell short, as is noticeable in the hesitations of the group and their difficulty in openly discussing troublesome issues. That may be a good time to call a break so you can take the leader aside and ask her or him how they feel the group is doing. This may elicit their own uneasiness, which you can then explore with them. Some coaching on your part, keeping the 10 principles of process consultancy in mind, may be appreciated by the leader, and applied as you return to the group. You might also keep in mind that some leaders are more task-oriented, focusing on what the group must do to achieve the primary task, while others are more focused on motivating team members and maintaining good working relationships among them.

Group Polarisation

In 1961, James Stoner presented individuals and small groups of people with 12 hypothetical problems that required a choice between two alternatives, like the eye problem at the start of Chapter 1, a *choice dilemma*: (1) a 'risky' venture that might deliver either a favourable or an unfavourable outcome; or (2) a 'sure-thing' inter-mediate outcome.[169] He found that individuals chose the risky alternative more often in groups, and subsequent research established it wasn't because of the diffusion of responsibility in a group. Dubbed the *risky-shift phenomenon*, subsequent research confirmed the findings in other countries and the number of published studies multi-plied. Closer study of the problems revealed that one of the 12 elicited a shift to the sure-thing alternative, a *cautious shift*, and that led to many new choice dilemma problems, some showing the cautious shift, so the findings were renamed as *group polarisation*.

Eventually, it became clear that two types of factors were causing the shifts: social influences and persuasive arguments. The social influence emerges during group discussions as individuals are constructing their preferences and listening to the preferences of other group members. They may nudge their own view towards the group norm, especially if others' arguments are persuasive. All this is happening quickly and repeatedly for each member, so in a short time it is possible for the group to agree a position that is more extreme than that held by anyone at the start. And this process of polarisation is more extreme when the group is composed of members whose preferences are similar at the start. Thus, polarisation can introduce bias in the judgements of a group. Later research showed that bias can be reduced by ensuring that members of a group are selected to ensure diversity of views on the primary task. And as I mentioned earlier, Reagan-Cirincione's research showed that task bias is further reduced with impartial facilitation and computer modelling.

Observational Research

Although all the above eight categories of research on group dynamics applied controlled studies to groups formed specifically to study the effect of selected features on the performance of the groups, this section reports observations of groups already engaged on tasks associated with their working roles.

Experiential Study of Groups

Learning about group dynamics by being a member of a group studying its own behaviour develops an ability to understand what is often going on in a group beneath the overt to-and-fro of interchanges between participants. Anxiety is a common experience of members as they feel uncertain about participating too little or too much, saying the wrong thing, feeling that the group is heading in the wrong direction, worried about their competence to make meaningful contributions to the primary task, or sometimes just a sense of unease without knowing why. Indeed, the facilitator may experience these feelings as well. It feels as if the group has a life of its own and participating can be daunting to individual participants.

Serious study in the UK of these issues began in 1957 by the Tavistock Institute of Human Relations, and later in the USA by the AK Rice Institute, as they organised temporary learning communities of people who were interested in exploring how a better understanding of groups could be applied to working teams in their public and private organisations. I participated in several of these sessions and discovered that I continued to learn more from each engagement. One particular Working Conference on Group Relations, as they are sometimes labelled, sticks in my mind. Twenty-four participants and several professional counsellors drawn from the helping professions, including psychotherapists and psychoanalysts, convened in a country residential hotel for a week of meetings, beginning with a plenary meeting of the whole group, three subsequent smaller study-group meetings of eight participants each, several inter-group exercises among the study groups and a daily plenary meeting.

In these exercises, one member of a study group might be charged with simply observing one of the study groups, with the authority only to observe, or observe and report back if the observed group agreed, or to try to persuade the observed group to adopt a particular point of view at the next plenary meeting, or to negotiate something between the two groups. In short, we were exploring how different levels of authority assigned to the observer could affect group processes in the sending and receiving groups. Our retreat was a closed system, as we had no contact with the outside world (no cell phones/mobiles then), which intensified our observing the interrelatedness within each of our small groups, between groups and in the plenary group, and in relationships with the staff – overall a controlled open system whose parts could interact with one another.

If you had asked me, as my wife did, after I had returned to the outside world, what I had learned, I would have found it difficult to provide a coherent answer. However, over the subsequent years, as I facilitated many decision conferences, it became clear to me that the experience had enabled me to better understand the dynamics of a working group and how the nature of different roles and interactions among participants can help or hinder work on the primary task.

For example, the group might implicitly confer on a participant whose contributions are usually optimistic and made with good humour, the role of a clown who jokes about a difficult patch in the group's work, which can defuse building frustration and anxiety. Alternatively, a normally pessimistic individual may adopt an 'I told you so' attitude, which relieves the anxiety of individuals as they can now dump their own uncertainties onto the sceptic, as I reported elsewhere.[170]

Other roles, observed in group relations conferences, include that of saviour, father, mother, victim, observer, spectator, commentator, expert, warrior or leader. This person, implicitly 'elected' by the group, becomes the spokesperson for feelings bubbling up in the group. The sceptic expresses everyone's scepticism, the saviour provides a vision for the group, the expert provides the knowledge to accomplish the primary task, the observer maintains a quiet, watchful eye on everything and so forth. While each of those implied roles may help a group, an excessive implicit demand by the group may show that the group is unwilling to take on those responsibilities and are relieved of anxiety as the nominated person takes over expressing what others are feeling. Usually, that person feels increasingly uncomfortable in the role thrust upon them without quite knowing why. The facilitator can ask the group if that person is perhaps expressing feelings that the rest of the group are experiencing. This may defuse the growing burden and shift responsibilities back to the whole group.

By explicitly acknowledging the role, the facilitator returns the task of working on the primary task back to the group, making clear that they own the problem and its solution, which you will recall is Schein's fifth process consultancy principle.

Another group of findings from these working conferences on group relationships is the way uncertainty and anxiety in a group can work as an emotional undertow, making it difficult to attend to the primary task, just as swimming in an ocean outward beyond the waves lapping the shore can prevent swimming back to land. To the facilitator, it feels as if the group has assumed it is more important to work on a new task, which is identified as *'basic assumption'* behaviour.[171]

So far, five such behaviours are recognised as associated with ways for a group to reduce its uncertainty and anxiety:

1. **Fight/flight**. A participant picks a fight with the facilitator or another group member, or they might threaten to leave the meeting, or actually walk out.
2. **Dependency**. An authority outside the group or an institutional process is invoked to act as the saviour of the group, or the facilitator is asked what should be done next.
3. **Pairing**. The group develops a relationship with two people in the group who are thought to be specially qualified to complete the primary task.
4. **Oneness**. Differences in the group are smoothed over by focusing on developing a sense of oneness in the group.[172]
5. **Me-ness**. One or more members of the group deny the reality of the social process and insist that only individual perspectives are real.[173]

Each of these reveals a different response to growing anxiety in the group and much time can be wasted by the group if the facilitator fails to recognise that members have shifted their focus away from the difficulties of working on the primary task by indulging in basic assumption behaviour.

The first response of the facilitator, once he or she has recognised basic assumption behaviour, is simply to ask, 'How does this further work on our primary task?' That question often causes an immediate shift back to the primary task. But it may be necessary to elaborate. For example, I've already reported in Chapter 10's sub-section, 'Dealing with Conflict', how Roy Gulick, an experienced facilitator, quickly responded to one senior person starting to walk out by saying that a quick phone call to that person's department could identify a new person to represent the department, causing the participant to turn around and resume his seat. Or the double-task example in the same sub-section, in which I applied the double-task method so participants could stop fighting and reflect on how well they were working on the primary task.

If a group member quotes an outside expert ('So and so says . . .') or an institutional process ('We don't do things that way'), the facilitator might ask, 'I see, but how is that relevant to our current work on the primary task?', neither agreeing nor disagreeing, but encouraging further engagement by the group, forestalling any attempt to become dependent. If you are asked a question, it might be appropriate to enquire, 'Why do you ask?', which really is an invitation to think for yourself. If a pair of participants begin to act as experts, the facilitator might intervene and ask, 'I hear what the two of you are saying, but I wonder what others here think', thereby justifying other points of view.

Sometimes the group assumes that consensus is required in a decision conference so participants may minimise their differences, a oneness that attempts to create agreement about the model's inputs. The facilitator can explain that it is important to test substantial differences of opinion in sensitivity analyses to see if they matter, perhaps adding that precision in the numbers, plus or minus about 5 to 10 per cent, rarely makes any difference to the final result.

Occasionally, one or more participants deny that agreement can be reached because it is only individuals and their different views that are real, a form of me-ness that denies the social reality of the group. The facilitator can acknowledge their perspective, but as individuals they are not a problem as they become observers and are rarely persuaded of other points of view (which calls into question their roles as experts, which as I've noted above disqualifies them as real experts, who are always open to new experiences and other points of view).

How do you recognise basic assumption behaviour? The data are there in how you feel as you are facilitating. Fight/flight behaviour exhibited as participants fight one another may arouse anxiety in you, or defensiveness if you are verbally attacked. For dependence, the group's inability to move forward may give you a feeling of hopelessness or annoyance as they deny their own expertise, which may tempt you to answer their question yourself as you feel an urge to be helpful. If a pair of participants engage in exploring how together their expertise might enable them to carry out the primary task, other participants will mostly remain silent and you may well feel excluded and, indeed, unnecessary. You could interrupt their dialogue with a summary of what they are proposing and ask the group if that was useful, or if others have alternative ideas. Displaying the me-ness basic assumption, participants concentrate more on agreeing with one another, which the facilitator might interrupt with the reminder that consensus isn't required, and that exploring the reasons for disagreements will sufficiently deepen understanding of what is required to achieve the primary task. I have occasionally said, 'We're not here to love one another: our job is to get the primary task done.' You may observe that the group is calm and inactive, even moribund, making you feel the same way, which may tempt you to inject some energy yourself, but that rarely succeeds. It's better to report your observation of the group's lack of energy and ask why this is happening. Especially with unfamiliar groups, you don't know much about them, and there are many good reasons why the group may be unwilling or unable to face working on the primary task as a group.

The five basic assumptions observed in working conferences are less likely to arise in decision conferences with familiar groups, but whatever the degree of familiarity, a decision conference is definitely not a therapy group, so there is no justification for the facilitator to make an interpretation back to the group about why the observed behaviour is occurring.

Action Groups

These are often referred to as *naturalistic decision-making groups*, whose main proponent has been Gary Klein. He studies teams of highly skilled people who perform tasks characterised by 'time pressure, high stakes, personal responsibility and shifting conditions', like firefighters.[174] He also developed his *recognition-primed decision model*, which combines pattern matching (does the current situation match the decision maker's expectancies, which are based on the individual's prior experience) with an evaluation model (if the situation is familiar, a well-tested action is taken; if not, more information is sought, the situation reassessed and simulated in thought, and a good-enough action taken). Thus, decision making is a sequential process, not a matter of comparing the best of alternatives at a fixed point in time.[175]

Nearly all the case studies in this book require time and reflection, so does Klein's approach have anything to tell us for decision conferences? I suggest it does, in four ways: (1) that decisions are contingent on the type of situation; (2) that experience may be sufficient for immediate action; (3) that when the situation differs from experience, simulation in thought is required; and (4) that when creating the future, a good-enough solution will do. All four characterise decision conferences, the main difference being that in addition to simulating in thought, we extend that capability by using a model to hold more features of the situation than we could ordinarily keep in mind. The main difference is in the immediacy of the situation and a decision conference's luxury of time to analyse the situation.

That said, I once facilitated a decision conference for a pharmaceutical company facing a crisis. A reputable newspaper in a foreign country claimed one of the company's main products was potentially lethal, which created a threat that it would be banned in that country, with possible similar government action in others. The pharmaceutical company's marketing director instigated a decision conference to provide a rapid response. Participants were confident in their research data, which showed the product was safe, and they believed the newspaper's claim was based on one published research study that the group felt was flawed; the reported deaths could be explained by a factor having nothing to do with the product.

The managers considered a wide range of possible responses, and they constructed a decision-analytic model to explore alternative strategic responses, which included a robust strategy to mount a legal offensive in every country threatening to ban the product, to engage in additional research that would settle the contentious claim, and to continue marketing the product as long as sound scientific research showed it was safe. That strategy, which took less than two days to establish, was adopted, kept the product on the market, and further research failed to establish that people using it were at risk.

High-Performing Teams

Field research observations of sports, performing arts and many other kinds of teams, including decision conferences, shows that high-performing teams:

1. are clear about their goals and objectives;
2. are motivated to achieve their objectives and are highly engaged in the primary task;
3. are operating competently on their assigned tasks;
4. draw on a diversity of work preferences;
5. have been given the requisite authority and resources to achieve the primary task; and
6. know the limits of their authority.[176]

Item 4, work preferences, is important because most people prefer to work in ways that are consistent with their personalities, so it can be helpful to know how participants in decision conferences can bring their different work preferences together in accomplishing the primary task. For example, some people prefer to explore the issues deeply, while others may wish to move quickly to possible actions. Still others may wish to explore and innovate in creating a decision-analytic model, while others focus on ensuring the quality of the model. These different forces can pull a group in one way or another, with different types of work needed to accomplish the primary task. Individual preferences associated with the types of work can be integrated to create a high-performing team, but this requires facilitator training that is beyond the scope of this book.[177]

Groupthink

Very occasionally, a decision conference doesn't work for a group. For example, a small group of inventors, who claimed that an autistic person with reading difficulties could manage to read better by wearing specially coloured spectacles, were invited to a decision conference whose primary task was to evaluate possible ways forward to attract investors in their invention. As we began to construct a decision model, I asked questions about the theoretical foundation for their invention, which they steadfastly refused to discuss, explaining that their trials with real people demonstrated clear improvement. I explained there must be some uncertainty about these results and that an understanding of how and how well the spectacles helped could be useful inputs to the model. Unfortunately, they just insisted that the scientific community was prejudiced against their work, and they continued to resist. Indeed, my questions about visual perception led me to wonder if they actually knew very much about the physiological and psychological aspect of seeing. Eventually, saying I was sorry that the decision conference couldn't continue without more satisfactory information, I closed the meeting.

On another occasion, the stratum 5 managing director of a UK company contacted me to say he was being promoted to become the executive director of the many other European companies like his that were under the control of the parent corporation located in the USA. He had used decision conferencing many times in the UK, and was delighted to now become a stratum 6 director who could engage with the MDs of all the companies in Europe to increase their reach, reduce unnecessary duplication of support functions and improve efficiency.

He instigated a decision conference to create a European strategy facilitated by myself and a colleague serving as the computer modeller, but after two days of discussion, we had not even turned on the computer, and the new director closed the decision conference. After a few months' reflection, he suggested we try again, but with a new approach to coordinating the companies, but that, too, failed. It was evident that the proposed coordination was a step too large, and the director resigned his position.

This happened shortly after the formation of the European Union in November 1993, which opened free trade across all the member states, so maintaining separate manufacturing of a full range of products in each country no longer made sense, and within a couple of years after the second failed decision conference, the European countries began to centralise manufacturing and make distribution more efficient. I suspect that increased pressure from the head office combined with the change in inter-company relationships made possible by the EU created sufficient pressure for the turn-around. Another example of the importance of context.

On reflection, I now think that another force prevented the earlier integration of the European companies, and that is the influence of *groupthink*, which Janis proposed after studying many problematical American foreign policy decisions between 1940 and 1970. He defined groupthink as 'a deterioration of mental efficiency, reality testing, and moral judgement that results from in-group pressures'.[178] He suggested that the signs of groupthink were:

1. A cohesive group making the decision.
2. Group insulated from information outside the group.
3. Participants rarely searching for alternative policy options to appraise their merits.
4. Group under stress.
5. Group dominated by a directive leader.

The EU group of directors were certainly a cohesive group as they supported one another, never referred to changes in the EU, suggested no alternative policy options, were clearly under stress as they knew the initiative came from head office, and now they were presented with a new corporate director who was attempting to move them in a new direction.

Janis also suggested how a group could avoid groupthink:

1. Leaders encourage dissent and criticism.
2. Leaders refrain from stating their preferences at the outset of discussion.
3. Establish other groups to work on the same issues.
4. Periodically discuss with trusted associates.
5. Invite outside experts to join discussions.

As you know, many of these features are built into the decision conferencing process, but we did not feel it necessary to invite to the meeting the chief executive officer (CEO), the stratum 7 director who was the new director's boss. Surely the CEO's longer-term vision for this global company would have established the necessity for the primary task of creating an integrated strategy for Europe?

It's also clear that groupthink had inhabited the minds of the inventors of the spectacles that were reported to improve reading ability for autism sufferers. They were such a tightly knit group that it was impossible to persuade them to obtain outside views of their invention, nor to seek reasons for why it seemed to work.

Summary

It should now be clear that many of the findings from laboratory and observational research about groups are relevant to decision conferencing. We saw that face-to-face decision conferences about the harm of psychoactive drugs gave more valid results and differentiated the drugs better than was obtained from summarising and/or discussing the results of questionnaire data in small groups. This is because the first task of the whole group, whose participants were chosen for their diversity of expertise and views on the issues, was to listen to others' views, discuss the issues, and identify the uncertainties and preference values that define the structure of a decision-analytic model. They then collectively make judgements through discussion, formulating preferences as they are needed. The facilitator listened to the discussions in the group and refrained from expressing his views on the content of the discussion, but acted as a guide, helping the group to achieve their primary task, an impartial stance that encouraged rational discussion among the participants. As a result, it was the full collective of diverse experts that squeezed the additional intelligence from the group discussion.

Laboratory research on eight topics proved to be relevant to work groups and decision conferences:

1. **Group size**. Depends on the complexity of the topic, can be as few as four or as large as 15, sometimes more.
2. **Stage of development**. Familiar groups settle into productive work more quickly in a decision conference than unfamiliar groups, and the calling note helps to minimise the time for both.
3. **Norms**. Qualities of fairness, equity and respect usually develop quickly in groups of experts, helped by the facilitator's stance of listening, asking questions and respecting alternative points of view. No need for establishing 'terms of agreement'.
4. **Roles**. Each participant speaks knowingly from their home organisation's role, ensuring that the emerging model accommodates that expertise.
5. **Status**. The facilitator makes clear that information is a neutral commodity, to be shared by all whatever their status, title or role. It helps to ensure all perspectives are aired if seating does not impose a 'head table' effect.
6. **Cohesion**. The facilitator encourages task cohesion in the group by keeping participants focused on the primary task. Cohesion can be quickly destroyed by anonymous voting.
7. **Leadership styles**. Both the facilitator and the leader of the group must be trustworthy, that is, competent, honest and reliable.
8. **Group polarisation**. Although group discussion can lead to a risky or cautious shift in the judgements of participants, this is minimised in decision conferences by impartial facilitation and computer modelling.

Experiential studies of groups have identified an emotional undertow in a group whose members are experiencing uncertainty and anxiety, which can lead to any of five, implicit 'basic assumption' behaviours in the group, fight/flight, dependency, pairing, oneness and me-ness, that can divert the group from its primary task, making it difficult to return to rational discourse, just as an ocean's undertow can make it difficult for a swimmer to return to the shore. By recognising these behaviours, the facilitator can help to steer the group back to the primary task.

Research on action groups, like firefighters, revealed several features in common with decision conferences:

1. Decisions are contingent on the type of situation.
2. Experience may be enough for consolidated action to be agreed quickly.
3. Further thought and discussion may be required for unique situations.
4. A good-enough (requisite) solution may be sufficient.

We covered the six characteristics of high-performing teams, all of which are seen in a decision conference. Finally, we suggested that occasionally a decision conference is stalled or unsuccessful when groupthink is present, but this rarely happens in decision conferences because they are purposely set up to engage differences in opinions. Anyway, the facilitator can spot the signs of groupthink and encourage thinking to broaden.

Epilogue to Part II

As these five chapters make clear, the social and technical aspects of creating a decision-analytic model are deeply intertwined. Indeed, a decision conference is itself a socio-technical system and although it is a (fairly) closed system, its impact will permeate the larger system from which its participants were drawn as they return to the workplace aligned with a new sense of common purpose.

Even more important, I have come to realise that this section of the book essentially maps out what my former colleague Lee Roy Beach suggests is a philosophy of decision conferencing, which explains why decision conferences are so effective: they provide a transitional object that can hold participants' uncertainties and anxieties as they safely explore 'what-if' analyses, anticipating the future under different assumptions, judgements and uncertainties, which never provides a single 'right' answer, but enables the construction of a new narrative[179] about the way forward. True decision support. And as one of my fellow graduate students from the 1960s, Dr Charlotte Doyle, now a professor of psychology at Sarah Lawrence College, points out, these five chapters add up to more than the sum of their parts.

A recent two-day decision conference for a major pharmaceutical company well illustrates the views of my two colleagues. Over 20 employees of a major pharmaceutical company gathered to explore their disagreements about how the company should respond to a recommendation by the World Health Organization to make available in poorer countries a single dose of a vaccine that is normally given to children as two doses. While not as effective as a double dose, it would at least provide protection for more children, but many in the company were worried the protection was not as sufficient as the double dose. Discussion about the issues on the first day became fraught as participants provided good reasons for preferring either option, with no compromise anywhere in sight. There simply were no other options; black and white. And while data was abundant for the double dose, almost none existed for the single dose.

However, early in the afternoon, I asked who decides between one dose or two, and participants agreed it would be the countries not currently offering two doses. I then suggested we construct a model to allow the two options to be evaluated for their relative values on criteria representing all the pros and cons that had been elaborated in the morning. An orderly discussion followed, as participants considered the effectiveness and safety of the vaccine to individuals, the extent of uptake in new countries, and the extent to which it creates herd immunity. In addition, costs of administering and screening were included along with the reduction in hassle and the health-care savings resulting from fewer people acquiring the disease.

Scoring proceeded apace because with only two options for each criterion the better option scored 100 and the worst a 0, and it was easy to reach agreement as to which was best and which worst. Weighting took more time as data about the single dose was incomplete, making it difficult to assess how large the 0–100 differences in value were, but all agreed they were not equal across the eight criteria. Thus, the usual question, 'How big is the difference and how much do you care about it?', was modified to include, 'And how sure are you?', an example of how more uncertainty about the data justifies lowering a weight as if it were multiplied by a probability.

The final result showed the single dose scoring 49 and the double dose a 51, almost identical, but for different reasons. Sensitivity analyses revealed that only very slight increases on any one of the four weights favouring the single dose tipped the results in favour of that option, as did very small decreases on the weights favouring the double dose. The group recognised that the model could be applied to help decision makers make choices for the future, so they agreed that the next step was to develop programmes tailored to the needs of individual countries, as expressed by each country's weighting of the criteria, and could include either or both doses.

This shift from heartfelt disagreement at the start of the decision conference to recognising a new way forward was the result of incorporating all the key issues raised at the start as criteria, and the 'holding' of the model as a transitional object. This enabled participants to safely change or form new preferences, see that both options are about equally viable, and agree several new ways to take forward their experience and knowledge about this vaccine so more children will be protected.

But this is only one isolated example of what decision conferencing can do. Many others are possible, as is demonstrated in Part III, which shows the many different ways in which organisations articulate their vision, values and purpose in decision-analytic modelling that stimulates creative thinking and creates strategic alignment.

Part III

Socio-Technical Modelling

Decision analysts over the past 50 years have developed six distinctly different types of models, so we begin in Chapter 12 by summarising those types, weaving together the technical with the social features of implementation. This taxonomy is based on a combination of experience and theory, with the simple distinction between value and uncertainty being an obvious place to start thinking about what type of model might best clarify the decision maker's sense of unease.

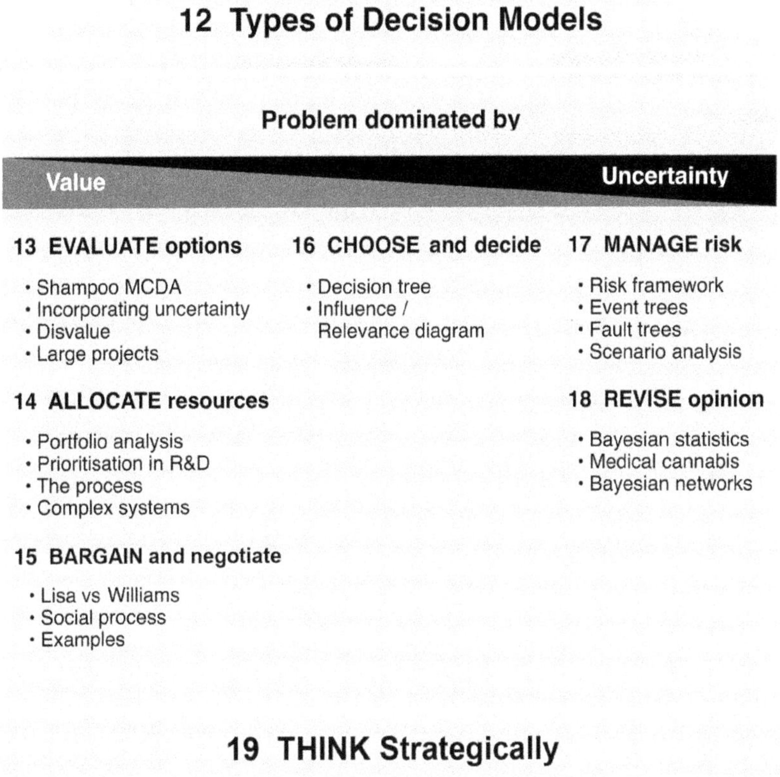

12 Types of Decision Models

Problem dominated by

Value		Uncertainty

13 EVALUATE options	16 CHOOSE and decide	17 MANAGE risk
• Shampoo MCDA • Incorporating uncertainty • Disvalue • Large projects	• Decision tree • Influence / Relevance diagram	• Risk framework • Event trees • Fault trees • Scenario analysis

14 ALLOCATE resources		18 REVISE opinion
• Portfolio analysis • Prioritisation in R&D • The process • Complex systems		• Bayesian statistics • Medical cannabis • Bayesian networks

15 BARGAIN and negotiate

- Lisa vs Williams
- Social process
- Examples

19 THINK Strategically

Figure 12.0

12   Types of Decision Models

All things are difficult before they are easy.

British clergyman and writer Thomas Fuller, 1608–61

This chapter provides brief summaries of six types of decision model and their variations, all of which are fully described with case studies in the succeeding six chapters. A final chapter discusses how, in any of these chapters, your client could be encouraged to think strategically, to consider what they wish to achieve and why, before moving on to creating a plan that explains how and by when.

But first, we need to consider what is meant by a decision model, which is only one of many model types that are mathematical in nature. A common dictionary definition of this larger class is a *mathematical representation of reality*, and this is what many clients will have in mind when they first hear about decision models. As a result, a potential client might object that it's too early to build any sort of decision model because there just isn't enough information. 'We'll get back to you when we have more data,' they say. This is an opportunity for the decision analyst to explain that decision models are different. Yes, they do usually include some aspects of the current reality, but they also describe the yet-to-be-created reality of the possible uncertain events, outcomes and consequences. Decision models are not just about *what is*, they go further; they consider *what could be*.

They are more like an architect's model of a new building, I explain, which allows a client to explore what the structure might look like, suggest changes and discuss alternatives. The model serves as a way for the client and architect to work together, think creatively and innovate.[180] That's what a good decision model will facilitate. I then go on to suggest that an initial decision model, based mainly on the collective judgements of the people in the organisation who do have at least some relevant knowledge and experience, can guide the search for more data. It does this via sensitivity analyses, which will identify the additional information that needs to be gathered. Too-early data searches expand, can cost a lot and end up providing far more data than is needed to take a decision. The initial judgement-based decision conference short-circuits that process.

It may also be helpful to explain that the role of a final decision model is not to provide an answer to the client's problem, but to explore the many possible answers that result from considering all the relevant issues that arise in discussions. Those issues felt to be important are included in the computer-based model, which holds them, allowing different combinations of uncertainties and values to be explored, thereby creating different scenarios about the future, which are explored and discussed. The model enables participants to express their anxieties about the change that is needed to resolve their initial sense of unease, so is serving as a transitional object that can contain and temporarily hold participants' reservations until clarity about the best way forward emerges.

The initial model enables participants to agree about the ingredients of the final model and provides an understanding of what information will be required. If the model is displayed while it is being built, participants will take part in their collective construction of preference values and probabilities, which eases them from what initially seemed very difficult, into what is now a clear view of the next steps for the decision maker.

Evaluate Options

Often referred to as multi-criteria decision analysis (MCDA), these models are characterised by several options, no one of which is best on all the objectives and criteria. The purpose of the model is to determine which option represents the best overall balance between the objectives. A hierarchical value tree depicts the structure of the model. An example is a company marketing its new women's shampoo in an Asian country but has been criticised by its US head-office as spending too much on television advertising, so the company is considering alternative options. The value tree is shown in Figure 12.1.

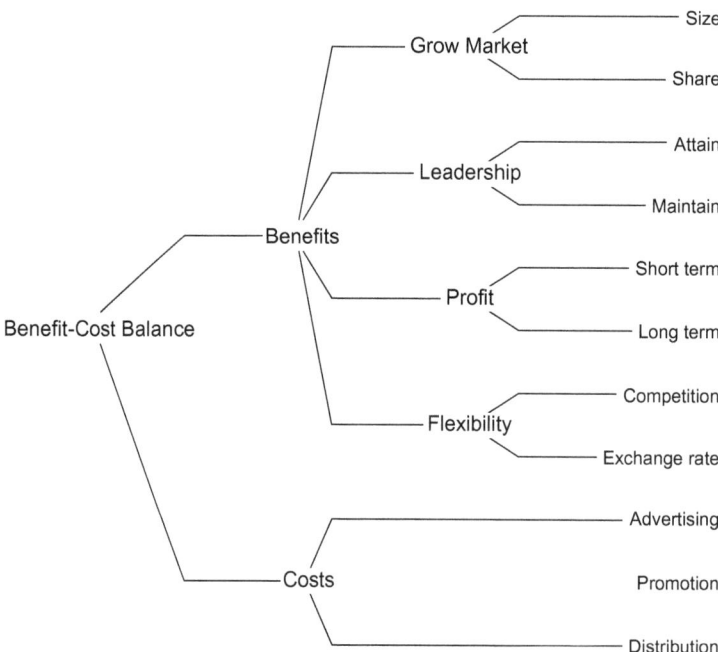

Figure 12.1

The two branches from the left node of the value tree suggest two main objectives: more benefit and less cost. These objectives become child nodes of the parent, the fundamental objective, to find the best balance between benefits and costs. Benefits are realised as four further objectives, with operational criteria defined for each: growing the market in size and share, attaining and maintaining leadership, etc. Three cost criteria, advertising, promotion and distribution, define the cost objective.

Options in MCDA models show practical ways in which the objectives might be achieved. They could be decisions, courses of action, strategies, systems, etc., but whatever they are it must be possible to finish this sentence: 'All of the options can be considered as _____', so there is a way in which they are homogeneous, for example, they are all holidays, or jobs, or schools, or strategies. For the above example, the options are ways of creating value for the company in the shampoo market, but they are later displayed at the stage of scoring the options, which is carried out separately for criteria under a node, then across nodes to establish weights at the nodes so that normalised weights can serve as scale constants that ensure weighted scores are comparable. Heterogeneous options are dealt with by applying portfolio analysis, which is described in the next section.

Allocate Resources

This model type is sometimes known as the multi-criteria commons dilemma. Imagine an organisation with several departments each engaged in many ongoing projects as well as considering new projects. The heads of those departments are accountable for ensuring that the organisation's resources (the 'commons') are best used to further the organisation's fundamental objectives. Each department creates an MCDA model comparing the adjusted benefit-cost ratio of all its projects, applying the same high-level objectives (although realised differently) for all departments.

The benefits are adjusted for their risks (namely, multiplied by each project's probability of success), then divided by cost, which establishes a *priority index* for each project, represented graphically as in Figure 12.2. These triangles are ordered from best to worst index for each department, then combined across all departments. The resulting *efficient frontier* identifies those projects that will make the best use of whatever total resource is available for the organisation's departments.

Figure 12.3 shows a graphic depiction of the ordered triangles for each of four budget categories and their combination into a single graph, where the horizontal axis is the cumulative cost of the projects, and the vertical axis is the increasing risk-adjusted benefit.

This example was an English Local Authority that developed the model to decide which projects to authorise over the next three years. You can see that if £1 million were available (the arrow), then the efficient frontier shows those projects up to point

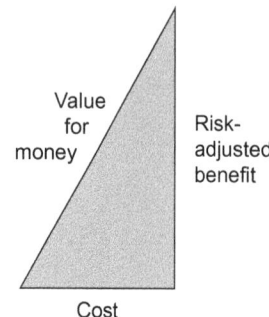

Figure 12.2

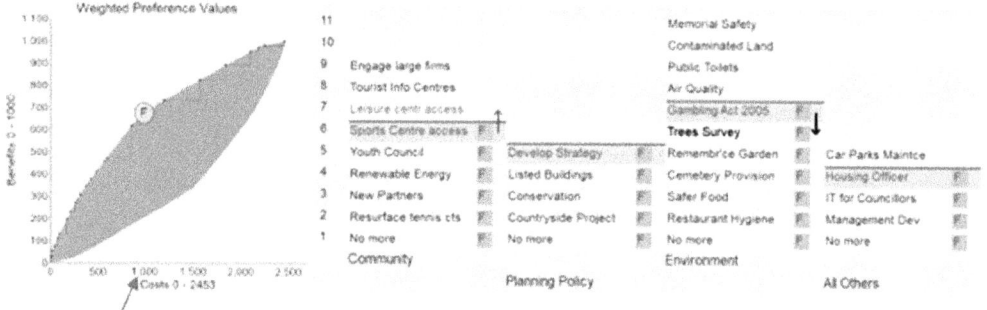

Figure 12.3

F are the best value for money. Previously, individual departments had pitched individually to the LA's Cabinet for more money, but this led to increasingly inefficient use of the total resource (therefore the term 'commons dilemma'),[181] so this approach arrived at a better allocation of the available budget.

Bargain

The clever feature of bargaining and negotiation models is that they take advantage of asymmetries of interest to find better positions for both parties. The issues that are the topics of bargaining are the decision analyst's criteria, while the stands taken on the issues by the parties are their agreed options. So, using the standard labels in the simple example in Figure 12.4 showing just 3 of 23 issues, value functions by Management and Union parties are represented by value functions. For the terms of agreement, management prefers one year and the Union three years, but the slight kink in the Union's value function suggests that they might compromise at two years. The length of the work week is very much a win-lose situation; no asymmetry there in the scores, but there is in the weights. And there are two asymmetries about Union recognition, one in scores and the other in weights.

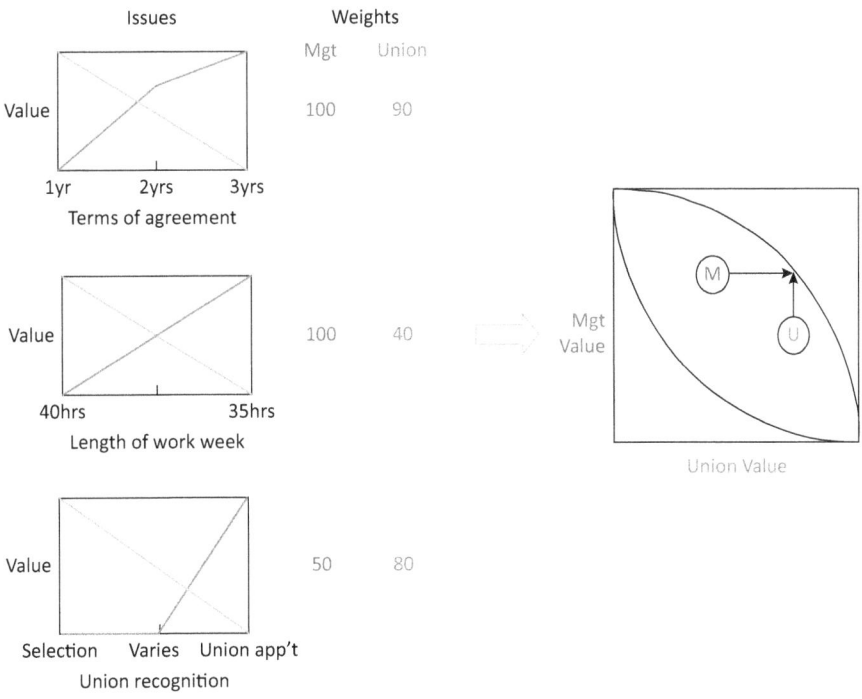

Figure 12.4

Once values are weighted and summed over all the many issues, a computer calculates the total value for each party of all possible combinations of issues (in this case, 3 × 3 × 3 × ...), which means that there are no agreements in the upper-right or lower-left regions outside the football shape. Each party proposed a contract, M and U, which gave more value to their own side and less to the other side. However, the arrows point towards a contract solution that would be better for both on the concave efficient frontier. Clearly, each side could benefit from negotiating to better positions for both. This can be made practical, with the support of computer modelling.[182]

Choose and Decide

Two different structures represent problems in which a single choice is to be made between one or more alternatives, but consequences are uncertain. Unlike MCDA, in which any number of options can be considered or chosen, the alternatives here are mutually exclusive; if one is chosen, it's not possible at the same time to choose another, unless combinations of options are also included as additional options.

Decision Tree

If the problem is characterised by many uncertain events and one or more criteria, then a *decision tree* might be appropriate. Figure 12.5 shows a real example of how

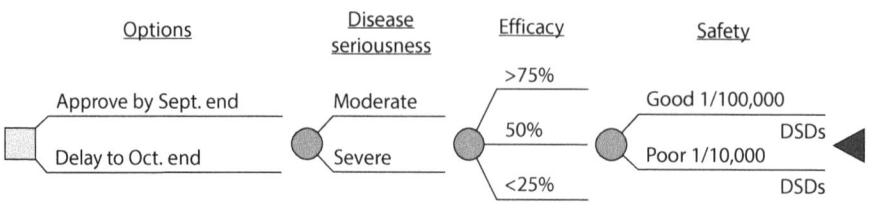

Figure 12.5

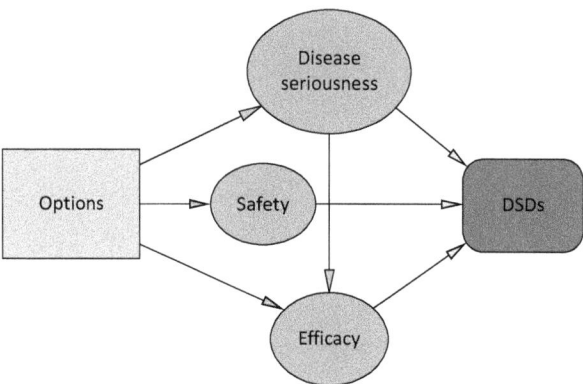

Figure 12.6

the European Medicines Agency explored how best to respond to the 'swine flu' virus (H1N1) when the World Health Organization declared a pandemic in July 2000. Should the applications for two vaccines be approved by the end of September to ensure all 500 million European residents could be protected, even though full clinical evidence had yet to be completed, or should they wait a month to be certain that the safety and efficacy of the vaccines was sufficient? The fundamental objective was to minimise the numbers of deaths and disabilities (DSDs).

Relevance/Influence Diagram

Decision trees grow exponentially as more nodes are created, so they can become very large with many branches from initial alternatives to consequences. In that case, an *influence or relevance diagram* more compactly shows the relationships between those elements in which knowledge or causation of one element affects the probabilities, values or timing of another element.

The influence diagram in Figure 12.6 shows that the options influence all three uncertainties, and all three events affect the DSDs, with only disease seriousness affecting efficacy. In Chapter 16, you will also see decision trees that include down-stream decisions, namely, once an initial decision is made, there are further decisions to be made depending on the outcomes of previous events.

Manage Risk

In decision analysis, risk always involves uncertainty, especially about undesirable consequences. But in everyday usage, risk has come to mean many more things, so an understanding of what your client means is essential to choosing a model. After all, the word risk can be used as a noun, verb or adjective, so it's best to pay attention to your client's use and avoid any attempt to explain what the 'proper' use of the term should be.

The psychologist Paul Slovic found that ordinary people may well experience a risk (as a noun) in terms of a feeling of dread, how little is known about it and the number of people affected by it.[183] These characteristics explain why many countries have found it difficult to agree on where they should bury their high-level radioactive waste (known as NIMBY, not in my back yard), as dumping the waste anywhere nearby scores high on all three characteristics. Ken MacCrimmon provided a summary of how risks can be managed, as we'll see in Chapter 17.

Event Trees

Sometimes the tree representation of risk is about a modest number of alternatives followed by many uncertain events that collectively define the feeling of risk experienced by the key decision maker. No subsequent decisions are taken at all. An *event tree* starts with the alternatives, one of which is to be chosen, with subsequent events resolving one way or another, leading to the final consequences.

The event tree in Figure 12.7 helped a UK manufacturing company decide what to do after one of its main products had been banned in two countries as unsafe. It would be unlikely that a new replacement product could attract the same level of sales as the old, reliable, recognisable product, but retaining the old product risked a possible ban in the UK for violating health and safety regulations. In addition, new technology being developed outside the UK posed a threat because it would replace the basis on which the old product worked. Given enough time, the MD intended eventually to replace the old product once the new technology was ready.

Fault Trees

When the problem is to make a corrective decision following a system failure so as to minimise potential damage, a *fault tree* shows the possible causes, intermediate outcomes and ameliorating events that may lead to a satisfactory correction of the fault, or signals what to do next.

In Figure 12.8, the decision was to install one of three possible warning systems, or not, that will warn drivers about a rare break on a bridge's surface, which would be invisible at night and lead to a vehicle toppling into the lake below. This tree included the cause of the situation, which influences the probabilities of subsequent events. The tree is entirely symmetrical; once the event branches are all attached to the previous

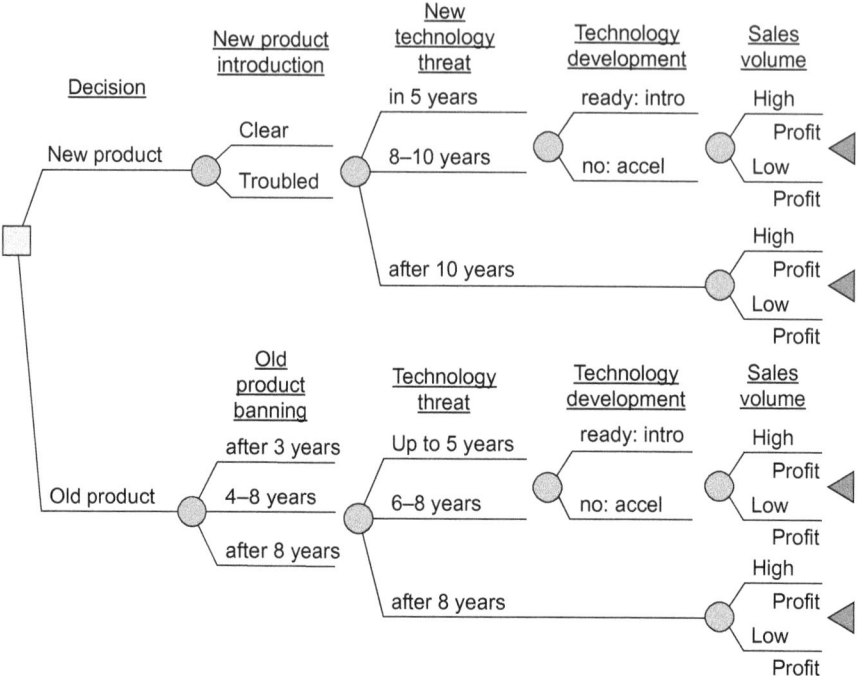

Figure 12.7

branches, this makes $2 \times 2 \times 2 \times 2 \times 2 \times 3 \times 3 \times 3 = 3{,}456$ paths through the tree, each a different scenario about what could happen in the future, with only a few paths culminating in loss of vehicles or life. This model requires only 11 probability assessments, so computer software makes the modelling easy. The hard part is ensuring all relevant uncertain events are included. The handbooks and online correction devices in nuclear power stations are the result of many fault tree analyses. More about this case study in Chapter 17.

Scenario Analysis

During my term as a reviewing editor for the *Journal of Forecasting*, I observed the result of a forecasting competition, which showed how difficult it was to accurately forecast time series of events that engaged people, like the financial markets, stock prices, exchange rates, etc. I came away with the sense that forecasts could at best be valid only for up to two years. I have since been sceptical about the validity of probabilities in any decision model that includes events affected by human activity systems with their long-term uncertainties that are often described in the literature as *deep uncertainty*.

I was, therefore, pleased when Paul Schoemaker came to London in the late 1980s to work with Shell's scenario group, which had been instrumental in developing a new way for the company to anticipate such future events. Paul published his view of the

Figure 12.8

Warning System	Potential Accident Situation	Potential Bridge Damage	Cause of situation	Action to avoid bridge damage	Action to avoid vehicle accident	Type of bridge damage	Vehicle accident	Loss of Life

LORAN-C + SLABOUT

LORAN-C only

SLABOUT only

STATUS QUO

None

Develops

Slabout

Non-slabout

Operator error

Other

Effective

Not effective

Effective

Not effective

Slabout

Non-slabout

None

Fall off   Vehicle_Cost

Damaged only   Vehicle_Cost

None   Vehicle_Cost

None   Value_of_a_Life

3 fatalities   Value_of_a_Life

6 fatalities   Value_of_a_Life

Shell group's work, which I found could be adapted to decision conferences, helping decision makers to broaden their perspectives about the future, thus counteracting many managers' assumption that the future can be reliably predicted from past trends. My 10-step adaptation has been tested in many decision conferences, as discussed in Chapter 17, with a case study drawn from an international health-care foundation in Chapter 19.

Revise Opinion

Revising opinion in light of new information is the theme for Chapter 18, where two approaches are discussed, both deriving from the laws of probability: Bayes' theorem, sometimes referred to as Bayes' rule. One is *Bayesian statistics*, which is increasingly applied to the analysis of data, enabling decision makers to attach probabilities to Yes/No hypotheses or the magnitude of consequences, and to the credibility of those probabilities. The other is *Bayesian belief networks*, which break down eliciting a probability of a complex event by creating a network of conditional probabilities that are related to the complex event.

Bayesian Statistics

My wife brought home a bunch of freesias, a South African flower, that I had never seen before. 'Very pretty, but a pity they have no scent,' I said. Surprised, she replied that she found them very fragrant. That set me to wondering if there was some genetic basis for our difference, and as I was teaching Bayesian statistics at the time, I constructed the left chart in Figure 12.9 to represent my uncertainty about the proportion of people who could smell freesias (no internet then to look it up). This probability density function, based on our differing experiences, shows that the proportion can't be either 0 or 1, but could be anything in between, with 0.5 as most likely.

I set out with the flowers and asked five neighbours if they could smell them. All said the scent was strong, so I applied Bayes' theorem to revise the gentle left

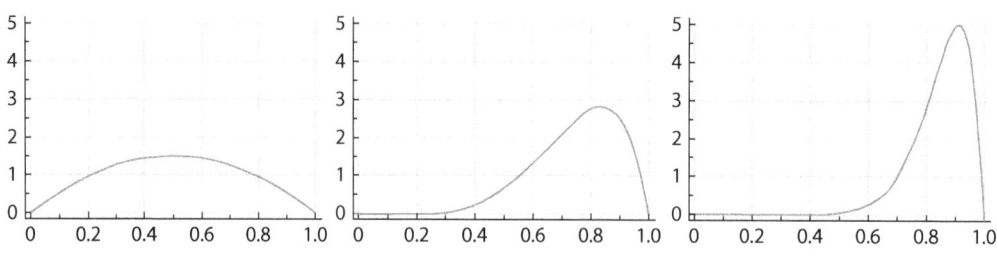

Figure 12.9
Proportion of people who can smell freesias:
Left, 1 can and 1 can't; middle, 6 can and 1 can't, and right, 11 can and 1 can't.

distribution, which resulted in the middle chart. Five more neighbours were consulted, and all smelled them, giving the right chart.

It was now very clear I was in the minority among my friends, as it appeared that the proportion of 'smellers' must be greater than 0.5. An internet search as I write this reveals that the average number of non-smellers is about 4 per cent for UK people of Celtic origin (I have both Welsh and Scottish ancestry) and around 10 per cent for others. And it took only 12 observations to be very sure I was in the minority.

These three graphs show the mean shifting as it moves closer to the 'true proportion' (if any such exists), and the credibility of the mean becoming narrower as a best guess. That is the main characteristic of Bayesian updating. Chapter 18 provides an elementary summary of Bayesian statistics.

Bayesian Networks

Figure 12.10 shows a real example, taken from working with a major UK insurance company in the late 1970s. In interviews with a small team of experienced head-office underwriters, I elicited conditional probability tables of 18 different types of building for the extent of risk they would pose to insure against threats like fire, flood and other sorts of damage. Figure 12.10 is a pared-down version for shops considering the five most important risk factors.

The probabilities were converted into risk factors, so a fair risk of 1.29 was converted to a worse factor of 2.2, shown in the bottom line of the Shop risk box. Including the other three factors, above normal in housekeeping, a small size, and in an above average location, showed a posterior probability of 62.3 per cent, representing a fair risk, with a final risk factor of 2.2, all explained in Chapter 18.

BBNs and Artificial Intelligence (AI)

BBNs are considered as one form of AI, but not so for any of the other five types of decision-analytic models. Why is this, and will DA become subsumed by AI? I tackle these questions at the end of Chapter 18. You might think about this yourself as my crystal ball is limited.

Computer Programs

As suggested at the bottom of Figure EP.2 in the introduction to Part III, the taxonomy of decision model types is based on experience of what works. Not surprisingly, decision analysts have developed computer programs that are specialised for each of the types. It's true that decision theory is at the heart of these computer programs, but experience has led to new features not anticipated by the founders of the theory, leading to successive versions as more capability is incorporated. Much of that experience isn't included in textbooks on decision analysis; indeed, it is the presence of the computer programs that first brought to my attention the taxonomy of decision model types.

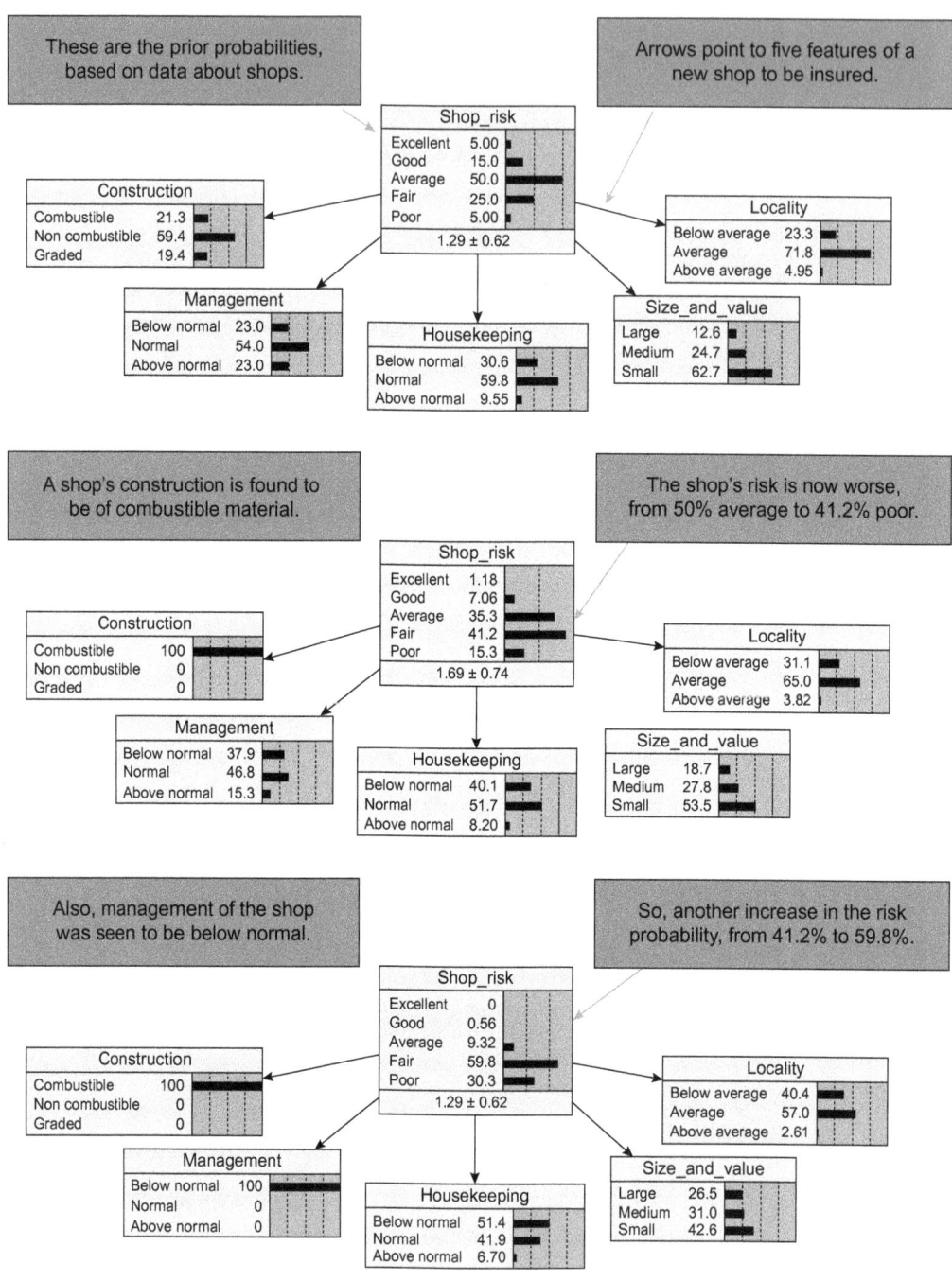

Figure 12.10

One of the earliest decision tree programs, DPL, is in its ninth version at the time of writing. Netica, for modelling Bayesian Belief Networks, is in version 5, while MCDA programs like Logical Decisions is in version 8, V•I•S•A in version 7, and Hiview and

Equity in version 3.[i] Many are free, even at professional level, and simpler versions, usually spreadsheet add-ons, are inexpensive or free, but limited in capability.

As the originally expensive professional programs become free, I suspect that the easy availability of open-source computer programs such as 'R' will see a blurring of the seven model types as they become incorporated into new, open-source decision modelling programs that also handle 'big data', using Markov Chain Monte Carlo (MCMC) methods that can manipulate the data to represent an unknown population distribution of any form. Whatever happens, the next 10 years will see an increase in open-source programs for the problem types.

---

[i] See www.catalyzeconsulting.com/downloads/executables/equity-3.4.0.6.exe. Enter this serial number in Help: 10741010EHDD.

See also www.catalyzeconsulting.com/downloads/executables/Hiview-3.2.0.7.exe. Enter this serial number in Help: 10061602KCDZ.

13 Evaluate Options

> It is only through evaluation that value exists: and without evaluation the nut of existence would be hollow.
>
> Friedrich Nietzsche, 1887

As Nietzsche makes clear, value exists through the process of evaluation. There is no such thing as absolute value, existing in some pure state, devoid of context. Value is created; that's why it is referred to in this book as preference value, and preferences are constructed on the spot when they are required for taking a decision. The ability to create value is what gives agency to humankind. We are goal-seeking creatures much of the time, even when our behaviour is instinctual (pre-programmed in our genes and brains), or habitual, or influenced by drugs. So, it is preference values that are the 'nut of existence'. It is the process of forming those values that is the topic of this chapter. It infuses all the remaining chapters, so this one is most definitely required reading.

Recall that at the end of Chapter 1, I outlined the five generic steps that guide the creation of any decision model. Here they are again in summary:

1. **Consider context**
2. **Frame the problem**
3. **Provide content**
4. **Explore results**
5. **Agree the way forward**

Answers from the client to questions posed at each step by the decision analyst drive the process of creating the model, as will be elaborated now with case studies showing how the 10 ingredients are structured to form a unique decision model. So, in this chapter, let's begin with models that evaluate options, when multiple objectives, some supporting, some conflicting, means that no single option is expected to perform best on all the criteria: some options are best in some ways, while others are better in different respects. It's called *multi-criteria decision analysis* (MCDA).

Women's Shampoo Case Study

We'll work through the five steps, showing how they guided the creation of an MCDA decision model, although when it was brought to my attention, I was unsure the conflict could be resolved.

1.   Consider Context

A new company, located in the Far East, only one of many companies throughout the world owned by a major US corporation, devised a grooming product for women that is used in other countries, but is not yet accepted in this particular country for a variety of reasons, mainly because grooming is based on cultural habits that do not include this type of product. The managing director (MD), a US citizen, had lived in the country for only six months and had determined that heavy television advertising would be the main approach to establishing the product's value to women. However, the main US corporation notified him that too much money was being spent on the TV adverts. The MD believed head office didn't understand the culture of the country, and that his approach would work. He didn't have time to test-market the product in a smaller part of the country.

The corporation's British company had successfully used decision conferencing many times, was willing to support the MD, and advised the MD to convene a decision conference to see if a solution could be found. He agreed, and the usual preparation, including a calling note from the MD, established that he, his various marketing managers, account directors, general managers and a management sciences manager from Britain would attend a two-day decision conference in the country, which I facilitated.

2.   Frame the Problem

At the start of the decision conference, after introductions, the discussion established several issues and concerns, largely supporting arguments for continuing the TV advertising, and focusing on attaining and maintaining leadership in the country of this new product, which was selling well in other countries. The MD asked the group to focus on the company's strategic direction over the next five years to ensure the product's success. It seemed to me that they were looking to evaluate the pros and cons of a single option, continue TV advertising. With only one option on the table, and wondering if other options might exist, I asked, 'If you reduced spending on TV, what would you do with the saved money?'

The MD said he hadn't thought about that, so the group spent another hour discussing where the funds could be used. The final list of nine options is here reduced to the five key ones, as the extra detail doesn't add anything important to this case study.

Options

1. STAT QUO: Continue advertising only on TV
2. +CNSMRS: Cut back advertising, extend use of the product to men
3. +PROMTN: Cut back advertising, spend more on promotion
4. +PRODUCTS: Cut back advertising, spend more on new products
5. HI QUAL: Cut back advertising, spend more on a high-quality version of the product
6. DISTN: Cut back advertising, spend more on distribution

During the discussion of options, participants emphasised the company's strategic direction, with objectives and criteria emerging from the discussion of how each of the options could add value in supporting the company's primary objective of establishing leadership in this product.

Criteria

Further discussion suggested that to achieve leadership wasn't sufficient; it also needed to ensure that a leadership position was maintained, and discussion broadened to consider both means and end objectives. These included growing the market for the new product in both size and share, but others argued that profit must also be considered, as must the company's response to being flexible to any competitive advances. Someone else pointed out that consideration should be given to exchange-rate fluctuations, because one ingredient of the product was imported. The finance director pointed out that all these options required spending within a given fixed budget, costs of advertising, promotion and distribution, although in different amounts for each option.

It became clear that the fundamental objectives were to achieve benefits and minimise costs, which are in conflict; that's the key trade-off. As the benefits were made explicit by answering my questions, such as, 'In what ways do you expect the market to grow?', the group formulated definitions of the criteria and these were typed into the computer, with criteria appearing under their associated objectives. The graphics displayed the structure, and text defined nodes, criteria and options that could be recalled at any point at the click of a mouse. Discussion bounced from one benefit to another, as the group defined the benefits, and could see the creation of the value tree, with definitions agreed and typed into the computer. The computer was 'holding' all these points of view and I explained that nothing was set in concrete, so could be recalled, edited, changed or deleted at any time.

Slowly, over a period of about two hours, an initial implicit understanding of the issues became increasingly explicit, with the emerging model projected onto a screen showing the computer's output. The value tree, with its 11 criteria, is shown in Figure 13.1.

(At this stage, Hiview3 displays names of the criteria as grey to indicate no scoring has yet been done, and the branch lines are dashed, a reminder that no weights have been assessed. What you see here is the model after completion of scoring and weighting.)

3.   Provide Content

With the exception of advertising costs, there was no data for any of the other criteria, and there were no probabilities, so the content was restricted to preference values and trade-offs. As this group had never encountered an MCDA model nor participated in a decision conference, I suggested we gain experience in making the necessary assessments by concentrating first on the Grow Market objective and its two criteria, Size and Share.

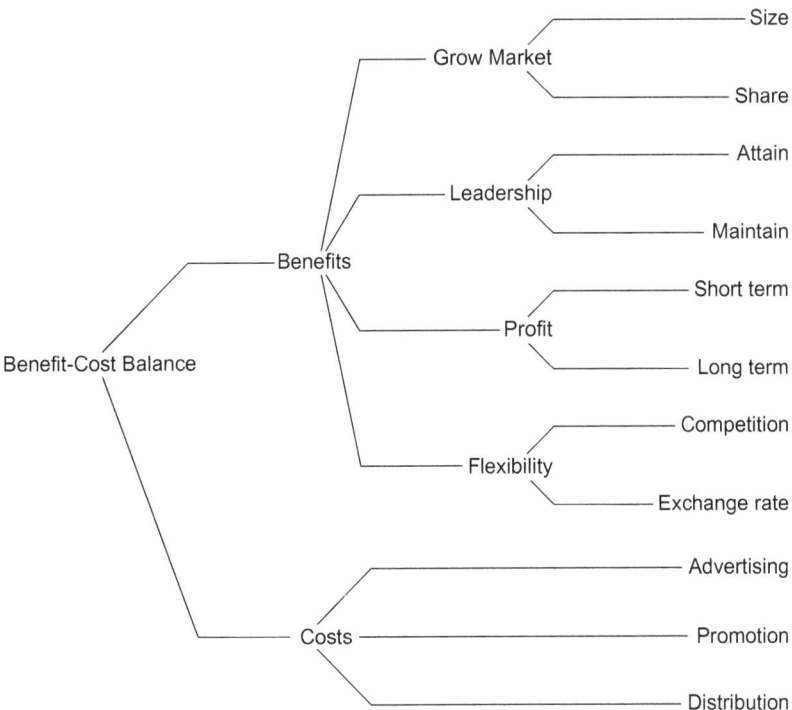

Figure 13.1 text labels: Grow Market — Size, Share; Leadership — Attain, Maintain; Benefits; Profit — Short term, Long term; Benefit-Cost Balance; Flexibility — Competition, Exchange rate; Costs — Advertising, Promotion, Distribution.

Figure 13.1

Scoring Preference Values

First, I drew on a flipchart the scale we would be using to score the options. I explained that this 0–100 scale was like a Celsius scale for measuring temperature, but for us, the numbers would represent the value associated with the consequences of an option's performance. For each criterion, we would assign a score of 100 to the option expected to perform best so would be most preferred, and a score of zero to the worst performing option considered as least preferred (see Figure 13.2).

Thus, these were relative values, so I warned that a score of zero might well be associated with some value, but it was less than could be said of any other option. I opened the scoring window for Size in Hiview 3, and asked if each participant could, without discussing it with anyone else, identify which two of the six options would be best and worst for Size. After a short pause, I asked them to say what they were thinking. Even after a short discussion, most agreed more consumers would be best and distribution least, so they were assigned 100 and 0, respectively. The group agreed that the remaining options should all receive scores less than 50, but it took a little time to agree the scores shown in the left panel in Figure 13.3.

During the scoring, I emphasised that these scores are relative, so it is their differences that are important to the final calculation, and those differences should feel about right. For example, I pointed out that the difference between +CNSMRS and +PRDCTS is 60 points, while the difference between +PRDCTS and DISTN is 40 points, a ratio of 1.5 to 1, so I asked if that felt about right, which they confirmed.

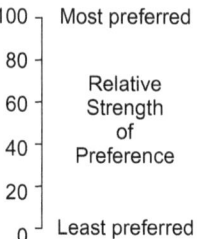

Figure 13.2

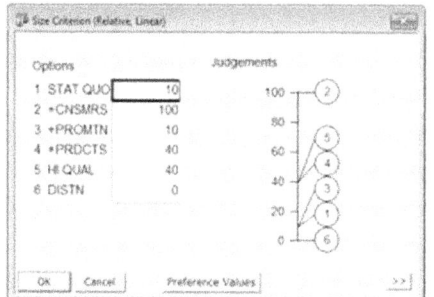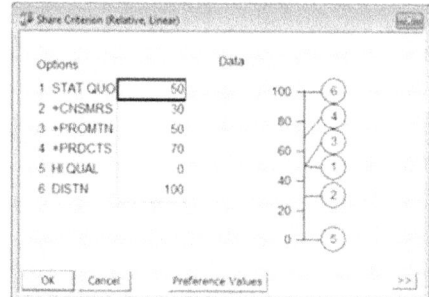

Figure 13.3

The group moved to the Share criterion and repeated the scoring process, shown in the right panel. At some point, I discouraged arguing about generating precise numbers, explaining that experience usually shows that preference values within plus-or-minus 5 points won't make any difference to the final results. And I suggested that if at any time someone wishes to hold a more extreme score, then they should write that score down, and raise it again when the model is complete so we can test it in sensitivity analyses to see if it changes the overall result.

It's important to show the scores for criteria under a parent criterion so the facilitator can see if any pair appear to be very similar, for if they are, then perhaps the scales are representing the same sources of values. If they appear similar, I ask if perhaps the scales were measuring the same thing, and if so, then suggest redefining the scales so the definition of the new scale encompasses the value in a more comprehensive way. Here, the flexibility benefit was a good example: almost the same scores, but these criteria represent different sources of value (Figure 13.4).

During the scoring, I quickly learned to direct my questions first to the participants rather than the MD, because if he spoke first, the others would not disagree, for that would be a failure to save face. This is an important consideration in any multi-ethnic setting, although there are also cultural norms that can affect the openness of discussions in many Western countries as well.

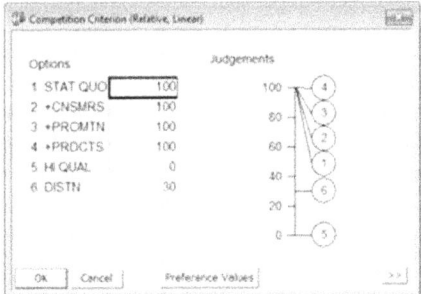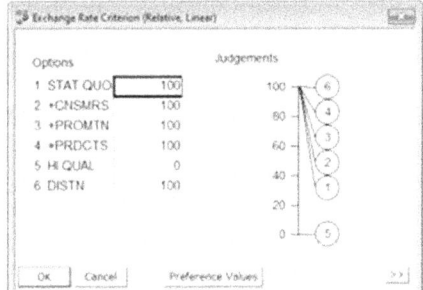

Figure 13.4

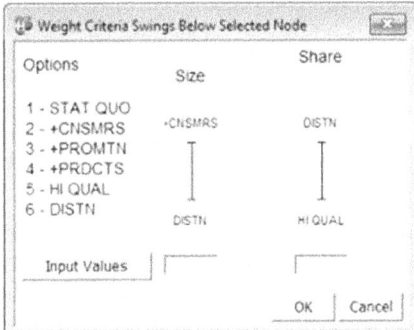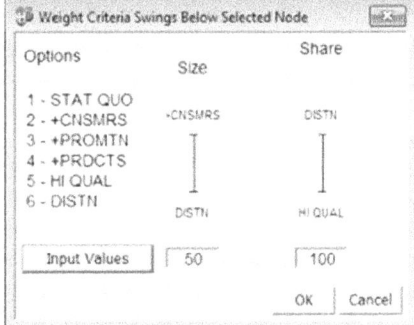

Figure 13.5

Trade-Offs between Criteria

With agreement reached about the scores for the Grow Market objective, I pointed out that the difference in value between 0 and 100 on the Size criterion might be different from that on the Share criterion. Eventually, we would like to combine the scores, so assigning weights to the differences on criteria is the way to ensure the units across the criteria are comparable. I then opened the weighting window, left panel, shown in Figure 13.5.

I asked participants, 'Think about the difference in size of the market between +CONSUMERS and DISTN, that is, how much bigger the market size will be for the top option compared to the bottom, least preferred option, *and* how much you care about that difference for the company.' I then gave them a moment to think about that, although a question or two required repeating the question. 'Keeping that in mind,' I said, 'now consider the difference in the size of market share between DISTN and HI QUAL and how much you care about that difference.'

Next, I asked, 'Which of those two differences, taking into account how much you care about each, is larger?' A short discussion led to agreement that the Share difference was larger, so I typed 100 into the white field below the thermometer display, and asked the group to assess the Size weight as a percentage of Share's 100. After some discussion, a 50 was agreed. I then explain that this process is called *swing weighting*, as it compares the added values as one swings from the bottom to the top of the thermometer scales.

As this was the group's first experience with weighting, questions arose as not everyone necessarily understood what they were asked to do. I explained that we are in the process of judging trade-off weights. That the larger one will be assigned 100, and the lesser one some percentage of that. Metaphors can help to clarify this. For example, in purchasing a new home appliance, when you make judgements about whether the extra capabilities of the more expensive machines are worth the extra costs, you are trading off the extra value of one or more capabilities against the additional costs. Chapter 5 gives other examples.

An Interim Calculation

With scoring of the options on the two Grow Market criteria and weights agreed for them, I suggested we look at their weighted average scores. The computer does the calculation, shown in Figure 13.6.

I explained that as the weights sum to 150, when normalised they are 33 and 67, therefore since DISTN scores zero on Size and 100 for Share, its weighted average is 67. I also asked if the overall lengths of the bars made real-world sense. At this initial stage, a few participants usually express their surprise that, yes, this does feel about right, and others agree. Occasionally, some disagree and we may need to revisit the scoring and weighting, making changes until the group can agree.

This process of making intuition explicit in the form of numbers will be easier for some participants than others, so I point out that nothing yet is set in concrete and we can at any time revisit previous work. Indeed, after all scoring and weighting is complete, some participants ask to revisit the first node's criteria. Most groups take quite a long time to get through this first stage of learning how to score and weight, which can be frustrating for the facilitator, but most participants learn quickly and the group speeds up. Patience on the part of the facilitator is soon rewarded as participants become acquainted with this new approach. And often the most severe critic at the start turns into an ardent supporter by the end of the two days.

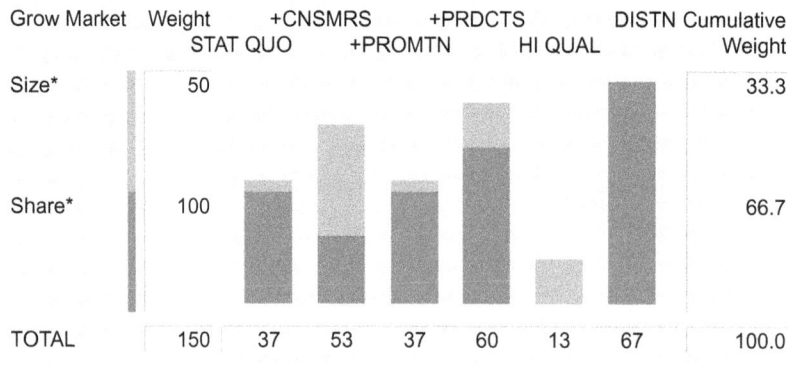

Figure 13.6

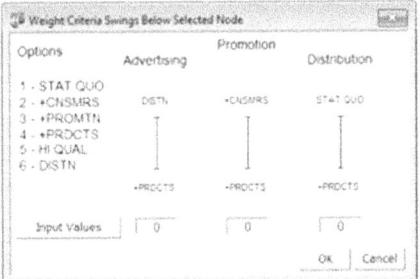 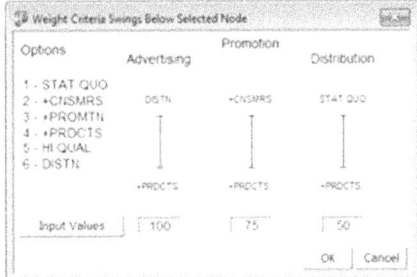

Figure 13.7

Completing the Model

Scoring the options and then weighting the criteria under each of the remaining three Benefit nodes proceeded apace. When scoring the options for the Cost objective, only the costs of the status quo were known, so I asked if they could directly score preference values, with 0 and 100 assigned to the most and least costly options, respectively, which they agreed was possible. (If actual costs had been available, I would have input them to the software and invoked the 'inverse' function in Hiview3 to convert those costs to preference values.)

Assessing swing weights for the three cost criteria was initiated by showing the three scales under the Cost node, as shown on the left in Figure 13.7.

I reminded the group that +PRDCTS was at the bottom of all three thermometers because it was the costliest option, while different options were at the top because they are least costly for their corresponding criterion. I asked the group which swing in value from bottom to the top created the most added value, that is, was the lowest difference in cost. The group agreed it was advertising because it would require an entirely new program for the added product, so that criterion was given a weight of 100. Comparing the swings on each of the two remaining criteria to the 100 as a percentage resulted in the 75 and 50.

That provided an opportunity to carry out a consistency check on the weights. I pointed out that the move from bottom to top of the two scales on the right, represented by the sum of the weights, 125, suggested that the two together are 25 per cent more costly than the Advertising bottom-to-top difference. And after some thought, someone who was informed about costs said that was right, but with an edge to his voice that suggested he now understood better what the weights represent: sums of differences in costs. Once again, relative differences come into play.

With scoring and weighting completed at the level of the criteria, I directed attention to the next step: comparing weights at the nodes. You might now look at Chapter 5's section 'Weighting in Hierarchical Models', which explains in more detail what is briefly presented here. I began by pointing out that one criterion under each node received a weight of 100, but swings in values for all these 100-weighted criteria might not be equal. Indeed, while assessing weights, participants might themselves ask if the 100 under one node means the same as under another, when it seems to them that's not

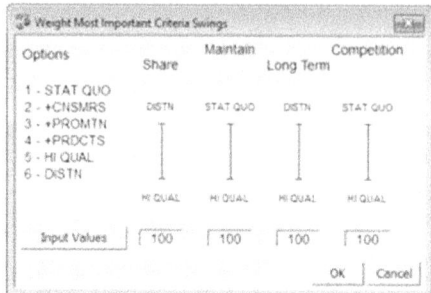 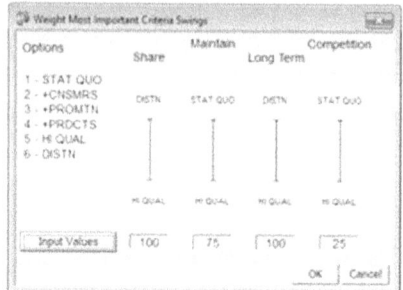

Figure 13.8

so. They are right, of course, and equating the units of value under all those 100-weighted criteria is our next task.

I started by opening Hiview3's 'Weight Most Important Criteria Swings' window for Benefits, which shows the four 100-weighted scales with weights of 100, as seen on the left in Figure 13.8, and explained that we now need to compare the swings in value on those four.

To clarify why we need to do this, I pointed out that both Fahrenheit and Celsius scales include 0–100 portions, but the difference in temperature is greater for the Celsius scale. Now, we need to know which of these scales is the greatest difference that you care about, and we'll then compare each of the other three to that, and as a consistency check, to one another. I emphasised that we're not just comparing the importance of these four criteria, rather we are considering how much better the top-rated option is actually different from the bottom-rated for that criterion, *and* how much you care about those differences.

During the discussion, participants argued that for Share and Long Term, DISTN was very much better than the HI QUAL option, particularly because four good commercial distribution companies existed in the country, which could be engaged; participants assigned 100s to both those swings. The other two criteria were given quite high weights until I added their weights for Maintain and Competition, which summed to more than 100. Nobody thought that was correct, so the group reduced weights to those shown in the right panel in Figure 13.8, as participants realised the added value of the status quo over the high-quality option was small because there wasn't any competition for their unique product as yet. The added values of 75 and 25 equalling 100 were felt to represent as much added value for either Share or Long Term.

The final step, comparing the 100-weighted criteria for Benefits and Costs, was a tough one, as it made very clear that weights represent trade-offs. It is at this level that it can be helpful to compare the Best–Worst and Worst–Best combinations to identify which criterion shows the largest value swing (Figure 13.9).

Standing next to the screen, I pointed to the top of one scale and the bottom of the other, asking, 'Imagine two new hypothetical options, A and B. Option A is the Long Term benefit of DISTN along with the cost of +PRDCTS. Hypothetical option B is the

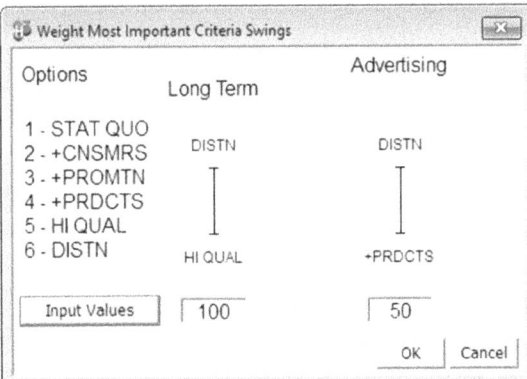

Figure 13.9

cost of DISTN for Advertising along with the HI QUAL benefit of Long Term.' That took a little time to sink in, and someone asked me to repeat it.

This time, pointing with left and right forefingers simultaneously to top left and bottom right, I summarised, 'A is best as for DISTN's Long Term benefits, but is most costly as for +PRDCTS' Advertising.' Then, pointing bottom left and top right, I continued, 'While B is worst as for HI QUAL's Long Term benefits, but is lowest in cost of DISTN as for Advertising. Which is better, A or B?' After a short discussion, the group agreed it was A, so the Long Term criterion was assigned a weight of 100. The group then suggested the swing on Advertising should be half as much, so was given 50.

Sometimes this doesn't work because the hypothetical options, A and B, are impossible, but in this case, although they were unlikely, most participants seemed to imagine the combinations.

4.   Explore Results

The next step revealed the overall results, the weighted scores for benefits, and for costs, then summed to give the table and its associated bar graph shown in Figures 13.10 and 13.11, respectively.

Although distribution wins and developing a high-quality product is a loser, the MD was concerned that the weights (inputs summed as in the Weight column, normalised to sum to 100 in the Cumulative Weight column) were in the ratio of about 4:1, which might not be giving enough attention to costs. That suggested a sensitivity analysis on cost, in which the overall normalised weight on the cost node was varied from 0 to 100 to see if that changed the overall result.

The graph in Figure 13.12 shows the result. The vertical axis shows the overall Benefit-Cost Balance, while the horizontal axis is the weighted sum of the three cost *preferences* (larger weights mean lower costs) at the Cost node. The vertical red line is located at the current weight, 19.8, and intersects the sloping lines at the TOTAL values shown under the bar graph, the total weighted values, with DISTN as most preferred at 79.

Benefit-Cost Balance	Weight	+CNSMRS		+PRDCTS			DISTN	Cumulative
		STAT QUO	+PROMTN		HI QUAL			Weight
Benefits	454	63	61	55	55	10	82	80.2
Costs	112	55	89	67	0	39	67	19.8
TOTAL	566	62	66	57	44	16	79	100.0

Figure 13.10

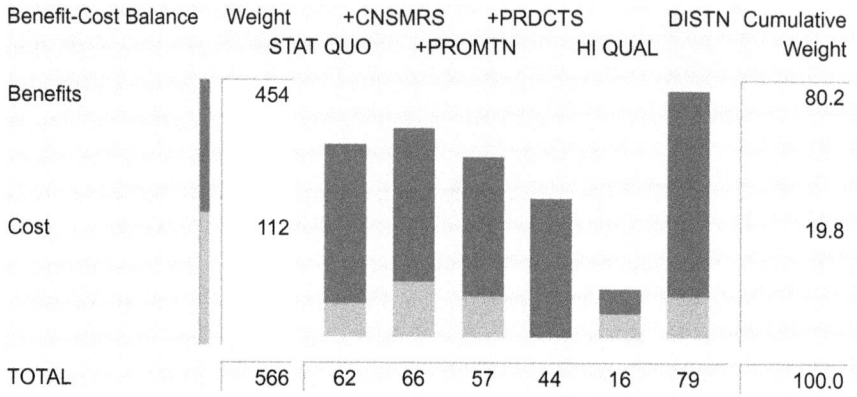

Benefit-Cost Balance	Weight	+CNSMRS		+PRDCTS			DISTN	Cumulative
		STAT QUO	+PROMTN		HI QUAL			Weight
Benefits	454							80.2
Cost	112							19.8
TOTAL	566	62	66	57	44	16	79	100.0

Figure 13.11

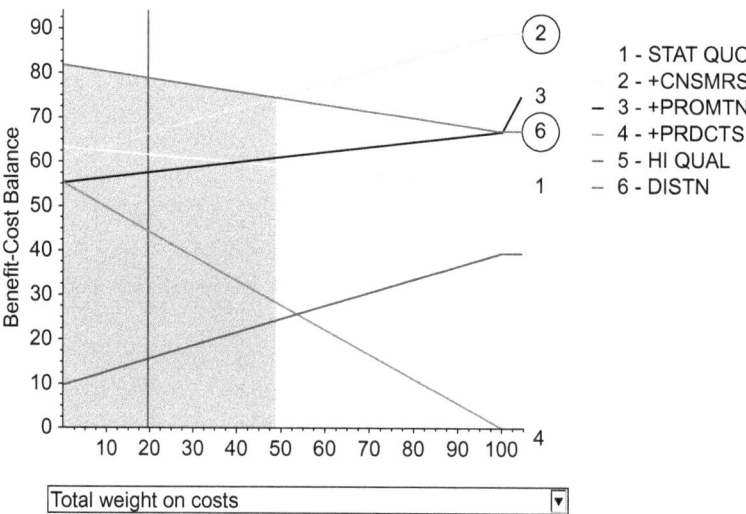

1 - STAT QUO
2 - +CNSMRS
3 - +PROMTN
4 - +PRDCTS
5 - HI QUAL
6 - DISTN

Total weight on costs

Figure 13.12

Now, imagine that more weight was given to the Costs node, which is the weighted sum of preferences for the three costs. That's equivalent to moving the vertical red line to the right, reducing the costs, with the result that DISTN would remain as most

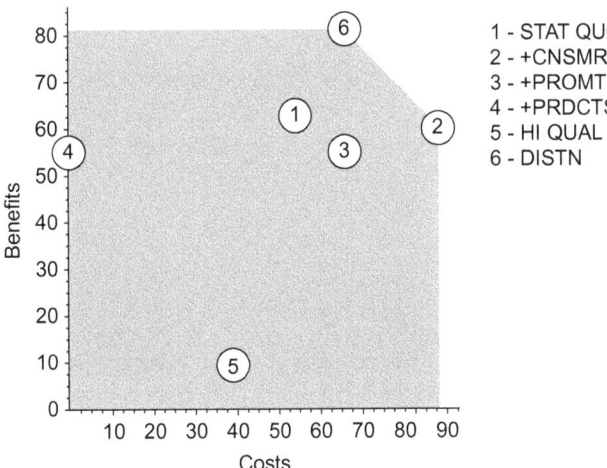

Figure 13.13

preferred until the weight reached nearly 50, so about equal to the weight on Benefits. Then, making the product available to more consumers, which wouldn't cost very much, would become most preferred.

That argument became even more clear when I suggested we look at the Benefits versus the Costs, without considering the weights between the two. Each circled number in Figure 13.3 shows its weighted benefit and weighted cost score as given in the table in Figure 13.10. For example, option 6, DISTN, is shown at (67, 82). I reminded the group that the computer's label is preferences for costs, so lower costs are to the right on the horizontal axis.

As the MD thought about this graph, he said he would reject +CONSUMERS because making the product available to another group of consumers would weaken the advertising and promotion to women. And he could see that 4 and 5 are either too costly and/or providing too few benefits, so he eliminated them. That left the possibility of reducing the current advertising spend and shifting some of it to promoting the product and/or improving distribution.

At that point, it seemed appropriate to compare those two options to the status quo by engaging Hiview3's Sort function, which sorts the criteria on the basis of the weighted difference between two options on each of the criteria. The left graph in Figure 13.14, STAT QUO minus PROMTN, shows that the status quo favours maintaining leadership, while promotion saves much of the cost of advertising. The right graph, STAT QUO minus DISTN, shows four advantages of spending more on distribution, one of which is also saving on advertising.

5.   Agree the Way Forward

This Sort arose at the end of the first day, and the MD said he realised that he may well have underestimated the importance of distribution in the country, so he asked me if we

Compare STAT QUO ▾ minus +PROMTN ▾

	Model Order	Cum Wt	Diff	Wtd Diff	Sum	
Leadership	Maintain	13.3	70	9.3	9.3	▬▬▬
Costs	Promotion	6.5	45	2.9	12.2	▬
Costs	DISTRIBUTION	4.4	10	0.4	12.7	'
Grow Market	Share	17.7	0	0.0	12.7	
Profit	Long Term	17.7	0	0.0	12.7	
Grow Market	Size	8.8	0	0.0	12.7	
Flexibility	Competition	4.4	0	0.0	12.7	
Flexibility	Exchange Rate	3.0	0	0.0	12.7	
Leadership	Attain	1.2	0	0.0	12.7	
Profit	Sort Term	14.1	-20	-2.8	9.8	▬
Costs	Advertising	8.8	-65	-5.7	4.1	▬▬▬
		100.0			4.1	

Compare STAT QUO ▾ minus DISTN ▾

	Model Order	Cum Wt	Diff	Wtd Diff	Sum	
Flexibility	Competition	4.4	70	3.1	3.1	▬▬
Leadership	Maintain	13.3	20	2.7	5.7	▬
Costs	DISTRIBUTION	4.4	60	2.7	8.4	▬
Costs	Promotion	8.5	25	1.6	10.0	▬
Grow Market	Size	8.8	10	0.9	10.9	'
Flexibility	Exchange Rate	3.0	0	0.0	10.9	
Leadership	Attain	1.2	0	0.0	10.9	
Profit	Sort Term	14.1	-40	-5.7	5.3	▬▬▬
Costs	Advertising	8.8	-75	-6.6	-1.4	▬▬▬
Profit	Long Term	17.7	-40	-7.1	-8.4	▬▬▬
Grow Market	Share	17.7	-50	-8.8	-17.3	▬▬▬
		100.0			-17.3	

Figure 13.14

could spend some time the next day figuring out what the right balance should be to spend on advertising, promotion and distribution. I was delighted to hear that, as this is exactly the kind of question that can be answered by portfolio analysis; he needed a portfolio of options that would achieve the best possible value for money. The next chapter will pick up from this point to carry out a portfolio analysis that enabled him to decide what to spend in the three areas.

Incorporating Uncertainty

How can uncertainty be accommodated in an MCDA model? There are several ways, so let's start by taking a look at the Effects Table for the drug belimumab (Benlysta), which when it was being considered for approval by the European Medicines Agency was the first new drug in 56 years for treating systemic lupus erythematosus (SLE).[184] Lupus is an incurable disease in which the immune system attacks its own tissues, and Benlysta is the trade name of a drug that works with other lupus medicines to help reduce disease activity.

SLEDAI (SLE Disease Activity Index) is a multi-item rating system used by the physician in observing the extent of a patient's disease activity at a point in time. The BILAG instrument is an ordinal scaling system of disease activity in eight organ systems. Measures before and after adding Benlysta to a patient's medicine provided the data, which are shown in the Effects Table in Figure 13.15 for three options: two different doses of the medicine, 10 milligrams and 1 milligram, and a placebo.

Because the regulator is charged with establishing the safety and efficacy of a new medicine, clinical trials for many patients established the figures. You can see they are percentages for five benefits, so larger numbers are more preferred, the default in Hiview. However, smaller numbers for flare rate and the three safety criteria are more preferred, so the inverse function in Hiview was adopted to change those numbers into preference values. A small group of EMA regulators constructed this MCDA model, using all the available data from trials, and assessed the weights, which are shown here after normalisation.

The first row of the table shows that the placebo performed better than either of the two doses. So, the three percentage-point difference between best and worst, when multiplied by a small weight, gives only a very modest contribution when the computer

Effect	Definitions	Units	Weight	10mg	1mg	PBO
FAVOURABLE EFFECTS						
SLEDAI 4–6% better	Percentage of patients with at least 4-to-6 points reduction in SLEDAI at week 52	%	2.3	16	15	18
SLEDAI > 6% improved	Percentage of patients with more than 6 points reduction in SLEDAI at week 52	%	5.9	37	33	23
PGA % no worse	Percentage of patients with no worsening in Physician's Global Assessment	%	1.2	75	76	66
BILAG A/B	Percentage of patients with no new BILAG A/B	%	3.5	75.2	70.1	69.0
cs Sparing	Percentage of patients that reduced the dose of cortico-steroids by more than 25% and to less than 7.5 mg/day	%	3.9	15.5	20.0	12.3
Flare rate	Number of new BILAG A cases per patient-year	number	39.1	2.88	2.90	3.51
UNFAVOURABLE EFFECTS						
Serious Adverse Effects	Potential for developing tumour, adverse interactions with vaccine and adverse effects on pregnancies	preference	16.0	0	90	100
Infections	Proportion of patients with serious infections that are life-threatening	%	23.4	5.2	6.8	5.2
Sensitivity Reaction	Proportion of patients with hypersensitivity reactions	%	4.7	0.4	1.3	0.1

Figure 13.15

calculates overall weighted scores of the options. Obviously, a reduction of 4–6 points in the SLEDAI score after a year's experience shows no statistical difference in effect; even the placebo is slightly better than the drug.

But the picture is different for the next row: a reduction of more than six points was experienced by more patients for the 10mg and 1mg doses, and both were better than the placebo; the weight of 5.9 reflects that improvement. Notice, too, that direct scaling of *potential* Serious Adverse Effects adds a future perspective to the model, and the zero for the 10mg dose suggests that these effects might appear in the future, while the 1mg dose and placebo were judged to be relatively safe.

If you had to read the above four paragraphs more than once, I'm not surprised, for this MCDA model captures the subtlety that emerges even from the simple additive mathematics of decision theory, which I hope is adequately expressed here in words, as you must in working with your client. And that includes unexpected results like those in the bottom two rows, where the 1mg dose resulted in more infections and sensitivity reactions than the 10mg dose. Usually, higher doses create larger side effects, but here the specialists were unable to understand the opposite result.

In addition to the subtlety issue, this example well illustrates the points I wish to make about incorporating uncertainty in an MCDA model. All the percentage data could be thought of as probabilities of success for the three options, especially as clinical trials are based on large sample sizes, so any sample proportion is a reasonable estimate of the population proportion. For each criterion, all the weights, then, represent judgements about best–worst differences in probabilities *and* how much the regulator cares about those differences on a given criterion, which is a value judgement. In calculating the overall score for each option, the data for every option is converted linearly to preference

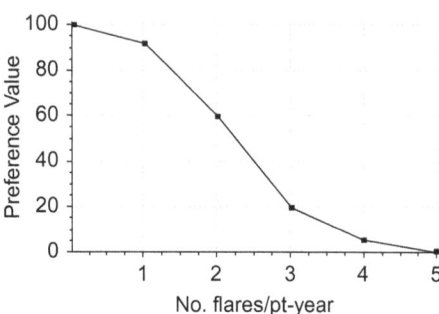

Figure 13.16

values (linearly for all proportions data to ensure that all patients are of equal value), then multiplied by the weights across the nine criteria. The resulting weighted averages are effectively the values of differences in probabilities.

But two exceptions also illustrate the flexibility of MCDA models. First, as we've already seen in other models, the ability to accommodate direct judgement when objective data are not available. That was the case for serious adverse events (serious enough to require hospitalisation), which required judgements based on regulators' knowledge of lupus and its pathophysiology because none had been observed in the clinical trials data.

Second, a non-linear conversion of number of *new* flares (incidents when lupus is very active in the body) to preference values, as seen in the value function, was assessed by the regulators. The graph in Figure 13.16 shows the loss of value from no flares is 10 points for one flare, 30 for two, 40 for three, then levelling off. This sort of inverted S-shape is often found to describe side effects of medicines. You may recall the QTc function in the Value functions section of Chapter 4, which showed a slight kink, but was all negatively concave.

The regulators were writing an interim report about belimumab, but were not yet agreed about whether it should be approved. The final results, shown in Figure 13.17, showed clearly why, as can be seen in the bar graph: the long portions of the 1mg and placebo (PBO) bar graphs for SAEs means they are safe from serious side effects, as shown in the research, whereas concern about extended use of the 10mg dose was judged as possibly occurring in the future. Assigning a weight of zero to Serious Adverse Effects gave overall preference values of 54, 30 and 24 for 10mg, 1mg and placebo, respectively, a clear win for the 10mg dose. Eventually, the EMA recommended approval, but required a 5-year follow-up of its use and to monitor any possible appearance of serious side effects.

Disvalue

The possible increase in flares following treatment with belimumab is effectively a loss of value. As we are limited in English for words expressing value as a noun (benefit,

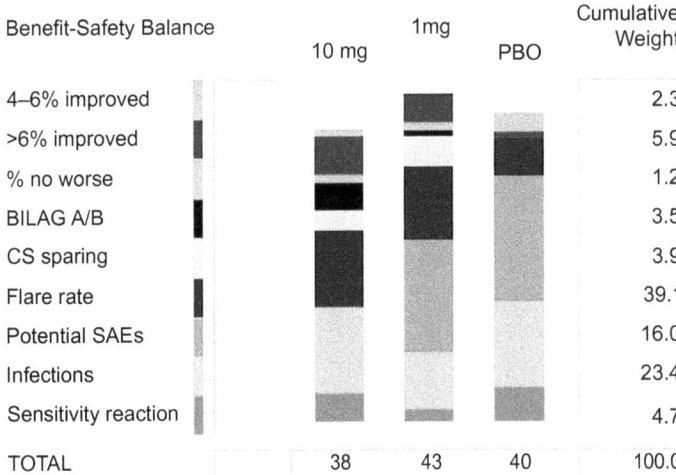

Benefit-Safety Balance	10 mg	1mg	PBO	Cumulative Weight
4–6% improved				2.3
>6% improved				5.9
% no worse				1.2
BILAG A/B				3.5
CS sparing				3.9
Flare rate				39.1
Potential SAEs				16.0
Infections				23.4
Sensitivity reaction				4.7
TOTAL	38	43	40	100.0

Figure 13.17

desirability,[i] utility, worth), it's even more difficult to express the opposite, although I think undesirability is pretty good, but so is the English word *disvalue*, meaning something of negative value, although it doesn't seem to be commonly used. But as decision analysts, we need to know how our clients think about disvalue, however they define it. The previous two case studies in this chapter provided examples.

In the benefit-cost example, participants assessed higher costs as larger disvalues, although I never used that word, and I showed how the software applied an inverse function so that higher costs received lower preferences. Everyone seemed to understand that, so they could understand the bar graphs. But when I showed any display with the benefit-cost balance on the vertical axis and cost on the horizontal axis, I had to remind the group that higher numbers of the x-axis meant lower costs.

For the Benlysta medicine example, the EMA experts were already using the descriptions of favourable and unfavourable effects, rather than the more commonly used terms benefits and risks, to ensure clarity about what the latter mean, as some may think of risk as also applying to benefits – for example, the risk of not achieving the benefit. There seems to be no agreement within disciplines about how risk should be defined, let alone across disciplines, so I've found it best to ask your client how they define the term; I say more about this in Chapter 17. Anyway, for this example, everyone agreed that more flares should receive lower preference values, and that was made explicit in the value function. But for infections and hypersensitivity reactions, I confirmed with the group that for both, lower percentages would be more preferred and that the linear function should be linear as all patients are to be considered equally. Thus, all these indirect functions can be considered as disvalue.

---

[i] Which didn't appear in Microsoft's Word thesaurus, but was suggested to me many years ago by Carlos Bana e Costa when he was searching for a word for value that he could use in the English version of his MCDA program, M-MACBETH. The original used the Portuguese word 'desejabilidade' and he asked me if 'desirability' would work in English. Very well indeed, thanks, Carlos!

The Harm of Drugs

A common view of risk is the possibility of something bad happening, the latter suggesting disvalue. And as I discovered at my first decision conference with the UK government's Advisory Council on the Misuse of Drugs (ACMD) in 2009, disvalue there was considered as the extent of harm and the number of people affected. It took an entire day for members to define the harms, which included physical, psychological and social harm, to users and to others, altogether 16 criteria, represented in Figure 13.18 in a disvalue tree.

Note that only overall harm was considered, not benefit-harm balance, as the ACMD's brief was to advise the government about potential harm. So, I defined harm scales as 100 representing most harm and 0 least harm. It took another day, several weeks later, to revisit the model, slightly revise the criteria, and complete scoring and weighting. Eventually, the ACMD put the model and the definitions of

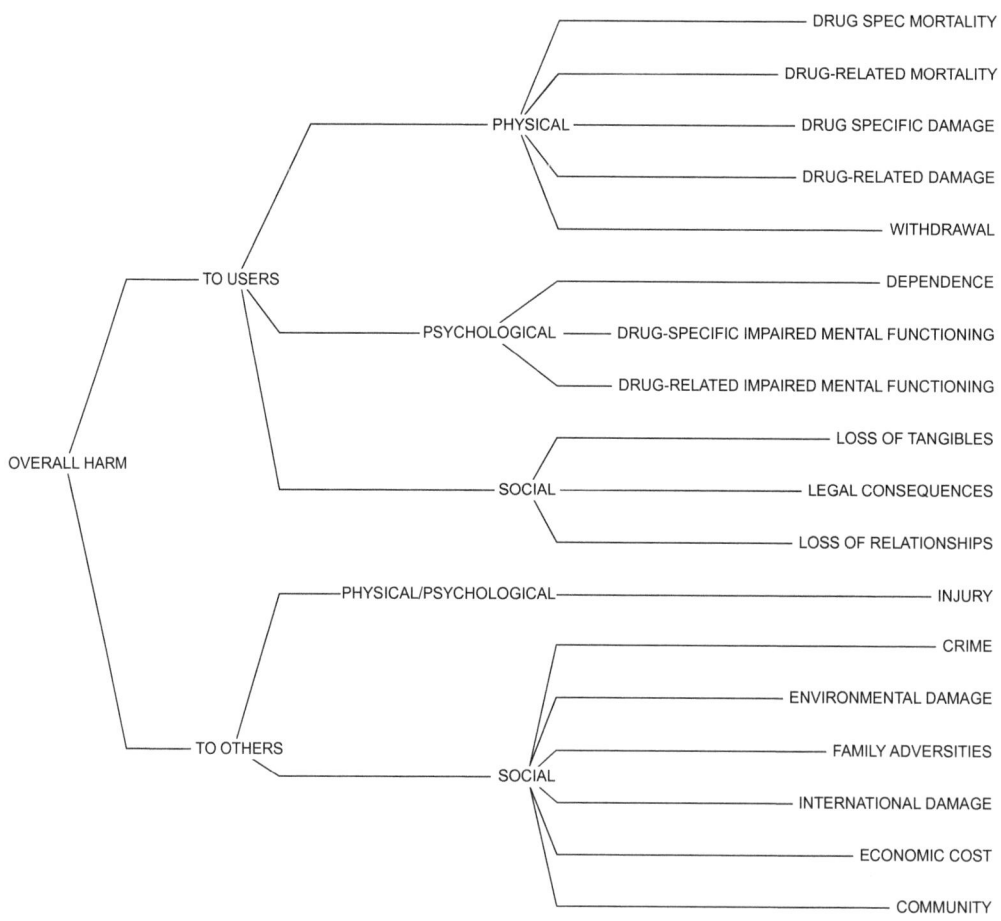

Figure 13.18

harms on their website, but did not report the full results on the grounds that more work would be needed to validate the findings as they were all based on judgements.

A few months later, the Chair of the MCDA, Professor David Nutt, gave a public talk in which he was critical of the Home Office's recommendation to reclassify the harm of cannabis from Class B to the more harmful Class A. He was promptly relieved of his position at the ACMD by the Home Secretary, Alan Johnson, which created outrage in the public media about scientists being punished for telling the truth. Nutt immediately formed a new charity, now known as Drug Science, whose remit is to provide science-based information about drugs. That new group, many of whose members had moved from the ACMD, met in mid-2010 for a new decision conference whose results could be made public.

After reviewing the structure of the ACMD's model, 20 drugs and the 16 criteria with their definitions, I suggested scoring the drugs on ratio scales, with 0 representing no harm and 100 assigned to the most harmful drug on the given criterion. That has the advantage of showing the ratings as horizontal bar graphs, as shown in Chapter 4 under the sub-heading of 'Ratio Scaling', which makes it easier for participants to compare lengths of the bars, and it facilitates consistency checking since it's easier to imagine how the sum of two bars would be greater or less than a single other bar.

Also, ratio scales reduce the complexity of weighting, which now becomes a task of comparing worst harm with no harm for each criterion, which, of course, reduces to the comparison of worst harm across the criteria. Figure 13.19, for example, shows the

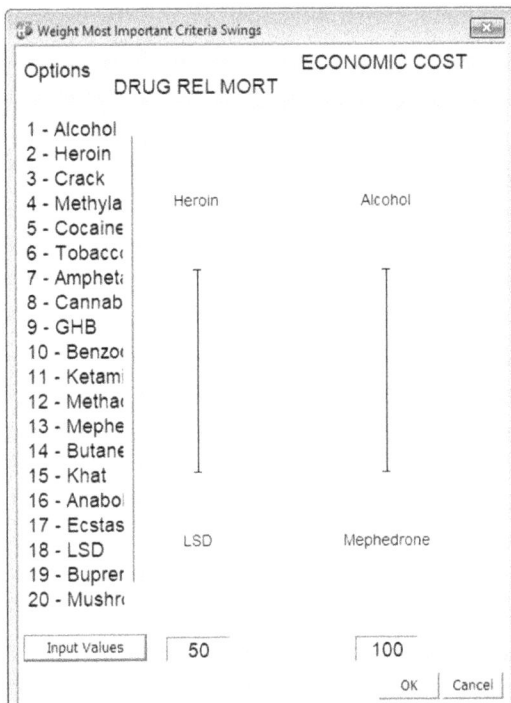

Figure 13.19

final trade-off assessment of the worst harm to users, drug-related mortality, compared to the worst harm to others, economic cost. Yes, LSD and mephedrone were both judged to be no harm on these criteria. So, the operative question was, 'How important is drug-related mortality to users of heroin, compared to the economic cost to others of alcohol?'

As I said above, participants considered harm to be two factors: the extent of the harm and the number of people affected, largely because harm studies include both. The group judged that death to the users from causes related to but not caused directly by heroin was about half as important as the economic cost to others from the misuse of alcohol (noting that the annual costs to the National Health Service in England and Wales were many billions of pounds sterling). The weights of 50 and 100 were agreed. The final result of this model was shown in Figure 11.2 (p. 188), and endnote 148 of Chapter 11, which contains details of the 2010 paper published in *The Lancet*.

Gap Analysis

By 2008, NATO's Allied Command Transformation (ACT) had identified 52 capabilities that could be improved in the medium to long term, and engaged me to help them prioritise products that could contribute to closing the capability gaps and improving the key capabilities. The prioritisation should also help to determine whether the allocation of ACT's budget should be broad and shallow or narrow and deep. With the help of Mara Airoldi, I facilitated a two-day decision conference in which 50 capabilities, each represented as a criterion under one of five objectives, were scored for the extent to which the capability added value to achieve a mission through effectiveness and interoperability (among the armed forces of all member countries).

The scoring was based on the 10-point scale shown in Figure 13.20.

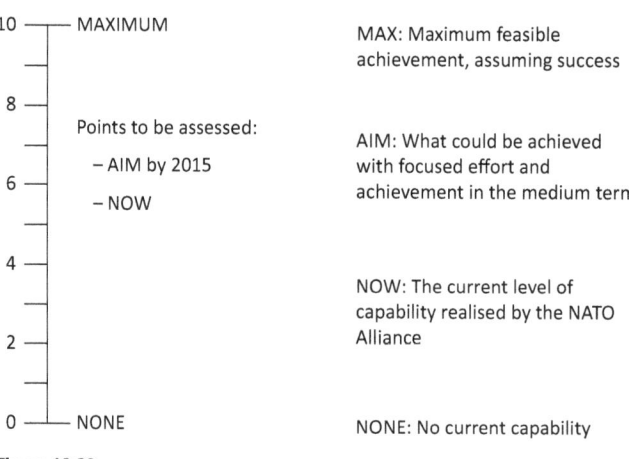

Figure 13.20

Each of the 50 capabilities was defined by a participant who was representing each criterion to let everyone know what the capability meant, whether that capability was wholly lacking, and what the definition of MAX should be. The discussion that followed defined where NATO was NOW and where it realistically could AIM to be by 2015. After scoring occurred at each node's criteria, relative weights were assessed as everyone could remember the best and worst scores on each of the criteria under that node, with at least one weight of 100 assigned under each node. After all criteria had been weighted, then the 100s across nodes were compared. The computer then calculated all the weighted scores.

A final sort of the weighted scores across all 50 criteria between AIM and NOW suggested which were most important capabilities in the short run, while a sort between MAX and NOW showed which capabilities should be prepared for in the long run.

In general, this gap analysis has proved useful when a senior decision maker needs assistance to discover why his or her sense of unease even exists. For example, one stratum 5 company's MD called a meeting of his stratum 4 directors along with their stratum 3 managers (who, you will recall from Chapter 8, are the managers of the company's direct product and service outputs, so are best informed about what is happening at the coal face) to carry out a gap analysis of all the major outputs. It didn't take long to discover where the weaknesses were, and what could most quickly be fixed. In one case, a health-care company discovered that marketing had managed to create bespoke insurance offers to a great many different kinds of customers, which made it easy to sell health insurance, but had overwhelmed the company's administration as the conditions in every product had been different, making it difficult to process all claims without making errors.

Large Projects

The case studies described here were sufficiently small projects that they could be completed within two days. But what changes for large projects, especially those with many criteria, and diverse expertise where a single meeting would be impractical as well as boring to those whose expertise is only required for a portion of the model? This was very much the case for the UK Government's Committee on Radioactive Waste Management (CoRWM), whose charge in 2003 was to recommend a long-term solution to the management of the UK's high-level and intermediate-level radioactive waste, and that the process of reviewing the options was to be open, transparent and inclusive, and should 'inspire public confidence'.

The committee commissioned a public stakeholder survey to identify issues and concerns, from which they generated several scenarios and eventually agreed on six storage options and three deep-disposal options for dealing with high-level waste. The MCDA model that my Catalyze colleagues and I helped the group to build required separate workshops over several months for teams of specialists who were knowledgeable about each of the 11 objectives and the 26 criteria, and later to score the options on the criteria. The Committee completed the model in a three-day decision conference early in 2006 by assessing weights and revising them as they were checked for consistency, exploring the model in sensitivity analyses, including examining all disagreements among members (none changed the overall results). The model helped to back up the 15 recommendations the committee forwarded to the government in July 2006, all but three of which were accepted. Since then, the search for a deep disposal repository location, which was a key recommendation, continues under the guidance of the Nuclear Decommissioning Agency, and many CoRWMs have been overseeing their work.

The point here is that MCDA models are not limited in their numbers of options and criteria, at least in theory. But to mobilise all the expertise required for creating the structure, obtaining data and eliciting judgements requires many meetings of workshops to prepare the model, with a final decision conference attended by those accountable for making recommendations. Producing a requisite model can be difficult as interest spreads about the ongoing model development and it becomes tempting to incorporate more and more issues, as this can lead to serious over-modelling in which the latest addition cannot possibly have any impact on the outcome. Sometimes that extra step has to be taken to prove it isn't necessary before the model can be simplified to make it requisite.

Summary

The focus of this chapter has been the modelling of value in achieving objectives, with different options working alone or together to achieve all the objectives, which may conflict with one another. The five-step process elaborated here for the first case study showed how to frame the problem by discussing the context and key issues, construct a value tree, score the options, weight the criteria, examine the results, conduct sensitivity analyses and agree what to do next. Interval scales in the first case study and ratio scales in the second demonstrated how the context of each study suggested which type of scale to use.

The women's shampoo case study served as a transitional object for the MD as the MCDA model shifted his sense of unease about answering a critique from his organisation's head office to a different issue, that the current allocation of resources to three functions could be improved. The anxiety arising from that recognition was literally held overnight as he and his staff constructed a resource allocation model described in the next chapter.

The Benlysta case study illustrated how probabilities can be included in an MCDA, which takes advantage of the unitless feature of both probabilities and weights, either of which can multiply by values; the computer doesn't know which is being used. The model served as a transitional object enabling the two EMA rapporteurs to agree on a recommendation in their final report.

The two case studies also showed how comparing pairs of options quickly and graphically can clarify the key differences in achieving objectives.

The third case study illustrated the concept of negative value, or disvalue, in the form of the harm of drugs, along with ratio scales, in a model of 20 drugs and 16 harm criteria, a matrix of 320 cells, every one of which required a disvalue score that was assessed by a group of specialists who were experts in drug harm. Development of the model served as a transitional object while diverse experts engaged collectively in scoring and weighting based almost entirely on their collective experience and very little hard data. It continues to serve as a transitional object and the original UK model serves as a template for replications in other countries with different teams of experts. Even though each country's results are different in ways that appear to reflect different cultures of drug use, high correlations for drugs held in common confirm the validity of MCDA for modelling the harm of drugs.

All three required the facilitator to consider whether an interval or ratio scale is required for each criterion; whether measured input data is to be converted to preference values directly or indirectly; and whether the conversion is linear or non-linear. Get any one of these wrong even for just one criterion, and the final results will most likely not look quite right to participants in a decision conference, and possibly to you.

As recently as 2022, I unintentionally chose the inverse function in Hiview3 for just one criterion, and it stopped work for about three months on the project until one of the participants figured out what had gone wrong. Since then, as a final step in creating a model, I review the Criteria Details in Hiview3 with the group to ensure that each criterion scale is labelled with the correct name for the input metric, that 0 and 100 are properly defined, whether the inverse box is ticked, and that the criterion value function is correct, either the default linear or defined properly as a piecewise function. The review only takes a few minutes, but is time well spent.

This chapter lays the foundation for the next chapter, which looks at creating portfolios of options across different budget categories that will make the best use of the available resources.

14   Allocate Resources

Action expresses priorities.

Mahatma Gandhi[185]

Priorities imply objectives, so prioritisation will be difficult when objectives conflict, the future is uncertain and trade-offs must be made, all of which were discussed in the previous chapter. There we dealt with comparisons of options that are all of the same sort, but now we broaden the discussion to options that are of different sorts and are brought together to form a *portfolio* that best meets the objectives for the available resources. In short, a value-for-money portfolio. Once again, the five-step process is applied.

Women's Shampoo Portfolio Analysis

Let's see how MCDA was applied to creating such a portfolio on the second day of a decision conference about the women's shampoo problem introduced at the start of Chapter 13. If you skipped that chapter, look at the short summary in Chapter 11's 'Allocate Resources' section.

1.   Consider Context

Resource allocation differs from simply comparing options, which was the topic of the first day's decision conference. The key task for the second day was to represent the value for money of each option with a right-angled triangle whose vertical axis is a value (or, as we will see later, risk-adjusted value) and horizontal base is cost, with the slope of the hypotenuse distinguishing the better and worse options – the steeper, the better. The objectives of growth, leadership and profit were adopted in the second day of the women's shampoo decision conference, together defining the overall benefit, which when divided by cost gave a single measure of value for money for each option.

2.   Frame the Problem

First, we identified the *areas* that define the resources, in this case, Distribution, Promotion and Advertising. A separate MCDA model was to be created within each

5		+ nationwide
4	Nationwide	Increase frequency
3	SQ, quicker & better	Heavy sampling	SQ: 80% area
2	SQ: 60%	SQ: sample, price off	Cut back freq only
1	Fewer areas	None	Cut back area & freq
	DISTRIBUTION		ADVERTISING
		PROMOTION	

Figure 14.1

area, such that the options within an area are all the same type, but different from options in the other areas. The group then engaged in creating the options for the areas. The structure shown in Figure 14.1 was created with the computer program Equity3. The first area considered was Distribution and I asked what defined the current strategy, which was described as covering 60 per cent of the areas in the country. I explained that for each area, we would start with the lowest level feasible for that area, and the group agreed it would be possible to cover fewer areas, probably focusing on just the larger cities. 'What would you do with more resource devoted to distribution than now?' I asked. 'We would do it quicker and better,' came the reply. 'And if you had even more resource?' I asked, 'Definitely go nationwide,' was agreed.

The resulting options were considered in Equity3 as incremental; starting at level 1, each an increment in preference value over the previous area. It is also possible for options to be independent as they were in the previous chapter's case studies. However, it was clear to me from the start that all these options needed to be incremental, some requiring less resource, others more. Once areas have been defined, Equity3 requires defining all levels for a given area as either all incremental *or* independent of one another because, as I'll explain later, scoring is different for each. However, an Equity model can include a mixture of incremental and independent areas, just not both in a single area.

Promotion was easier, with a modest expenditure on samples accompanied by a price off on the first purchase, but heavy sampling if more resources were available. Advertising currently reached 80 per cent of the country, with the most cutback aimed at both area and frequency, but preferably only a cutback of frequency.

Just making all this explicit, with the help of the managers of the three areas, revealed some potential combinations that didn't make much sense, like advertising to 80 per cent of the country, yet only distributing to 60 per cent. When each manager defended the current expenditure, it became clear that their reasons were good, but engaged different objectives, so I asked the group to think about a set of objectives that could be shared in evaluating all the options. The group easily suggested the first three objectives from the previous day, growth, leadership and profits, all defined by yesterday's criteria.

3.   Provide Content

Scoring began by considering Costs and Benefits for the distribution area. The current five-year budget across the three areas was 23 million (in the currency of that country), 10 million for the status quo (SQ), distributing to 60 per cent of the country's areas. The MD suggested shaving off 2 million for level 1, fewer areas, and adding 2 million for each of the higher-cost levels. The group then scored the benefits, using the familiar 100 and 0 representing most and least preferred levels, respectively (Figure 14.2).

Consistency checks compared differences in scores with one another, for example, that the 30-point differences on the growth criterion between levels 2 and 3 truly represented twice the difference between 1 and 2, and three times as much as the 10-point difference between levels 3 and 4. Confirmed. However, note that going nationwide was judged to be the worst level for profit, which defined the least preferred position because even with fewer areas profit would be reasonably good. These are interval scales, so zero doesn't necessarily mean no benefit. The group then turned to scoring for promotion and advertising. The results are shown in Figure 14.3.

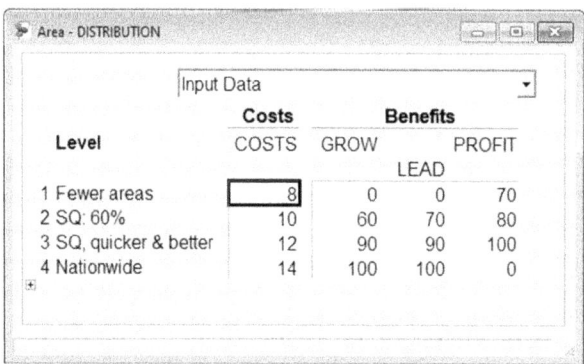

Figure 14.2

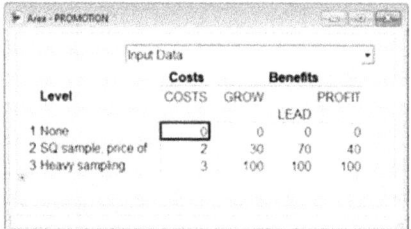
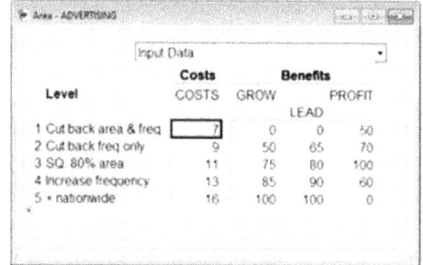

Figure 14.3

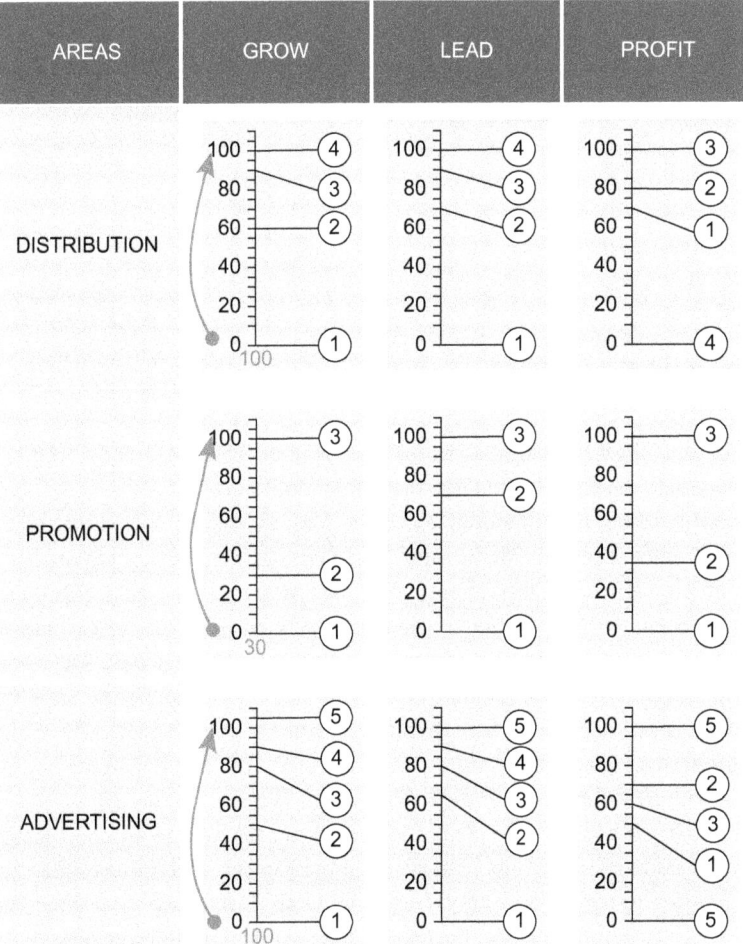

Figure 14.4

With scoring complete, I explained that with three 0–100 scales in three areas, we have nine scales that do not necessarily represent equal differences in preferences, therefore two different sets of weights are required to complete the model, not just between the criteria, but also between the three areas. Figure 14.4 shows all nine scales.

Within-Criterion Weights compare the three area scales under the same criterion. The group started by comparing the swings on the three GROW scales, as indicated by the red arrows. (To show the three scales in Equity, double click on the GROW scale in each of the three Area Input Data tables and display the thermometers on the screen side by side.) The group considered which of the three swings is the largest, and decided it was a toss-up between distribution and advertising, so gave each a weight of 100, then judged the swing for the promotion scale compared to (either) 100 to be 30. These three weights were entered into Equity's Edit Weighs chart, shown in Figure 14.5. The group repeated this process for the three LEAD scales, and again

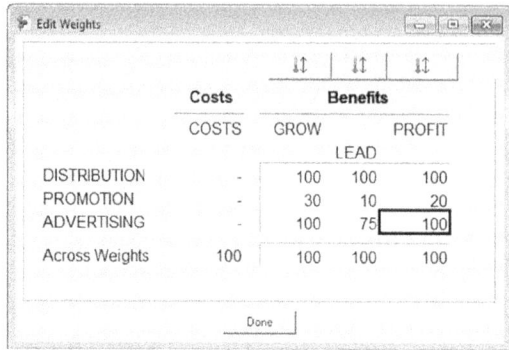

Figure 14.5

for the PROFIT scales. After swing weights for LEAD and PROFIT scales were assessed, the chart looked like that shown in Figure 14.5.

Remember that all these weights are scale constants; they ensure that the weighted preference values are all the same unit. Thus, an increment of any size means the same value for any of the three areas, *given* the criterion. If instead of PROFIT, the criterion had been NPV, expressed in that country's currency, Equity would automatically rescale the financial values proportionally into 0–100 scales. The weights can then be assessed by the program, as the input monetary figures were all the same unit for each area.[i] However, here human judgement must supply the weights. And in Figure 14.6 the weights just assessed are displayed along with the original scales.

The 100s for Across Weights in the Edit Weights display are default values, so the next step was to assess them. These compare the Within-criterion weights of 100 in each column across the criteria. If they all occur in the same area, that makes the question to participants easy. Here, DISTRIBUTION achieved three 100s, so I said, 'For distribution, consider the added value in going from fewer areas to nationwide for growth and for leadership. Which is larger?'

The group agreed it was definitely growth, and commented that leadership was comparatively small, so I then asked the group to compare that difference for growth with the difference for profit between nationwide and the status quo, quicker and better. Again, they opted for growth, and said the profit difference is small, like the leadership difference. Finally, the group agreed across weights of 100–10–10.

That's difficult to think about, and I assume you took some time to follow the above comparison of three differences two at a time, which actually is exactly as done in Hiview treating distribution as a single model. However, usually the 100s fall in different areas, and that's a brain-bender because participants are required to compare 0–100 differences in different areas. But if you always use paired comparisons, then it's possible to display the original scores for the two areas and compare the relevant scales, looking for the largest difference to establish which across-criterion weight should be 100 so the others can be compared individually to that 100.

---

[i] By simply clicking on the up-and-down arrow above the NPV criterion in Equity's Edit Weights display.

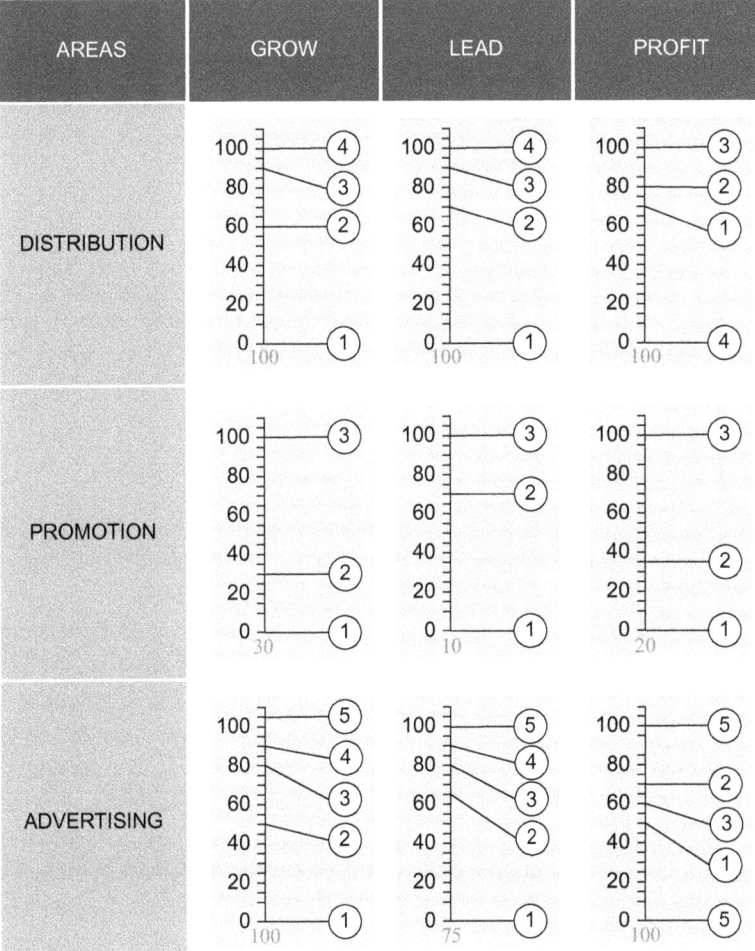

Figure 14.6

This process of comparing swing weights is effectively establishing trade-offs between areas, which ensures that the double weighting process equates units across both the criteria and the areas.

The first step for you to develop clarity about the difference between within-criterion and across-criteria weights is to construct this model for yourself, and work your way through it. As this isn't a case study you own, it's difficult to imagine why some weights should be larger than others, but participants who understand swing weighting will often pitch in with the right questions. You may need to re-read the above several times to ensure you understand that within-criterion weighting means holding the criterion fixed while you make judgements from one area to the next. And that across-criteria weighting means making judgements across the largest within-criterion weights, which are often across different areas, but could be all in the same area.

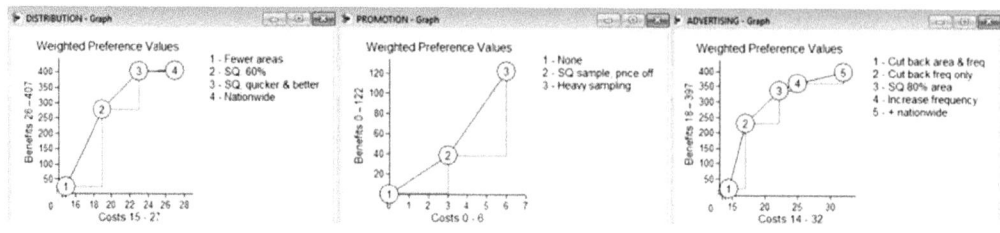

Figure 14.7

Of course, this whole process of weighting in resource allocation models could be made easier with paired comparisons incorporated in a wizard for Equity; let's hope that someone does that in the future.

4.   Explore Results

Equity now computes a triangle from the doubly weighted, summed benefits for the vertical side of the triangle and the costs on the horizontal side, so a steeper hypotenuse represents the value for money of each option (Figure 14.7).

For distribution, doing it quicker and better looks good, but going nationwide doesn't at all; the triangle is almost flat. For promotion, the slope for heavy sampling is better than for the SQ, so either do that or not at all. The slope for cutting back the frequency only of advertising is the best slope of all, but the slope to the status quo doesn't look as good as the best slopes in the first two areas. The computer then starts at level 1 in each area, and chooses triangles in order of decreasing slope, stacking them to the right of each other, whose upper surface in the left figure is the *efficient frontier*, the convex curve at the top showing the tips of the triangles as dots (Figure 14.8).

Once all the feasible options for the three areas are stacked in one graph, it is possible to show the *Order of Priority* (OoP), with level 1 the starting point in the lower-left corner, followed by the triangles in order of their slopes. Equity facilitates doing this one step at a time, and each of the area 'owners' participating in the modelling becomes engrossed in seeing how many of their options are higher priority than the others, a sort of race to the top. It's easy to see that the last three are the flat triangles in distribution and advertising.

Also of interest is where the status quo sits. The computer adds the weighted benefits and costs of the SQ and shows them as a point that here falls below the efficient frontier at point P. The right-hand image in Figure 14.8 shows a better B package at about the same cost as the SQ, and a cheaper C package at about the same benefit as the SQ, so it is clear the SQ can be improved.

5.   Agree the Way Forward

After discussing these results with the participants, and using the software to try out a new strategy, we found another package that was almost on the efficient curve, slightly to the left of B and below it, but allowed for some cutback in advertising and heavy sampling.

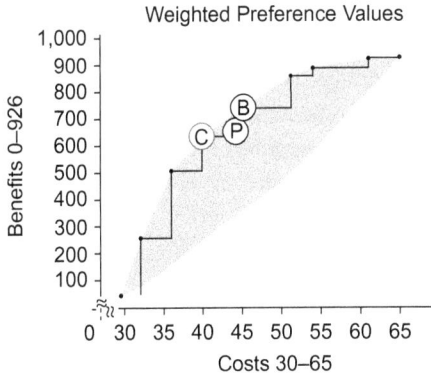

Figure 14.8

The MD then pointed to the two advertising agency participants, who attended the decision conference as observers, and told them their budgets were cut by 10 per cent and asked them to put forward proposals to accomplish the reduction. He then turned to the promotion manager and said his budget was doubled and he was to submit a new promotion campaign within two weeks. Finally, he asked the distribution manager to put forward a new plan for quicker and better distribution. Within the month, all strategies had been implemented.

Normally, some time would elapse to allow for reflection and perhaps further exploration of the model. But the urgency of responding to the criticism of head office required a response soon. The managing director, an American who had been in the country for only six months, admitted that he had underestimated the importance of distribution in the country, and that the existing networks, which he could use, were very effective. In addition, the decision conference format enabled full discussion of the issues for each of the three functions, regardless of seniority, which allowed the managers to propose new ideas without being disrespectful to the MD, an important consideration in the country's culture.

***

This case study well illustrates the role of computer programs as transitional objects. The women's shampoo Hiview model in Chapter 13 enabled the MD to safely explore new ideas as it held several options in abeyance while he considered advantages and disadvantages of pairs of options and could see how they related to one another in a Benefit versus Cost space. This led to his insight that perhaps a better allocation of resources among distribution, promotion and advertising could be devised. The Equity model of this chapter provided time for the group to bring their expertise about the three activities to invent new options for each, followed by the whole group assessing trade-offs between the areas and the criteria, and exploring alternative strategies.

Although the computer holds all the structure and numerical inputs, it also puts the elements together by applying some simple mathematics, literally 'handing back in changed form' what it has already been told, so it is an *active* transitional object, much like a human expert who listens carefully and then acts as a sage in suggesting something useful and perhaps unexpected. Indeed, sometimes a participant will disagree, arguing that what the computer says is wrong. I remind the group that the computer isn't saying anything, it is just reflecting back the logical consequences of what it has been given by the group. And that can begin a fruitful examination of why these particular results were obtained, which often leads to an 'Ah-ha, now I see!' reaction as new insights are forthcoming, but can also provide justification for changes in the model as the group realises some things need changing. Of course, increases or decreases in weights can lead to results that are unexpected in other parts of the model because the computer renormalises all the weights to accommodate the change in a single weight. Thus, it is difficult to change a weight to get the result someone wants.

Although this real project was small and provides an understandable introduction to the fundamentals of portfolio analysis, you might well wonder if it is manageable for large portfolios. The answer is yes, particularly when many areas or budget categories are required, which characterises the next two case studies, but it isn't always easy. The first is about research and development portfolios of projects, and the second concerns the design of a new system, a warship, that must be capable of performing many functions. Indeed, Equity was originally called Design, as it helped an organisation to design a new combined office, warehouse and distribution system, much to the annoyance of the architects, as they and the client working together, in a decision conference facilitated by an impartial outside facilitator, found ways to substantially improve the architect's design.

It is mainly the social processes of applying the portfolio technology that distinguish complex applications of prioritisation, as illustrated by the next two studies here, both of which have been published in some detail. Here, the focus is on how to manage the complexity arising from ownership of different parts of the model by very different stakeholders and experts, and how collective working can be organised to ensure that the right participants are developing the right parts of the model at the right time. In addition, several technical issues that arise especially in large problems will be introduced, with suggestions about how they can be resolved.

Project Prioritisation in Research and Development

It was the MD's sense of unease about how to respond to his head office's criticism that he was spending too much on advertising, a question of resource allocation, that only half-way through the decision conference turned into a problem about prioritising the allocation among advertising, promotion and distribution. And you may have noticed from the Order of Priority that he didn't exactly follow it: although he chose quicker and better distribution, he cut back on advertising and chose heavy sampling, choices that better fitted the culture of the country, a 'softer' objective that hadn't been explicitly included in the model.

In general, the action of allocating resources follows from the process of prioritisation, as Mahatma Gandhi said more eloquently. But none of the organisations I have worked with modelling priorities ever slavishly follows the Order of Priority as there are always many more practical restraints and soft objectives left out of the model because it would have been too tedious to include them.

Modelling everything is a waste of time because all that is needed for decision makers to do their job is a requisite model. This is especially true for prioritisation and resource allocation models. In your initial contact with a client, if you ask them at some point what they think the problem is, you may be told that they have too many projects and too few resources, or that their organisation needs to find a better way to allocate a limited budget, or that cutbacks are needed to reverse falling revenues, or they need to reprioritise their projects and so forth, none of which enables you to be very clear about how you might be able to help.

That's because we don't have in English good ways for expressing the meaning of project prioritisation. My daughter-in-law is a manager of projects, which means she is in charge of several project managers, each of whom is accountable for managing one or more projects. She and they get on with doing stuff, which means creating plans and following them, adjusting and rearranging as obstacles require changes to the plans so they can accomplish the tasks that will achieve the objectives they are pursuing. The decision analyst's language of prioritisation and resource allocation just isn't used.

Definitions

So, let's back up and first agree on four key terms: task, project, area and portfolio. I've used task well over 100 times so far in this book, assuming its ordinary meaning of a piece of work to be completed within a limited time. For our purposes, we need to be more specific and expand it:

Task: An assignment to produce a specified output by a targeted completion time, with sufficient allocated resources and by applying adequate methods, all within prescribed limits.[186]

Project: Work to create or modify a particular product or service that has well-defined start and finish times, along with the resources required to complete the work, and with the authority to do the work.

Area: A budget category composed of projects that are in some way similar, but different in kind from projects in other areas.

Portfolio: Any collection of projects across areas, along with the authority to provide resources to complete the projects.

This paints a picture of an organisation in which staff at all levels are carrying out tasks to meet well-specified goals, with project managers accountable for doing their best in assigning tasks to subordinates to achieve the desired outputs, and managers of portfolios of projects held accountable for the outputs of the project managers, for example, Chapter 8's requisite organisation.

This may seem rather obviously needed, but I once encountered the R&D division of an organisation that simply hired scientists to get on with the job of developing new products. They had no well-defined projects, just tasks, let alone records of what percentages of time their scientists spent on each of the assigned tasks. They were keen to make the development process more efficient, but it took them about a year to redefine tasks into projects, cost the projects and assign accountabilities for projects, with the most senior person given authority over the portfolio.

That is one difficulty you may encounter, but hopefully it will be rare. Here's another, the manager who says, 'Projects are easy to prioritise', and explains how it is done in just five steps:

1. List all the projects in one column.
2. Calculate the net present value (NPV)[ii] (or any other index of performance) for each project and enter it next to the projects in a second column.
3. Calculate the forward cost of each project and enter it in a third column.
4. Sort the projects from highest NPV to lowest.
5. Starting with the highest-NPV project, go down the list accepting each project until the total cost exceeds the budget.

That's it. A portfolio emerges that uses all the available resource. But is it the best use of the resource? Absolutely not!

The Priority Index

A better way to prioritise requires answering three questions for each project:

1. What is the project's benefit, assuming it is successful?
2. How probable is the project's success?
3. What is the forward cost of the project?

If the answer to any of the questions is, 'I don't know', then the next question might be, 'So why are you doing the project?' The questions also apply to projects that are being considered, for if they are to be included in the portfolio analysis, then to avoid thinking the grass is greener on the other side of the fence, some attempt to answer those three questions is required. The answers provide inputs for the Priority Index, first introduced in the 'Allocate Resources' section in Chapter 12.

$$Priority\ Index,\ PI = \frac{Benefit \times Probability\ of\ Success}{Cost}.$$

In working with clients, it's better to draw the triangle shown in Figure 14.9 on a flip-chart, displayed throughout the modelling process, emphasising that eventually every project will be described by a single triangle. Indeed, I've often reminded participants to think of the process we're going through as creating a triangle for each project, for as research or development proceeds, changes to any of those three quantities can affect a project's priority. 'Become accustomed to thinking in triangles', I advise.

[ii] Defined in the section 'Means and End Objectives' at the start of Chapter 4, also known as discounted cash flow (DCF) models. Further, read there the critique of DCF models.

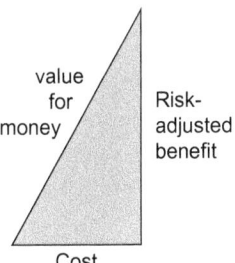

Figure 14.9

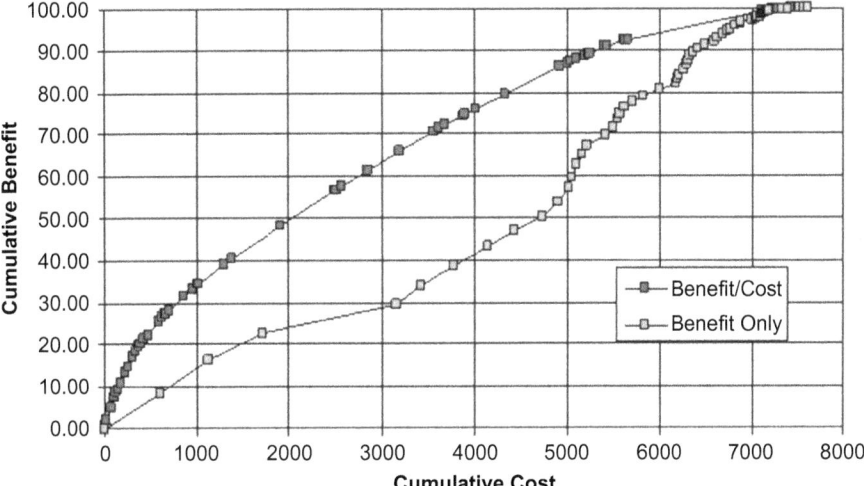

Figure 14.10

One project for a UK Government department always prioritised their projects on the basis of benefits. I've shown in the chart in Figure 14.10 that this always provides less value for money than prioritising by the priority index. The projects as originally ordered by benefit only are shown by the lower line graph, while the upper line graph shows the same projects reordered by the benefit/cost ratio (assuming all would be successful and with costs in thousands of pounds sterling). Only the hypotenuse for each triangle is shown to avoid clutter.

You can see that if the budget is limited to £5 million, then the first 11 projects on the lower benefits-only curve absorb that cost, obtaining about 60 per cent of the benefit of the upper curve projects if all of them up to that half-million point were chosen. Note that the fourth project on the lower curve, with its gentle slope, defines the costliest project, which also shows at the upper right of the top curve. Participants insisted that project was statutorily required, but at least that kind of insistence, often argued by civil servants, can begin to be challenged by insisting on 'thinking in triangles'.

In short, a lot of costly projects with high benefits absorb so much resource that the low-hanging fruit, projects that are very low cost with low benefits, appear at the upper right of the benefits-only curve. Some critics argue this is a bias of the PI method, but my counterargument is that the current allocation is biased towards big, impressive projects which can be publicised and used as evidence that the organisation is doing its job. My evidence for that is that after helping Allergan prioritise its development portfolio over several years, the low-hanging fruit of the early years almost completely disappeared in later years. Anyway, whether this is a bias or not, a benefits-only curve *always* lies below the benefit/cost curve.

Another reason to avoid defining benefit as a single quantity is that there is no reliable figure, financial or non-financial, that defines benefit. A very popular one is NPV for commercial organisations, and good practice requires modelling the key assumptions using event trees with probabilities, so the output will be a probability distribution of NPV. But this may well be greeted by senior management with a frosty, 'Don't give me probabilities, I want a single figure!' If the mean is then suggested, it might be followed by, 'Think again, and provide a better figure.'

Some organisations require that any investment must make a return of at least 8 per cent, or some other figure. You can then bet that internal staff will do their best to find a set of plausible assumptions that yield the required figure. I'm not making up these two reasons; I've encountered both in my consultancy practice, especially with large organisations whose senior executives are so busy they don't have the time or competence to look at the assumptions, and it is well known that the results of discounted cash flow models are very sensitive to the assumptions.

As I pointed out in Chapter 4, there is good reason not to rely on a single criterion when prioritising projects. Actually, the bias towards financial models is simply that many organisations don't have any processes in place for incorporating non-financial objectives, and when I explain that decision-analytic models can incorporate any combination of different types of criteria, they become interested. For example, in one major pharmaceutical company, the president of marketing insisted on NPVs as inputs to the company's annual development portfolio model, while the president of R&D required application of their unmet medical need algorithm, so both were included in a portfolio model and given equal weight. Today's clients welcome this flexibility and make good use of it.

Silo Decision Making

Perhaps you are now wondering if it isn't easier for senior management to review a portfolio periodically and make some changes by reducing resources from the projects that are coming along less well and allocating it to the projects that appear to be progressing well, thus speeding up the time to success. In many companies, that's known as *silo decision making*: you let each project manager do their best with the available resources, rewarding the more promising projects with some additional resource at the expense of the weaker projects. That keeps the project managers reasonably happy, mildly disappointing the losers, but rewarding the winners suffi-ciently to keep the enterprise moving forward. But is that the case? Let me show you a real case that calls this into serious question, to the extent that a senior executive

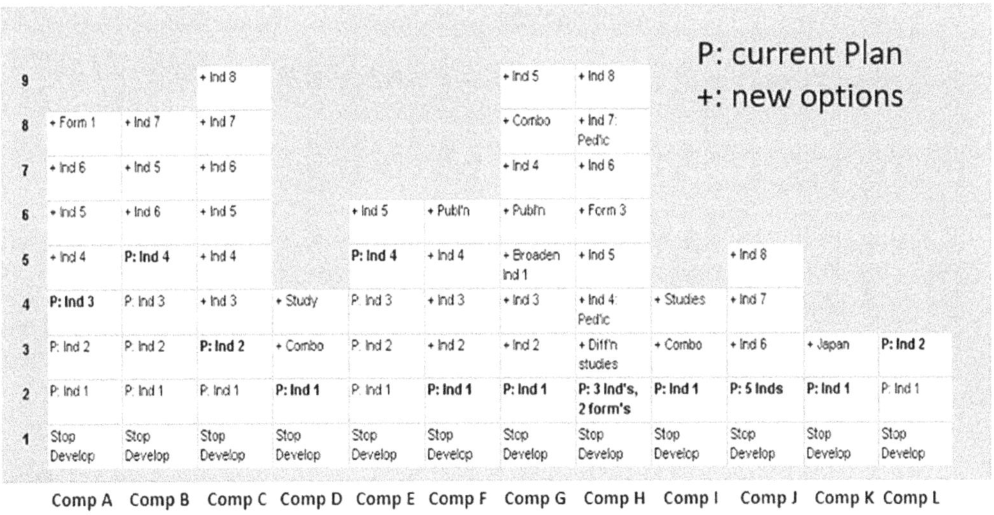

P: current Plan
+: new options

	Comp A	Comp B	Comp C	Comp D	Comp E	Comp F	Comp G	Comp H	Comp I	Comp J	Comp K	Comp L
9		+ Ind 8					+ Ind 5	+ Ind 8				
8	+ Form 1	+ Ind 7	+ Ind 7				+ Combo	+ Ind 7: Ped'ic				
7	+ Ind 6	+ Ind 5	+ Ind 6				+ Ind 4	+ Ind 6				
6	+ Ind 5	+ Ind 6	+ Ind 5		+ Ind 5	+ Publ'n	+ Publ'n	+ Form 3				
5	+ Ind 4	P: Ind 4	+ Ind 4		P: Ind 4	+ Ind 4	+ Broaden Ind 1	+ Ind 5		+ Ind 8		
4	P: Ind 3	P: Ind 3	+ Ind 3	+ Study	P: Ind 3	+ Ind 3	+ Ind 3	+ Ind 4: Ped'ic	+ Studies	+ Ind 7		
3	P: Ind 2	P: Ind 2	P: Ind 2	+ Combo	P: Ind 2	+ Ind 2	+ Ind 2	+ Diff'n studies	+ Combo	+ Ind 6	+ Japan	P: Ind 2
2	P: Ind 1	P: Ind 1	P: Ind 1	P: Ind 1	P: Ind 1	P: Ind 1	P: Ind 1	P: 3 Ind's, 2 form's	P: Ind 1	P: 5 Inds	P: Ind 1	P: Ind 1
1	Stop Develop	Stop Develop	Stop Develop	Stop Develop	Stop Develop	Stop Develop	Stop Develop	Stop Develop	Stop Develop	Stop Develop	Stop Develop	Stop Develop

Figure 14.11

wishing to make the best use of the available resource will never do this 'salami slicing' again.

The Equity3 *cityscape* in Figure 14.11 shows 12 areas, whose real names are *compounds* that a pharmaceutical company's research division created and tested in early development research to ensure they are safe and well handled by the patient's body, and have the potential to be developed to treat one or more specific human medical conditions. All the white blocks in each area are *projects*. Most projects are defined by the medical condition it is intended to treat, namely, an indication, as it's known in medical parlance, and a compound might be considered for any number of indications.

Projects identified with a 'P' are currently being developed, but those with just a '+' are new possibilities. And projects other than indications are possible, which includes a new formulation of the drug, a new study, a combination with another drug, a paediatric indication or even a new market in Japan, and so forth. Note that level 1 is to stop development, which provides a level playing field against which all projects will be judged.

To summarise, areas are compounds and options are projects, except for level 1. This case study will now be further developed using the terminology of the pharmaceutical company. The levels in all areas are cumulative in Equity3, but at the end I'll say more about the structure as Equity provides more capability than is needed in this case study.

After scoring and weighting the options in each area, they were ordered by applying the PI. The ordering for Compound A is shown in Figure 14.12.

It's clear that current indications (levels 2, 3 and 4) are best, then there is a kink in the curve, with the remaining projects showing less good slopes, and the level 8 a project to develop a new formulation (way of entering the body) for the compound,

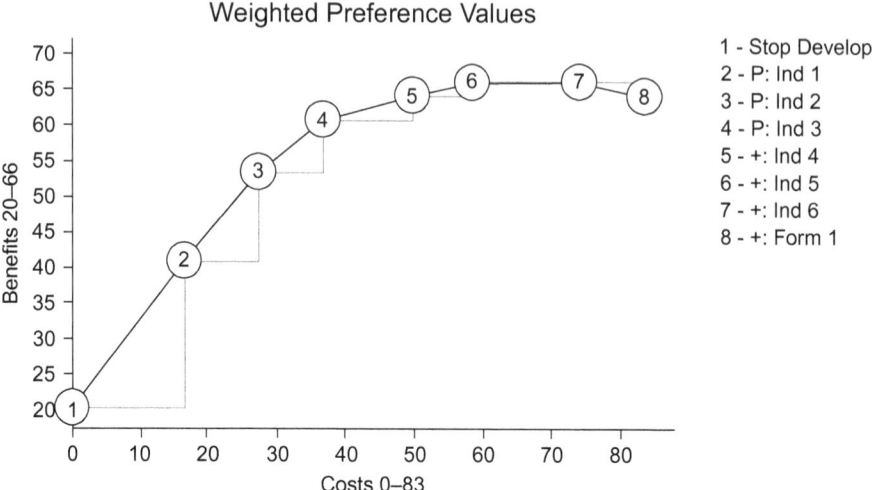

Figure 14.12

showing a negative slope, indicating that the risk of that project outweighs the benefits (more about how that can happen later).

However, applying the PI changed the ordering for several other areas. For example, the original ordering for compound B, as shown in the cityscape by the numbering of the indications, was slightly modified; the PI for indication 6 PI is better than that for 5.

Now let's look more closely at where the current plan falls. The computer adds the costs and also the weighted benefits of all the planned P projects and plots that point at the circled P (in Figure 14.13), but it also shows a better portfolio B at about the same cost, and a cheaper one at about the same benefit at C. Therefore, any portfolio within the darker area is both better and cheaper than the current plan.

But does that matter? Indeed, it does. B shows 35 per cent more benefit than P, which in terms of probability weighted NPV, one of the benefit criteria, is *1.023 billion US dollars*! That's equivalent to a blockbuster drug hidden away in the inefficient use of the resources currently spent on its existing P portfolio. This is one of four times I have encountered a gap of more than a billion dollars in any project prioritisation. However, in a survey of my decision conference reports to clients, one of my master's degree students found considerable variability in the P-to-B difference, and the average was 25 to 30 per cent. However, the graph in Figure 14.13 is a typical result, even for smaller financial values.

How is it that so many organisations do not use their available resources more wisely? Perhaps it is the way accountabilities are defined. The R&D executive would be held accountable for providing a pipeline of medicinal products that will gain approval, while the Marketing and Sales (M&S) executive would be held accountable for maximising the income, and the Operations executive for manufacturing at the lowest cost that maintains quality and safety. Nothing is said directly about the *portfolio* of products. But some Chief Executive Officers (CEOs) recognise that they

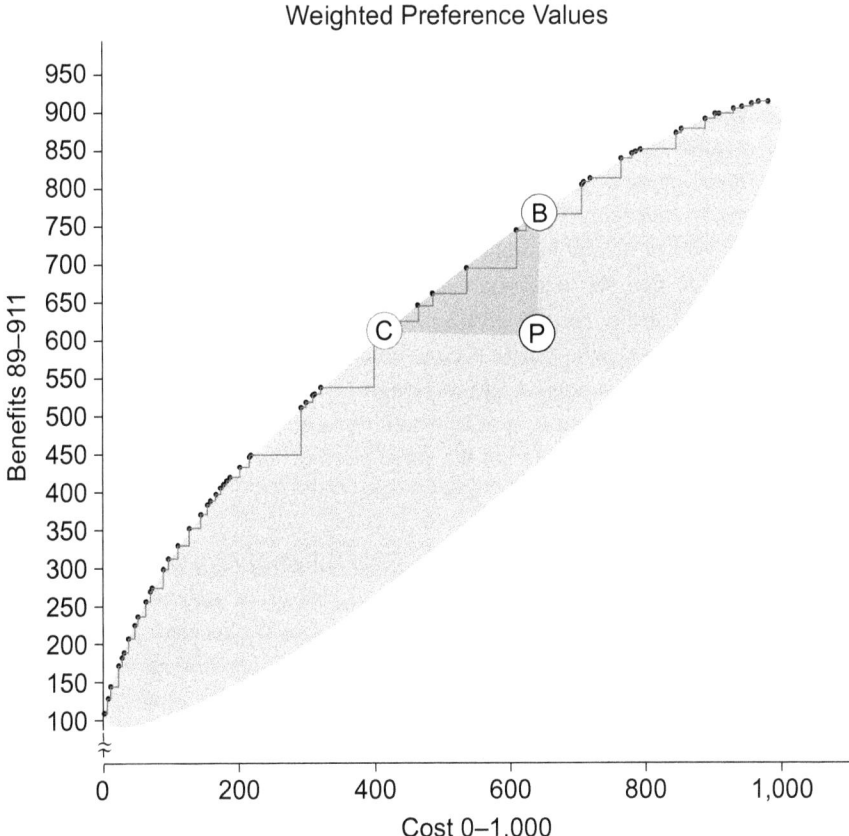

Figure 14.13

are accountable to the company's Board for the performance of the portfolio, although they rarely attend the final decision conference meeting, a *merge meeting*, that brings together the work on the individual projects to assess the within criterion and across criteria weights that determine the efficient frontier. Consequently, both the R&D and M&S executives attend, where value for the former is how well each product realises unmet medical need, and the latter thinks more in terms of NPV, with both those criteria included in the model, along with others, as defined here later.

An additional problem is known as the *commons dilemma*, a term proposed by Garrett Hardin in 1963, entitled *The Tragedy of the Commons*, which describes a situation when farmers' herds are grazing on common land and each individual farmer considers it makes economic sense to add more cattle to their herd without considering that can cause overgrazing, definitely not in their collective best interests.[187] Present-day examples are over-fishing in parts of the world, water shortages in the southwest of the USA and even traffic jams. In organisations, this over-use of resources can arise from the existence of fiefdoms, as managers protect their organisational units, and lack of accountability, as small groups of people research and develop projects outside agreed objectives.

However, even if all project managers are doing their best with the resources they have been allocated, it will still not be collectively best. That was very much so in the above case study, for prior to the MCDA portfolio model, resources were granted to each project to ensure its continued existence, a salami-slicing process that spreads the available resource among all projects too thinly. That is a top-down approach to maintaining control over the budget, but with many projects and options for each, no senior manager or executive can be expected to understand the details sufficiently to find the best combinations of projects.

You can see that establishing accountability for projects is not the same as accountability for the portfolio. In my initial contact with an R&D organisation, I usually ask who is held accountable for the portfolio, and I have never been told it is the organisation's CEO, although I have known more than one CEO who was fired by the Board or quit as a result of a serious failure of the portfolio to deliver. In one project, that led to the share price of the company halving and to this day it has never recovered. So, you can see that getting the portfolio right is desperately important.

How can that be assured? The Nobel laureate Elinor Ostrom suggested it is through collective action.[188] She argues for a 'second-order' rationality to offset the selfishness of individuals seeking to maximise their own expected utility. This second-order rationality depends on the trust individual participants have of one another, efforts by individuals to establish and maintain a favourable reputation, and willingness to follow norms of reciprocity, that is, 'individuals tend to react to the positive actions of others with positive responses and the negative actions of others with negative responses'. Thus, she believes these three necessary conditions define a new theory of collective action that can ensure better allocation of resources.

These conditions establish relationships among participants during a decision conference for prioritising resources. Trustworthiness and reputations build as all project managers engage with the group in reporting current and proposed new projects and discuss costs and benefits of all options (which for large models are the results of individual workshops), receiving from participants their views and agreeing proposed changes. Reciprocity emerges as a guiding principle in assessing all weights fairly and realistically without attempts to unduly bias one's own projects. By building in these social aspects of effective problem solving to portfolio analysis, an organisation's board can be assured that the CEO has done his or her best to ensure that subordinates are effectively pursuing the right projects as agreed at the final decision conference.

Organising the Process

After meeting(s) with senior managers and/or executives, briefing them about what portfolio analysis can do for their organisation, I suggest that the whole process is best guided by a senior strategy manager, who would be responsible for implementing the portfolio process, as suggested by the graphic in Figure 14.14, which shows only the key stages.

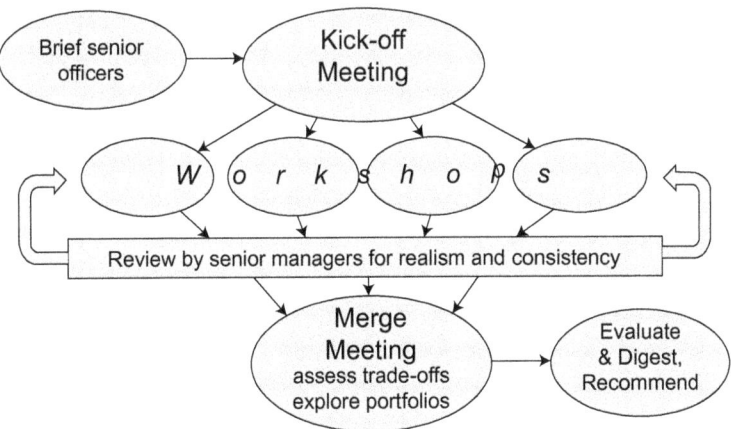

Figure 14.14

1. A kick-off meeting with the area managers to explain the portfolio model.
2. Workshops with the project managers and their teams to develop options which are reviewed by the strategy managers with feedback to the compound managers about changes.
3. A merge meeting to bring everything together, creating the final agreed portfolio model.
4. The order of priority is then considered by an executive group who evaluate it and make final recommendations to the R&D executive.

The senior strategy manager forms a team of area project managers, often the vice-presidents whose subordinate compound managers encompass all the compounds and projects to be made explicit in the portfolio model. Once this strategy team is in place, the strategy manager and I facilitate a meeting with them to explain the portfolio model and process, agree which compounds and projects are to be included in the model, and agree the criteria against which all projects are to be scored, although that might have been carried out at the briefing with senior officers. Also, an agenda for a Kick-off Meeting with the compound managers is agreed.

I also explain the commons dilemma, for there are always winners and losers, so some compound managers will be happier, some won't see much change, and some will lose resource. I point out that this is the inevitable consequence of resolving the commons dilemma, even though each manager is making the very best use now of the resources available to them. This usually helps to dampen critics of the process, and there are always some, because this implies change. And it is essential that everyone knows it has the backing of the CEO. That backing usually emerges after my initial briefing with the R&D president and his or her staff, who presents the new process to the CEO and gains that person's approval.

If you have read Chapter 8, you may recognise that at this point as many as five organisational strata participate in portfolio analysis: the CEO, R&D president, vice-presidents, compound managers and project managers. This is necessary in portfolio analysis because the process needs the lower-level managers to apply understanding of the actualities about what's going on in developing drugs as they do the scoring, but the higher-level executives will have a more accurate sense of trade-offs because they work as colleagues (at least in a requisite organisation), not competitors. As the decision analyst, you will need to ensure that scoring and weighting are done by those who are most knowledgeable and experienced.

In discussions with senior staff, I have found that five generic criteria can effectively cover the main concerns of R&D project prioritisation, and may even be applicable to other types of projects:

1. **Financial Value**. Whatever measure is best suited to the projects – for example, NPV, profit, revenue, share of market, within a defined timeframe, assuming a plausible level of success. (And definitely not any form of percentage, where both numerator and denominator can vary, making it impossible to make valid comparisons.)
2. **Core Value**. Related to the fundamental value of the organisation – for example, the extent to which an option meets unmet medical need for a pharmaceutical company, or is sustainably innovative for a technology company.
3. **Business Impact**. Extent to which an option protects the business from competitors – for example, expanding a franchise, building a barrier to entry by competitors.
4. **Future Potential**. The extent to which an option will sustain the above benefits beyond the defined timeframe. This is particularly relevant to recognise value created beyond any discounting applied within the timeframe.
5. **Probability of Success**. The probability that the project will be a success – for example, a drug is approved, a project overcomes technical hurdles.

These might be revised somewhat at the Kick-off Meeting and subsequently applied, subject to approval by the strategy group.

In preparation for the workshops, ask the project managers to provide a list of each compound's proposed projects along with their forward costs and any information from account managers about prospective financial performance, like assessments of possible profits or NPVs.

Workshops

The development work for each compound is carried out by a team usually managed by one individual who is held accountable by the R&D manager, and these teams are often operating independently, although any one manager might be assigned to head up more than one compound. To ensure that the benefits and costs for each compound are current and accurate, separate facilitated workshops are organised for each, usually lasting a day for more projects and a half-day for fewer. Each workshop sees participants drawn from two organisational levels, certainly those who are in their laboratories and their manager, but possibly also others, depending on how the organisation operates.

To ensure diversity of perspectives, I ask who the key players are, that is, who can contribute to discussions of benefits and costs for products. When they are identified, I double check by asking if there is someone who might see the workshop report and disagree with anything; if so, that person should have been in the workshop. Thus, attendees will include not only scientists developing the compound, but also representatives from accounting, global marketing and other relevant disciplines. With good forward planning, the workshops can be completed within several weeks, even for large models with up to about 20–24 areas, and longer for more.

The primary task of each workshop is to create and score options for the given compound. Explain to the group that to do this, they will be guided by the following four steps:

Step 1: **Agree the compound's name and definition**. This usually causes a lot of discussion because the name is still in flux or it hasn't been agreed by all those working on the compound, or the definition is so technical that not everyone agrees. If that happens, I ask the group to give it a name and definition that would be understandable by any scientifically savvy layperson. Surprisingly, when that is achieved, some participants feel progress has already been made because they weren't entirely sure of what it was they were working on. Enter the name in the software as a new area.

Step 2: **Explain what projects are currently funded and underway**. This is sometimes difficult because participants haven't yet been clear about what the drug can do, but usually each project is all the current projects at levels above the name of the compound. Whatever is shown at level 1 stays there in Equity3, so to give an even playing field, level 1 could be 'stop development'. That is likely to be met with the objection that it isn't realistic because development is well advanced. Point out that it will then score well for benefits with low forward costs, which will establish it as high priority. You also know that if some projects are allowed to show at level 1, then others may feel they have been unfairly penalised. This approach is a version of zero-based budgeting, which helps to engage all participants for its fairness.

Step 3: **Consider additional projects *assuming* more funds were available**. This step usually provokes the objection, 'But we don't have sufficient funds for what we're doing now, so there is no point is suggesting more projects.' I ask the question in a different way by saying, 'Are there any unexplored opportunities for this compound that would be considered if there were more funding?' Usually there are, but it's worth suggesting options that other pharmaceutical companies typically pursue, or even that have come up in other workshops.

If that doesn't work, try a directed SWOT analysis. Write one of these words, Strengths, Weaknesses, Opportunities and Threats, on four separate flipcharts. Ask the group to consider only this compound, list its internal Strengths and Weaknesses, and external Opportunities and Threats. I like to do this in open discussion, with me doing the writing, but you could also use sticky notes in a free-for-all. Stop the process

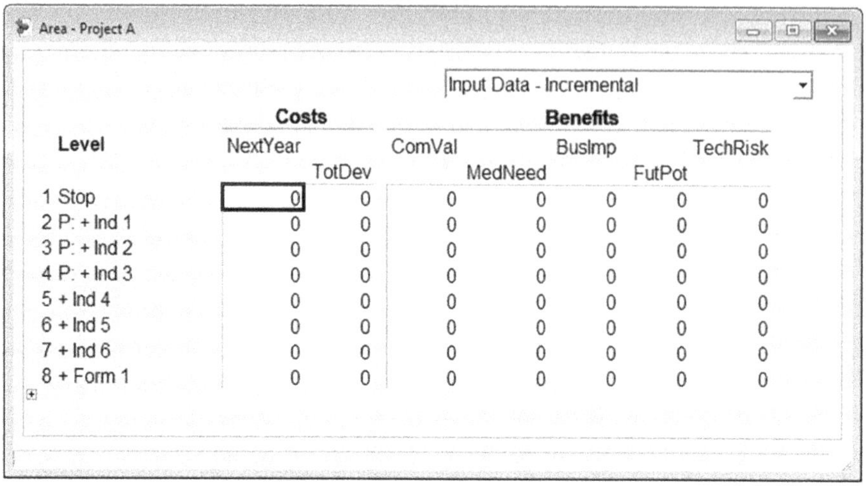

Figure 14.15

when it slows down, and ask the group, 'Now generate new options for this compound that could capitalise on the strengths and fix the weaknesses, as well as grasp the opportunities and stave-off the threats.' Write the options on a separate flip chart.

Then reduce the number of projects to those that could be seriously considered alongside the existing projects, perhaps by voting, giving each participant three to five votes to be spread across different options. Explain that the finally agreed new options provide an opportunity for gaining recognition by senior management of their compound's potential. Any back-up research strengthens their inclusion in the final list.

Step 4: **Score all the projects on all the criteria**. In Equity3, open the Area display. Figure 14.15 shows this for compound A, showing the two cost and five benefit scales, altogether 16 zeros for costs and 40 to be replaced with 0–100 benefit scores.

Advance preparation for the workshop is, of course, limited to the current projects, but at least their forward costs should be available, along with NPVs or other commercial value figures. For a first-time client, these data may not be available, but enough may be known by participants to provide estimates. For drug development companies, the main costs may be staff salaries, so at least an estimated average of person-months remaining for the current projects may be sufficient. If one or more participants is a specialist in modelling commercial value, they may be able to estimate NPVs during the workshop.

Remember that whatever the benefit units of measurement are, the MCDA software converts inputs into preference values; the default is relative (100 most preferred, 0 least preferred) or fixed (specific input metrics define 100 and 0). Unfortunately, non-linear functions are not accommodated in Equity3, although I have very rarely needed them for portfolio analysis. On the rare occasion when they arise, as in the next case study about the design of a warship, the objective metric is converted independently (for example, using Hiview3), with the resulting preference scores read off and input to Equity3.

In my second year of work with one pharmaceutical company that constructed NPV models for all projects, I suggested to their accounts manager that they extract from their records about 30 past NPVs that were reasonably representative of all they have done, and carry out risk analyses on all the input values to determine which values mainly influence the final NPV (this is easily done with DPL software, but can also be carried out with @Risk or similar software). They discovered that only a few variables really matter, so they were able to establish different levels for those variables so they could ask a few questions about a new proposed drug, enter the answers into their laptop and come up with a representative NPV on the spot.

I suggested this based on previous research with other companies in which I varied NPV figures used in former models to see how much variability could be tolerated without making much difference to the final OoP. Surprisingly, plus or minus about 25 per cent was the answer. In general, precision for portfolio models is not required, for small errors or bias make no difference at all to the OoP, and even modest errors usually move a project's priority up or down only one or two places. This insensitivity to precision in the PIs isn't too surprising as the single PI for the above Project A is based on 56 numbers, so no single one will make any difference at all, within ±25 per cent.

Many pharmaceutical companies spend a great deal of resource modelling NPVs for every project, sometimes by hiring outside experts to ensure 'good' NPVs, but *this is a waste of resources*, as I'll soon show in sensitivity analysis on the effects of changing NPVs for this case study.

Some pharmaceutical companies model the degree of unmet medical need for a given medical condition, so their model can provide those figures. Otherwise, this criterion will be based solely on judgements in the workshop, and that's true of business impact and future potential as well. As for the probability of success, the Equity3 software provides four different interpretations, as this extract from the Criteria Types Help screen explains:

1. **Manual**: This is the normal Criterion, benefits are scored and weighted in the normal way. If in doubt use this. Use as a 1–100 preference score when the client sees this criterion as a measure of *confidence* in the other benefit scores, which will be weighted and added along with the other weighted benefits.
2. **Risk Adjusted (Negative Benefit)**: Used to model risk within the Equity3 model. Probabilities of achieving the benefits given the resources are entered into Equity. These are used to penalise the benefits by way of a logarithmic scale. This is a proper scoring rule (described at the end of Chapter 6). The resulting negative scores subtract from the benefits, which is how the negative slope for project 8 in Figure 14.12 was created.
3. **Risk Adjusted (Multiplicative)**: An alternative way to model risk. Probabilities of achieving the benefits given the resources are entered into Equity. These are used to scale the benefits. Equity multiplies the sum of the weighted preference

scores on the other benefit criteria by this input probability to give an overall weighted preference value.

4. **Formula**: Allows a benefit Criterion to be derived from other Criteria using a number of supported mathematical operators. This is a pragmatic way of partially adjusting the benefits for one area or for a single criterion, as explained in more detail in the Help Screen, but it isn't consistent with MCDA theory, so I can't recommend it.

In the pharmaceutical case study here, I used the negative benefit approach, so the technical risk column contains all negative numbers for all compounds, with one exception: the probability of success for level 1, stopping development, is 100. Yes, because the stoppage prevents any benefits being realised for that project, so you are 100 per cent sure the benefits will score zero. The other probabilities were assessed in the workshop by the whole group after they had received a little training in probability assessment. See the section in Chapter 6, 'The Process of Eliciting Good Probabilities'. At the very least, I engage the group in the bones-in-the body exercise, which always finds at least a third of the group being over-confident. It also helps to ask the group to suggest ways their project could fail, which usually elicits many reasons, and only then assess a probability of success. Research shows that making explicit how a drug might succeed or fail, especially the latter, helps to obtain realistic, less biased probabilities.[189] If time permits, ask the group if they know the probability of technical success revealed by surveys, such as from Biotechnology Innovation Organization, for all drugs at this phase of development. If not, give someone in the group the task of looking it up. Then ask the group why their assessment was larger (as it usually is) than the average, which will stimulate more discussion and perhaps a revision downward.

Merge Meeting

After all workshops have reported, and before the merge meeting, the work of each compound team is presented to the members of the strategy panel, which then sends their suggested changes to the compound managers, with a deadline for making changes so that the revised workshop reports can be assembled and sent at least a week before the scheduled merge meeting. This gives all its members, who include the compound managers and the senior staff, such as vice-presidents and executives, time to acquaint themselves with the material to the extent they will be able to engage in scoring the non-financial criteria, and be able to think across the compound areas to judge the within-criterion weights.

The merge meeting begins with an overview from the senior strategy manager, sometimes with the assistance of the facilitator, who reminds the group that its primary task is to complete the portfolio model. Even if the organisation has engaged in portfolio merge meetings before, this overview is necessary to ensure that new members are not left behind in the understanding of the portfolio process. This may be followed by giving each compound manager five minutes to provide an overview of the important points raised in his or her workshop and a few minutes for questions, limiting them to questions of fact to avoid raising issues that should have been raised with the strategy managers. All this might take the entire morning of a two-day decision conference.

The scoring and weighting process then commences, guided by the facilitator, usually with the help of the strategy manager, whose seniority, knowledge and experience will help the group to stick to its primary task, and forestall diverting technical discussions.

With all inputs now in the computer, resist the temptation to see the overall result, for it is now necessary to ensure that each area's projects are sorted in order of their PIs, *subject to dependencies between them*. As a first step, the decision analyst sorts them by their PIs and the group then looks to see if some projects must come first because they will provide information about the compound that other projects depend on. In the second step, those required projects are moved to the early positions. Therefore, the costs of those first projects won't be incurred for the compound's further indications, whose PIs will always be higher than that for the earlier indications.

Take compound C as an example. The first P project, at level 2, Ind 1, has a poor PI compared to all the other projects because it is costly, having to bear the burden of all the early development stages that won't be necessary for any further indications. To deal with this dependency, the position of Ind 1 was moved to just above Stop Development. This forced the computer's sorting algorithm to start at level 2 for compound C, and for many of the other compounds, too, thus creating convex portions of their benefit-cost curves (Figure 14.16).

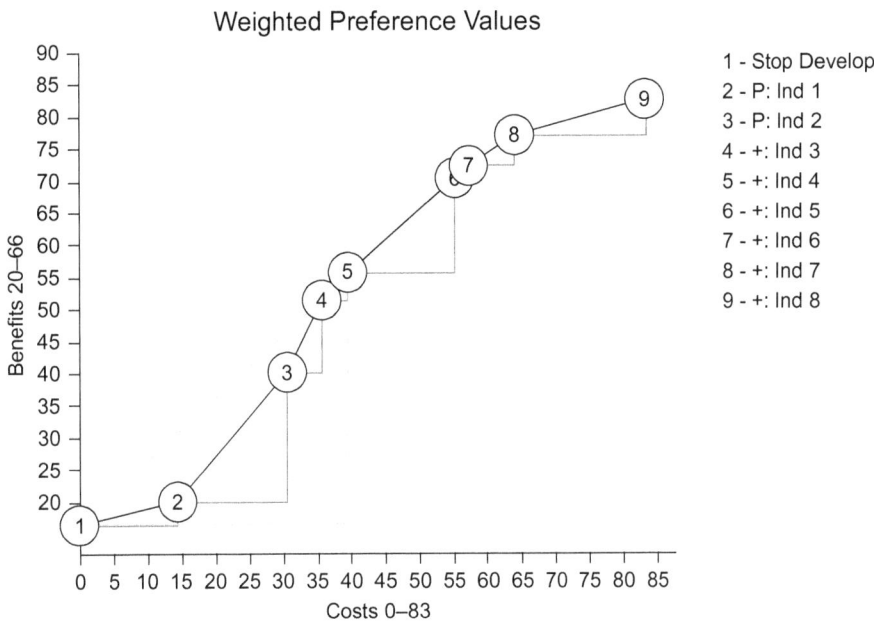

Figure 14.16

The algorithm is very simple: it starts at the bottom level 1 in the cityscape, and looks across all areas for the best slope, then the next, and the next, and so forth until it has run out of positive slopes. You'll note that I said 'slopes', not PIs. For compound C, and others whose initial indication was forced into first position, the consequences are instructive. Starting at Stop Development, the computer sees the hypotenuse of the big 1–5 triangle (which I've drawn) is tangent to point 5, Ind 4, so it skips over all the preceding projects, suggesting that all four projects together constitute a comparative best strategy for this compound. It turns out that Ind 1 is required for getting started, but is not itself value for money.

For compound J, the group moved the planned five indications into first position and defined them as one project, which eliminated the convex portion, and made sense to the group because they were certain that not all five would be approved by the regulator, but weren't sure at this stage of development which ones would fail. As the group examined the curve for each of the areas, a great deal was learned even before the efficient curve (Figure 14.17) was shown. Once that was displayed, we saw the

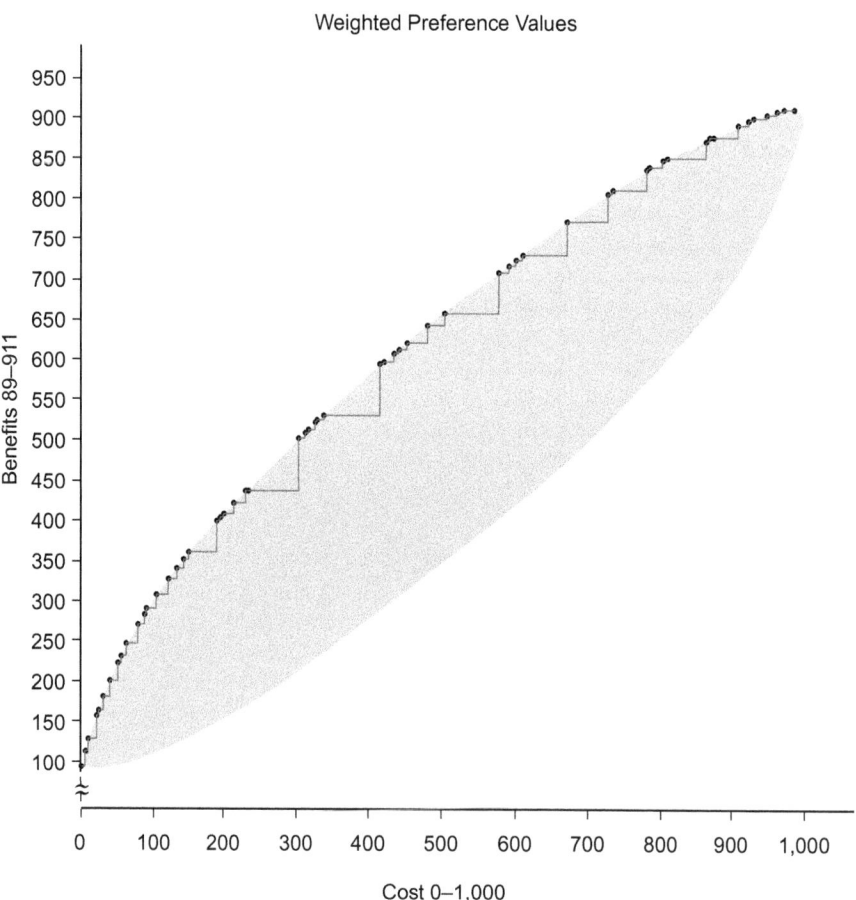

Figure 14.17

usual cluster of low-hanging fruit, typical of any R&D company's first portfolio analysis, followed by a mixture of projects displaying expensive projects that create considerable value, and clusters of less expensive projects that collectively provide only modest increments of value.

Of course, this examination inevitably provoked interest in where each project was located on the efficient curve. To show this, the software enables the decision analyst to define a Frontier point, starting at level 1 in all areas on the cityscape. It draws a solid green line on top of level 1 in all areas. It then finds the best slope in any of the areas, and moves that area's green line up to the next best triangle. It repeats this process of stepping up one triangle at a time, moving green lines upward, in the order of decreasing slopes.

As you can imagine, this process always creates great interest as anxious compound managers hope their projects will be brought into the portfolio early, and fearing *all* theirs could be left to last. It's also possible to show the OoP as a separate table.

For this pharmaceutical portfolio, it was more instructive to define a frontier point whose cost would be available from the beginning of the next year. The horizontal green (dark grey) bold lines on the cityscape in Figure 14.18 define the projects below them that together are affordable at that cost. (The up-arrow for compound E points to the next project that would be chosen if more resource were available, while the down-arrow points to the project that would define the portfolio if slightly less resource were available; both movements chosen on the basis of differences in PI.)

You can see that the computer chose all the projects in the large triangle for compound C, as we expected, but excluded the planned project of 5 Inds for compound J. But that was unacceptable, because research had established five possible indications that were about to be filed with the regulator. So, the decision analyst used Equity3's Trade-off function to turn the cursor into a 'T', drag and drop it to the 5 Inds cell, which

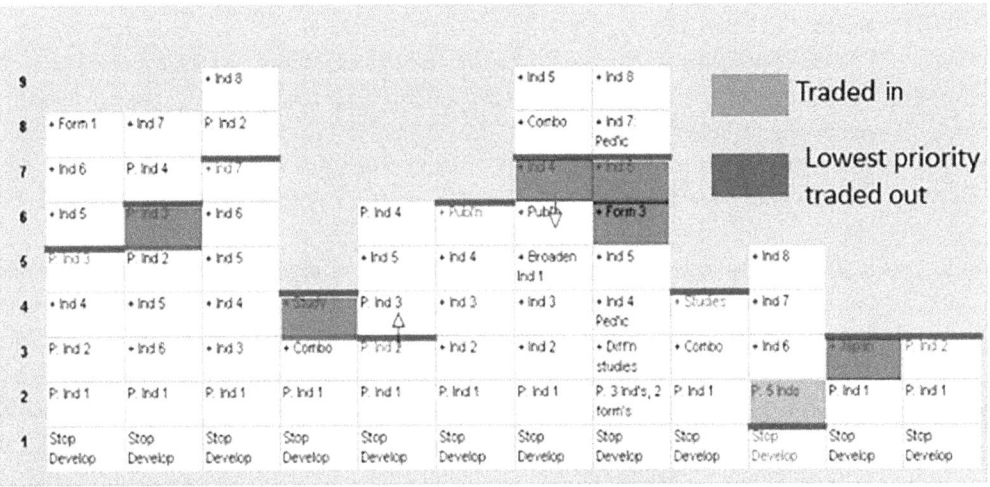

Figure 14.18

tells the computer to bring this project into the affordable portfolio, turning it green (light grey). But to pay for it, the computer selected the next lowest PIs across all areas, turning them red (dark grey) and trading them out to provide sufficient resource to cover the cost of 5 Inds, thus ensuring the budget was not exceeded.

This is a very powerful display. In the first instance, some senior executives have said this is the first time they have seen all their projects displayed at once, and, second, how easy it is to explore trade-offs without having to consult tables of costs and benefits. You will see in the case study in the next sub-section that this had a profound effect at the highest level of the UK Navy and resulted in a radical change of plan.

You may wonder why I haven't shown the PCB point for the pharmaceutical portfolio we've been discussing in this sub-section, and the answer is something I learned only later in my career: it was seen as a severe and hurtful critique of current decision making in the organisation, which participants felt was at least reasonably adequate, so something must be wrong with the model, and it was rejected. So, I never show the PCB graph during a first-time client's decision conference.

Sometimes a portfolio model opens eyes to reality, and is painful but now faced, as we will see in the next case study about a warship design. But first, I would like to say more about how sensitivity analysis of the portfolio can elicit further insights.

Sensitivity Analyses

There are many ways to see the effects of changing scores or weights in portfolio analysis. For example, a change in one project's score can easily be seen by opening two screens: the Area display to change a score; and the Graph display to see if the change is reflected in a new slope for the project. If the new slope preserves the order of all projects in the graph, then it is very unlikely that the new score will have any impact on the OoP, and even if it did, the order would be only one position up or down, which could be seen if the OoP display is also kept open when the change is made.

One approach that capitalises on our in-built capability to spot differences is to provide all participants with a paper copy of the cityscape showing the green lines that define the affordable frontier point. Then make any change asked for by the group, using the same cost for the affordable frontier point. Ask compound managers to look at their compound areas and report back on what if anything has changed – gains and losses.

For the pharmaceutical portfolio, one participant argued that the five indications for compound J might fare better if the portfolio were driven only by the financial criterion. It was easy to change the across-criteria weights to 100–0–0–0, re-sort the areas, impose the same cost constraint and ask the compound managers what changed. My report of the decision conference showed that result in Figure 14.19, which I've overwritten with green (lighter) and red (darker) dollar signs on the original model. Indications 6 and 7 for compound J are now included in the portfolio, but the five indications planned are still not selected, so to pay for these two indications, 14 indications are foregone.

Drive the portfolio by NPV and risk only: gain $ options and lose $ options.

	Comp A	Comp B	Comp C	Comp D	Comp E	Comp F	Comp G	Comp H	Comp I	Comp J	Comp K	Comp L
9			• Ind 8				• Ind 5	• Ind 8				
8	• Form 1	• Ind 7	P. Ind 2				• Combo	• Ind 7 Pedic				
7	• Ind 6	P. Ind 4	• Ind 7				• Ind 4 $	• Ind 6 $				
6	• Ind 5	P. Ind 3	• Ind 6	P. Ind 4	• Publn		• Putih $	• Form 3 $				
5	P. Ind $	P. Ind 2	• Ind 5 $		• Ind 5	• Ind 4	• Broaden Ind 1 $	• Ind 5 $			• Ind 8	
4	• Ind 4 $	• Ind 5	• Ind 4 $	• Study $	P. Ind 3	• Ind 3 $	• Ind 3	• Ind 4 Pedic	• Studies		• Ind 7 $	
3	P. Ind 2	• Ind 6	• Ind 3	• Combo	P. Ind	• Ind 2	• Ind 2	• Diffn studies	• Combo	• Ind 6 $	• Japan	P. Ind 2 $
2	P. Ind 1	P. Ind 1	P. Ind 1	P. Ind 1	P. Ind 1	P. Ind 1 $	P. Ind 1	P. 3 Ind's, 2 form's	P. Ind 1	P. 5 Inds	P. Ind 1	P. Ind 1
1	Stop Develop	Stop Develop	Stop Develop	Stop Develop	Stop Develop	Stop Develop	Stop Develop	Stop Develop	Stop Develop	Stop Develop	Stop Develop	Stop Develop

Figure 14.19

Nobody liked that result. We also drove the model just by unmet medical need, and that, too, gave a very different result, which was also rejected. Many other sensitivity analyses were tried, but eventually the group agreed that the most preferred portfolio was the one at the start, which enabled all five criteria to contribute to the final result.

This was an important learning point for the group as some had argued against including both NPV and unmet medical need criteria, arguing that if a project meets unmet medical need, then it will make money. These criteria are correlated, so they are double counted. That led me to explain the difference between statistical correlation and preference independence, for nobody had asked to see the NPV figures when they were scoring the projects for unmet medical need. So, I put to the group the following scenario. Imagine two projects X and Y that are given exactly the same scores on all the criteria except that project Y is scored higher for unmet medical need. Would you now have any preference for either project? The group agreed they would prefer Y. 'Why?' I asked. 'Well, that's what we are in business to do, meet medical need!' 'Because we will be seen as a progressive, innovative organisation.' 'It will be easier to attract top-rate scientists to our company.' Those were some of the replies, and ever after, I ensured that we defined the unmet medical need criterion in whatever terms ensured we weren't double-counting financial return, but ensuring preference independence.

Requisite Modelling for Portfolio Analysis

It should be clear by now that I believe any organisation whose modelling of R&D projects relies mainly on financial modelling of each project independently is wasting time and money. I know of one large pharmaceutical company that spent over $20 million each year hiring outside consultants to model NPVs for their late-development projects. Of course, that amount is peanuts compared to the amount they spent on developing drugs, from initial discovery to approval, which is now well over $2 billion for a single drug. So, what benefit is obtained from NPVs? I argue that it is mainly social. First, imposing the DCF structure on each compound helps to give a degree of reliability in the numbers, even if they are short of validity (recall the distinction made near the end of Chapter 3). Second, NPVs provide a language for top management to communicate information about their pipeline of drugs, especially to the financial world, although that should be accompanied by statements of uncertainty, such as confidence intervals, to avoid over-promising.

For portfolio analysis, we've already seen that we don't need precise numbers, so from a requisite point of view, all we need is 'good enough' numbers. Of course, with the benefit of hindsight, it's easy to discover that some elements of a model weren't needed as they didn't influence the results. But how can that be established earlier? Here are five things you can do:

1. Restrict the model to currently funded projects that are looking so good they absolutely would not at this stage be stopped. Place them at level 1 in the model, where they will stay whatever happens to projects above that level, but their inclusion allows their forward cost to be included in the total budget.
2. Don't include projects whose forward costs are small compared to the total budget. Decisions about them can be made independently.
3. Don't include projects which are in their very early stage of development because benefit judgements about them would be more about hope than reality. In pharmaceuticals, for example, compounds showing promise (*leads*) for different medical conditions might best be the subject of an evaluation model (Chapter 13) to find those that can justifiably be put forward for inclusion in next year's portfolio.
4. For a first-time portfolio, restrict the number of new projects that can be taken forward from the workshops, say the best three or four.
5. Better yet, in the second or later year, examine the benefit versus cost graph for each area from the previous year's portfolio analysis to see which areas last year put forward too many new projects that were rejected, and those areas whose graphs were still rising. This analysis helps to legitimise areas of greater opportunity being allowed more options than areas of lesser opportunity. It also encourages project teams to prepare better for subsequent years' portfolios.

Is it possible to conduct a portfolio analysis during research and discovery? Many companies argue that it isn't possible because they don't yet know enough about a compound to calculate an NPV. That's true, so explore with a potential client what the fundamental objectives are of the organisation's discovery research and how they now make choices to achieve those objectives, in particular to learn what outputs the scientists are expected to produce. Some pharmaceutical companies only require papers that can be published in refereed journals, while others focus on new compounds that look sufficiently promising to be passed on to the organisation's early development division. You might enquire if the numbers of papers or of new compounds is looking good. Eventually, an enquiry about why these numbers are as they are might prompt you to ask if these outputs are being produced in a cost-effective manner. If the answer is that they are, you may well wonder why you were asked to help.

Disease States as Areas in MCDA Discovery Portfolio Models					
Allergy and Respiratory	Anti-infectives	Atherosclerosis	Cardiovascular	Dermatology	Diabetes and Obesity
Gastro-Intestinal	Immunology	Infectious Diseases	Inflammation	Metabolic	Neuro-degeneration
Oncology	Osteoporosis	Pain	Psychotherapeutics	Tissue Repair	Urogenital

Figure 14.20

More likely, they will say the process could be improved, so the door may be open to your suggesting that instead of NPV, it's possible to make preference judgements about *commercial potential* alongside criteria that are appropriate to early development. These could include meeting unmet medical need, future potential, clinical do-ability and innovativeness, as well as numbers of papers or new compounds. The areas in a discovery portfolio are disease states, such as those shown in Figure 14.20.

So, the answer to my question two paragraphs ago is yes, it is possible to create meaningful portfolio models for guiding decisions in discovery and early research.

But that can raise another issue you may encounter, which is whether innovative products are best produced by leaving scientists to their own devices, or by exercising some degree of control over their behaviour or their outputs.[190] Although research shows that control seems to improve efficiency and create more desirable financial results for both small and large companies, the organisation's culture may or may not be sympathetic to a new value system. As a process consultant, you first need to establish whether a portfolio system is already in place, then explain that a portfolio model doesn't favour either type of control, but it does improve the cost-effectiveness of research and development in all stages.

Allergan reported that there has been little controversy to the proposed portfolio at the executive committee level due to consensus and commitment gained during the process, that the process provides a useful tool for thinking and a serious guide to decision making. They also noted that it has demonstrated how significant increases in return can be obtained with a modest increase in overall risk. Over time, they observed, the starting point each year has become more realistic, prioritisation has improved and resources are now allocated more rationally.

The next prioritisation project shows how it is possible to design an entirely new technical system, and we'll see how it totally upended traditional ways of thinking, provided a result that was approved more quickly than usual for such complex systems and was successfully implemented.

Project Prioritisation for Complex Systems

As I said earlier, the precursor to Equity was called Design because its first application resolved disagreements between a client and their architects. But it soon became apparent that the new program could be generalised to assist the allocation of resources in many other situations, especially those involving budget restrictions. Over its many

Figure 14.21

years of use, Equity acquired functionality to handle the vagaries of clients' different needs and can now accommodate single budgets, like those for groups of stratum 5 individual companies, but also of a stratum 6 or 7 corporation to create a budget of budgets (which also requires a team of experienced facilitators).

This chapter's final section describes how Equity3 and decision conferencing were applied to the design of the UK's Type 45 destroyer, which was completed and approved in record time with minimal subsequent changes to its design during construction. Figure 14.21 shows HMS Daring, first of its class, launched in 2006.

Background

Although the UK had worked jointly since 1992 with France and Italy to design a frigate, it became clear by 1999, after the UK had left the joint effort, that the frigate model could be adapted by the UK for their new Type 45 destroyer.[191] I worked with an Integrated Project Team of senior naval officers in several workshops, one for each of the ship's 25 functions, over a period of two years refining the model, to recognise that it could only be firmed up by face-to-face engagement with all the key players. This took two major decision conferences, beginning in 2002, which I and two naval officers facilitated, including a Brigadier General army officer to oversee the financial costs, scrutineers to oversee the process and operational research participants to oversee the methodology, as well as major equipment manufacturers to provide their expertise on what sub-system capabilities were possible for what costs.

This last point about including competing companies, whose systems might eventually be purchased for the new ships, solved the Gordian knot of how a company could give a realistic cost for a sub-system without a precise specification for what was needed, and how the Navy could provide a specification without knowing what it cost. Here is how this problem was solved:

To overcome the stalemate the naval officers pointed out that systems were not being costed – capabilities were. The facilitators pointed out that the Equity model is not sensitive to precise costs, that 'ballpark' estimates are sufficient. And the armed forces specialists in costs asked that only representative realistic costs be presented by the contractors. The contractors realised that if they gave costs that were too high, that could call into question the viability of the project, and could lead to its cancellation. If the contractors gave costs that were too low, they might eventually be held to them. Everyone knew that costs had to be squeezed, now and in the future. Realism was encouraged.[192]

From then on, the dialogue was about capability, namely, military value, not about any specific existing system, which sometimes frustrated the operational research attendees, who were accustomed to modelling effectiveness or performance. Recall the NATO commander mentioned at the start of Chapter 4, who recognised that his family's three cars provided different personal value for him, his wife and two children, although all three were identical models.

Structure

At the end of the second decision conference, the Equity model showed the ship's 25 functions as areas, with 113 capability options as levels, but the cityscape is tipped on its side to enable a readable rectangle of short names (Figure 14.22).

	1	2	3	4	5	6	7	8	9	10	11
PROPULSION	CODAD	CODAG b	CODOG SP	COGAL	CODOG b	CODAG a WR21 2 GT WR21	CODLAG SP	COGAL WR21	CODOG a		CODLOG WR21
MANOEUVRE	NOTHING	BOW-THRUSTE									
STRUCTURE	Commercial	Lloyd's Naval	Scaled T23	Full Military	+part composite						
STEALTH	Basic	Some	Better	Best							
VULNERABILITY	Basic	Better	JTS requiremnt	Superior							
ACCOMMODATE	NES Issue 4+	NES Issue 4+*	2SL Z	2SL Y	2SL Min	MN full					
SPECIAL FORCES	None	Partial	Full								
PMS	Basic	LPD	LPD plus								
HELO facilities	Lynx	Lynx+ land	Lynx + Merlin	Lynx + Merlin							
CS Architecture	Open consoles	Fully open	Growth	Partially open							
CMS Functions	Control PAAMS	+ Full Link 16	+ Enhncd TPC	+ Force TEWA	+ Link 22						
CSS Functions	Stand alone	SA CSS + auto	Integ part'd CSS	IntCSS&SDD in							
SSGW	None	Fit for but not	SSGW								
MCGS	None	FBNW	Fit refurb'd 114	Fit 127 mm	Fit 155 mm						
MULTI-ROLE VLS	None	proud platform	flush platform								
UWW det	FBNW	FBNW + Mine	FBNW+	MF sonar	MFsonar + mine	Multi-function					
ASW	None	FBNW	Int torpedo								
ASW TORP DEFNCE	None	Towed o-m	Towd o-m, exp	Layered							
ESM	FBNW	OTS intell binkg	OTS MI full	OTS MI LPI DF	AIEWS	Horizon					
ECM/C2	Def aids only	Def aids & C2+	Def aids,	Def aids,	Def aids,	Horizon UK					
CESM	None	FBNW	Fitted								
AAW (IFF)	SIFF ltd Mode S	SIFF full Mode	Horizon Frlt								
Visual Det/VID	Unaided vis surv	Day only	Day & ltd night	Day & night full							
ILDS	No ILDS	CIWS 1a	CIWS 1b	CIWS (GK)	Missile system						
COMMS	LPH	LPD(R)	LPD Integrated	Multi-service	LPD Developed	Horizon	Horizon				

25 functions (rows)
113 options (cells)

FBNW: Fit But Not With (i.e. provide fitting, but don't install the system)

Figure 14.22

You will notice that compared to the pharmaceutical Equity model, there are no 'P' or '+' options, with one exception (CMS Functions), as this is an entirely new venture, and most options don't accumulate, they are all independent and must be so defined when they are input to Equity. Also, independent options must be ordered by cost for each function. Equity will eventually find just one capability option for each function that overall gives the most capability at no more than the allowed budget.

The first area, Propulsion, shows 11 different engines that will give a maximum speed of at least 26 knots and provide power sufficient for all the ship's functions. The least costly solution was at level 1, CODAD, with subsequent solutions rising in cost. The benefit versus cost plot for this area was very jagged, making clear to participants that the added value from one level to the next was not at all linear. Indeed, many solutions showed less capability at more cost than the previous solution. This happened many times and provoked considerable discussion and revisions throughout the two meetings.

Also, level 1 for several functions was to do nothing, which enabled debates of pros and cons to be heard and tested in the model. CMS Functions shows the PAAMS air defence system, which was from the work with France and Italy, at level 1, so certain to be included, but adds a few incremental options suggested by participants.

Criteria

Five benefit criteria were included in the Equity model. The first two are positive benefits, while the remaining three are dis-benefits.

1. **Performance**: capability of an option to add value in a mission.
2. **Growth Potential**: ability of an option to grow in capability as new technical features are introduced.
3. **Time to Deliver the Solution**: score 100 if first-of-class solution delivers before September 2007, otherwise zero.
4. **Risk**: lower probabilities of success were associated with larger negative penalty scores.
5. **Logistic Costs**: includes all costs of operating the ship over a 25-year life – the higher the cost, the lower the preference values.

Separate workshops developed their own models of performance judged on criteria that were unique to each function for Performance, Growth Potential and Logistic Cost.

Two costs were defined in the Equity model: Unit Production Cost (recurring for each ship) and Non-Recurring Cost (the cost of developing each solution). Different weights were used to ensure that the full NRC wasn't borne by the first-of-class ship.

Scoring

All military personnel are clear that they exist to satisfactorily complete missions in times of peace and war. Any mission requires the exercise of good military judgement, a phrase I often heard from my first project in 1995 with the UK Navy, especially from sceptics who doubted no model could take the place of the extensive training and experience of seasoned military personnel.

Although I made clear that models support thinking and extend human capability, they don't replace it; minds were not changed until I suggested that we try supplementing how they already make decisions with some additional modelling. That was accepted as a trial, but by the end participants in a decision conference agreed it had helped them to understand one another better, to surface assumptions, develop new insights and even solve a knotty problem. In short, modelling helped them to move from intuitive and qualitative to explicit and quantitative.

By the time of the Type 45 work, all that was well understood by the military personnel, but not so of the civilians who had not yet been engaged in decision-analytic modelling, let alone decision conferences. However, as they knew that the Navy favoured the approach, they pitched in and contributed when they could, especially during the scoring as they contributed their expertise and knowledge about systems they had studied. And it was their knowledge about performance and effectiveness that helped the military personnel formulate preference values about military capability.

The constant focus on capability, *what* the system could do, now *how* it would do it, avoided committing to any particular system that could deliver the capability. Working together, face to face, they were able to judge scores that were realistic and consistent, as trust was built within the group.

For example, scoring the performance criterion for living-quarter accommodation enabled the military participants to be explicit in constructing preference scores at options of increasing square metres on flexibility, effectiveness, contentment, motivation, morale and retention in the Navy. As I reported:

The modelling enabled military judgement to be made explicit, as in the case of the S-shaped value function for accommodation space. Indeed, the accommodation team argued during the first two decision conferences about the importance of good accommodation to morale, which led to the development of the value function. (A judgement later confirmed by the glowing pride of a seaman as he showed his personal space on the Daring to the interviewer in a national network TV program broadcast in 2010.)[193]

Finally, costs were provided by the Brigadier General's team, who admitted that precision at this stage was difficult, but they had attempted to provide figures that were realistic.

Weights

The two sets of weights, within a function and across functions, required judgements from the experts who know about the performance and effectiveness of the systems for a given function, but also from senior military personnel who were better acquainted with the relative importance of systems across the functions for their contribution to a mission's success.

A large gun on the forward deck of the ship, for example, was considered more important in peacetime, when manoeuvring in seas outside an unfriendly country (as we will see later).

At the final decision conference, the senior military officers sat at a separate table, resolving any final disputes about scores, and they were the major players in assessing the across-criteria weights. As Chris Lloyd, the marine architect, told me:

Another revelation of decision conferencing to the Type 45 programme participants was how it dealt with the subjectivity of capability requirements, prioritisation and arriving at shared conclusions. This social process of joint workshops with all leading stakeholders was fundamental to its success. In my 25 years in naval procurement, it was the first and only time I have seen flag officers openly debating the relative merits of radars and electronic warfare systems with senior procurement managers, technical specialists and ship designers. The exchange of knowledge and thus convergence on a jointly understood solution was phenomenal. Much is made of Integrated Project Teams and customer/industry collaboration in defence, but this is one of the few occasions when I have seen an approach that actually steers the participants towards a conclusion in days, not weeks or years.[194]

Results

Figure 14.23 shows the efficient frontier for the design of the Class, with zero weight on the time criterion, along with the frontier point at the £150 million budget for each ship.

The steep initial portion provides 81 per cent of added benefits at 23 per cent of added cost. The 'F' cells constitute the solution. However, the group needed a solution for both First of Class as well as the whole class (12 ships), so they re-ran

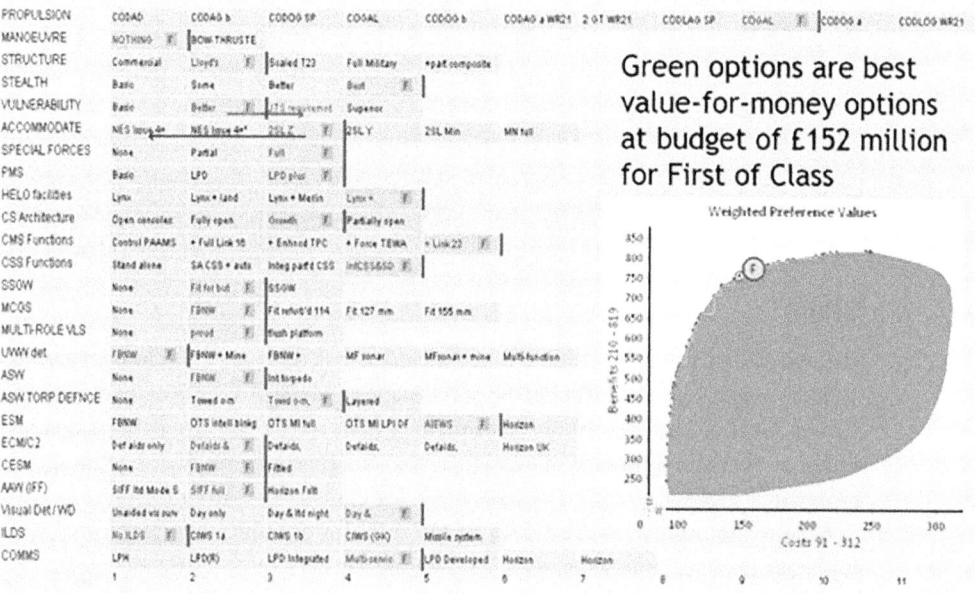

Figure 14.23

the model including the time criterion, and examined the result at its target cost of £280 million.

The result was wholly unsatisfactory as it didn't allow for migration paths to the Class solution for at least some functions.

Constraints

Many modellers build in the constraints at the start. I've discouraged this, as it encourages participants to bias the model for their preferred solution. Equity provides a *blocking* function that enables the constraints to be added at the end of the modelling, which alleviates the need to spend time at the start agreeing and including the constraints, many of which would be found irrelevant at the end. So, it's best to recognise possible constraints at the start, but ignore them when constructing the model.

To handle the problems of migrating to a feasible solution, participants used the buffering function in Equity3 to iterate towards an acceptable Class solution, focusing on only those constraints that would provide a migration path. The constraints changed the shape of the possible portfolios of solutions, but Equity shows the original (lighter) and restricted shapes (darker), assisting participants in agreeing a final solution. However, that took five iterations of discussions and revisions to achieve the result shown in Figure 14.24.

First, however, I was asked to attend a briefing of the model at a key meeting of several Admirals and Commodores, in the presence of the Royal Navy's First Sea Lord. His reaction changed the strategy for the Type 45.

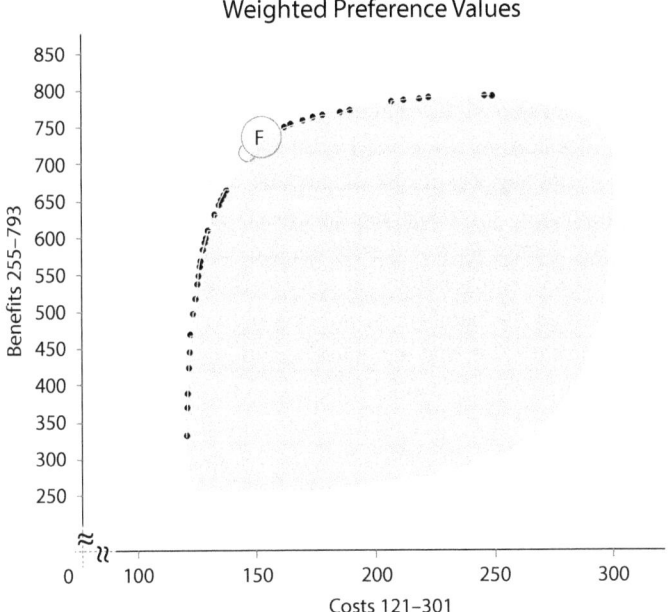

Figure 14.24

Trade-Offs

The November 1999 briefing began with introductions and a short statement of the meeting's purpose, followed by explanations establishing the main constraints of time, cost and capability. I provided a resumé of the 25 functions and a few of their benefit-cost graphs, with the full model displayed on a large screen.

In less than 20 minutes, we arrived at the full display of the cityscape, and I could see he quickly scanned what was included in the affordable portfolio. He suddenly rose from his seat and exclaimed, 'I'm not going to sea without a gun!' He had seen in the MCGS row that the gun was FBNW (Fit But Not With); the limited resources meaning that a fitting for the gun would be constructed, although the gun itself would be fitted later as more resource became available. But to the First Sea Lord, that was unacceptable.

In our preparation for the meeting, we suspected something like this would happen, as by then it was generally agreed that the plan for 12 ships would have to be reduced. Even so, I recovered from his forthright response and said, 'Yes, sir, you can have a gun. We can force it into the portfolio, and the computer will then display what must be lost in order to pay for the gun.'

I then invoked Equity's Trade Off Select function to bring the 155mm gun into the portfolio. Equity highlighted 10 capability solutions that would be lost. This brought home to the Navy Board the severity of the budget constraint, and after further study, the MoD contracted BAE Systems to construct, first, eight ships, and later just six ships. The last of the six ships entered full service in 2014. At that time, they were considered by many to be the best air-defence destroyers in the world.[195]

Summary

From a simple extension of the women's shampoo problem that enabled the MD to decide a new allocation of resources in just one day, to assisting a pharmaceutical company in constructing a portfolio of the best development options for 12 newly discovered compounds, to establishing the most cost-effective design of a new ship's 24 functions, this chapter shows the richness and diversity of applying MCDA to the allocation of resources across budget category areas involving any number of projects. It also shows that as the numbers of projects grow, the complexity of the model's structure grows linearly, but that the human effort requires additional workshops and back-room tasks to inform the work of the decision conferences. There it is reported, discussed and modified, the remaining weights are assessed, the completed model is subjected to sensitivity analyses, and new scenarios about the future are explored to see how priorities might change and be accommodated.

The three case studies vividly illustrate the role of the decision model as a transitional object that holds its basic structure even as it changes, and also holds the data and expert judgements required for the content, enabling participants to safely make changes and see results, trying out differences of opinion, exploring the effects of uncertainty and trying out different judgements about the future. The model provides a safe way of testing the effects of alternative inputs to see which options consistently fall within the affordable frontier, so will be more robust to a changing future, and can be considered as the core of the portfolio. Those options that consistently fall outside the affordable frontier might be discarded, at least for now, if deciding further research could strengthen their positions, such as finding ways to reduce their costs with minimal reduction of benefits or engaging in joint ventures with another company.

Throughout the modelling process, preferences are constructed and reconstructed, as deliberations shape and reshape value preferences, especially during exploration of the model, as participants see results they hadn't expected and are helped by the facilitator (who may also be puzzled) to dig into the working of the model to see why. This process itself can change a group's risk tolerance.

An MCDA model is not a black box, and its simple weighted averaging arithmetic is readily understandable, so puzzles will yield to close examination of the parts of the model. Many times, I have seen an overall result that was not even considered at the time of assessing scores and weights, but became clear once the weighted averages were examined. This observation is simply the consequence of the whole being greater than the sum of its parts. All decision models deconstruct a complex problem into its pieces, but once the scores and weights have been obtained, the whole is reconstructed – the model is handed back in changed form. This can be startlingly true of portfolio analysis, and that is why portfolio MCDA is so effective in overcoming the commons dilemma.

15 Bargain and Negotiate

Compromise is the best and cheapest lawyer.

Robert Louis Stevenson[196]

Let's start with a simplified two-sided bargaining and negotiating situation, borrowed from Howard Raiffa, in which both parties are open about their preferences and willing to work together, although they differ about many issues. Later, we will explore other bargaining situations, including some that start with one side imagining the other side's preferences.[197]

Lisa vs Williams Negotiation

This hypothetical situation is intended to illustrate how an MCDA efficient frontier can be developed using the technology from Chapters 13 and 14.[198] The five-step process for creating any decision model outlined in Chapter 1 is applied here.

1. Consider Context

A young woman, Lisa, has applied for a job with a company called Williams. Discussions about a possible contract have stalled because the two sides don't agree on three issues: salary; length of a year's vacation; and the number of staff Lisa will require for her to do her job properly.

2. Frame the Problem

A bargaining and negotiation MCDA framework for this problem begins by establishing the numerical data associated with the options for each issue, shown in Table 15.1.

3. Provide Content

The next step is to construct preference values for each of the options, from Lisa's point of view and from Williams' perspective. For each issue, 0–100 preference values are assessed independently by the two parties (Table 15.2).

This chapter has been written with Cameron Peterson, who I'm pleased to acknowledge is definitely the first author.

Table 15.1

Issue	Options	Lisa	Williams
Salary ($000s)	34		
	37		
	40		
Vacation (Weeks)	3		
	4		
Staff Size	10		
	15		
	20		

Table 15.2

Issue	Options	Lisa	Williams
Salary ($000s)	34	0	100
	37	70	60
	40	100	0
Vacation (Weeks)	3	0	100
	4	100	0
Staff Size	10	0	100
	15	70	90
	20	100	0

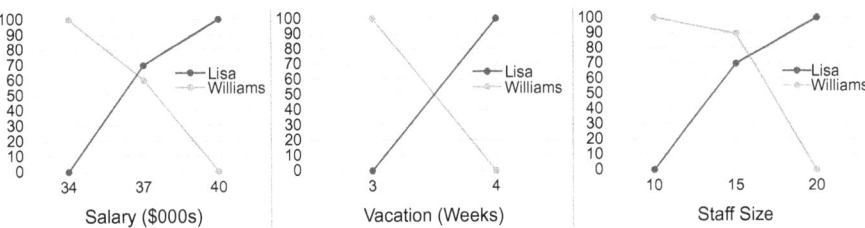

Figure 15.1

Each side's value functions make clear their disagreements (see Figure 15.1).

Recognising that the six 0–100 scales don't necessarily represent the same differences in preferences, the facilitator assists each side in assessing their own swing weights. Multiplying the above preference values by their corresponding weights gives the weighted value functions shown in Figure 15.2.

The largest differences between the two parties are the $40,000 salary, which Lisa favours, and staff size, which Williams favours. Neither cares much about the length of the vacation. The asymmetries of the value functions suggest that the efficient frontier will be fairly concave, as we will see next.

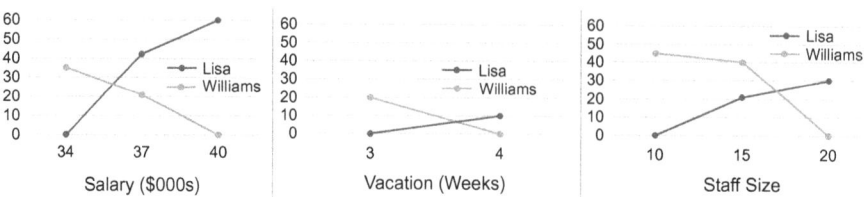

Figure 15.2

Contracts	Lisa	Williams	Sum
34-3-10	0	100	100
34-3-15	20	95	115
34-3-20	30	55	85
34-4-10	10	80	90
34-4-15	30	75	105
34-4-20	40	35	75
37-3-10	40	96	136
37-3-15	60	81	141
37-3-20	70	41	111
37-4-10	50	66	116
37-4-15	70	61	131
37-4-20	80	21	101
40-3-10	60	65	125
40-3-15	80	60	140
40-3-20	90	20	110
40-4-10	70	45	115
40-3-15	90	40	130
40-4-20	100	0	100

Figure 15.3

4.   Explore Results

Multiplying scores by their corresponding weights gives a table of weighted preferences for all 18 potential contracts (3 for salary, times 2 for vacation, times 3 for staff), with a scatterplot of Williams' weighted preference scores summed for the three issues versus those for Lisa (Figure 15.3).

The line shows the efficient frontier: the best six contracts, with no contracts above and to the right of the concave line, defined as the efficient frontier. Each of the remaining contracts is dominated by at least one of the six (sometimes only roughly). Of course, the (0, 100) contract very much favours Williams, while (100, 0) favours Lisa. Many people might feel those contracts aren't fair, that at least both sides should be reasonably rewarded. Perhaps the lower-right (91, 40) contract is fairer than the upper-left (21, 95) contract. You might argue that the sum of their two weighted preference values should be as large as possible. But scanning down the Sum column reveals there is no single best contract. Rather, there are two sums, the (61, 81) and (81, 60) contracts, so how to choose between them (surely, we won't argue about one point)?

5.   Agree the Way Forward

Well, there isn't any technical justification. Agreement depends on the social situation. Perhaps Lisa and Williams can agree on one or the other without further discussion. Of course, (70, 70) would be ideal, and it might be possible to select different salary and staff size options than the three considered here to achieve that. Indeed, in Raiffa's handbook, a salary of $38,000, vacation of 3 weeks and staff size of 15 achieved a value of 70 for Lisa and 73 for Williams. But it may well be that this simpler model is requisite: it is good enough for the two parties to fine-tune the result sufficiently that both will be satisfied without further technical help from the decision model. We'll soon see some real case studies that show that in action.

The Social Process of Bargaining

Consider now the process of creating a bargaining model. Let's assume that you, as a decision analyst who is familiar with the technical aspects of modelling, are the negotiator between two parties who wish to work collaboratively to develop a contract that will be acceptable to both. How do you help them to identify the issues and the stands (options), while maintaining your impartiality to ensure they eventually agree a final contract? You might go back to Chapter 9 and scan the 10 principles of process consultancy to see which principles would be relevant to your bargaining and negotiation situation. And many of the facilitation skills in Chapter 10 will be helpful. Much depends on what you have learned during your initial questioning about why both sides have come together and what they expect of you.

In a real application, it will be important to think about the social process because you will be assisting them in making explicit and quantitative what is now mostly implicit in their thinking about creating a contract of work. You will see in the next six real case studies how considerable initial explorations enabled the negotiators to be effective in arriving at an agreed solution, which also required experience in working with groups, the subject of Chapter 11.

Negotiation Examples

Cam Peterson and his Decisions and Designs Inc. (DDI) colleagues were involved in six governmental and private company negotiations in the late 1970s, which as far as I know was the first use of this type of decision analysis modelling. Indeed, their work was the basis for the subsequent development of Design, the computer program that eventually became Equity, which enables many combinations of options to be analysed in a way that provides an efficient frontier of benefits versus costs. The main difference between Equity compared to bargaining models is that the latter develops an efficient frontier representing the benefit of one party compared to the benefit of the other party.

Panama Canal

DDI first applied the bargaining model to the US Government's Panama Canal treaty negotiations, which was mediated by one government official who was interested in trying out the new methodology. However, by the time DDI became involved, the problem was so familiar and over-studied that little was learned from the extra modelling. DDI learned much; for example, if any utility function is single-peaked, as we met in Chapter 4, it is necessary to split the function into two separate issues, one increasing in value and the other decreasing, possibly with kinks, so that they compete with each other for value in the final result.

Base Rights and Arms Negotiation

Pentagon and State Department negotiators applied the model to negotiate agreements about US base rights in another country, which turned out to be fairly easy, and was found to be useful. A more important application was in arms negotiations, which is often seen as a zero-sum game – what one side wins, the other side loses: one side's increasing value is mimicked by the other side's decreasing value. But that is often the overall viewpoint before breaking the problem apart into separate issues, to reveal asymmetries of interest, which has the effect of making the efficient curve more concave, bending upward to the right, as in the Lisa-Williams case. The more scope can be given to the problem, the easier it is to get away from a zero-sum result. For example, to include inspection of both sides' armaments, or to extend the issues beyond strictly military functions, like wheat sales to a country needing them from the other country's surplus.

Cold War Negotiations

DDI also worked with several US agencies in negotiations with Soviet Russia during the Cold War, with one US intelligence agency role-playing the Soviets, and the State Department and other US agencies, including the Department of Defence (DOD), prioritising issues from their perspective. DDI found inter-department differences were often substantial, and not subtle. For example, the State Department wanted scientific exchanges, whereas the DOD didn't. So, a major role for the decision-analytic model was to help the team members confront their differences and effectively develop the issues, preference values and weights that could represent the US position, thus preparing the teams for any subsequent development in the negotiations.

In the past, the typical US position was to go into negotiations with a single agreement, not with their own value functions. It became clear to DDI that a bargaining and negotiation model also serves as a method for scoring how well negotiations are progressing. At the end of each negotiating day, the US team could see how well they had done – if poorly on important issues, then overall they would see they did poorly even if they did well on the unimportant ones, which might be seen as a disadvantage of explicit modelling by negotiators wishing to come back saying they won. Fortunately, that risk was considered by most of the US players as worth the benefit of going into negotiations ready and prepared for anything the other side might throw at them.

Commerce

A large commercial organisation hired DDI to help them reduce featherbedding (overmanning in the UK). Initial work identified about 43 issues, although the focus was initially on only a few, such as the terms of the agreement (1, 2 or 3 Years), length of the working week (35 or 40 hours) and union recognition (only by National Labor Relations Board election and various other methods, or based on card check), plus direct wages, cost-of-living adjustment, health insurance, life insurance, pensions and so forth. The head of labour relations was the negotiator, helped by DDI staff. The main finding was the great value of the modelling approach in coordinating the negotiator with the views of his boss.

Cam explained that if the negotiator wants to act as a witch doctor, keeping an aura of mystery about how he or she works, then the boss is more likely to interfere, and the less value the model will contribute. Fortunately, the organisation's negotiator used the model, which extended eventually to 28 issues, with differences between management and unions in both scores and weights, to find a mutually acceptable contract, as can be seen in the 'Bargain' section of Chapter 12.

Oil Tanker Standards

Perhaps the most successful of all the DDI negotiation models was establishing worldwide standards for oil tankers to reduce pollution of land and seas. Various oil tanker mishaps in late 1976 and early 1977 attracted much media attention in the USA, prompting government action to improve tanker safety and pollution prevention. With support from President Carter in 1977, the United Nations' Intergovernmental Maritime Consultative Organization convened an international conference to be held in February 1978, with preparation for the conference to be carried out in meetings throughout the rest of 1977.

The US Coast Guard, in cooperation with the State Department and other agencies, represented the interests of the USA, but with so little time to prepare, they engaged analysts from DDI to help form and implement a negotiation model that would engage many other parties in the negotiations. This was, effectively, a construction of final recommendations for the February 1978 conference in which the issues accommodated the interests of all participating countries and their differences in preferences.

Eleven issues eventually emerged from these preliminary meetings, quoted here from the paper by Jacob Ulvila and Warren Snider reporting this case study:[199]

1. *World Oil Outflow.* The amount of oil discharged from tankships into the world's oceans (in metric tons per year).
2. *Oil in Own Waters.* The amount of oil from tankships that is discharged within 50 miles of the coastline of each country (in metric tons per year).

3. *Safety.* The reduction in deaths, injuries, and property damage due to a reduced number of tankship accidents.
4. *Cost.* The total cost in 1977 U.S. dollars of implementing various standards.
5. *Dollars per Ton* (of oil discharge prevented). Cost (criterion 4) divided by World Oil Outflow (criterion 1).
6. *Ease of Passing Cost to Consumer.* The ease with which a particular country's economy allows increased costs to be passed to consumers (of particular concern to countries with planned economies).
7. *Charter Party.* The impact on existing tankship charter agreements. (Some proposals may invalidate some existing charter agreements.)
8. *Tanker Surplus.* The reduction in the surplus of oil tanker capacity resulting from various changes to standards.
9. *Shipyards.* The amount of increase in ship construction and conversion work generated by new standards.
10. *Competitive Advantage.* The competitive advantage gained by operators of modern tankers.
11. *Enforceability.* The extent to which enforcement of the standard relies on equipment design rather than human performance.

These criteria were carefully developed by the team working with the participating countries to ensure the wording of the definitions was agreed and understood, as well as preference independent so that an additive model could be applied, thus making it more transparent for the users. The team started development of criteria by considering the technical measures set out in President Carter's message to Congress, but these were found to heavily interact with one another, making it difficult to define value functions, which didn't reflect preferences of the participating countries anyway. However, by attending to differences of opinion among the countries, the team formulated anew the 11 criteria, which were accepted by the countries.

In the next preparatory meetings, three packages of proposals were developed showing how to realise each of the 11 criteria to reduce oil pollutions from tankers and increase tanker safety: US Proposal, Package 1 and Package 2. A fourth package defined the status quo, that is, what the case would be if the 1978 Conference failed to reach agreement, which defined the 1973 International Convention for the Prevention of Pollution from Ships, MARPOL 73, and the 1974 International Convention for the Safety of Life at Sea. In addition, the team developed an MCDA model just for the World Oil criterion, which acted as a 'plumbing' model that distinguished the sources of oil pollution, operations and accidents, and the various ways these could lead to outflows of oil, including size of tankers, types of oil, types of operations and types of accidents. These four packages essentially defined the different viewpoints of the participating nations, so can be considered as the main parties to the negotiations.

Over a period of six months, the team initiated many bilateral discussions, both within the USA and with many countries, gradually becoming clearer about the key criteria and how best to describe them. After several iterations, the team felt sufficiently confident that objective measures of the reduction of oil outputs derived from the MCDA model could proportionately be rescaled to 0–100 preference values, with direct assessment by the experts for the remaining nine criteria, which are shown in Table 15.3.

Table 15.3

	Scores of the Alternatives			
Issues	MARPOL 73	U.S.	Package 2	Package 1
1 World Oil	0	81	100	80
2 Oil in Own Waters	0	100	0	100
3 Safety	0	100	50	85
4 Cost	100	0	95	30
5 Dollars per Ton	0	0	100	32
6 Ease of Passing Cost	100	0	95	30
7 Charter Party	100	0	95	10
8 Tanker Surplus	0	100	20	90
9 Shipyards	0	100	20	90
10 Competitive Advantage	0	100	20	90
11 Enforceability	0	100	10	90

As expected, each row contains at least one zero and one 100. For example, Package 2 was deemed to be best for World Oil, and just one of many in worst position for MARPOL 73. It's clear that no one alternative is better on all 11 issues, so no dominating single winner here. Thus, it's also clear that trade-offs must be considered to see if there is a compromise that would be acceptable as a world standard.

After creating short descriptions of the best and worst impacts for each issue, the team facilitated swing weighting with small groups of Coast Guard respondents, who role-played the foreign countries they had engaged in bilateral discussions, and other US interest groups, always obtaining rationales for the swing weights. Throughout the preparations period, these assessments were revised as each country's interests became clearer.

Scores and normalised weights were constructed across US and county interests by Coast Guard members of the team and weighted preference scores calculated for each of the four alternatives (Table 15.4).

Differences of numbers within each of the four interval scales can be meaningfully compared, but not between the columns. However, similarities of interest are evident. For example, differences are small between countries A, B and C for the US and Packages 1 and 2. Countries A, B and C agree that the US Alternative and Package 1 are the best, but perhaps bringing in the best issues for D, E, F and G in Package 2 might constitute an overall acceptable agreement. Sensitivity analyses showed that general conclusions drawn from this table are little affected by minor variations in scores and weights.

Those are just some of the team members' insights, which led them to further explorations with the participating countries and with other US stakeholders. The authors explained a major value the model played in this stage of the project:

By exercising the model, the delegates could creatively explore possible compromises and examine their likely consequences. Examinations of the scores of the alternatives on the criteria

Table 15.4

	Scores of the Alternatives			
Country	MARPOL 73	U.S.	Package 2	Package 1
US	9	79	47	79
A	3	88	29	83
B	15	85	25	81
C	12	85	25	81
D	61	22	80	43
E	52	41	66	54
F	36	55	77	63
G	29	62	76	67
H	50	47	55	55
I	27	58	62	62

Table 15.5

Scores		Preferences	
Issues	New package	Country	Value
World Oil	105	US	81
Oil in Own Waters	100	A	47
Safety	100	B	51
Cost	90	C	57
Dollars per Ton	80	D	79
Ease of Passing Cost	90	E	71
Charter Party	90	F	81
Tanker Surplus	15	G	85
Shipyards	25	H	53
Competitive Advantage	35	I	65
Enforceability	10		

and the sets of criteria and weights of the countries enabled the delegates to identify possible compromise positions, in terms of their technical components, that might be evaluated favourably by both the United States and other countries.[200]

As a result, a new package, shown in Table 15.5, emerged from their discussions.

Needless to say, the explorations benefited from trying out different judgements on the computer model, which minimised the bias that inevitably accompanies verbal discourse. Indeed, a final agreement was developed, which the participating countries found to be acceptable. This agreed model helped the team to brief stakeholders in the USA, including members of Congress, and the new measures were mostly implemented. William Usery, then the US Assistant Secretary for Labor, who had gained experience in union-management labour relations in the late 1960s and early 1970s but left government service in January 1977, was hired by DDI to serve as a consultant on the Oil Tanker negotiations. He mainly advised the team when to negotiate and when to listen, and later told Cam he had never seen a team so completely in control of negotiations.

And did the agreement reached have an impact? We know, of course, that cause-and-effect are hard to prove, and that good outcomes don't necessarily follow from good decisions. However, data from ITOPF, a not-for-profit organisation that keeps track of oil spills, shows substantial, sustained reductions. In the 1970s, 788 tonnes of oil had been spilled from large and medium-sized tankers, reducing every decade to 27 tonnes in the 2020s. Perhaps the DDI project was a contributor.

Overall, DDI's experience with MCDA bargaining and negotiation models can be summarised as follows:[201]

1. Helps negotiators prepare in advance
2. Allows negotiations to be flexible
3. Helps users to maintain control
4. Facilitates coordination between negotiators and their organisation
5. Forces negotiators to widen the scope of the issues
6. Facilitates implementation
7. Provides negotiators with a thorough understanding of the situation
8. Helps negotiators anticipate positions of other delegates
9. Encourages development of new alternatives
10. Improves communications within the negotiation team

All of this happened in the late 1970s, and times may have changed in the world of bargaining and negotiation. To learn more while writing this chapter, I asked ChatGPT this question:

What are the main characteristics of two-party bargaining that a negotiator should address to develop a contract that enables both sides to feel that their issues have been addressed?

And this is the response, unedited:

When engaging in two-party bargaining to develop a contract that satisfies both sides, a negotiator should address several key characteristics. Here are the main characteristics to consider:

1. Mutual Interests: Identify and understand the shared interests between the parties. By focusing on mutual interests, negotiators can uncover areas of potential agreement and develop solutions that meet the needs of both parties. Finding common ground is crucial for creating a contract that satisfies both sides.

2. Effective Communication: Clear and open communication is essential for successful negotiation. Negotiators should ensure that all parties have the opportunity to express their concerns, priorities, and desired outcomes. Active listening and effective articulation of ideas help build understanding and trust between the parties.

3. Compromise and Trade-offs: Negotiators should be prepared to make compromises and explore trade-offs to address the concerns of both sides. It involves seeking creative solutions that meet the core interests of both parties while accommodating their respective preferences. A willingness to give and take is crucial for achieving a mutually acceptable agreement.

4. Win-Win Solutions: Aim for win-win outcomes where both parties feel that their issues have been addressed and their goals achieved. A negotiator should actively seek opportunities to create value and expand the overall pie of benefits, rather than focusing solely on claiming

a larger share for their own side. This approach helps build a cooperative and collaborative environment.

5. Fairness and Equity: Addressing concerns about fairness and equity is vital in developing a contract that satisfies both parties. Negotiators should strive to ensure that the agreement is perceived as fair and reasonable by both sides. Transparency in the negotiation process and equitable distribution of benefits can help foster a sense of satisfaction and acceptance.

6. Long-Term Relationship: Consider the long-term relationship between the parties beyond the immediate negotiation. A negotiator should be mindful of preserving the relationship and avoiding tactics that might damage trust or create animosity. Building a foundation of trust and goodwill can facilitate future collaborations and make future negotiations smoother.

7. Flexibility and Adaptability: Negotiators should be flexible and adaptable in their approach. Circumstances may change during the negotiation process, and new information or unexpected developments may emerge. Being open to adjusting positions and exploring alternative solutions can help navigate challenges and find mutually acceptable outcomes.

By addressing these characteristics, a negotiator can create a contract that acknowledges the concerns of both parties and enables them to feel that their issues have been addressed effectively.

All of these seemed reasonable and certainly reflect what happened in the Oil Tanker case, under the wise guidance of Usery, helped by the use of a computer model that could encompass all points of view. Sadly, the DDI software is not available, nor has one been developed, as far as we know. An opportunity here for a reader skilled in programming!

Conclusions

DDI's engagement in bargaining and negotiation with decision-analytic models pre-dates the 'discovery' of decision conferences in 1979, which you may recognise shares many characteristics, such as the importance of developing trust (item 6, above). Of particular note is the role of the computer program as a transitional object (Chapter 10), able to hold and contain multiple points of view as the users confront the current reality while they set about finding ways to reduce their sense of unease about worldwide oil spills, or anything else. It's a process of creating a better world based on current data, breaking a problem down into its pieces, holding them while exploring different points of view, looking for ways to find win-win outcomes, ensuring that all points of view are heard.

A second observation about a bargaining and negotiation model is its eventual irrelevance. At the start, its role is to quantify participants' intuitions, with preference values representing extent of impacts and swing weights the relative importance of the impacts, which are not easily distinguished in words. But in the end, numbers are only a route to a better understanding of the issues, which then can better be expressed in words, a constructed narrative that directly addresses the problem in natural language.

Finally, in none of the examples given here did any party draw a red line at the start of negotiating, which is essential for keeping lines of communication totally open. Red lines can easily kill any hope of compromise. They are best kept implicit, as they can forestall an effective negotiation.

16 Choose and Decide

Sometimes the right path is not the easiest.

Disney's Pocahontas, 1995

The simple decision tree about the blind problem shown at the beginning of Chapter 1, a risky choice compared to a sure-thing, with more than one criterion describing the consequences, is occasionally useful for deciding what to do in a simple situation, as it can serve as a warning against the 'certainty bias', giving more weight to a sure-thing alternative because its outcomes are familiar and it feels safe. However, for more complex problems, with several uncertainties and perhaps multiple criteria, more complex decision trees are required.

To see how larger decision tree models are developed, I'll first report here how Graham, a design engineer who attended a once-a-week seminar about decision analysis, asked for help on a real problem he was facing. I'll report the conversation he and I had over a period of only 45 minutes. Then I'll apply this type of model to more complex problems.

Graham's Decision Problem (Decision Tree)

On the seminar's first Wednesday, after I had introduced the blind case study in the morning, Graham asked if decision analysis might help him decide how he could use this approach to his choice of how to design a particular piece of equipment that his boss needs early next week.

'Well, let's give it a try,' I replied. 'What's the problem?'

'I know how to design what he wants,' he explained, 'and it is an old, reliable method which involves various tables and charts and look-ups that are tedious to apply, which takes two or three days. I know a bit about computer programming, and thought I might be able to design a computer-aided method that I'm pretty sure would work and save time for me to work on other projects.'

'You seem hesitant to do that, so what's stopping you?' I asked.

'I'm worried that if my program doesn't work, I could be short of time to go back to the old method, and I'm very concerned about my job security. Delivering late would be a black mark.'

'Sounds to me this looks a lot like the blind problem, an uncertain option versus a sure-thing.'

'Yes, the certainty is moving me in that direction.'

'So, is this what you are thinking?' I said, drawing on the whiteboard a choice node with two options: Write program and Use old method. I then drew at the end of the Write program branch an event node with two outcomes, Program works and No: use package.

'Yeah, that's it,' he replied.

'OK, and can you tell me more about the consequences, like what objectives are you considering?' I asked.

'My boss is expecting the new design before the end of the week, which the old method will permit. But if I take too long trying to get a computer program working and it doesn't, I could be in trouble with him. Completing on time is crucial.'

'Is speed the only objective?'

'The program would add an element of flexibility unlike the old method, which doesn't allow much leeway. And, of course, it would be more accurate. Oh, and a quick completion would reduce the cost of my time to be charged against the project.'

'So, you want to consider all four criteria? Let's call them speed, flexibility, accuracy and cost.'

'Sounds good,' he added. 'But now you've got me thinking there are a lot of advantages for the computer-based approach. Actually, I did quickly explore the possibility of applying an existing commercial program that is very inexpensive, but I rejected it as I wasn't sure it would work for me. Might be worth a try, as it would take less time than writing my own program.'

'I see, and if it didn't work, would that still leave time for you to try writing your own program?'

'Ah ... yes, I see now I had considered them simply as alternatives.'

Let's now look at Graham's problem under the usual five headings for creating a decision model.

1.   Consider Context

Graham was very much concerned about his job security. He wanted to be sure of solving this problem by the end of the week so he could present the solution at the start of the next week. Anxious to do a quality job in time, he said he was inclined to apply the well-accepted look-up design process, without considering any risky options. That's a common mistake: one option only is considered, and it will always be possible to find reasons for going ahead or not. But this isn't decision analysis, it is decision rationalisation. When someone says there is only one option, that's to be challenged.

2.   Frame the Problem

The mix of uncertainty and multiple objectives in Graham's narrative of his task, in particular the decision he would face if the computer package doesn't work, suggests

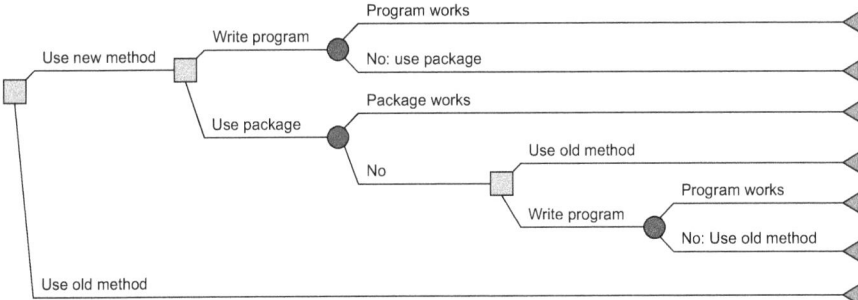

Figure 16.1

that a decision tree could accommodate that 'if-then' feature. Decision trees always begin with alternatives, so it's tempting to begin the structuring process by considering those initial options. But it's better to start by considering the objectives first, then identifying the uncertainties and decisions.

A little more discussion resulted in agreement about definitions of the four criteria: speed of results, flexibility (ability to change a parameter to see its effect on the overall design), accuracy of the results (better with the program) and cost (of his time in producing a result), all of which seemed to be preference independent.

About 20 minutes of diagramming on a whiteboard, erasing, rearranging and changing pieces of the problem resulted in the decision tree shown in Figure 16.1, redrawn using DPL software (p. 226).

Graham's tree shows seven possible future scenarios, seven paths through the tree, which effectively represent his dilemma more clearly than any verbal description of it. But it's obviously more complex than the simple tree he started with. It was only at the point where he began to think not only about his fundamental objective, to protect his job security, but also about the more immediate goals, that he began to consider the four criteria that led to his insight that he had time to consider another choice after finding the package didn't work.

Provide Content

I invited Graham to assess probabilities for the uncertain outcomes (which he had already learned in the course), with the results shown in Figure 16.2.

It's clear that at the start he feels most confident about his own ability to write a program, a little less about whether the package will work and even less if the package didn't work, as that would reduce his confidence about his ability to write a program himself.

We turned next to consider the four criteria and score each of the seven scenarios on the criteria, applying interval scaling, with a score of 100 for the most preferred option and 0 for the least preferred. I wrote the scores on the whiteboard in a table of four columns, enabling the best and worst consequences in each column to be identified so Graham could assess swing weight. After a few consistency checks, he calculated

Table 16.1

Scenario	Speed	Flexibility	Accuracy	Cost	Weighted Totals
A	90	100	90	90	**92**
B	25	0	0	20	**20**
C	100	100	100	100	**100**
D	30	0	0	30	**24**
E	60	100	90	80	**70**
F	0	0	0	0	**0**
G	40	0	0	40	**32**
Weights	0.7	0.15	0.05	0.1	

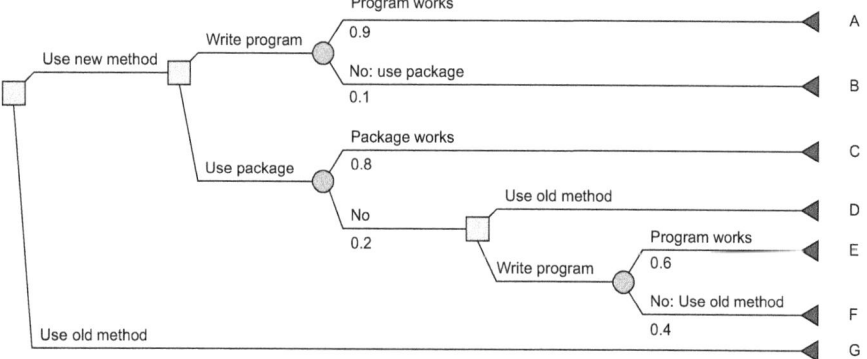

Figure 16.2

a total weighted value at each event node, and rolled the tree back for each scenario (Table 16.1). (Sorry to say that although multiple attributes can be accommodated in DPL, the process is complex and swing weighting is not transparently easy.)

Interesting that using the package could lead to either the best scenario, C, or to the worst, F, on all criteria. That's often the case with taking a new approach and is why we've learned that the status quo is often the safest approach. It's the 'least bad', but using that consistently as the basis for making decisions means never taking advantage of opportunities.

Placing the totals at their respective locations at the right end of the decision tree enables the computer to roll back the decision tree to show the results.

3.   Explore Results

We saw the process of rolling back in Chapter 1. Starting with the total values at the right, it is a matter of calculating expected values at the event nodes, then moving left to compare the alternatives, taking the larger value leftward, and repeating the process, stopping at the initial decision node. That was done by Graham, with the help of a calculator. In Figure 16.3, DPL did it.

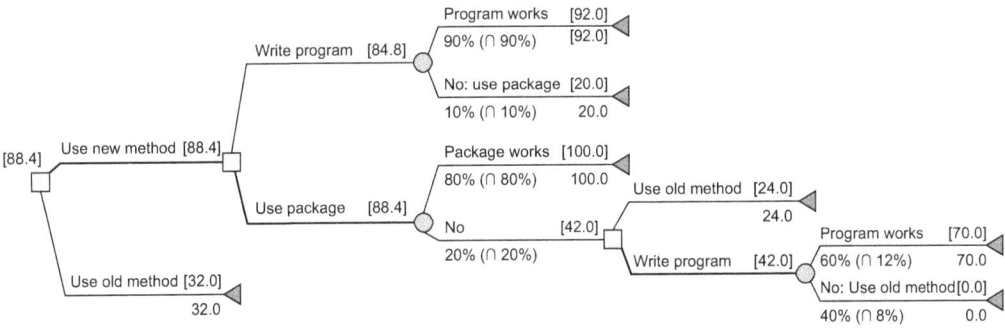

Figure 16.3

Numbers above the branches, in square brackets, are calculations, while those below are values. Starting, at the lower-right event node, the values of 70 and 0 are multiplied by the probabilities of 0.6 and 0.4, to give a weighted total of 42, shown in square brackets on the previous Write program branch. That 42 is then multiplied by 0.20 on the No branch, and that product is added to the Package works product of 100 by 0.80 to give 88.4, the value of Use package.

When the event node at the top is rolled back, this gives a value of 84.8 to Write program. That weighted total is less than the 88.4, and that is much better than the 32 for Use old method, so the software highlights in bold the best decision, Use new method. Note that the percentages in round brackets below the branches are the products of all the probabilities up to that point on each path. Thus, the chance of the worst outcome is 8 per cent (the ∩ symbol means intersection, which here refers to all previous branches), 40 per cent times 20 per cent.

Sensitivity analyses on probabilities act differently for decision trees than on criteria weights for MCDA. The reason is that in decision trees the probabilities of a node's outcomes must sum to 1.00, so their effects are local, whereas in MCDA changing a single weight can affect other weights at other nodes to ensure that the normalised weights across the value tree sum to 100, thus influencing results in other parts of the tree.

For example, how low must the probability of the package working be for the choice of a new method to shift from Use package to Write program? Lowering that probability to 73 per cent (and increasing the probability of No to 27 per cent) causes the shift. Although Graham wasn't sure about that probability, he said it was at least 75 per cent, and thought 80 per cent was more realistic.

4.   Agree the Way Forward

Graham was surprised by the low value of using the old method (recall the quote at the start of Chapter 6 by Sir Francis Bacon), and he felt much encouraged to try the new method. The process had changed his severe risk aversion. When he returned to the course the following week and we asked him what he did, he replied, 'I decided to write my own program, and it worked!' Someone asked, 'But that wasn't what the model said to do. Why didn't you use the package?' 'Well, because the difference between the two new options was only a few points, so I decided to apply a fifth criterion that is very personal: the pleasure I would experience if my own program worked and I could use it again, if needed.'

That exchange shows again that decision models simply give back in changed form what was given to them. At best, they recommend, but usually they feed back a different perspective that causes the decision maker's original sense of unease to be sufficiently reduced that he or she can comfortably decide. As Graham rightly did.

This simple problem well illustrates how further decisions after initial ones can be represented in decision trees (which are often referred to as 'real options analysis'), but this flexibility can be quite cumbersome if the same event trees keep popping up, making it impossible to physically show all branches of the tree. It has now become standard to show event nodes detached from decision branches where the same structure would otherwise be repeated at each branch. This is well illustrated in the next case study.

MEM Case Study

In the 1960s and 1970s, textbooks usually positioned decision analysis as supporting individual decision makers, largely because decision theory makes explicit the consequences of an ideal person's preferences that are consistent in the sense that they obey simple axioms, as described in Chapter 2. Preference values, trade-offs and probabilities were characteristics of individuals, not groups. Thus, applications of decision analysis in the early years largely focused on the decision maker, although some organisations established decision support groups that applied decision analysis to formulate recommendations to the accountable decision maker. Some academics suggested that these features might also exist in groups and have proposed schemes for combining individual cardinal preferences into a group preference. Others have shown that any such scheme won't satisfy all the axioms of decision theory, such as Kenneth Arrow's Impossibility Theorem.[202]

In this book, I presume only that a group is capable of agreeing preference values, trade-off weights or probabilities in a single requisite decision model that any member of the group could support, even if their individual preferences may be different. The oil tanker spillage case study in the previous chapter well illustrates my claim.

1.　Consider Context

I was led to that mindset only after accepting in 1979 a consultancy project from a medium-sized British firm manufacturing outboard engines and motors for pleasure craft, Maritime Engines and Motors (MEM).[i] For over 20 years, MEM's main product maintained a solid 70 per cent market share, largely because of its reliability and sound engineering, as well as its attractive design. MEM's managing director (MD) explained that the product had just been banned in the inland and coastal waterways of the USA because it did not meet new federal regulations for emissions, and the MD was worried that the UK might also ban it. Although there was no suggestion the UK Government would tighten emission standards, he wanted to anticipate a possible threat to MEM's main product, so was considering redesigning the carburation system of the motor, which would include a new microchip currently being designed by an in-house team. That would meet the US standard, and presumably any new one in Britain. In addition, these changes would provide an opportunity to introduce robotics to the firm. But all this would meet resistance from the company's Board, who were known for their conservative approach to any new initiative.

2.   Frame the Problem

It took two months of meetings with individual Sales, Finance and Production Managers, and some of their staff, and the MD, to flesh out a decision tree. The flavour of some meetings was like a Luigi Pirandello play in which each new character explains a different social reality from the previous, leaving me guessing about what to include and exclude in the decision model. More than once after I left a manager's office and explained what I had learned so far, the next manager would disagree or say that wasn't the real crux of the problem. So, back and forth I would go, and only during a final meeting with the MD to show him the preliminary model did he add the 'Troubled' branch of the left-most event node in the decision tree, on the grounds that the previous launch of a new product had not gone smoothly. In the meantime, I elicited probabilities from those who were willing to provide their views.

The relative order of event outcomes on the decision tree is important: always in the order their outcomes are expected to become known, not necessarily in the order they will actually happen. This keeps the decision tree grounded in reality, for decision makers can only take subsequent decisions once the earlier event outcomes are known. Recall how that led the gas-gathering pipeline decision tree at the start of Chapter 7 to provide a better solution than designing the whole system in one go. For the MEM case, including the timing of event outcomes led to different outcomes and final values.

3.   Provide Content

During the iterations of the structuring process, the probabilities began to coalesce in agreement, with the MD resolving any remaining differences at my last meeting with him. The final structure of choice and event nodes resulted in a hand-drawn decision tree of 70 paths that is more compactly displayed by using DPL (Figure 16.4).

---

[i] The name of the company and its products have been changed, but the report here accurately describes the problem, the model and what subsequently happened.

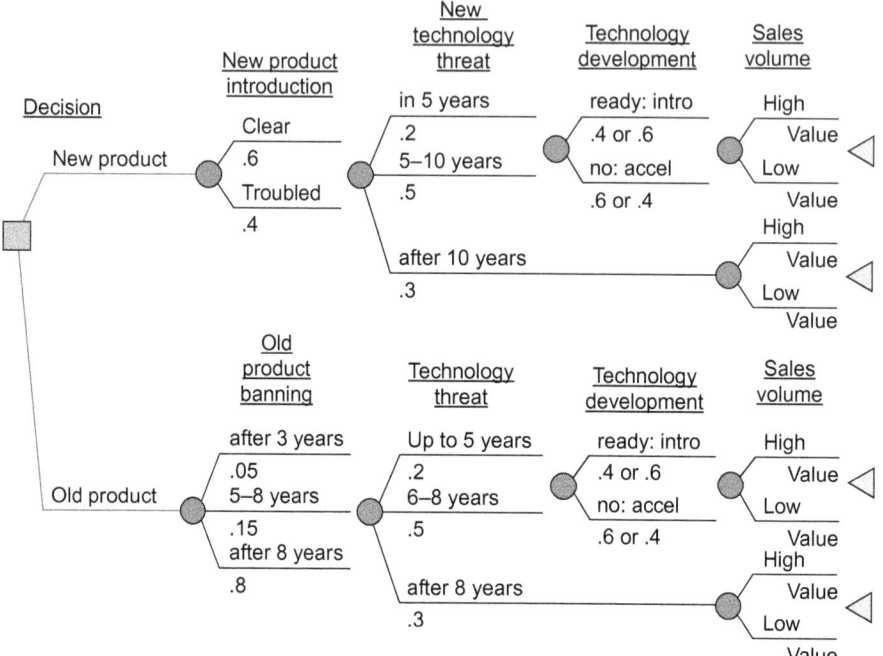

Figure 16.4

It is now standard practice of decision tree software to leave nodes that are children of parent nodes unattached if they are repeated under other parent nodes and their descriptions are unchanged. Thus, the three-branch technology threat node floats to the right of the nodes to which it will be attached when running the model. Once everything is attached, there are 20 New product paths through the tree, and 30 Old product paths, 20 less than the original model as it isn't necessary here to show branches for which profit calculations were made about the new product.

The paths show all the assumptions needed to describe the Value consequences evaluated against three criteria:

- Net present value of the old or new product, a monetary scale.
- Value associated with the chip-based product, a 0–100 preference scale.
- Value of new manufacturing technology, a 0–100 preference scale.

A few assumptions enabled the two preference scales to be converted to monetary figures, accompanied by weighting factors of 0.5 on both scales to allow sensitivity analyses about the values. Because the technology threat is unaffected by MEM, those three-branch events show the same probabilities (one must remember for sensitivity analyses to change both similarly), while the in-house technology development probabilities reverse when that node is attached to the threat branches, namely, 40–60 for 'in 5 years' and 60–40 for 'in 5–10 years'. The ranges of NPVs extended from £30 million for the worst scenario to £110 million for the best.

4. ## Explore Results

At a Board meeting in November, large paper drawings of the complete decision tree, showing the probabilities and values for all three criteria, were distributed to the members so they could comment on any part of the model. The trustworthy IBM 5110 portable computer was present, enabling me to test the effects on any new judgements or disagreements. Once the MD had introduced the decision tree model and justified the probabilities, the Business Planning Manager discussed the NPV model and the basis for monetising the other two criteria. I explained the simple weighted-averaging roll-back procedure for attaching financial values to the decisions.

When the tree was rolled back, it showed that the New product choice was valued at £81.6 million, and the Old product at £77.2 million (Figure 16.5).

Not a big difference, so the MD wanted to see the values at Clear and Troubled. He saw that clear introduction of the new product was valued at £88.8 million compared to £77.2 million for the old product, and he asked me if that difference would justify his spending up to £11.6 million to ensure a clear introduction (88.8 minus 77.2). I agreed, and he replied that he could increase the probability of a clear introduction at considerably less than £11.6 million.

However, some Board members expressed their concerns about other aspects of the model. The first issue concerned the 0.6 for a clear introduction, which some thought might be lower, but nobody thought it should be lower than 0.5, which when entered into the computer gave a new expected value of 79.6; still, the new product was best.

One member suggested that probabilities of 0.2, 0.3 and 0.5 for the microchip threat were too optimistic: more weight should be given to the upper two branches. A survey of the Board revealed that the most pessimistic view was 0.5, 0.3 and 0.2. Once those probabilities were entered into the computer for the two technology threat nodes, it confirmed a lower expected value for the new product, 79.2, as expected. But the figure

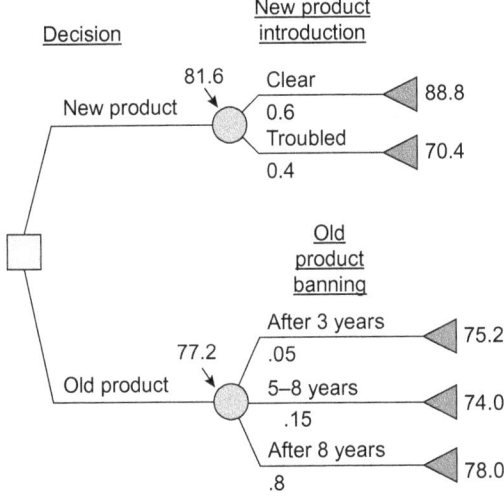

Figure 16.5

for the old product also decreased, 75.6, still favouring the new product. Finally, some Board members suggested that the weight of 0.5 on the second criterion, the value associated with the chip-based product, should be increased. It was increased to 1.0, giving new expected values for the decisions of 86.4 and 84.0; again, the new product won.

The original decision tree included an extra event at the end of all the new product paths, the difference between the sales price and the manufacturing cost. Two branches for each of the 20 paths showed outcomes of High and Low, with probabilities of 0.8 and 0.2, respectively. One Board member suggested reversing all those probabilities, which was then carried out, giving an overall weighted value for the new product of 82.8, now smaller than the 84.0 for the old product obtained at the previous sensitivity analysis.

5.   Agree the Way Forward

Reminding the group that the changes made so far had been cumulative, I pointed out that adopting the old product would be justified only if everyone agreed to the more pessimistic probabilities of the ban. Returning at least one change back to the base case would lead to the new product being most preferred. It quickly became clear that no member believed all the pessimistic assumptions. The Board agreed to go ahead with the new product, and the MD hired a design consultant to redesign the product.

The decision tree only represents many possible future scenarios, but it doesn't display the strategic plan that was being constructed in the mind of the MD before the Board meeting. Here's what I wrote in the 1982 paper:

If the ban is announced in 1981, effective in 1983 [the top branch, After 3 years], the Managing Director decided that he would shift to the new product (not the chip-based product) but produce it using conventional methods. This would save the cost of robotics which would be too risky to introduce in the light of the chip threat. If the ban was not announced by 1984 [second branch], and the chip threat had developed by then, he would immediately commit the Company to shifting to the chip-based product. But if the threat had not developed by the time the ban was announced, then he would recommend manufacturing the new, conventional product on old equipment. Development of this strategic plan occurred when the parts of the tree were put together and the need for a plan became obvious. However, the contingent actions were the subject of considerable debate, which was settled only when the problem was put to the Managing Director.[203]

This case study provides three insights into how to create a better future. The first is that a decision model can deepen thinking about a problem. It wasn't until near the end of the model's construction that the MD realised it should include the possibility of a troubled introduction for a new product. And the model revealed he could reduce that problem by spending a substantial sum to increase the probability of a clear introduction.

The second is that the model helped the Board to expand and clarify their thinking about the problem, which had mainly focused on a possible ban, but the model showed that the MD's strategic approach had made the ban largely irrelevant. If the Board had applied their usual approach of arguing the pros and cons, that would have positioned the microchip threat as applying only to the new product, whereas in fact it applies to both the new and the old.

Finally, engaging the MD right from the start in the model-building process helped him and the Board to own the problem. His staff spent much more time than he did, but the graphics greatly helped him to quickly grasp the intricacies of the problem solutions. Overall, the model served as a transitional object, holding the completed elements as they were elaborated over several months, and allowing all key players to try out new judgements and assumptions.

If you have read the chapters of Part II, you will see intimations in the MEM case study of what was to come next: requisite models rather than optimal models, how a requisite model can reduce the decision maker's sense of unease, that engaging the key problem owners helps to ensure that everyone is pulling in the same direction in creating the future, and that the process consultancy stance of the facilitator ensures full ownership by the client of the problem and its solution. And you can see how all this came together when I decided to adopt decision conferences and develop them with my US and UK colleagues as a socio-technical modelling approach.

Finally, as I finished this chapter, I was curious to know if MEM survived, so looked up their history on the internet. I was pleased to see they continue trading, with a reputation for reliable, innovative products, as part of a larger organisation which bought them only a few years ago, but continues to use the MEM name for all that company's products. Perhaps it was the MD's courageous step into the future with new technology and robotics that built such a positive image and a stable company able to flexibly respond to new challenges (and, no, it wasn't about outboard motors).

Relevance Diagrams

Logically, relevance (or influence) diagrams belong in this chapter, for they are an alternative way of structuring a decision tree. They show two things: how earlier decisions and event outcomes can either cause or be relevant to later ones. For example, knowing the time on my electronic wristwatch reduces my uncertainty about what your wristwatch shows. There is no causal relationship between our two watches; it is the time signal from GPS satellites that causes their displays to be identical.

For example, Figure 16.6 shows a relevance diagram for the blind problem of Chapter 2. The options and event outcomes are not shown, which makes the graphic simpler. What it does show is that the value of the consequences depends on both the patient's decision and the outcome of the operation, while the absence of an arrow from the rectangle to the oval shows that the decision maker has no control over the operation's outcome. That can only be confirmed on a decision tree by inspection of the probabilities. You can see that if there were many events, outcomes and subsequent decisions, the relevance diagram easily shows where sets of event probabilities and

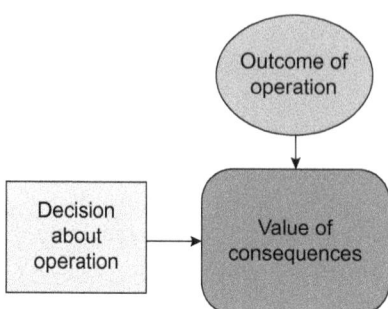

Figure 16.6

preference values are independent and where they are conditional. This will become clearer in the next chapter.

Recall that in the 'Choose and Decide' sub-section of Chapter 12, there is a simple decision tree, with only one decision to be made, but three uncertain events that in combination determine the final consequences. We return to that case study in Chapter 18, but for now you can see that knowing the outcomes of all three events is relevant to assessing the consequential deaths and disabilities, but among the events, only disease seriousness affects efficacy. But sorting out whether the arrows can be interpreted as representing 'knowing' or 'causing' is here (and usually) very tricky and doesn't affect the creation of a requisite decision tree. And it's an issue that doesn't overtly arise when assessing probabilities and values in decision trees. For that reason alone, I always prefer the decision tree diagram, as it makes intuitive sense and is easy for the client to follow if the outcomes of events are shown in the order they will become known to the decision maker as time moves forward. However, relevance diagrams reappear in the next chapter, as they are convenient ways to supplement risk and fault trees.

The Value of Information

Recall that when the MEM MD saw only a modest difference between the expected preference values of the new and old products, he wanted to see the expected value for a clear new product introduction. That was larger, so he felt justified in spending up to £11.6 million to ensure the introduction would be clear and that he could effectively gain control at considerably less than that. The additional information would effectively give him control over that uncertain node.

When working collaboratively with the decision maker, I usually find that when a decision model includes several subsequent decisions and their outcomes, the accountable manager's sense of unease increases as he or she sees a series of worse cases developing on one branch of the tree, rather like branch F in Graham's decision problem. That's when the manager reformulates the tree, often by stepping back and changing the context, revising initial parts of the tree and/or adding corrective nodes later on to ensure at least a tolerable worst-case scenario.

When it is desirable to find the value of information at each or any node to see if buying more information would be justified, software can help by allowing the user to drag a worrisome event node to the start of the tree, so it can calculate the *expected value of perfect information* (EVPI). This simulates what the decision maker should do as if they had perfect information at each node. That is rarely needed in collaborative modelling because clients find ways to develop decision trees that recover from worst-case consequences. Thank goodness, for explaining to clients how EVPI works is not for the faint-hearted.

Summary

Building models collaboratively *with* your client is the theme of this chapter's case studies. Of course, decision trees can be built *for* a client as well, and many consulting companies do that. But the tide is changing as the process consultancy approach is generally more effective at gaining acceptance of the solutions and implementing them. But it isn't easy. It takes time and patience to gather available information, think creatively about the future, imagine what might happen and how to react, then formulate flexible strategies that include many 'If this, then that ...' responses. Decision analysis had yet to be born in the time of Pocahontas, but as a trail guide, she certainly was correct.

Two final observations. The first is that structuring a decision tree can itself impact the risk attitude of both the decision maker and the group, echoing the findings of the group polarisation phenomenon discussed in Chapter 11. Graham's risk aversion initially led him to favour the old method and his view of the problem wasn't as nuanced as the seven paths of the value tree. MEM's MD added the potential for a troubled introduction of a new product to the decision tree, and rolling back the decision tree allowed him to see how he could control that uncertain event with an affordable investment.

The second observation is how both decision models served as transitional objects, enabling the process of thinking about their problem, allowing the detail and complexity to be held temporarily in abeyance while constructing the model and after exploring the completed model. And for the MEM case study, it showed that the individual preferences of the Board members could be maintained without affecting the decision, effectively a risky shift for the group, but still a requisite model for the group.

17   Manage Risk

Great love and great achievements involve great risks.

Dalai Lama[204]

Imagine there is a history of heart problems in your family, and you have done your best to maintain a healthy body. In a recent health check-up, your doctor tells you about a newly approved drug and says, 'There is a risk that this new drug won't help your heart risk and there are risks from taking the drug.' You probably know what is meant without being aware that the doctor has invoked three different definitions of 'risk':

- New drug risk: failure to experience a benefit.
- Your heart risk: a biologically inherited condition.
- Risks of taking the drug: possible side effects.

As a decision analyst, you are certain to encounter risk in many assignments, but simple concepts of risk, such as 'the possibility an unwanted event may occur', hinder attempts to make explicit what your client actually means. Here are examples I've encountered:

1. Insurance industry: The probability of a loss times the severity of the loss.
2. British Medical Association: The probability that something unpleasant will happen.
3. Nuclear industry: The probability of an individual dying from radiation, integrated over the number of doses received and the number of people receiving them.
4. Financial industry: The volatility of financial outcomes, measured by their variance.

Even within an industry, there may be different definitions:

5. Pharmaceutical industry

   a. Research scientist – probability a compound merits further development.
   b. Development scientist – probability of regulatory approval.
   c. Marketing manager – probability the drug will be a commercial success.

The experimental psychologist Paul Slovic carried out a psychometric study that identified three factors of how people *perceive* risk, which has been replicated across different people and interest groups.[205] Factor 1 captures the feeling of *dread* by people exposed to a risk (as a noun). Factor 2 is the extent to which the risk is *familiar*. A third factor, the *number of people exposed* to the risk, has been found in several studies. These dimensions explain people's reactions to many risks, such as mad cow disease, which became a serious concern in the late 1980s as people worried about its possible transmission to humans. Despite the belief of scientists that the probability of transmission was very small, that did little to allay concern, an attitude that can be explained by invoking the three factors. If the disease were to infect humans, we would dread the destruction of our brains and spinal cord, the possible transmission of the disease was unfamiliar, and it could affect a high number of people – everyone who had recently eaten a hamburger.

These three factors capture both objective and subjective aspects of risks, so it is no wonder that an objective definition is not agreed. The take-away for the decision analyst is that when your client raises concerns about risk, you may not understand what they mean without further questioning them. Their answers will help you to think of some combination of the 10 elements of good decisions (Chapter 1) that you can assemble in a decision model, enabling your client to explore their perceptions about risk.

So, are risk and decision analyses really different? I think they differ only in their purposes. A decision analysis shows the favourable and unfavourable events whose uncertain outcomes may help or hinder achieving desired goals, whereas a risk analysis is intended to mitigate occurrence of unfavourable events in the pursuit of goals. Both represent uncertainties associated with event outcomes and may include multiple criteria. However, the decision analysis model will show mutually exclusive decisions at the start of a decision tree and also possibly after the outcomes of subsequent outcomes, as in Graham's decision model, whereas the risk analysis model may show only events and their uncertain outcomes. If the latter does include initial and subsequent decisions, as in the MEM case study (Chapter 16), then it will look very much like a decision analysis model, but as I've said, the purposes are different, as can be seen in the two case studies of this chapter.

Risk Framework

To create a decision model that incorporates features relevant to risk, MacCrimmon and Wehrung's REACT model of managing risk, whose five phases and the features of risk, may help you to engage with your client's feeling of risk, so here is a brief summary of their approach.[206] Their model for managing risk consists of five phases: (1) *recognising* and structuring the risk; (2) *evaluating* the risk; (3) *adjusting* the risk; (4) *choosing* among risky options; and (5) *tracking* the outcomes. They also provide guidance on how to adjust risk by gaining time, information or more control, so as to increase chances of success, maximise the value of outcomes and reduce exposure (Figure 17.1).

We'll see the REACT model in operation with the two case studies to follow. Both cases start with decisions that would adjust the risk in two very different situations that attempt to minimise deaths. *Event trees* start from a particular undesired initiating event followed by decisions and key uncertain events. *Fault trees* start with a particular

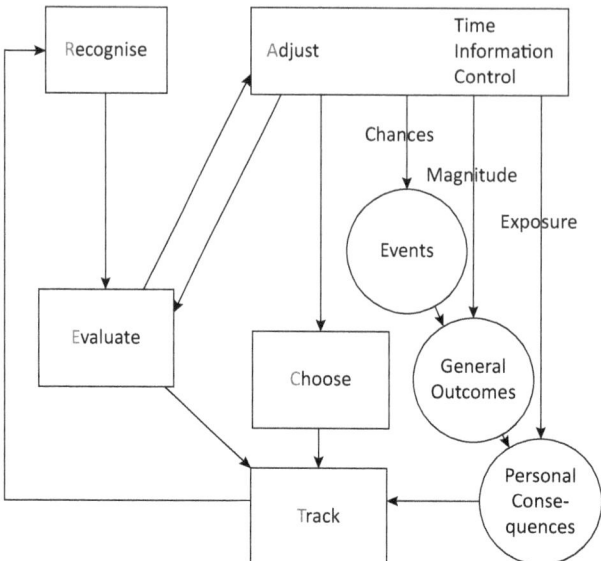

Figure 17.1

undesired final event that could occur and work backward to identify the component failures needed for it to have happened, so the tree starts with decisions to control the causes. The two techniques build the tree from opposite ends.

The following case study provides an example of an event tree; decisions to be taken now to adjust the later uncertain events that together define the riskiness of the problem.[207]

Event Trees

The European Medicines Agency (EMA) established a small team, which I led, at the beginning of 2009, whose purpose was to explore how regulators could be more transparent in approving drugs and better at communicating their decisions. After interviewing regulators in six European countries to find out how drugs were approved, we suggested that quantitative modelling might be helpful, so presented an internal seminar on decision-analytic modelling.

In August, the head of the EMA, Thomas Lönngren, asked me if modelling could clarify an urgent problem facing the Agency's drug approval committee. I suggested it might, but we would only know if we tried. Here, reported in the usual five stages, is what we did.

1.   Consider Context

The Agency's concern was whether to approve in September two vaccines still under development to treat swine flu, caused by the H1N1 virus, which in July had been deemed by the World Health Organization to be a pandemic, or wait until October, when clinical trials would be complete. Approval without full data could lead to criticism if the vaccines were found not to be as safe and efficacious as expected, but if the Agency waited and the pandemic turned out to be serious, they would be criticised for not acting sooner. A real damned-if-you-do and damned-if-you-don't situation.

2.   Frame the Problem

A brief discussion led my team and I to believe that this could be modelled as a simple event tree, so a meeting of EMA specialists in vaccines gathered a few days later for what turned out to be a day's decision conference. Its sole purpose was to test the applicability of explicit modelling, 'with no legal or regulatory implications or formal connection to the ongoing work in the EMA on the H1N1 vaccines', for improving the regulator's understanding of the available data and communicating the results of their deliberations, which we had discovered in our interviews, are conducted mainly by discussion and debate, and only, if necessary, by voting.

3.   Provide Content

After an initial introduction by Dr Lönngren about the purpose of the meeting, the first person to speak said there was no point in continuing because there simply wasn't enough data, but after a brief discussion the group agreed to go ahead, arguing that this was just a trial, and judgements about probabilities would have to depend heavily on the collective knowledge of the group. The group quickly agreed that the crucial decisions were to approve by the end of September to ensure the rapid availability of the vaccines, or to wait until the end of October, thus ensuring the vaccines were safe and efficacious. But they emphasised the considerable uncertainty about the disease's progression, the vaccines' efficacy and safety, and possible death rates among the European population of 500 million people.

On the spot, we constructed a decision tree using an Excel-based decision tree program, which was projected as it was built and during the assessments. Its DPL version is shown in Figure 17.2. As all the nodes are detached, once they are assembled there are $2 \times 2 \times 3 \times 2 = 24$ paths through the tree.

I've included the influence diagram to show that the probabilities for disease seriousness depend on the timing of the decision, that probabilities for efficacy depend both on timing and the seriousness of the disease, and that probabilities for safety depend only on timing. The numbers of deaths and serious disabilities (DSDs), which depend on all three event outcomes, was the single criterion.

Considerable discussion attended the definitions of the event outcomes, the timing of severity, the attack rate of the new pandemic, the numbers of deaths for each of the 24 scenarios and many more concerns. Three of the group's experts who were knowledgeable about the current pandemic and past ones, worldwide, assessed probabilities. Surfacing and agreeing assumptions enabled participants to assess probabilities and DSDs for all 24 scenarios, which broadened and deepened their collective

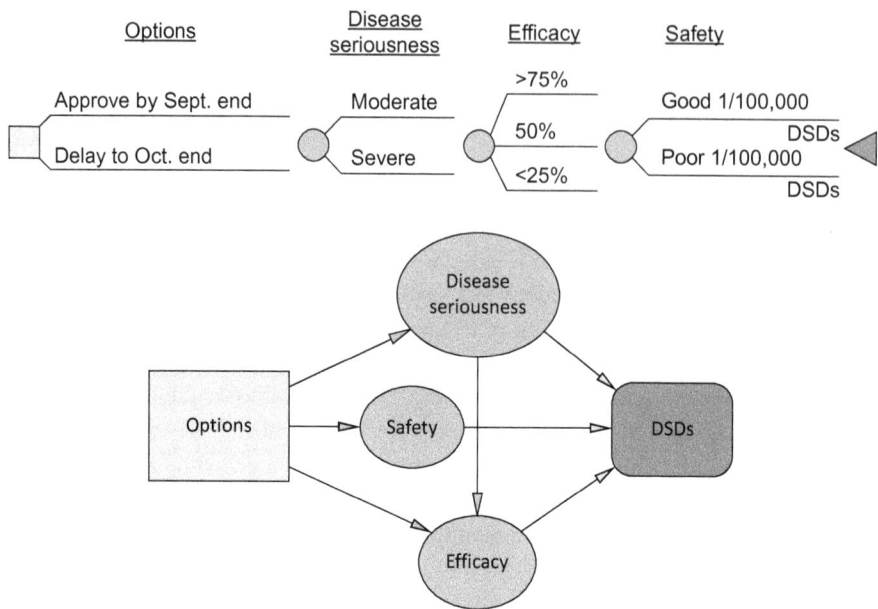

Figure 17.2

understanding of the problem. Many sensitivity analyses highlighted the need for more epidemiological information, so a subset of participants were appointed to engage an expert from the European Centre for Disease Prevention and Control after the meeting to elicit the information, which led to an update of the data.

4.   Explore Results

The best path through the tree is for a September decision with all three of the best outcomes, which results in 42,500 DSDs, whereas the worst path, following an October decision, at the bottom, shows 1,268,750 DSDs, nearly 30 times larger. This is a decision that matters!

Rolling the tree back gives the expected (weighted average) number of DSDs for each of the 24 scenarios: it is lower for approving at the end of September, 216,500.0, than waiting until October, 291,546.9. The difference between the expected DSDs, of 75,047, makes clear that acting sooner is better.

Sensitivity analyses played an important role in the project, as participants challenged assumptions, tried out new ones, disagreed about probabilities and explored the effects on results over all ranges of disagreement about anything at all. And eventually the group discovered that over the group's agreed ranges for probabilities of safety and efficacy, the September approval remained best. Only with very extreme probabilities that nobody considered reasonable did the model favour October. On the other hand, October would be preferred if the probability of moderate was judged to be not 0.75, but more than 0.84. At the time of the decision conference, the trend pointed in the opposite direction, but, fortunately, it soon reversed.

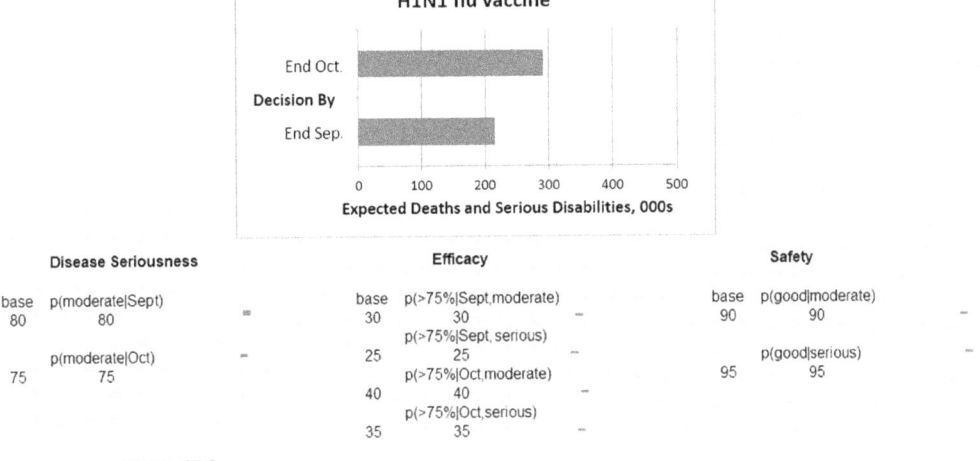

Figure 17.3

5.   Agree the Way Forward

This team's brief was to test the desirability of quantitative modelling, which they confirmed had changed the minds of many attendees at the decision conference. But that was all, so the model was not shown to the decision makers from all the European countries, who did, however, at their September meeting, approve the H1N1 vaccines.

In the meantime, my team felt that if a quantitative model were to be presented to the decision makers, they would mainly be interested to test differences in their judgements. That could be done easily via a dashboard, which can be created within Excel, like the one shown in Figure 17.3.

The model served as a transitional object during the process of creating it, modifying it with better expert judgement and providing the dashboard. With reference to the REACT model, we worked with the client through the first two steps, Recognise and Evaluate, leaving them with a tool that enables them to Adjust their *perception* of the risk they face so they now feel confident in taking a decision.

The next case study provides an example of a fault tree; decisions to be taken now to reduce the undesirable consequences and their likelihood of occurring if a fault occurs in a complex system.[208]

Fault Trees

The Lake Pontchartrain Causeway is today two parallel bridges linking northern New Orleans, Louisiana, to Mandeville, a northern suburb of the city (Figure 17.4). The longer of the two bridges is 23.83 miles (28.35km) long, which is the longest continuous bridge in the world. The first bridge was built in 1956, the second in 2011. As the lake is shallow, the bridges are slabs of concrete

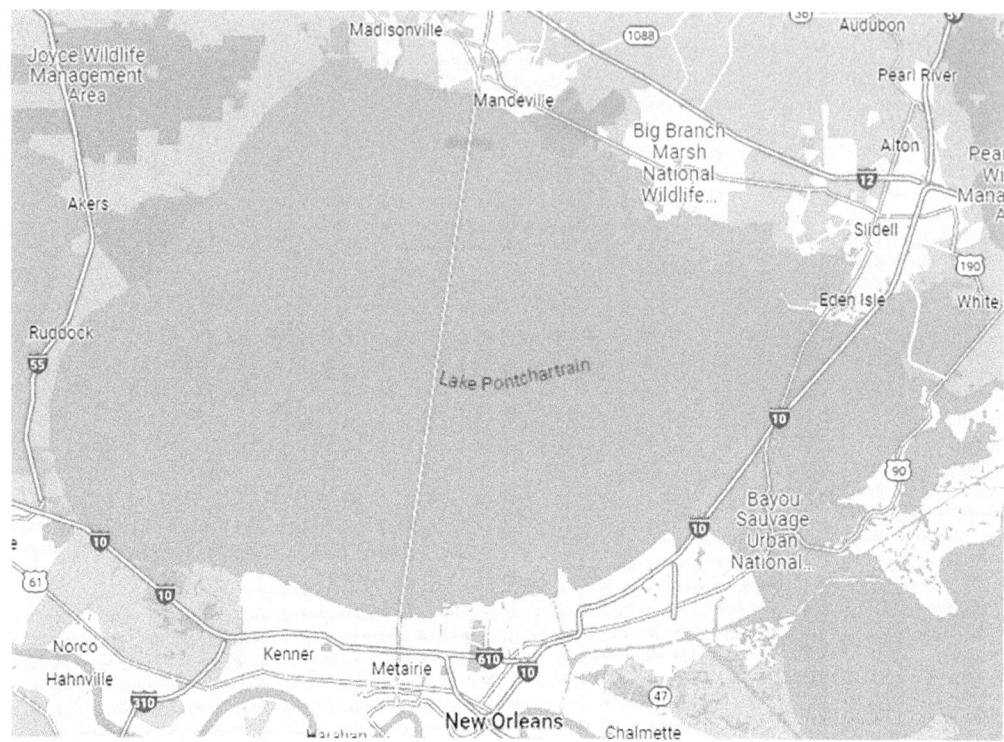

Figure 17.4

supported by 9,500 concrete pilings. Eight miles south of the north shore, a counterweight supports a draw bridge that can be raised to allow boats to pass through.

For most drivers, the convenience of going north from New Orleans over the bridges is considerably more convenient than driving around such a large lake, and is a major reason why the second bridge was built. There is, however, one safety problem that can occur if a tug or barge loses control, hits one or more pilings, causing slabs of the bridge to collapse into the lake, taking any vehicles with it. If such an event occurs at night, a driver is unlikely to see a gap in the bridge, so braking is too late. For example, a slab-out accident in January 1964 led to a bus falling into the lake, causing six fatalities, including the driver.

Taking a year off from teaching in 1976–77 and honing my then-underdeveloped decision-analytic skills at Decisions and Design, Inc., I assisted one of DDI's analysts, Judith Selvidge, to work on a project studying warning systems for the Lake Pontchartrain bridge that could sound alarms in vessels that came too close to the bridge, and alert drivers about slab-out events. This is a summary of our work.[i]

---

[i] This study was authorised in 1977 by the Greater New Orleans Expressway Commission through David Volkert and Associates, who contracted Decisions and Designs, Inc. to conduct this decision analysis.

1. Consider Context

The client's main objective was to improve safety by reducing fatalities when vehicles go off the bridge after a slab-out accident. Additionally, preventing damage to the bridge and to vehicles was also desired. Our first task was to establish what had happened in the past, which we represented by a timeline starting when the bridge opened in 1956 to 1 January 1977. During those 21 years, seven accidents occurred, two with fatalities. The later of those two, in August 1974, resulted in three fatalities, prompting the US National Transportation Safety Board to send a letter in January 1975 to the Greater New Orleans Expressway Commission recommending that they 'install a warning system on those sections of the Lake Pontchartrain causeway that are vulnerable to impact by errant marine vessels. The system should activate automatically to warn motorists of danger ahead, should the causeway span collapse.'

This established the primary function of a warning system that could reduce fatalities in three ways: by reducing the chance of a slab-out occurring in the first place, by reducing the chance of vehicles going off if a slab-out occurs, and by reducing the number of people killed when their vehicles go off. As a warning system couldn't affect the number of deaths, we concentrated on two methods for dealing with the other two events.

One method that could prevent damage to the bridge, thereby reducing the number of slab-out accidents, and also alert the bridge police to any danger of an accident so they can halt traffic, was a land-based radio system, known then as Loran-C, which was then a navigation system operated by the US Coast Guard. Ships could have a Loran-C receiver installed, whose function was to accurately determine the ship's location, much as we do today with GPS. Installing a Loran-C system in every large vessel operating on the lake would automatically sound an alarm in any ship coming too close to the causeway bridge, also setting off an alarm for the bridge police, thus reducing the number of vehicles being driven off the bridge.

We also considered a system that would warn drivers whose vehicles were already on the bridge, a slab-out warning system, such as a continuous electrified wire strung alongside the bridge, which would break in the event of a slab-out, triggering an alarm system on sound and lights on the bridge warning drivers to stop.

These two systems together, the Loran-C system and the slab-out system, would reduce the chance of a slab-out and reduce the chance of a vehicle driving off more than either system by itself.

We recognised that our primary task was to identify the uncertainties attending the number of accidents and their consequences, then to explore how alternative warning systems could reduce or eliminate those uncertainties, thereby improving safety. Determining the feasibility of the alternatives would require examining the extent to which the cost of improving safety saved lives and reduced the cost of lost vehicles, as well as repair costs to the bridge.

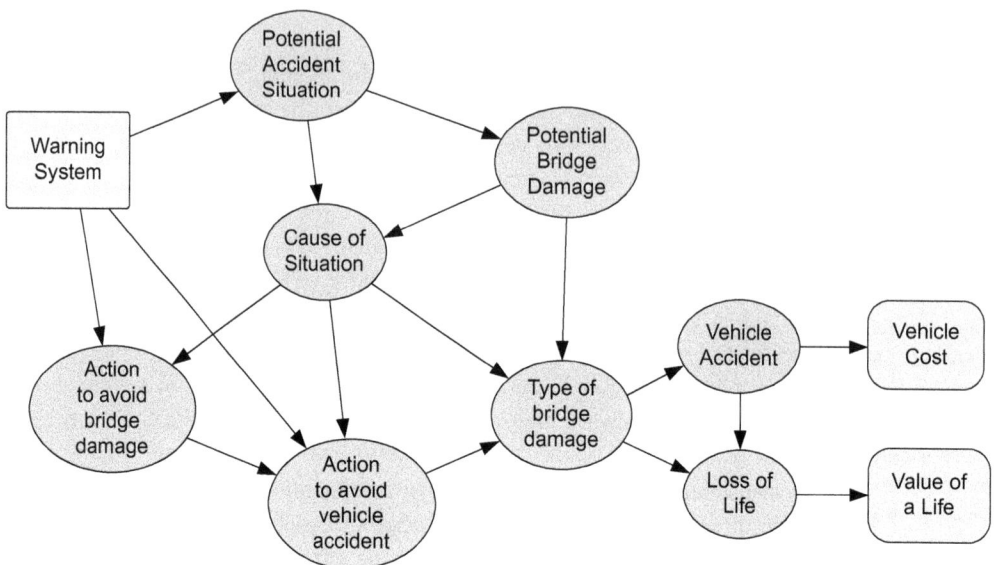

Figure 17.5

2.   Frame the Problem

Details about past accidents led us to establish eight uncertainties, shown in the relevance diagram in Figure 17.5 by the darker ovals. The arrows show how decisions and uncertain events define possible scenarios that in their different ways determine vehicle costs and the value of losses of life.

The four options include both Loran-C and slab-out systems by themselves, or both together, or maintaining the status quo. Following the upper arrow from the rectangle shows that the warning systems differ in their ability to detect a potential accident situation, and that events' outcomes in turn are relevant to assessing probabilities about the cause of the situation and about potential bridge damage. The latter is relevant to assessing probabilities about both the cause of the situation and the type of bridge damage, and that in turn affects both the probabilities, numbers and costs of vehicle damage, and uncertainties about the numbers and values of lives lost. And, of course, the vehicle accident impacts uncertainty about loss of life. Following the lower branches of the influence diagram shows the relevance of actions on the type of bridge damage. It is all these dependencies of one event's outcome on another that is captured with conditional probabilities in any decision tree, and especially in a fault tree.

Putting all the logical combinations together into a fault tree gives 47 branches. You may wonder how it could be shown to a group of experts today in a decision conference. It's difficult, but can be done one event node at a time, depending on the software, by zooming in first on a parent node, then extending the view to include the next child node, making it possible to assess the conditional probabilities at the child node. Then repeat for successive children. There will be times when it is possible to copy and paste identical structural elements, but it takes some skill to do this in front of a group of experts. Try it first with your team before you bring the experts in.

3. Provide Content

For the Pontchartrain problem, the team itself assessed the 15 event probabilities on the basis of available data (over 90 accidents up to 1977), after making various assumptions that were later tested in sensitivity analyses. We also projected forward 20 years to show how each of the options was expected to perform. This enabled us to extend the timeline of the past, seven fatalities in 21 years, a probability of 0.33 per year, for continuing without a warning system into the future, showing an accident every three years, with fatalities every seven. The two slab-out accidents before 1977 led to three and six lives lost, giving a probability of 4.5 fatalities per slab-out accident.

Prior to 1977, timing of accidents had been irregular, so could not be predicted in the future, but at least we could then model the effect of a warning system to *reduce* the number of accidents over 20 years, although not their actual timing, to arrive at probabilities per year (Figure 17.6).

With the exception of the 0.33 mentioned above, all other probabilities were conditional on the outcomes of previous events. We also assessed eight costs over 20 years, which included costs of the Loran-C system including set-up and operating costs, and the same for the slab-out warning system, cost of repairing slab-out costs, various costs of temporarily closing the bridge, and the costs of fatalities defined as the value of a human life, the latter after considering many studies, which ranged from $240,000 (the figure used in traffic studies by the US Department of Transportation), to

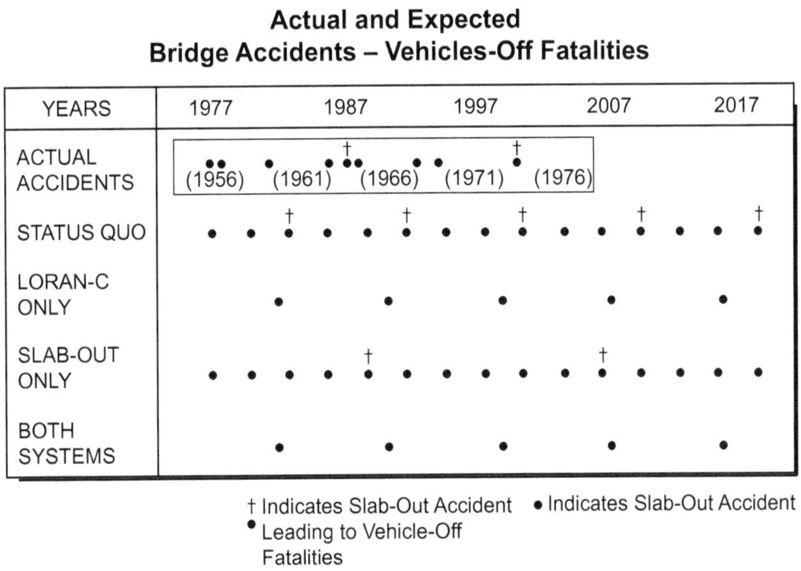

Actual and Expected
Bridge Accidents – Vehicles-Off Fatalities

YEARS	1977	1987	1997	2007	2017
ACTUAL ACCIDENTS	•• (1956) • (1961)	† • •• (1966)	• • (1971)	† (1976)	
STATUS QUO	• • † •	• • † •	• • † •	• † •	• • †
LORAN-C ONLY	•	•	•	•	•
SLAB-OUT ONLY	• • •	† • • •	• • •	† • •	• •
BOTH SYSTEMS	•	•	•	•	•

† Indicates Slab-Out Accident   • Indicates Slab-Out Accident
• Leading to Vehicle-Off
Fatalities

Figure 17.6

Table 17.1

Safety method	Expected number of accidents over 20 years	Probability of vehicles off, given occurrence of a slab-out, per year	Joint probability of slab-outs and vehicles off, per year	Expected number of slab-out accidents with vehicles off over 20 years
Loran-C and slab-out warning	2.4	0.53	0.0064	0.13
Loran-C alone	2.4	0.10	0.012	0.24
Slab-out alone	6.6	0.18	0.053	1.1
Status Quo	6.8	0.33	0.11	2.2

a range of $2–2.5 million in a study by Professor Ron Howard at Stanford University. We ignored who incurs the costs. All costs per year were estimated, with capital costs amortised over 20 years, and identified at the end of the full decision tree by the letter C and its subscript.

4.   Explore Results

The first roll-back of the fault tree was based solely on the joint probabilities of an accident at each of the ends of each of the 47 paths through the tree. That is, the computer multiplied together all probabilities from left to right in the fault tree, then added the products for each safety option to give a joint probability of an accident per year for each option, or the expected numbers over 20 years (see Table 17.1).

The final column shows that safety is best with Loran-C and the slab-out warning systems alerting drivers of an accident. Both systems together are about 20 times safer than the status quo. A second analysis explored the numbers of deaths that would be prevented by the combined safety systems, but as there were then only two of nine accidents before 1977 that led to losses of life, the team did not feel comfortable making any assumptions about how the systems might reduce that number, especially as the expected number of vehicles passing over the bridge would increase in the next 20 years.

We realised that the results are sensitive in particular to two assumptions, the value of a single life and the average number of fatalities per slab-out accident with vehicles off, so we constructed an indifference curve so the client could see what combinations of those two quantities would show one or the other system as most preferred (Figure 17.7).

Any pair of assumptions above the solid convex line favour Loran-C plus slab-out, while pairs below the line favour Loran-C only. Interestingly, if one takes the value of a single life to be at the high end, between $2 and $2.5 million, and assumes the future will continue to average no more than 4.5 fatalities per slab-out accident, then the short vertical dashed line between the upper two horizontal dashed ones shows that either system could be justified. But from the government point of view, with its much lower value of a life, $250,000, the Loran-C system alone would be judged sufficient.

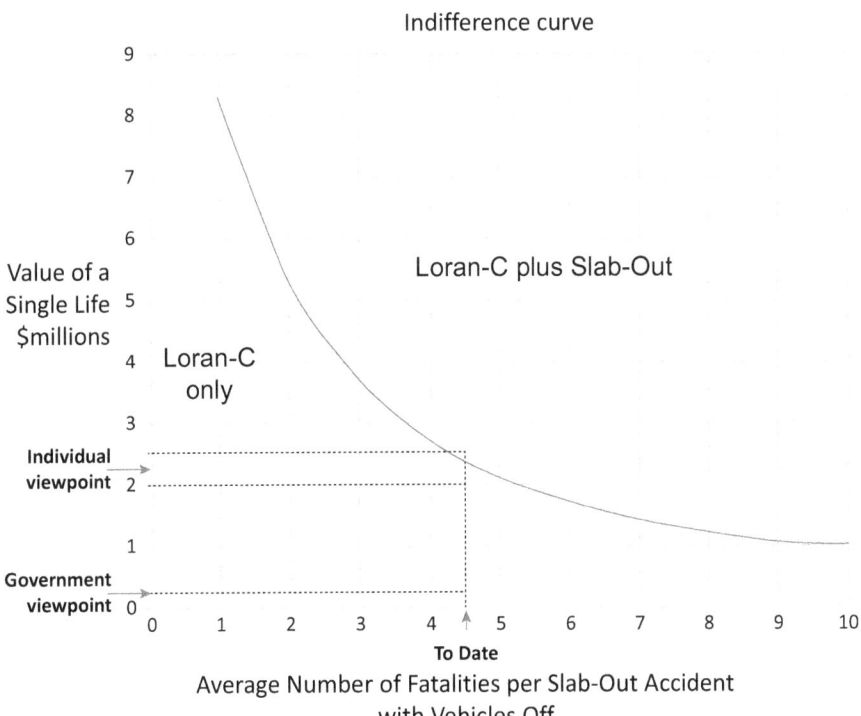

Figure 17.7

Even with the high values for an individual life, nobody argued that 4.5 fatalities would be maintained as the Loran-C system alone would substantially reduce deaths. As can be seen in the indifference curve, over a 20-year timeframe, there is no expected advantage from adding the slab-out system. On balance, the team then felt justified in recommending the Loran-C system only.

Remember Chapter 1's 10 ingredients of good decisions? Number 10 is risk attitude – the extent to which the possibility of harm is judged to be tolerable. We collectively felt that the Loran-C system itself was well within our tolerance for driving on the causeway, even though none of us ever had. (We had been told that after the first slab-out accident with lives lost, local residents driving at night would slow down as they approached the causeway until a car bearing an out-of-state licence plate would overtake them so they could follow closely enough to be able to slam on the brakes if the car ahead disappeared.)

5.   Agree the Way Forward

On 1 January 1980, the National Transportation Safety Board classified their 1974 recommendation to the Greater New Orleans Expressway Commission to install a warning system was 'Closed – No Longer Applicable'.

You may wonder if it was necessary to develop a fault tree of 47 scenarios about the future to establish what looks obvious: the Loran-C system had been operational along the east coast of the USA since 1957 as an aid to navigation under the aegis of the Coast Guard. Its usefulness, accuracy and affordability had long been established. But it was a new departure for achieving the safety for a bridge over a shallow lake, so any expenditure would require justification. In hindsight, the study came to a clear and satisfactory conclusion, but in 1977 it wasn't obvious to our team, and the consideration of a slab-out system alone seemed sensible then.

You also might be critical, as I am today, about any model's probabilities for outcomes of events over a 20-year time horizon if they are in any way associated with human activities. There simply is no evidence for the validity of such probabilities; people are unpredictable, individually and collectively. However, the probabilities in these two case studies represent expert judgement about how harm can be reduced now by applying objective procedures, whether vaccines or alarm systems, for which evidence confirms that they work in the longer term.

Referring to the REACT model, the case studies show the effects of *reducing* the harm, by adjusting timing, information, and control about chances, magnitudes and exposure. Of course, uncertainty remains, so whatever the baseline probabilities are for doing nothing (or waiting, as for the vaccines), it is the extent of the reduction in probabilities *and* the magnitude of harm that is represented in the model. And it is the final difference between the decisions that matters, aided by sensitivity analyses to further reduce the decision maker's uncertainty about which option is best.

Scenario Analysis

Another approach to dealing with 'radical uncertainty' is to postulate that the future is unknowable.[209] While that is often true, it should not lead to a position of despair, for human agency often must be deployed now. In the early years of decision analysis, I was often told to 'come back after enough information is obtained' to justify modelling. As I've said earlier, it is at the start of such difficult projects that decision analysis can helpfully guide the search for data that is truly relevant to the decision. When an organisation actually did get back to me, although most didn't, much time and money had been wasted in gaining information that wasn't relevant to any decisions at all.

I had the good fortune to meet up with Professor Paul Schoemaker when he came to London on an extended sabbatical leave from the University of Chicago in 1982–84 to study how Royal Dutch Shell's strategic planning group was creating scenarios about how their business might be affected by different future events than one expects from trends. Managers at Shell were asked to incorporate this in their thinking when developing strategic plans, and I was pleased to learn more about what Paul developed with the planning group: scenario analysis.

He defined a scenario as 'a script-like characterization of a possible future presented in considerable detail, with special emphasis on causal connections, internal consistency, and concreteness'.[210] Discussions with Paul occurred at a time when decision conferences were just being developed, and I wondered if they might be helpful in broadening a decision maker's future perspective, ability to think strategically, acknowledge uncertainty, avoid 'best guesses' about the future and create decisions that can respond flexibly to unexpected future events. I adapted Schoemaker's 10-step process[211] so I could help a group to construct scenarios in two to three hours. This is my summary:

1. Agree the scope and timeframe of the scenarios.
2. Create a list of the key strategic options facing the organisation and the objectives they are intended to achieve.
3. Identify important events over several past time periods, each roughly equivalent to the timeframe of the scenarios.
4. Scan the events over the time periods; extract important trends and step changes, and note their possible impact on your organisation.
5. Discuss the pros and cons of the trends and model their relationships (for example, cause and effect).
6. Identify the key uncertainties and their possible outcomes, and the impact of the outcomes on your organisation. Assess the interdependence of the uncertainties (for example, qualitative intercorrelation matrix, high, medium or low).
7. Break into three sub-groups, each to construct a plausible scenario that addresses the trends and resolves the uncertainties. Two scenarios might be bounding scenarios, one pessimistic, one optimistic. The other scenario extrapolates the trends with a mixture of pessimism and optimism. All groups imagine they are at the future date and are describing the world as they see it then, and not be concerned about how we got there. All scenarios to include one or more unexpected step changes.
8. Main group reassembles to examine the scenarios. 'Live' the scenarios: imagine how key players outside the organisation would behave. Assess the internal consistency and plausibility of the scenarios, eliminate combinations that are not credible or plausible, and create revised scenarios.
9. Discuss the differences and similarities between these scenarios as a means of identifying further the strategic issues that are important to the organisation.
10. Test the strategic options against the scenarios by imagining consequences: If we follow this strategy and that scenario transpires, here are the consequences. Generate new strategies that will be robust to turbulence in the future.

After completing these steps in a decision conference, participants' horizons are usually broadened, making them better able to consider and complete a modest decision model that enables the group to agree a new way forward. The IFHF case study in Chapter 19 includes a scenario analysis as an early step in developing a vision statement and strategic plan for their organisation's next 10 years.

Conclusions

Risk is a slippery concept, so explore what it means if your client mentions it or even if they appear hesitant to think afresh in a troubling situation. Recall Graham's decision problem in the previous chapter, who initially felt he should apply the old, reliable look-up method for producing the design. Or the reluctance of the EMA participant who argued there was insufficient evidence to justify an early decision, or the dropping of the slab-out warning system from the combination with the Loran-C alerting system on the grounds that the extra warning system was unlikely to add any value over the 20-year time span. In their different ways, each of the decision models shifted participants' risk tolerance, enabling them to accept a modicum of risk in order to achieve their objectives.

For some people, the fear of failure can motivate avoiding any course of action that might lead to an undesirable consequence. Different levels of risk tolerance typically are found by staff at different levels in their organisation, with those at higher levels often complaining that their subordinates are insufficiently willing to take risks, which is a natural consequence of two main contributing factors: (1) the extent to which the organisation's culture rewards innovation and creativity without punishing failures; and (2) the range of resources for which the decision maker is accountable.

For example, the manufacturing company 3 M has developed several processes to encourage and facilitate innovation. These include its '15 per cent rule' (dedicating 15 per cent of employees' time to innovation), its 30/4 rule (targeting 30 per cent of sales from products introduced in the last four years), and its commitment to science and sustainability. The company expects some things won't turn out to be successful new products, so failures are tolerated. The culture of innovation coupled with leaving time for their staff to try out new ideas is the opposite of the blame culture found in other organisations, in which employees are careful to cover their tracks for fear of losing their jobs if things go wrong.

Risk tolerance generally increases as employees achieve more senior roles, largely because the range of resources increases so as to cover many projects. Thus, while a subordinate with fewer projects and a smaller budget will take care to avoid failure, the more senior person will recognise and accept more risk, knowing that the success of many projects will more than balance failure of a few. As a result, senior people often complain that their subordinates are not taking enough risks. Clarity about accountability and authority can help to lessen this difference in risk attitude if managers explain to their subordinates that they, the managers, hold the subordinates accountable for doing their best with the resources allotted to them, recognising that some projects will fail through no failure of the subordinate, but purely by chance or unexpected outcomes.

Of course, some people are more motivated to avoid failure than to achieve success, and they are more likely to flourish in an organisation whose culture does reward or punish on the basis of an accountable manager's outcomes. But whatever an individual's propensity to take risks is, creating the future involves uncertainty, and more benefits inevitably are associated with more risks. The organisation that understands that is in large part the story of organisations built to last.[212] By all means, engage subordinates in building decision models that address the uncertainty, and ask them to assess probabilities about those events for which they are better informed than their bosses, but it is the risk tolerance of the accountable decision maker that is to be engaged when taking the decision.

Finally, recall from Chapter 10 that the decision model serves as a transitional model, holding in one place all the key uncertainties and values of the key players as the model is used in sensitivity analyses to explore imprecision in the data and differences of opinion. This enables participants to construct their preferences and revise their risk tolerances to the point where the accountable manager will feel more confident in taking a decision.

18   Revise Opinion

When my information changes, I change my mind. What do you do?

Paul Samuelson recalling John Maynard Keynes, 1978

When finished with a day's writing this book, I always go back the next morning and revise what I wrote yesterday, changing, deleting, adding and rearranging to make what I wanted to say clearer and simpler. But this chapter isn't about that kind of revision. Nor is it anything like revising for exams. Instead, it is concerned with the process of revising one's opinion as new information becomes available, and the crucial role of Bayes' theorem in modelling that process for assembling the new information.

The freesias example in Chapter 12 captures exactly what I mean. Recall that my wife found freesias as sweetly scented, whereas I could smell nothing at all, so I asked friends and neighbours to have a sniff of the native South African flower to determine which of us was in the minority. By applying Bayesian statistical methods, I developed three probability density functions (PDFs) showing how with more and more data I became clear that I was in the minority.

In a moment I'll explain how these PDFs are easily created, but first it's necessary to explain the mathematics of Bayesian statistics. Once that is clear, I'll apply it to some recent data exploring whether medical cannabis can reduce the frequency of epileptic fits in children, and how the finding that it does so dramatically can best be explained to prescribers and the medical profession more generally.

This chapter will end by explaining how the insurance underwriting example in Chapter 12 was created by capturing the experience of senior underwriters in a Bayesian belief network (BBN), a form of artificial intelligence that in a test case of 500 real situations resulted in risk assessments that were more consistent and valid than the intuitive assessments of local underwriters.

Bayesian Statistics

Let's meet the reverend Thomas Bayes, non-conformist Presbyterian minister, philosopher, statistician and Fellow of the Royal Society, among whose papers was found, after he died in 1761, the theorem that now bears his name. There is no known image of him other than the drawing shown in Figure 18.1, but no one is sure that's really him.

Figure 18.1

Today's version of the theorem is a simple consequence of the multiplication and addition laws of probability theory, so the rule isn't debatable, and it is now being applied in a great many disciplines, worldwide, from medicine and pharmacology, to business and finance, to engineering and machine learning, to environment and the law.

Bayes' theorem informs us in different ways. It can act as a normative principle about how people should deal with new information, or it can provide a descriptive model of how they actually behave. Between those extremes we will find it most useful as a model about how people *could* think and behave, as has characterised most of the decision analysis models in this book. As I said in Chapter 12, I was surprised it took only 10 more people after my wife and I discovered our differences for me to learn that I was probably in the minority, at least among our friends.

Let's see what was behind the revision of my uncertainty about the proportion of people who can smell freesias. At the heart of Bayes' theorem is a *conditional* probability, *p(x|context)*, where x is an uncertain quantity or event. For the freesias example, x is the proportion of people who report the flower as highly scented (let's call that the *smellability proportion* or SP for short). The context is freesias purchased at the local florist, and friends asked to engage in my experiment.

Bayes' theorem relates my *prior* probability *p(x|context)* to a *posterior* probability after obtaining data, *p(x|context and data)*. Let's just keep in mind the context, but drop it to simplify the notation, with *d* standing for observed data. The term that makes the link between my prior probability, p(x), and a revision of that probability after observing data, *p(x|d)*, is another conditional probability, *p(d|x)*, the likelihood of the data actually observed given a value of *x*:

$$p(x|d) = \frac{p(x) \times p(d|x)}{p(d)}$$

To further simplify matters, let's drop $p(d)$, the probability of the data, because it is merely a scaling constant that ensures probabilities over the values of x sum to one. Thus, the core of Bayes' theorem, summarised in words, is this:

$$\text{Posterior probability} \propto \text{Prior probability} \times \text{Likelihood},$$

where the symbol, $\propto$, means 'proportional to'. This equation is the core of Bayes' theorem, which is often referred to as the theorem of inverse probability, for it transforms $p(d|x)$ into $p(x|d)$. However, whereas probabilities, either prior or posterior, must sum to one over all values of x for a fixed d, that isn't true of likelihoods, because both d and x are fixed.[213]

Failure to distinguish a likelihood from a posterior probability can lead to an error of judgement, called the *inverse fallacy*.[214] For example, a physician may diagnose a patient as having a particular disease because the patient's symptom (the data) is usually found in people with the disease. But that doesn't mean this particular patient has the disease; although the evidence is associated with the disease, that doesn't mean the disease is certain. And the inverse fallacy can work the other way around: absence of evidence isn't evidence of absence.

For the freesias example, Bayes' theorem becomes

$$p(SP|data) \propto p(SP) \times p(data|SP)$$

So, the probability of SP *given* the observed data is proportional to the SP *without* considering the data, multiplied by how likely it would be to observe the data for any given value of SP. Thus, if the prior probability of a disease is very low, even if the data is more likely given the disease than without it, that may not be enough to overcome the low prior probability, resulting in a posterior probability that may still be low, but not as low as the prior.

As the quantity x we're interested in is a continuous uncertain quantity (uq), Bayes' theorem must be calculated for all possible values of the uq, from 0 to 1.0, for the data actually observed, with my uncertainty about the uq also represented adequately in some form that is appropriate for the binary data, smell-or-no-smell. What is known as a Beta distribution suits very well for the prior and posterior because it can take on an infinite number of shapes, including those that are symmetrical, as well as those with longer left or right tails. The exact shape is determined by only two parameters, a and b, whose values can be modified depending on the observed data.[215]

Beta distributions are also easy to revise with binary data. Here's how:

1. Let S represent a success: the number of people who say they can smell freesias, and F the number of failures, people who can't.
2. To change a prior to a posterior Beta distribution, increment the numbers of success and failures by 1: $a = 1 + S$ and $b = 1 + F$.

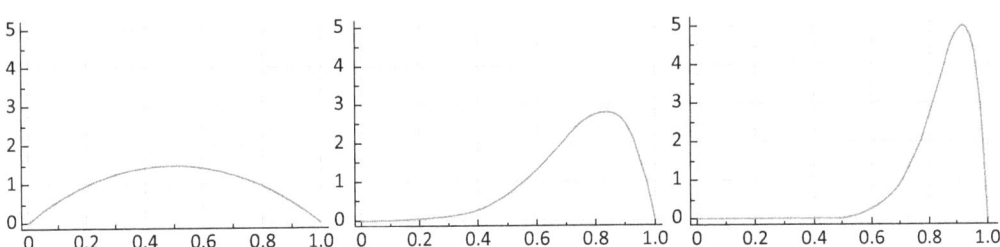

Figure 18.2
Proportion of people who can smell freesias. Data: Left, 1 can and 1 can't; middle, 5 can and 1 can't, and right, 11 can and 1 can't.

Figure 18.2 shows the Beta distributions that describe my uncertainty about the proportion of people who can smell freesias, beginning at the left before collecting data from friends and family.[i]

The graphs were obtained by entering values of a and b into an online Beta distribution calculator, described in the Appendix to this chapter. Each PDF to the right is a revision of the one to the left, the first representing just my wife's experience and mine, showing that proportions of 0 and 1 are impossible, but anything in between could be correct, most likely 0.5. Four more people resulted in the middle PDF, and six more are incorporated in the right PDF.

It's also easy to calculate the central tendency of the distributions from the values of a and b. (The median equation is an approximation.)

$$mean = \frac{a}{a+b} \qquad median \approx \frac{a-1/3}{a+b-2/3} \qquad mode = \frac{a-1}{a+b-2}$$

Thus, the means of the above three distributions are 2/4 = 0.5, 6/8 = 0.75 and 12/14 = 0.86. Those are the proportions I would have reported if asked for a single number rather than a distribution, but would also have commented on how sure I was to give those single proportions. 'Could go either way from 50–50', after just two observations, then 'Pretty sure it's more than 50 percent' and, finally, 'Definitely more than 50'. We'll see in the next case study how to quantify your uncertainty about a 'best guess' can also be represented.

Medical Cannabis for Childhood Epilepsy

I'm a member of the Scientific Committee of Drug Science,[216] a UK charity that provides the 'public in the UK and internationally with high quality, scientifically based information on drugs and evidence-based comment and analysis of new research ... free of all political and commercial interest'.[217] During a meeting a few years ago, I presented a possible application of Bayesian statistics to

---

[i] For readers unfamiliar with probability density functions, the vertical axes are simply numbers that ensure the area under each curve is 1.0.

observational data then being collected by the leader of the group, Professor David Nutt, a neuropsychopharmacologist and psychiatrist who studies drugs that affect the brain. He suggested that Bayesian revision appears similar to what doctors do with patients as they ask questions, gather information about symptoms, diagnose and choose actions to improve the patient's condition. Indeed, *Medical Decision Making*, a journal of the Society for Medical Decision Making, is devoted to that process, often reporting studies of Bayesian inference and the use of revised probabilities in decision trees to support rational decisions.

Shortly after the meeting, I suggested how one of David Nutt's PhD students, Rayyan Zafar, could best communicate his surprising finding about the positive effect of medical cannabis on children with severe epilepsy, in whom previous medications had little or no effect. This summary of his work applies the usual five-step process, even though it didn't happen this way.

1.   Consider Context

Although medical cannabis has been known to treat seizures in infants since 1843, cannabis in any form has been illegal in many countries since the early 1900s, but beginning in the new century, decriminalisation particularly for *medical* cannabis has increased, with licenced products appearing in the USA from 1996 in California, and many states and countries from 2001. In the UK, both recreational and medical cannabis were made illegal in 1971, but medical cannabis was rehabilitated in 2018, although at this time of writing, it is rarely prescribed in the UK's National Health Service.

2.   Frame the Problem

Case reports suggested that medical cannabis might reduce the number of seizures suffered by children with chronic epilepsy whose treatment with conventional anti-epileptic drugs had failed, so two UK charities dealing with childhood epilepsy were contacted to ask parents for their approval to evaluate the use of medical cannabis on their children. Twenty participants, from 1 to 18 years old, eventually participated in the study, with funding of whole-plant medical cannabis by private prescription or in a couple of cases through the National Health Service.

3.   Provide Content

Parents and participants' carers provided data on their children's seizures via telephone or video conference calls, some based on memory and diaries of seizures, that were confirmed with clinicians' reports where available. The primary question addressed in the study was the percentage change in the frequency of seizures each month after taking medical cannabis.

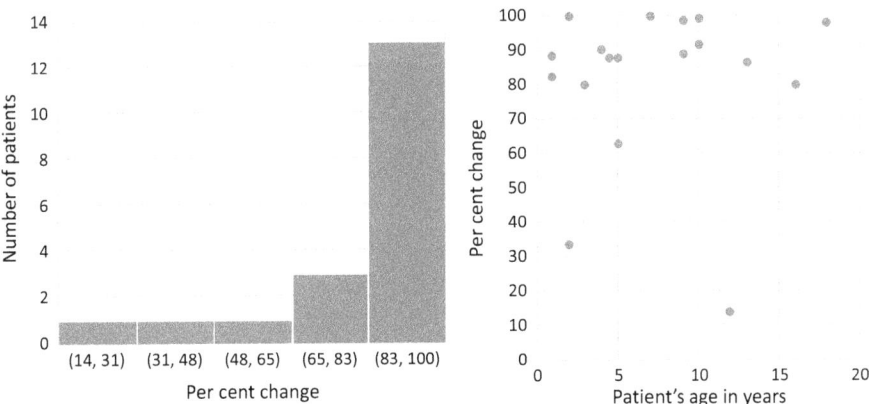

Figure 18.3

4.   Explore Results

In two published studies of this research, the authors showed the before and after frequencies as bar graphs, a pair for each of the first 10 patients in one paper, which was considered as a field study, then a second 10 patients in the next paper, positioned as a confirmatory follow-through.[218] The frequency of seizures reduced in all 20 cases. After eliminating one 24-year-old who had been included in the first paper, I have re-analysed the 19 to show how a Bayesian analysis of the data, which was absent in the two papers, gives potential prescribers the information they need in deciding to prescribe. More to be said about this sequence of scientific discovery in a moment. But first, the results are shown in Figure 18.3.

Rather than show the before and after bar graphs for all the patients, here are two descriptive statistical displays that tell the whole story, a simple histogram of the per cent improvement on the left, and a scatterplot of the per cent change of each patient's number of seizures and their age on the right.

The tall bar, the mode of the histogram, and the spread of patients shown by the dots in the scatterplot, show that most patients improved greatly. Three patients' seizures stopped altogether (the age 7 dot at 100 per cent is for two patients), and three others were in the high 90s. The mean change is 82.4 per cent. Only three patients show improvements of less than 70 per cent. Might the effectiveness of the drug depend on the patient's age? Not so, the correlation is only 0.03, so physicians can be reasonably sure that younger or older will both benefit about equally.

That is the story so far based on summary descriptive statistics. But more can be said as we move to making a judgement about the future by applying Bayesian analysis, thereby providing a probability that a new 20th patient, a child with intractable epilepsy, will benefit from medical cannabis. We apply the same approach as for the freesias example, now with 19 successes and 0 failures. The parameters of the posterior PDF increment those numbers by 1, so a = 20 and b = 1, giving a mean of 21/22 = 0.95, a 95 per cent chance the next patient will experience a reduction in seizures. And how sure of that percentage should the physician be? The posterior distribution gives a 95 per cent

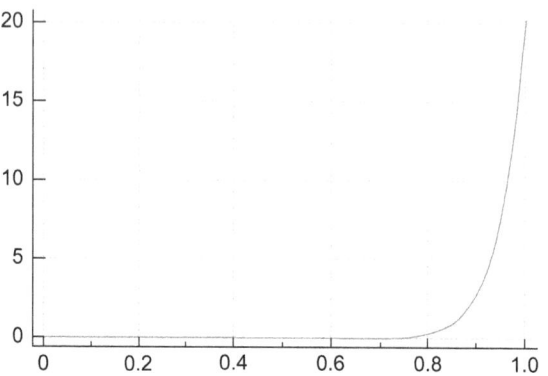

Proportion of epileptic children who will benefit from medical cannabis

Figure 18.4

credible interval that the true proportion is between 0.86 and 1.00 (Figure 18.4). This is a description of a rational prescriber's uncertainty in light of the available data.

Why wasn't this analysis included in the *BMJ Paediatrics* paper? After all, the Bayesian analysis addresses the decision to prescribe, which is substantially less than can be ascertained just from consulting the published bar graphs. My view is that the journal's editor was concerned about this being an observational study, not a random-ised controlled trial (RCT), still considered by many medical practitioners as the gold standard for establishing that a drug is the cause of the patient's improvement, not some uncontrolled, unaccounted-for effect unrelated to the drug.

The paper's editor could see that 20 successes out of 20 didn't need statistics to establish the potential for medical cannabis to reduce the number of infant epileptic seizures. Furthermore, after a paper about the first 10 patients had been rejected by the journal's editor, Rayyan had kept on studying more patients as the data continued to reduce his uncertainty about the effectiveness of medical cannabis, so a sample of 20 emerged; it wasn't an initial goal, as is required in a classical statistical analysis of RCTs. So, the *BMJ* editor for this paper suggested that the first 10 patients be considered as a field trial, and to consider the latter 10 patients as a confirmatory trial.

In effect, we were asked to throw away the data from the first set of patients and only present bar graphs for the latter 10. Thus, the message to paediatricians was not as strong as it could have been with all 19. Also, the editor, apparently unaware that a Bayesian analysis models the researcher's uncertainty, for which the stopping rule for collecting data is irrelevant, considered that our Bayesian analysis added no value. We decided not to argue with him as that would cause further delay, so we reported only the descriptive statistics.

5.   Agree the Way Forward

We, the authors of the first two papers, have learned a lot from our attempts to communicate these exceptional findings in research papers, which we consider is desperately needed, as the numbers of chronic epileptic children worldwide who are drug-resistant is large, around 17,000 in the UK and 70,000 in the USA. Childhood epilepsy creates a substantial burden on parents and carers, and limits the ability of affected children to realise their full physical and mental capability. Some die before reaching adulthood. We continue to feel it is important to spread the word about how well medical cannabis can alleviate such suffering.

Other DrugScience researchers exploring the effects of medical cannabis on other medical conditions joined with us to write a third paper that champions the use of real-world evidence (RWE) in establishing cause-and-effect of medical cannabis. We discuss the limitations of RCTs, which establish the efficacy of a drug but not its effectiveness in actual use, describe the advantages of RWE that uses subjects as their own controls, providing a direct picture of the drug's effectiveness, Bayesian analysis of data (including the bar graphs of Rayyan's 20 original patients), basket protocols in which medical cannabis is given to patients with different medical conditions, and limitations of RWE, culminating in 12 key recommendations.[219] We hope that this paper will contribute to a deeper understanding of how RWE can contribute to health care.

Bayesian Networks

Now for something that looks completely different, but is in fact another application of Bayes' theorem, this time in a commercial setting. It shows how professional experience can be encoded in a Bayesian model that assembles many pieces of data and their interactions to give a posterior distribution that facilitates decision making.

The area of professional expertise is insurance underwriting. My first sustained consultancy as a decision analyst was in the 1970s with Commercial Union (CU) insurance company, whose CEO, worried about a recent downturn in the market, directed the head office to find ways to improve underwriting decisions. This prompted a search by two senior underwriters to enrol in an executive programme that I was then teaching about decision analysis. At the end of the four-day course, they told me they were surprised to learn that decision theory makes explicit all the features underwriters take into consideration when making decisions about insuring potential clients.

This led to my working with the two senior underwriters to develop insurance case studies that could benefit from decision analysis, which were subsequently taught to all the senior staff and underwriters at CU over a four-year period, initially by me and subsequently by Dr Howard Thomas, a decision analyst at the London Business School, and Professor Dennis Lindley, a Bayesian statistician and Head of the Statistics Department at University College London. The course introduced the fundamentals of probabilities, values and trade-offs, along with decision trees and multi-criteria structures, so that underwriters could become more adept and better at applying those concepts in making underwriting decisions, not to turn them into decision analysts.

Follow-up questionnaires to all underwriters after the course suggested we had failed. All participants said they enjoyed the course and had learned a lot, but we saw no direct evidence that everyday work had changed at all. It occurred to me that the business of underwriting pre-dated the invention of probability theory in the seventeenth century, and even much earlier in the form of risk-based pricing when it was applied to ships as far back as about 3,000 to 4,000 BCE. So, although mental modes for anticipating expected loss must have changed over many years, persisting in the minds of today's underwriters despite the development of probability theory in the seventeenth century, it was not to be overwritten by decision theory concepts. But more about this later, as I've seen the same problem in other disciplines.

However, CU management recognised that decision theory could help in other ways, so they established a once-a-week consultancy service at their main office in the City of London, which I manned ready at the end of a telephone to respond to any request for help in making decisions other than underwriting ones. It was hoped that others would gain confidence in applying decision analysis with my guidance. And that exposed to me the many other business decisions that are common to all organisations, a good start to my career, for which I'm grateful to CU.

And now, I would like you to see what happened at the end of my consultancy with CU. I had worked at DDI for a year in 1976–77 where I learned about a mainframe computer that had been turned into a desktop luggable computer, the IBM 5100. At DDI, I was able to persuade a CU underwriter from Canada to work with me in testing the potential for a BBN to capture the experience of senior underwriters in the form of conditional probabilities, which could then be used in Canada to cover the whole of the country, increasing the ability of the company to expand across all the country as they had too few experienced underwriters to cover that long but narrow territory.

After a few days' work, we had created a test case that seemed to be working reasonably well. When I returned to London, my research unit purchased an IBM 5110 which I lugged to CU's Head Office and showed to the head of underwriting in the UK. He was so impressed he engaged me to start work in January 1979 with senior underwriters to create models for insuring commercial buildings against fire, damage and theft.

I've now recreated and simplified one of the fire models using Netica, a widely used commercially available computer program with good displays, to model shops using data that are now probably out of date, but you'll get the idea of how the BBN works. The five-step process well describes the procedure in this case, which consisted of many meetings over nearly a year, attended by two to five senior underwriters, and a statistician colleague at Brunel University, Tom Wisniewski, who eventually developed a new statistical model for insuring fleets of vehicles.[220]

1.   Consider Context

At the first meeting with the senior fire underwriters in the spring of 1979, we clarified that the purpose of the project was to determine the feasibility of using BBNs to serve as an aid to an underwriter's decision about insuring a building against fire, damage and theft. At some point, I asked how decisions to insure were currently made, and the *average line* method was explained, a process of four steps that apply to many types of insurance, but not to life and vehicle insurance, which are the provenance of actuaries (Figure 18.5).

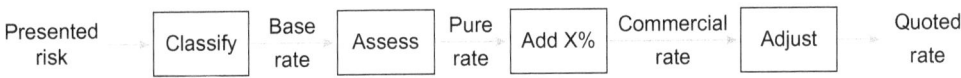

Figure 18.5

A potential client requests fire insurance for their building, which from the underwriter's perspective is a presented risk that must first be classified as a building type to establish the *base rate*. For each class there is an associated base rate, which is a predefined amount per £100 to be insured that applies to an average or normal building. The base rate is determined empirically by examining claims for a given building type, paid out in previous years, so losses will justify increasing the base rate, and excessive profits decrease it. Various features of the building to be insured are then assessed to enable the underwriters to adjust the base rate, raising it for unfavourable features shown by claims to be sources of risk, called *loadings*, and lowering it for favourable features, *discounts*, resulting in a *pure rate* considered to be unique to the building. A further adjustment for profits, commissions and other expenses adds a percentage to the pure rate to give a *commercial rate*, and even that may be subject to further adjustment to take account of market forces, competition, changed company policy or other considerations.

I had seen a role for BBNs in assisting underwriters in transforming the base rate for a particular class of buildings into a pure rate for insuring an individual building of the class. The BBN was certainly a process of transforming underwriter uncertainty about a class of buildings into their uncertainty about a specific building to be insured, and that is how the project was formulated; probabilities replacing one step in the average line method of underwriting. But was it a step too big? We'll see and report the answer at the end of step 5.

2.   Frame the Problem

When I asked how risk is currently defined by underwriters, everyone agreed it was the probability of a loss times the magnitude of the loss. As that product is a continuous uncertain quantity, it was interesting to discover that underwriters communicate their views with words indicating more or less, so we agreed a simple discrete numeric value system associated with the words, shown in Figure 18.6.

The numbers are multipliers on the base rate for a given type of building, and it is those numbers that transform the base rate for buildings of a given class into the *pure rate*. Thus, larger base multipliers act as loadings and the numbers less than 1.00 as discounts.

The point of the BBN is to associate a probability with each base rate multiplier and then calculate the mean base rate multiplier, which itself is multiplied by the pure rate to create the pure rate associated with the building. It's interesting to see that compared to Average risks, Fair to Poor risks are more severe than Excellent risks are good (as we saw in Chapter 17, emphasising the importance of understanding your client's definition of risk). It became clear that for underwriters, Average means normal, not weighted average, but perhaps the mode, in standard statistical parlance.

Level of Risk

Excellent	0.50
Good	0.75
Average	1.00
Fair	2.00
Poor	3.00

Figure 18.6

Table 18.1

Feature	Level of risk		
Construction			
Walls, roofs, floors forming perimeter of rateable range	Combustible	Non-combustible	Graded
Management			
Financial standing, moral hazard, fire loss incidence record, labour relations, attitude to risk improvement and fire protection, economic viability of business in this situation	Below normal	Normal	Above normal
Housekeeping			
Waste arrangement, conditions of storage, use of hazardous materials and inflammables, firefighting equipment, electrical installations, smoking facilities, general maintenance of buildings/plant/ equipment.	Below normal	Normal	Above normal
Size and Value			
Defined by a graph. (Confidential to CU)	Large	Medium	Small
Locality			
Location's suitability for easy access by firefighting equipment. Market values of surrounding properties. Prevalence of vandalism.	Below average	Average	Above average

The next step was to identify a list of the *features* to be included in a BBN. In the course of several meetings, we identified 13 features, eight common to all buildings, two further features omitted for some buildings, and a final three factors defined differently for each building. CU employed over 200 trained inspectors to visit each building, using a checklist of features to report the observed *level of risk* for the type of building. For shops, 11 features were considered, but the five most important features are sufficient here for demonstrating how BBNs work (Table 18.1).

Figure 18.7

At this point, the reader might download Netica, which is free to use for small models such as this insurance example. Also, download the User's Guide. To become familiar with BBNs, click on File → Open, then select 'Asia', and follow the Guide's construction of that model, playing with it to see how instantiating each item of data changes all the bar graphs, particularly the one about diagnosing tuberculosis or cancer. Click on Help → Help for information.

To construct the insurance model, close the Asia model, click on File → New, then click on the yellow oval, a 'nature' node (in our terms, an event node) in the ribbon, drag the cursor to the empty screen and click. Then right click or double left click on the letter A, which opens the Properties window, and type 'Shop_risk' in the Name field. In the State field, type the top level of risk, Excellent, tab to the Number field and enter 0.50, then click on the New button and repeat this process, assigning names and values as shown in the table shown in Figure 18.7. Then click on OK. This is the target node where the final results will appear. The dimmed numbers and bars show equal probabilities, for now.

Repeat the process for the remaining five data nodes, but this time only enter the Title of the features and the State Names, for example, for the Construction feature, enter states of Combustible, Non_combustible (the underscore will disappear when you click on OK) and Graded. Then insert the links by dragging the arrow in the ribbon from Shop_risk to each of the other nodes. After all five have been given Titles, State names and links, this simplified model is complete.

When structuring a new BBN for a client, it's also advisable to include descriptions in the Description field for each feature so you can instantly call them up to remind your client what is meant by the feature. No need to do that here, although you can, if you wish, copy the descriptions from Table 18.1. The descriptions were the subject of much discussion among the underwriters, as they were not then all written down. They were understood implicitly, which was one reason why it took many years of experience to become a fully-fledged underwriter; you apprentice yourself to an experienced underwriter and watch.

3. Provide Content

With the structure of the BBN model agreed, the team of head-office underwriters gathered to assess the conditional probabilities for shops. They began by discussing the

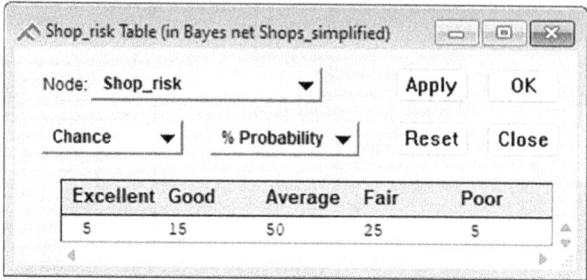

Figure 18.8

Construction Table (in Bayes net Shops_simplified)

Node: Construction

Chance   % Probability

Shop_risk	Combustible	Non comb...	Graded
Excellent	5	65	30
Good	10	65	25
Average	15	65	20
Fair	35	50	15
Poor	65	27	8

Figure 18.9

prior probabilities for shops, which are close to the relative frequencies of all the shops they have already insured. To input their priors, right click on the Shop_risk node and select 'Table ...', then type 5–15–50–25–5, pressing the Tab key to move to the next part of the field, as shown in Figure 18.8.

Yes, these, too, are conditional probabilities, conditional on CU's database of shops, adjusted by the underwriters to include the proportion of shops they have rejected in the past. So, largely objective, but some subjective adjustments, all conditional on the available information and the experts making the judgements.

The next step was to call up the five conditional probability tables, one at a time, and assess the required probabilities, starting with the Construction table. Right click on that node and select 'Table ...' to input one probability distribution for each row. I'll explain in a moment how that was done, but Figure 18.9 shows the result when the table is completed.

I asked the underwriters to think about all shops that are average risks, and briefly to discuss actual names of such shops, ensuring they all agree about what Average means. This turned out to be an important question, because in the 1970s underwriters knew no statistics, so they didn't know the definitions of mean, median and mode, and their descriptions often seemed to me to be closest to the mode (most frequent).

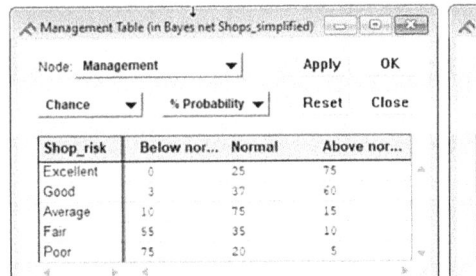

Figure 18.10

Next, I asked, 'What proportion of those average shops would Construction be judged combustible, non-combustible and graded? Think about it first, then when everyone has made their judgements, let's talk about them to see if we can reach a consensus.' As I've explained before, this 'Think, Reveal, Discuss, Agree' process ensures that the first person to speak doesn't bias the others. If at any time the row probabilities don't sum to 100, Netica will give an error message. The underwriters assigned probabilities for the Average row, noting that of all the average shops they have underwritten, 65 per cent are constructed of non-combustible materials, 15 per cent of combustible materials, and the remaining 20 per cent graded (again, tabbing to move right).

Note that the Excellent distribution, compared to the Average one, shows a 10 percentage-point increase for Graded, while the Poor distribution substantially increases the probability of Combustible. This shows a modest difference in risk between Excellent and Average shops, but a 50-percentage point increase between Average and Poor for Combustible. Remember that these numbers are percentages of shops described by the row and column titles; they're not risk scores.

Moving to the Management table gave the data in the left table, and then Housekeeping, right, as shown in Figure 18.10.

Naturally, these relative frequencies aren't stored as numbers in the heads of the underwriters, but they quickly become adept at constructing row distributions that sum to 100, reflecting their knowledge and experience gained over many years, and respecting the logic of how the three states, Below normal, Normal, and Above normal, require smaller or bigger numbers. And they benefit from doing this collectively, as their experiences are not identical, so they learn from each other during the discussion. Quite literally, the numbers are constructed as they are required.

Figure 18.11 shows the last two tables, if you want to complete your model.

4.   Explore Results

With priors and likelihoods all entered, click on the lightning bolt in Netica's ribbon to compile the model. It should look like the image in Figure 18.12.

The probabilities shown by the bar graphs in each of the six nodes should represent the approximate proportions of buildings currently funded by the company. Of course,

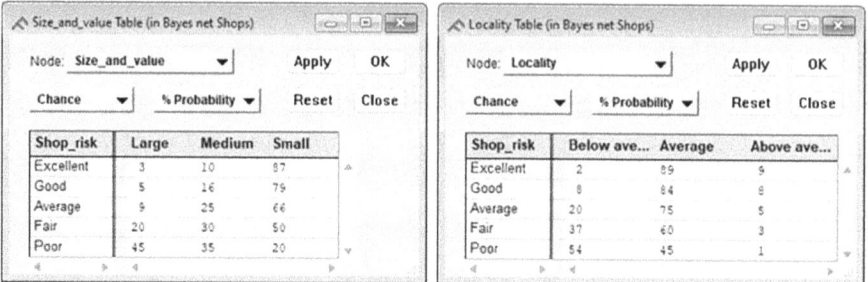

Figure 18.11

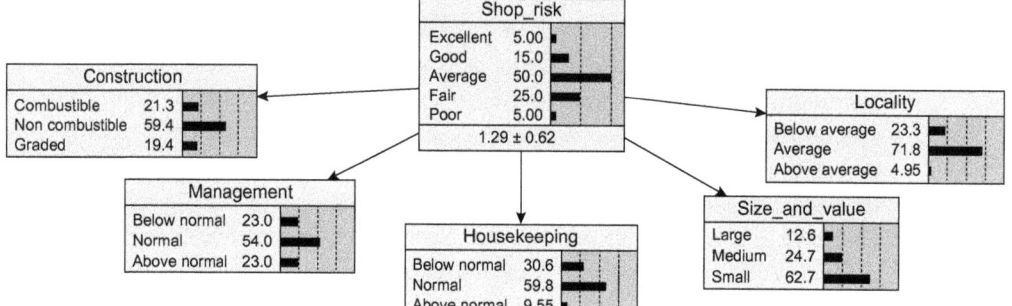

Figure 18.12

the Shop_risk probabilities were directly assessed by the underwriters, but all the others are calculated by the computer from the conditional probability tables. This provides an opportunity to check their face validity by asking the experts if they look about right.

First of all, the middle level is the highest of each set of three probabilities in four of the features, but not for Size_and_Value, where there are more small than medium or large shops. The underwriters confirmed (to their surprise) that was correct, and they noted that equal probabilities for above and below was right for Management, and below average in the other two features was more likely than being above. Only very occasionally did they not agree with the calculation, so we returned to the table for that feature to adjust it until it gave a believable distribution that closely matched the proportions in CU's database of shops.

Note that the bottom field in Shop_risk shows the product of the risk scores times their probabilities, giving a mean score of 1.29, with a standard deviation of 0.62. As the underwriters had defined average risk as 1.00, that is less than half a standard deviation away from 1.43, but perhaps shows a slight bias in underwriters' views of risk. I should have asked them at the time, but didn't think of it. It would have been a further reality check.

We then explored the model by clicking on one of the three alternatives in each of the five features to see the effect on the shop risk, and how that information changes probabilities at all the other four nodes. If you haven't created your own model, look at the example in Chapter 12 to see how instantiating a feature changes the overall risk assessment. You might also try this example, or just read the results here. Click on Combustible, which causes Shop_Risk to move from 50.0 per cent for Average to 41.2 per cent for Fair. All levels in the other features are changed as well, as would be expected now we know that construction is combustible. The reduction in uncertainty is propagated throughout the network. Click on Below normal for Management, and Shop-Risk changes to 59.8 per cent for Fair.

As you instantiate a level for each feature, the more you choose features that are undesirable, the higher the mean risk score becomes, and the reverse for desirable levels. Note how some data create larger changes than others, which should be consistent with underwriters' experience. Bayes' theorem requires calculations of ratios of likelihoods, which automatically gives more weight to ratios that are different from 1.0, so creates bigger changes in the revisions of the posterior probabilities.

Toggle on and off to change a single finding. To cancel all findings, right click on the background and click on 'Remove findings'. Even if the other three features were judged to be above average, the shop remains Fair at 62.3 per cent, and overall Shop_risk is now 1.67, slightly less risky than at the start. That seemed right for a small shop in old premises on a corner in a reasonably safe neighbourhood.

Validation
Several branch offices were briefed on the factor model and asked to identify factor levels for actual fire risks presented to them in the normal course of business. Pure rates assessed by the branches using their normal procedures on over 500 risks in eight classes of business were subsequently compared to rates generated by the Bayesian models. Separate scatter plots of actual rate against Bayesian rate were constructed to facilitate identification of risks for which the two rates were substantially different. Experienced head-office underwriters judged the Bayesian rate to be the better rate in nearly every case. Very substantial inconsistencies were noted in the relationships between the actual rates offered to clients and the factor patterns for many risks, not just between the branches, but also in a given branch. (If you didn't like the offer, hang up the phone, wait, then call again and hope a different underwriter at the branch will answer. If so, give him the information he asks for and you will most likely be given a different quote.[ii]) Finally, if all 500 presented risks had been written at the pure rate, total premium income using the Bayesian model would have been within 10 per cent of the total premium income generated by the usual average line procedures.

Credibility Factor
During the process of creating and exploring the models with the IBM 5110, our programmer, Scott Barclay, pointed out that in the (original) shops model of 11 features, each of which could be in just one of three states, there are $3^{11} = 177,147$ possible combinations, each one a *pattern* of states, which are summarised by the

---

[ii] He, him? In the late 1970s, underwriters were always men.

Bayesian model as a mean risk multiplier.[221] Now imagine a frequency distribution of all those risk multipliers; very few are low, others very high, but most will be concentrated in between, like a bell curve. Once the computer stores that bell curve, it can then look to see where any particular building's pattern lies and feedback the probability of a more extreme result, which we called the *credibility factor*.

If the credibility factor is very low, say 5 per cent or less, the computer was programmed to warn that the input pattern of features might indicate that (1) the wrong type of building had been chosen at the first stage, or (2) an error had been made in assessing the features, or (3) this building was simply an unusual combination of states, as a few must reside in the tails of the distribution. Thus, the BBN is issuing a warning that further checks might be needed before its result is accepted. As BBNs are the foundation for some forms of artificial intelligence (AI) systems, this kind of self-monitoring seemed to me as very important, and it is only human judgement that can decide between the three alternative reasons.

Subsequent research with one of my colleagues, Stuart Wooler, found that when such a credible factor message was obtained in a laboratory experiment, participants often persisted in assuming there was an error in assessing the features, and appeared to be strongly anchored on their initial choice of building type. Sad to say, we never published the paper, as I have noticed that once an initial frame for a decision model is agreed, but final results are not accepted, it is difficult for groups to accept they may have erred at the framing stage.

Feature Interactions

Some underwriters expressed a concern that some of the features may interact, in particular, that Housekeeping's conditional probabilities might be influenced by Management, requiring an arrow from Management to Housekeeping to represent causation. This would require a more complex table, the same five columns from the Shop_risk node, but nine rows, combinations of Management's three rows and the three for Housekeeping. We tried to assess that large table for shops, but gave up when the underwriters decided the two features were indeed independent. But they thought it might be true for sawmills, but again, looking at the 5-by-9 table, one row at a time, top to bottom, 45 cells altogether, proved too difficult.

Not willing to give up easily, I invented an on-the-spot method which started by the underwriters identifying highest-and-lowest-risk cells, then making paired comparisons between cells while holding constant either Management or Housekeeping states, finding clusters of very similar cells, judging the required relative frequencies, and making consistency checks between them once the computer calculated the revised base rates. In the end, the underwriters found numbers about which they could agree, but admitted that the number of sawmills they insured were too small for them to judge relative frequencies in all 45 cells, so agreed that assuming independence of the features was good enough for all buildings. Particularly as that was how the levels of risk for each feature had been defined. I now see that this event may well have instigated my later concern for requisite decision models. But interactions may well exist for other applications, and research on how best to assess them is needed.

5.   ## Agree the Way Forward

By November of 1983, we had completed 14 models, usually meeting for only a few hours once a week for most of four years, with many revisions over several months as the team learned more about the process of constructing conditional probabilities.

As I said earlier, the Canadians picked up on the work, extended it themselves, and used the models at their head office following reports by the inspectors. The Bayesian model solved their problem of insufficient branch offices in a country that is about 4,700 miles (7, 560 kms) from east to west, covering six time zones, but with 90 per cent of the population living within only 100 miles (160km) north of the USA.

Here in the UK, a new head of fire underwriting sent a very long letter to me in 1983 discussing the project, now known as CARE (Computer Assisted Risk Evaluation), suggesting that it might be possible to develop it as an alternative to the tariff system then offered by the UK Fire Office Committee (FOC), which was established in 1868 to regularise previous informal collaboration among fire insurance companies. He was concerned that although CU subscribed to and was one of the major underwriters contributing their data to the FOC, the tariff might soon become illegal, so the CARE work would need to be extended to include more building types. But he was worried that its current format would require revision and additional investment to make it available on CU's mainframe computers. He estimated a new project would take until 1986 to develop a prototype system, with a production version by 1987.

The FOC system was a simple anchoring and adjustment algorithm, which for a given type of building established a base rate for each type of building along with the loadings and discount adjustments. At periodic meetings of the FOC, base rates were raised if the five major companies contributing their data had lost money in the previous year, or lowered if profits were high. Also, adjustments were subject to actual financial performance, although they must have been associated with only a subset of the features developed for CARE. No systematic statistical analyses of the data from the five insurance companies were undertaken. A 1988 report, *Commercial Fire Insurance*, explained how the tariff schedules were created:

The schedules were based more on underwriting 'feel' than exact science, but nevertheless incorporated many years of business experience. As a result, at the overall level, the Tariff was successful in prescribing premium rates that gave offices a very adequate level of profitability. But it was not always so satisfactory in terms of fine tuning, and some problems were experienced with the system as the 20th Century progressed into its later years.[222]

I thought CARE did a better job, especially as the fire tariff was increasingly felt by insurance companies to be insensitive to the actual causes of fires and unable to respond on a more individualised basis. CARE enabled CU to decide their own base rates by examining statistical analysis of year-on-year trends, not necessarily just last year's performance, and they could 'fine tune' and include new features. In addition, the conditional probabilities could become modified by actual claims data, and by underwriters' abilities to anticipate future changes in political, economic, social, technological, legal and environmental conditions.

The tariffs were abolished in 1985 by Margaret Thatcher's government as an element of her various deregulation measures and broader economic liberalisation agenda. At this point, adopting CARE appeared to be a step too big, so CU decided to continue underwriting building insurance by the anchoring-and-adjustment method that had worked since 1688 when merchants, bankers and ship owners met at Edward Lloyd's coffeehouse in London. CARE simply didn't fit a centuries-old culture of underwriting. CU merged in 1998 with General Accident to form CGU, which merged with Norwich Union in 2000, later renamed Aviva.

BBNs and Artificial Intelligence (AI)

The first section of this chapter mentioned that a BBN is a form of AI, and you can now see how a BBN can outperform an individual expert's judgement in the sense that the BBN is more consistent and valid. We also saw the MCDA model for the harm of drugs, in which preference values were entirely based on the collective judgement of experts whose UK results have been replicated in other countries, so can be considered valid. The conditional probabilities in each of the underwriter BBNs were assessed as relative frequencies, adjusted by the head-office underwriters based on their collective experience, while the disvalue judgements about the harm of drugs were assessed by experts who were experienced in dealing with people who misused drugs. Yet the BBN could be considered as AI, whereas the MCDA model would not. Why not?

Let me answer the question from the point of view of a decision analyst acting as a problem solver. I draw on the 10 ingredients of good decisions, combining them in different ways, as I follow the five steps for creating a decision-analytic model, which acts as a structured framework for thinking about the problem and teasing out a requisite solution. The model acts as a transitional object, aiding the decision maker in thinking about the problem.

But in using AI, as I've done many times in writing this book, I'm usually searching for summaries that can help me distinguish A from B, provide strengths and weaknesses of A and B, report about a specific historical event, explain the current status of X, what is best practice for Y and so forth. In short, stuff I might do myself by searching the net, or find in Wikipedia, but hope that AI will do the job, in depth, relying on its very large database and its neural network to do the job quicker and better. I'm not problem solving, I'm using AI as an expert consultant.

So, where is the real difference? I believe it is in how the two approaches deal with context. In the underwriting BBNs *and* the harm of drugs MCDA, groups of experts discussed their different experiences to arrive at a consensus judgement about conditional probabilities for the BBN matrices and about harms (disvalues) for the MCDA. However, the BBN provides a probability distribution over the risk measures (Excellent, Good, Average, Fair and Poor), while the underwriter takes the mean of the distribution as a measure of the pure risk, and then adjusts it for the contextual factors. Similarly, the MCDA for the UK harm of drugs is taken as a template and adjusted for the territorial context of different misuse and even different drugs from one country to the next (the high correlations are only for the drugs that are the same across the countries).

However, there is a substantial difference in how the original models are updated as more information becomes available. BBNs can update their conditional probability matrices by incorporating new cases. This can be done automatically, so will reflect changes in the political, environmental, social, technological, economic and legal contexts, as seen in the new probability distribution of risk measures. If the context changes, it will be reflected in the automatic revision. For the MCDA, however, changes in any of those six contextual features will require gathering a new group of experts to revise the harm-of-drugs model. In short, Bayesian revision of uncertainty is accomplished because new knowledge is automatically incorporated as revised relative frequencies, a form of Bayesian updating. But there is no formal theory for updating preference values. Nor, of course, is there any formal theory for updating trade-offs, which are wholly context dependent.

So, I thought, AI might be limited in its ability to implement decision-analytic modelling. To test that working hypothesis, I gave Graham's decision problem (a one-paragraph summary of the dialogue at the start of Chapter 16) to ChatGPT, and asked it what Graham should do. It replied with a tidy summary of the problem and suggested four steps, the first of which was to try the commercial program, given Graham's risk tolerance and the given probabilities. That was the recommendation of the original model, so apparently ChatGPT can engage in some reasoning from stated probabilities and verbal descriptions of risk attitude, without calculating expected preference values.

That led me to wonder if ChatGPT could draw a decision tree, so I asked it, and it said 'Certainly,' but added, 'while I can't draw the tree directly here, you can visualize it like this' (see Figure 18.13).

Well, that's a bit incomplete, but roughly correct, and even shows that success with the commercial software would produce a design in less than a half day. So not quite full marks to ChatGPT, but one day it may be able to draw a proper decision tree and perhaps even do the calculations required to roll the tree back.

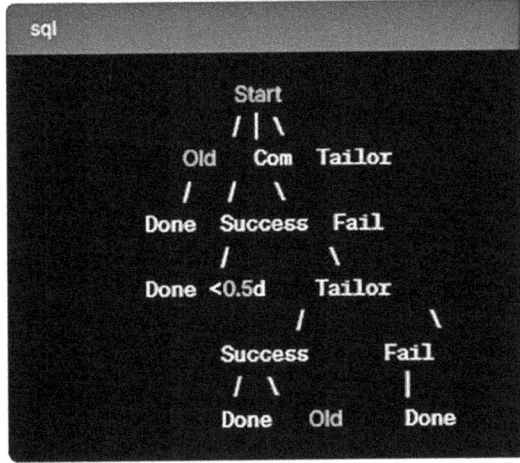

Figure 18.13

So, I'm now assuming that decision analysis and AI may help each other, maybe even in the near future, but there will always be a clear role for human judgement to adjust relative frequencies to ensure their relevance for the future, to assess value functions when metrics describe consequences, to assess preference values directly when metrics are not available and to judge trade-offs. I am sceptical about AI ever being able to fully anticipate future changes in context.

And, indeed, that is what happened with Graham. After giving the decision analysis due consideration, he did not follow its recommendation; he wrote his own program, and it worked. Was this a bad decision that resulted in a good outcome? Not so, Graham admitted his initial view was to use the old method as it was certain to produce the result in time. But the decision analysis had changed his risk attitude, he could now afford to try writing his own program. Little did I know then that the decision model served as a transitional object for him, enabling him to try writing his own program, and he would enjoy the pleasure if it were successful, but he still had sufficient time if it wasn't. Note, too, that in summarising the dialogue with Graham for ChatGPT, I assumed the clarity that simply didn't exist at the start of structuring the problem. Could AI have dealt with the messiness of formulating the MEM problem?

Conclusion

The freesias example introduced Bayesian statistics, while the Bayesian Belief Network demonstrated how a hierarchical model of conditional probabilities can combine multiple sources of information to make an inference about the future. Both approaches extend our brain's limited ability to combine many pieces of information and synthesise them, which I commented on in the Epilogue to Part I.

But there is a problem. Many experts hesitate to accept a new algorithm that replaces an older, familiar one. Recall from the section, 'What Defines an Expert?' in Chapter 11, the observation that insurance underwriters and drug regulators 'eschew modelling in favour of implicit, qualitative and subjective thinking'. Of course, experts consider the available evidence, but they somehow assemble it in their heads and apply an implicit rule, guided by their feelings, to arrive at a conclusion. But we saw in comparing the CARE model's risk assessment with that of underwriters' intuitive judgements, for 500 real-life cases, two important findings, that underwriters substantially disagree with one another, and that the CARE predictions were always preferred by head-office senior underwriters to local underwriters' judgements when the two approaches substantially differed. Of course, they often agreed, so perhaps the extra cost of CARE wouldn't have been justified. Then again, any improvement in underwriting might help to beat the competition. Perhaps Bayesian systems only for the types of buildings that generate the most net income and with only the main building features would justify the extra cost of CARE. A challenge to any insurance company reading this, but today translating CARE to local desktop computers would be trivial, compared to the cost and time in the 1980s for translating to mainframes, so I was told (although they did it in Canada).

Research findings now agree that algorithms make better, or at least as-good, decisions than unaided intuitions. Fortunately, a great many unaided decisions are 'good enough', or requisite for the problem at hand. It may well be better to make a quick, good enough decision now and wait to see the consequences, perhaps adding a few adjustments, than wait for the help of an algorithm. That said, I'm reminded that Ralph Keeney has shown that the main cause of premature deaths worldwide is bad decisions.[223]

What, then, is the proper role for the many algorithms derived from decision models that use Bayesian ideas? Let's start with Bayesian statistics. Modern books on the topic are vastly different from the early textbooks. Then, you learned about significance and hypothesis testing, p-values, confidence intervals, Gaussian (normal) distributions and data-generating functions, which today litter the published scientific literature, all now considered as 'classical' statistics. Today's Bayesian statistics textbooks subsume all kinds of testing within what is known as the Generalised Linear Model and calculations are now entirely carried out by a range of computer programs that engage in Markov chain Monte Carlo techniques that enable you to fit a model to any data.[224]

In the past 50 years, the various Bayesian approaches to data analysis have grown. Even today, objections to Bayesian statistics are based on the difficulty of determining prior distributions, which is no longer a problem, as is evident in the freesias example, where my prior was based on just two observations. More generally, reports of data analyses using Bayesian methods usually show not only a base-case prior, but also one or more sceptical priors that can establish the vigour of the results. Note that even the classical statistician relies on some sort of prior evidence in order to power a classical study. Basically, there is no way to avoid judgement in applying either classical or Bayesian approaches, so Bayesians prefer to make their judgements public.

But the more important consideration, in my view, is that a Bayesian analysis neatly complements a decision analysis. You can use a Bayesian posterior probability distribution to inform the event probabilities in a decision tree, as shown in the evacuation case study in the next chapter. More simply, recall that the mean of the posterior probability distribution in the epilepsy project communicated exactly what the prescribing doctor wants to know, the probability that the next patient will improve, whereas classical p-values are useless – and frequently misinterpreted as the probability that the null hypothesis is wrong. Even worse, that the confidence interval shows there is a 95 per cent probability that an effect is genuine.

As for Bayesian Belief Networks, the fire underwriting case study makes clear that creating this type of model requires a mixture of hard data and judgement. It is expert judgement that defines the features to be included in the model and their definitions, what the levels of the features are and the likelihoods. Priors were closely associated with the relative frequencies of the five levels of risk in the company's portfolio of buildings, so were more objective, initially, than the judgements of likelihoods.

More generally, the objective-subjective distinction is not useful in describing the difference between priors and likelihoods because either or both can be based on hard data or judgement. And the reality is that judgement always plays some role in creating numbers that will work best to aid decisions about the future. Dennis Lindley once suggested to me that the distinction might better be based formally on substantive and collateral information, representing likelihoods and priors, respectively. Indeed, he never used 'prior' and 'posterior' in his last book, instead always referring to how new information contributes to revising your knowledge base, K.[225] That interpretation, which associates probabilities with an individual's degrees of belief, better describes BBNs in a real-life setting.

Appendix: Obtaining Charts of Beta Distributions, Given Parameters a and b

Two computer sites show how to calculate Beta distributions given its two parameters a and b. The first gives the probability density function and the second shows how to obtain a highest density interval.

Beta probability density functions:
Log on to www.medcalc.org/manual/beta-distribution-functions.php.
   Below the graph, replace the default values 2 and 5 with the desired values of a and b.
   Click on Replot to see the revised graph. The values on the vertical axis readjust to ensure the area below the curve integrates to 1.0.
   If comparing prior to posterior distributions, you may need to adjust the gentler distribution's vertical axis so the maximum and minimum are identical to the posterior distribution.

Highest density interval:
Log on to https://real-statistics.com/bayesian-statistics/bayesian-statistics-for-bino mial-distributed-data/analytic-approach-binomial-data/high-density-interval-hdi.
This shows two ways to calculate a highest density interval (HDI). Both use Excel Add-ins.
   If you are familiar with Excel's Solver Add-In, you could apply the process described in the section Using Solver.
   Alternatively, you can use the Real Statistics BETA_HDI function, which is included in the Real Statistics Resource pack at https://real-statistics.com/free-down load/real-statistics-resource-pack. Be sure to carefully follow the instructions there, which include downloading Excel's Solver, which the BETA_HDI function uses in the background, so you don't need to know how Solver works.
   There is also useful information here: https://real-statistics.com/real-statistics-envir onment/accessing-supplemental-data-analysis-tools.
   In either of the above cases, applying them in Excel requires you to create the following text and the desired values of a, b and alpha (1.00 minus the credible interval, so 0.05 for a 95 per cent credible interval) in a blank spreadsheet (here showing in rows 2, 3 and 4, the values for the epilepsy posterior distribution). Then, in B6, enter the

	A	B
1		
2	a	20
3	b	1
4	alpha	0.05
5		
6	lower	0.860892
7	upper	1
8	length	0.139108
9	pdf lower	1.161586
10	pdf upper	20
11		

Figure 18.14

formula =BETA_HDI(B4,B2,B3,TRUE). As soon as you finish entering the data, Excel calculates and displays the results in rows 6 through 10 (Figure 18.14).

You can see that B6 and B7 define the 95 per cent credible interval for the epilepsy data, and that the interval between them is just 0.139 percentage points wide. B9 and B10 are the vertical axis values at the CI points; they are irrelevant for our purposes.

19 Think Strategically

> Strategy is the great work of the organization . . . it is a unifying theme that gives coherence and direction to the actions and direction of an organization.
>
> Sun Tzu, *The Art of War*, fifth century BC

The types of decision models in the previous seven chapters focused on the many ways in which the 10 ingredients of good decisions can be combined to help resolve the decision maker's sense of unease. Now it's time to look at the larger picture to make explicit what is implicitly felt, and find out how decision analysis can provide coherence and establish direction to actions.

I first learned how this can be achieved, not from Sun Tzu, but from Peter Denyar Hall, whose work with International Computers Ltd (ICL) was focused on how computers could become decision support systems. He had studied decision analysis at Stanford University and suggested in the early 1980s to ICL's MD, Robb Wilmot, that decision analysis could play a role in the newly emerging field of decision support systems. Robb agreed and the two of us, often working together and sometimes with help from other ICL staff, facilitated over 70 decision conferences from 1983 to 1987.

We quickly learned that Robb had a problem. As an electrical engineer whose former job was at Texas Instruments in the USA, he believed that one day computers would become commodities. In the early 1980s, that was an unusual view as mainframe computers were everywhere in the UK, at universities, local authorities, government departments, the Ministry of Defence and many commercial organisations. Nobody even dreamed that we would today have vastly more computer power in our mobiles/cell phones. How could Robb, assisted by his then marketing manager, Peter Bonfield, turn this substantially mainframe ship onto a new course?

It was Peter Hall's familiarity with just three concepts: *mission*, *objectives* and *strategy* (MOS) that did the trick. He was formerly an Army Commander in the British Army, and brought to ICL what military leaders worldwide understand well are the steps that must be taken before engaging in a mission. He believed that ICL was now in a position to establish a clear mission for the future, define the objectives to be achieved and establish clear strategies for realising the value that achieving the objectives would bring. This would align decision makers in the organisation and ensure everyone was pulling in the same direction. And ever so slowly, it would turn the ship around, ready to confront the digital future.

CONTEXT

External: Political, Economic, Social, Technological, Environmental, Legal
Internal: Mission–Why are we here? Core Values–What do we deeply care about?

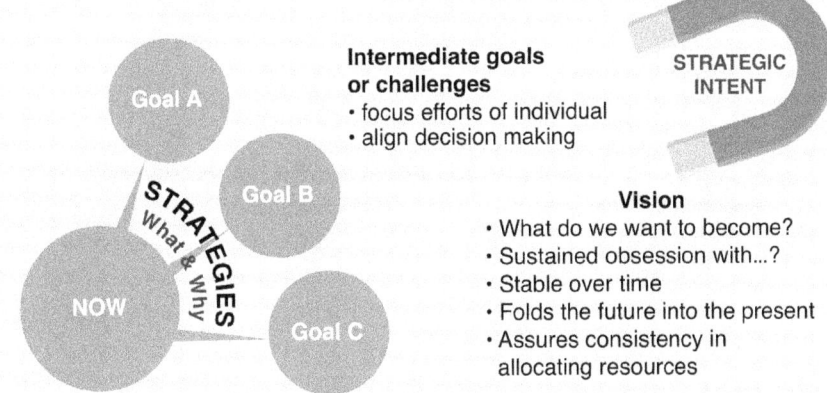

Intermediate goals or challenges
• focus efforts of individual
• align decision making

STRATEGIC INTENT

Vision
• What do we want to become?
• Sustained obsession with...?
• Stable over time
• Folds the future into the present
• Assures consistency in allocating resources

Figure 19.1

From the 1980s onward, I've enhanced MOS, through trying out various of its concepts after reading about them largely in many books about strategy, initially a problem as there are a great many definitions of all the MOS concepts. I found Hussey to be particularly informative and coherent,[226] and I was also influenced by Gary Hamel and C. K. Prahalad, whose research revealed that success is often driven by a company's obsession with winning out of all proportion to its resources and capabilities.[227] They argued that a company's *strategic intent* was key.

When working with Pfizer, I was discussing strategy with a senior vice president, Dr Nancy Hutson, who interrupted me and said, 'Strategy is simple. It's *what and why, not how or by when.*' That fit well with the 10 ingredients of good decisions, especially with value-focused thinking. And I found it useful to distinguish Mission from Vision. Over time and borrowing from many sources, testing them in many decision conferences, I put together a model that summarises the key concepts of strategic intent, shown in Figure 19.1

The magnet is a metaphor for the aligning properties of strategic intent, just as a magnet held under a sheet of cardboard creates an invisible magnetic field which aligns iron filings sprinkled onto the cardboard. To understand where we are NOW could be described by the organisation's internal strengths and weaknesses, and its external opportunities and threats, a SWOT analysis directed to the problem at hand.[228]

Vision answers the question of what the organisation wishes to become, the fundamental objective(s), possibly as a sustained obsession about something that many in the organisation may feel will be difficult to achieve, is unlikely to change as a destination, requires the achievement of intermediate goals that will be understood by implementers, and are the areas to which resources will be allocated.

STRATEGIES are options that describe *what* is to be done, with the question of *why* answered by objectives and criteria summarised as goals.

CONTEXT influences Now, Vision and Strategies in three ways. First is the PESTEL features: the political, economic, social, technological, environmental and legal situation relevant to the organisation for the problem at hand. Second is the Mission of the organisation, its reason for being, answering the question of Why we are here. Third is the organisation's Core Values, what it deeply cares about, which distinguishes it from other similar organisations, contributing to its longevity.[229]

That's a lot to digest, let alone remember, so the next case study describes how strategic thinking was realised by one organisation in preparing for the next 10 years. Following that case study, another real-life case will show how the US military responded to a Middle East crisis by simultaneously adopting three different frames, a decision tree, multiple objectives and a Bayesian Belief Network for probabilities, to ensure the success of a mission.

What and Why, Then How and When

Many companies see the goal of strategic management as creating the future, which requires organisation-wide clarity and acceptance of mission, vision, goals, objectives and challenges. Effective strategic planning capitalises on an organisation's core values and historical strengths, and goes beyond strategic evolution by managing discontinuous change. However, if the historical strengths are insufficient to meet new challenges in the environment, then strategic management is needed to develop the new capabilities needed to survive.

Strategic thinking can occur at all levels in the organisation. It requires that before acting, a manager considers *what* must be done and *why*. With this clearly in mind, the next step is to consider *how* to do it and by *when*. Focusing only on how and when, such as tactics, leads to frantic activity, distraction in putting out bush fires and constantly reacting rather than taking a more proactive stance.

Groups can easily slide into defining options that are tactical, with arguments arising because participants are assuming different objectives. The short-term nature of tactics provides a clue for the facilitator to redirect the discussion to longer-term objectives by asking, 'What are you trying to achieve with these options?' And the answer might need to be followed by, 'And why do you care about that?', repeatedly, until a fundamental objective is reached, as suggested in Chapter 4.

Now let's turn to consider how one members-only organisation applied the strategic intent framework to position their organisation for the next 10 years. I'll apply the usual five-step framework to describe what occurred in a two-day decision conference. As you will see, the majority of the group's work was at step 2, framing the problem.

1.   Context

The International Federation of Health Funds (IFHF) was in 1992 a worldwide, members-only network of health-care organisations, an umbrella organisation of small funds and large global health-care businesses, governed by a Council of Management composed of chief executives drawn from their membership. Their Secretary General, Kenneth Groom, met with me and my late wife, Mary Ann, a group-process specialist with whom I often worked in facilitating decision conferences, to discuss what issues should be the main focus for the organisation's next annual conference.

A major concern arose in the discussion about how the individual missions and visions of member companies, which were often very different from one country to the next, could be accommodated at the level of this umbrella organisation, which itself had no clear vision or mission other than to offer a portfolio of activities that would assist members in meeting opportunities in their own countries. Developing an agreed mission and vision for the Council itself appealed to Ken, so he consulted many of the chief executive members to obtain their views. They were enthusiastic, so Ken devised an open-ended questionnaire, sent to all members in August, asking for their answers to four questions:

1. What are the major opportunities for health funds in your country?
2. What are the major threats facing health funds in your country?
3. Recognising that additional resources would be required, what new activities, if any, would you like to see IFHF address to help you meet the opportunities for funds in your country?
4. What other changes would you like to see in IFHF's portfolio of activities?

Ken's summary of the 55 replies highlighted the difficulties experienced by members in adapting to fluctuating changes between public and private provision of health services, lack of innovation and imagination on the part of members' organisations, increases in costs, consumption of services by an ageing population and so forth. In particular, some respondents felt that any new activities should add cost-effective value for members.

To ensure that all IFHF activities were capable of delivering value, Ken felt that the current portfolio of activities could make better use of its limited resources by clarifying the IFHF's reason for being and acquiring a better view of what might develop over the next 10 years. And so, VISION 2004, Opportunities and Threats, was born as the topic of a two-day decision conference. Eleven CEOs from Ireland, Canada, the USA, New Zealand, South Africa, Australia, Holland, Belgium, the UK and Zimbabwe gathered in January 1993 at Kilkea Castle in Ireland.

2.   Frame the Problem

After introductions, Ken reiterated the objectives of the meeting as stated in the calling note:

1. To reconsider the mission of the Federation
2. To establish a Vision for the year 2004
3. To agree strategies for achieving the Vision

I then explained the overall structure of the meeting, which drew on an early version of the strategic intent model. Because what might happen to health care in the future had been a frequent topic of the questionnaire answers, I suggested we first carry out a scenario analysis, and quickly described the steps given at the end of Chapter 17.

Key Events in Funding and Provision

We started with a free-for-all discussion of the key events about health funding and provision throughout the world over the past decades. We quickly established seven time periods to list political, economic, social and technological influences relevant to health care since 1850. Thereafter, a lively discussion identified a great many events, and it was interesting to see how none of us fully appreciated the extent of different events, especially in provision.

Pre-1930s

- exodus from rural areas
- unions and mutualities emerge in Europe (1850–90 Europe, earlier in England)
- per-capita system in Holland
- cash payments
- 1914 subsidised private socialised initiatives in Continental Europe
- other parts of world – increasing government action

1930–1945

- beginning of tension between public and private provision
- private side seen as failing egalitarianism
- low-cost care
- 1936: New Zealand first nationalised health system in the world

1946–1950s

- emergence of egalitarianism; access to health care
- 1948: GB NHS breaks tension
- specialisation in medicine
- economic growth
- UK: funded partly by taxation, national insurance; after 1950 by co-payment
- co-payment in Belgium, Netherlands and Luxembourg

1960s

- 1966: Medicare and Medicaid in the USA
- 1967: nationalised care in Canada
- extension of coverage to vast majority of populations
- growth in standards of living, expectations

1970s

- Australia: nationalised health (mixed system)
- economic growth slows
- development of for-profit delivery

1980s

- medical cost inflation escalates
- demographic changes: ageing population
- increased expectations in health care
- growth in technology
- prevention measures
- beginning of awareness of state funding difficulties
- emphasis on healthier lifestyles
- high public interest in health care and health insurance

1990s

- state funding difficulties
- shifts for most countries in the mix of state and private regarding provision and financing
- break-up of USSR leads to loosening of socialist ideology in health care
- emergence of criteria for outcome measures, effectiveness, return for investment, quality of life
- reappraisal of role of medicine
- governments developing new schemes for financing
- integration of medical insurers

Identify Main Themes and Key Uncertainties

The group then looked to find trends over the decades, extracting several main themes and identifying key uncertainties that could impact health care. This is what they agreed:

Main Themes:

1. Relative contribution and involvement of government vs private.
2. Search for marriage between social justice and innovation/flexibility.
3. Balance between individualist vs collectivist ideologies.
4. Role as health-care financiers as part of larger financial world.
5. Measures of outcome.
6. Rationing.

Key Uncertainties

1. What encompasses 'health care'?
2. What will be financed by the public and private sectors?
3. Split between profit and not-for-profit organisations.
4. Impact of globalisation.
5. Degree of government regulation.
6. State of global economy.
7. Extent of spread of AIDS.
8. State of medical technology including genetic engineering.

Create Optimistic, Pessimistic and Trend Scenarios

The group next divided into three sub-groups which addressed the themes and resolved some uncertainties in developing pessimistic and optimistic scenarios that would bound actual subsequent developments, and a trend scenario that extrapolated the trends. I emphasised that the scenarios should describe 2004 as if you have arrived without concern for how you got there. These scenarios, which describe the anticipated year 2004, are as follows:

OPTIMISTIC SCENARIO

Global economy booms. We all continue to get healthier. Advances in medicine. We live longer. Nevertheless, still insufficient resources to fund all health services for ALL. Governments agree they cannot fund everything and draw line. Others will be compelled to opt out. Sensible management of interface between public/private. Long-term opportunities for funding (e.g., pension style) for later life health expenditures. West feels social responsibility towards Third World health care, which presents opportunities for IFHF. Responsible medicine develops to replace confrontational relationship between funding and medical practitioners.

What is encompassed as health care in 1993 will be widened and Funds will expand coverage, but exactly where and how much is not clear. Oregon-type approaches will be evident. The public/private split will not be relevant. No unexpected step-function changes incrementally are foreseen between 1993 and 2004.

TREND SCENARIO

Environmental pollution and nuclear accidents and continued thinning of ozone layer have reached levels where they cause ill health significantly. There have been great advances in biogenetics and a reduction of genetic-based chronic illness. These and other improvements have however only led to displacement of demand towards the diseases of old age. HIV has plateaued with the new vaccine, but AIDS will continue to spread for the next ten years forcing developed countries to give health care aid to those most affected. The public and private systems are under great pressure for psychiatric care. We have a mixed health care economy where the Government provides or mandates a basic level of health care, but requires extensive co-payments to ease funding. People are free to obtain further benefits from private insurers. The high proportion of reasonably well-off elderly are cared for privately. State funding to health care is capped and the content of the basic package is determined by increasing proven cost effectiveness of treatments. There is an international shortage of nurses and richer countries are poaching them from poorer countries.

PESSIMISTIC SCENARIO

There will be increased dichotomy between the developed and developing economies. Stagflation will continue in the developed economies, leading to shortage of

> funding for health care. Diagnostic ability will continue to outstrip therapeutic ability, leading to increased cost. There will be growth in 'heroic' measures – e.g., primate transplants. A loss of 'friendly' environment for providers and funds, through growth in consumer law, product liability for medical acts, more litigation, ageing populations. Competition between private funds will lead to 'cherry picking' and uninsurable groups, provoking increased government involvement which also facilitates rationing leading to higher costs.

Discussion of the differences and similarities between these scenarios led the group to identify several concerns about the future for health-care plans:

Key Issues

1. Two-tier system (where is the line drawn?)
2. Shortage of capital
3. Tight economies
4. Changing consumer attitudes
5. AIDS

At this point, I felt that the group needed to get down to the nitty-gritty of exploring strategies for each of their areas of activity, so we began the process of building a multi-criteria portfolio model using Equity software.

3. Provide Content

The areas of activity were well known to participants as they defined budget categories for the IFHF. The latter are shown here in boldface, with text describing current and new activities, which were treated as strategies because they described only what the activities did, not how they did them.

1. **Conferencing**: shorten and focus biennial conference, more regional conferences and special interest conferences, study tours, wider audience activities and more frequent.
2. **Information exchange**: publishing, proceedings, newsletter, information series, etc., conference pamphlet or other enhancement, cataloguing, upgrade commentaries.
3. **Studies**: commission two studies per year for Conference and sponsor major research project.
4. **Recruitment, Members**: continue to react to enquiries, target recruitment, actively woo prospective members, hold council meetings in target countries.
5. **Inter-Fund Relationships**: more inter-Fund transfer schemes and study tours, plus staff exchange.
6. **Standards**: gather information re. EDI, influence standards, develop dedicated expertise.

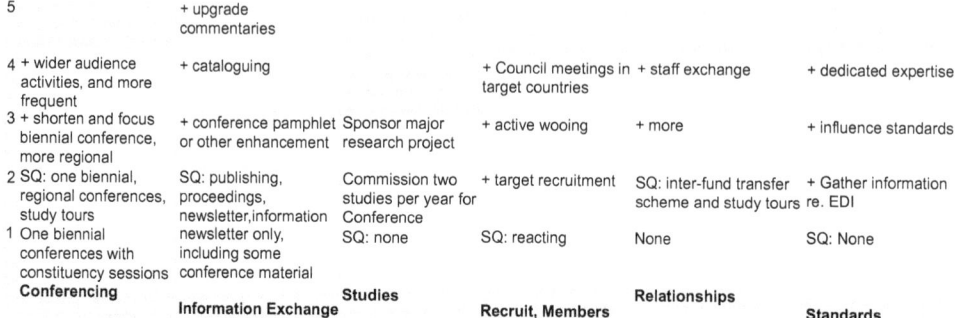

Figure 19.2

In Equity, the strategies were shown at levels within each relevant area, which resulted in a cityscape of 24 strategies, including the 'none' ones, shown in Figure 19.2.

Note that at the time of the decision conference, IFHF activities were limited to the Status Quo (SQ) strategies in Conferencing, Information Exchange, Recruitment and Relationships. All strategies preceded by a '+' sign were new suggestions. Also, cutbacks from the SQ were considered. This is the cityscape before sorting the strategies by their benefit-to-cost ratios, the indices that establish value for money.

With only limited time available, I suggested evaluating the strategies on just two criteria: estimated annual cost and expected relative benefits. First, participants discussed the goals that were to define the benefits, and they agreed on the following:

1. Exchange information
2. Facilitate contact between funds
3. Promote and foster useful studies
4. Establish the Federation as authoritative and credible (added during model building)

Thus, two strategies could be given the same benefit score, but for different reasons. The group then started scoring the strategies in each area on the usual 0–100 scale, representing least and most preferred strategies. As participants discussed the area of Recruitment, I sensed that they were skirting around their basic values, so Mary Ann and I asked the group to talk about them. It didn't take very long for participants to agree the following:

IFHF Core Values

Members of IFHF

- care about their members.
- try to improve health services.
- actively contribute to the Federation's mission.
- are committed to learning from and supporting each other.
- share a sense of social responsibility.

Figure 19.3

These are the values they would explain to prospective members. With that clarification in mind, participants completed the scoring process. As I've said before, the process of creating a decision model isn't necessarily linear. Here, an interruption was needed to ensure participants were working from similar values.

With just one benefit criterion, the process of weighting the six 0–100 scales of benefits required comparing only the added value from 0–100 from one area to the next, and entering them in Equity as within-criterion weights. With the model completed, the computer program calculated the priority index, the ratio of benefit to cost in this case, creating a triangle for every strategy, as illustrated in Chapter 14.

4.   Explore Results

After sorting the 18 above level 1 strategies in each area for their priority indices, starting with the largest at level 2 (the level 1 strategies are the fixed starting points for calculating the upward benefit-to-cost ratios), the cityscape looked like that shown in Figure 19.3.

Only strategies in Studies and Relationships have remained in the same order. By selecting the SQ strategy in each of the six areas to create a Proposed (P) package of strategies, the computer displayed where that package sits compared to the efficient frontier of all strategies, as compared to a Better (B) package at the same cost and a Cheaper (C) one for the same benefit, as shown by the chart in Figure 19.4.

Participants were surprised to see that all three packages were far to the left of the efficient frontier. Even the C package was slightly more beneficial than the P package, as there wasn't a cheaper one horizontally to the left of P. The total cost of the SQ package was only £29,000, whereas participants wanted FHF to do much more. I suggested to the group that they chose different points on the curve to create increasingly beneficial, and costly, packages, but Mary Ann interrupted me and said that her reading of the group was that most participants wanted to do everything.

I noted how thin the shaded area was and that the efficient frontier continued to grow upward almost linearly, suggesting there may be even more that FHF could do for its members.

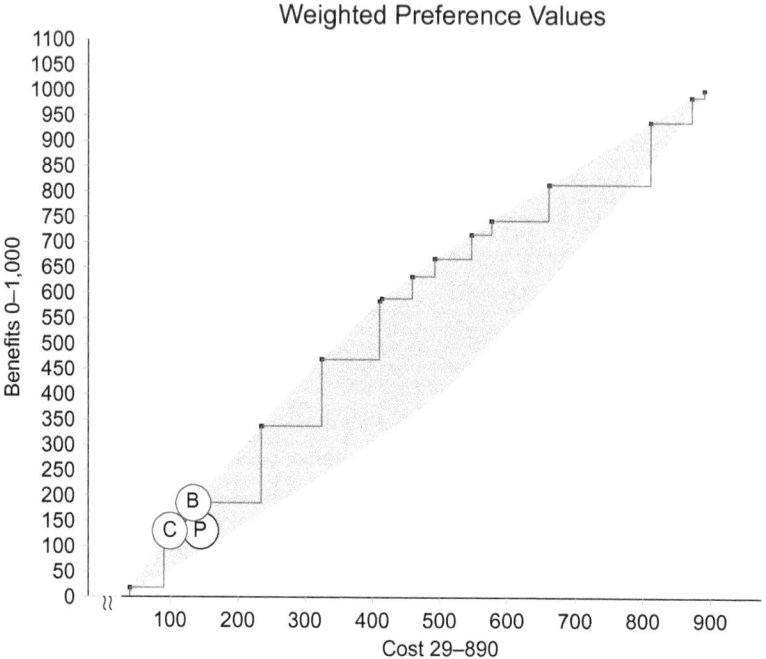

Figure 19.4

5.   Agree the Way Forward

Participants enthusiastically agreed with her, so I asked if they could formulate their vision for 2004, which they did, with my thinking that this was certainly a sustainable obsession. They also clarified their mission and reason for existing, as follows.

FHF Vision for 2004

The FHF will be the premier international source of information about non-governmental health-care funding, providing a forum for members to obtain and exchange information.

Mission for FHF

- To promote international contact between member organisations.
- To exchange information and expertise.
- To further advances in health-care financing and delivery by facilitating international studies and debates.

What Is FHF?

FHF is an international body of non-governmental organisations which exist solely to help their members afford health care for which charges are levied.

Interesting that this group of high-level CEOs needed to take a hard look at the activities they wanted FHF to support before they could formulate the vision and mission, and explain the FHF's reason for being. That concluded the decision conference.

What Happened Next?

Two years later, the FHF held an invitation-only forum at the Grand Hotel in Noordwijk, in the Netherlands, that included selected CEOs of Federation members, other compatible organisations and a few people with relevant expertise about the topic: Leading Change in Independent Health Care Finance. The aim of the forum was to synthesise views about broad trends in health care, strategic options for independent health-care providers and the qualities required of leaders to effect change for the independents.

Keynote speeches were followed by facilitated small-group discussions and then attempts were made to summarise the discussions, which showed the many differences and similarities in how health care is funded and provided across the countries. As Mary Ann and I facilitated many sub-groups, we left feeling that almost everyone had learned a lot, including the speakers and facilitators.

In writing up this case study, I looked up what FHF is doing now or even if it still exits. I was pleased to see that they are now the iFHP, International Federation of Health Plans, and very much alive. Interesting to see 'Funds' replaced by 'Plans', perhaps shifting the emphasis from member organisations known by the noun 'funds' to the more active role of the iFHP in helping members to 'plan', as an active verb, not just for their organisations, but also to improve planning generally for better health.

At a luncheon with the iFHP's current Chief Executive, Chris Watney, to whom I had sent the above summary, and his assistant, Barbara Vanneuville, I was surprised to learn that the above description was entirely unknown to them. Further discussion revealed that the iFHP moved from an emphasis on funds to the broader perspective of plans, and that the organisation had pretty well implemented many of the plans from the 1993 decision conference and the forum in 1995.

It was made clear to me that the organisation had been operating as Ken Groom had hoped might be possible by 2004, and the leadership in the new century had joined when Ken's vision had been achieved. The transitional decision model in 1993 had helped to guide developments in the previous century until so much had been achieved that it was no longer needed; indeed, it was forgotten by the organisation. The longest use of a transitional object of the many presented in this book.

Combining Decision Frames

The next case study is based on a real political situation, showing how advanced planning can track events occurring in the future, enabling decision makers to respond rationally as uncertainties are resolved. Although based on a conflict in a Middle Eastern country, it demonstrates how any developing crisis, such as a government's response to a developing health crisis or a threat from a competing organisation, could enable decision makers to respond actively and quickly, while ensuring that competing objectives are met with minimum monetary and non-monetary cost.

By the mid-1970s, Decision and Designs Inc. (DDI) had built an organisation of decision analysts as well as military experts who were retired generals and admirals, funded largely by the US Department of Defense's Advanced Research Projects Agency. Most of their projects showed how decision analysis could be of use to the US military. One of them, a contingency planning problem, consisted of options followed by key uncertainties about several outcomes, with the combinations of options and outcomes evaluated against benefit and cost criteria. The many political events that could go one way or another were modelled by a Bayesian Belief Network (BBN) to model risk, with its associated uncertainties.

All these features were combined in one software program, OPINT (Operational Intelligence), for the IBM 5100,[230] and in June 1976 a team from DDI had been invited to demonstrate it to NATO personnel. However, on arrival they were told that no time was available for a briefing as a new Middle East crisis needed their full attention: the possible evacuation of US and European personnel from Lebanon. The DDI team explained that was exactly the kind of problem that could be modelled by their software, and suggested they help. I suspect that the presence of military experts on the DDI team helped to persuade the NATO personnel to give it a try. Surprisingly, they did.

1.   Context

In June 1976, the ongoing civil war in Lebanon, which had started in 1975, worsened to the extent that it endangered the lives of many US and NATO personnel and their families. In particular, fighting in Beirut between Lebanese Christian militias and the Palestinian Liberation Organization (PLO) had provoked the Christian faction aligned with the Lebanese Government, potentially disrupting elections in 1976. All this threatened the safety of foreign nationals, so NATO launched Operation Fluid Drive in June to carry out the evacuation, just as the DDI team arrived.

2.   Frame the Problem

The immediate operational problem facing NATO was whether and how to position NATO training exercises for the US and European navies then operating in the Mediterranean. In part, the choice of options depended on how permissive the evacuation would be by those fighting, which was uncertain, and on the benefits and risks of the consequences of the action taken and its outcomes. Furthermore, the uncertainty about the permissiveness of the evacuation situation depended on the outcomes of several political issues.

The DDI team helped NATO and the intelligence experts to establish possible options and agree the criteria against which consequences would be evaluated, in short, the structure of the problem. DDI also helped the intelligence analysts to 'extend the conversation' about the permissiveness of the evacuation situation to include the outcomes of key political events, expressed as a relevance diagram in the form of a BBN.

Each of the two teams contributed their findings to the computer, but with considerable to-and-fro as the structure of the evacuation problem developed into

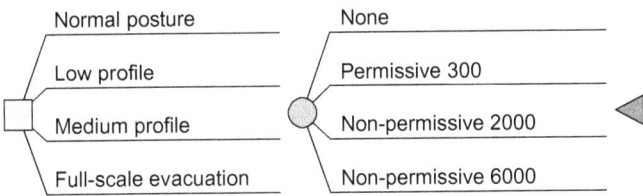

Figure 19.5

a contingency plan, enabling the military side to explore how to position the ships in the Mediterranean as the future unfolded, describing any of the combination of outcomes.

3.   ## Provide Content

Let's start with the military decision of the posture to adopt for the evacuation. The decision tree is shown in Figure 19.5, displayed using DPL. The tree starts with four alternatives followed by an event node of four outcomes, the latter agreed with the intelligence analysts.

Alternatives. Here are the definitions of the posture options:

- Normal posture: no action taken beyond alerting subordinate commanders that evacuation is a distinct possibility.
- Low profile posture with modest capability to airlift 500 personnel out of the area. (Requires minimum forward staging and a permissive evacuation environment.)
- Medium profile naval posture with capability to evacuate 2,000 personnel. (Requires selected fleet units to operate in eastern Mediterranean; does not require a secure in-country airfield.)
- Full-scale evacuation posture with capability to evacuate 6,000 personnel. (Requires major fleet units to be located offshore; has good capability to operate in hostile environment.)

Uncertain outcomes. And here, the definitions of the uncertain outcomes defining the event about permissiveness:

- No evacuation necessary because a ceasefire agreement has been negotiated.
- The fighting continues, commercial airlines have cancelled flights into the area, and a small number of personnel, about 300, wish to leave the country. Indigenous (friendly) security forces control the airport and access routes from the city.
- Fighting has increased in Beirut and about 2,000 personnel, mostly US nationals living in the immediate area want to leave. The airport is subjected to sporadic gun fire, therefore armed helicopters and security forces may be required.

- Heavy fighting has spread throughout the country and up to 6,000 US and allied nationals may want to leave. The evacuation force must be prepared to operate in a war-like environment.

Criteria. With the round event node and its four outcomes repeated at each of the four alternatives, this gives a decision tree of 16 paths, each defining the consequences to be evaluated against four criteria established by the military group:

- **Exposure**: Safety of US and other nationals once the decision to evacuate has become necessary – namely, exposure risk.
- **Readiness**: Loss of combat readiness while in unusual or advanced deployment postures.
- **Flexibility**: Loss of normal crew proficiency training while in advanced alert postures.
- **Political**: Adverse consequences of either 'over' or 'under' reacting to a sensitive situation.

Influence diagram. Now we turn to the final influence diagram developed by the intelligence group:

This shows possible outcomes of elections in Lebanon, with prior probabilities assessed by the intelligence analysts. Elections were anticipated to influence the level of hostilities in Lebanon, which could provoke Syria to invade Lebanon. But Israel might react to the invasion to push back Syria with its own invasion of Lebanon. Finally, both the level of hostilities in Lebanon and Israelis' reaction influence the permissiveness of the evacuation. The probabilities shown for these events are the result of the many likelihoods assessed on the spot for each of the three bottom events' outcomes (Figure 19.6).

In today's world, either DPL or Netica can accommodate the three pieces of the problem given above, options, permissive events and their probabilities, and criteria, but it's easier to do this with Hiview. The permissive event outcomes are the four nodes below the overall result we expect at the Contingency Planning node, that is, a table and bar graph showing the overall weighted value of the four options. Below each of the permissive nodes we place the four criteria. Thus, the task is to value the four options on each of these 16 nodes and assess criterion weights within each node and then across the nodes (Figure 19.7).

Hold on, you say! Value tees require weights, but the influence diagram produces revised probabilities, not weights, for the permissive outcomes. True, but Hiview only requires weights that are just numbers from 0 to 1.0, so the probabilities are just weighting the relative outcomes, which seems logically satisfactory. And sensitivity analysis on any one of the four nodes would automatically in Hiview cause the other three node weights to be adjusted proportionately so the sum of all four would be 1.0, and the following scenario analyses showed coherent results.

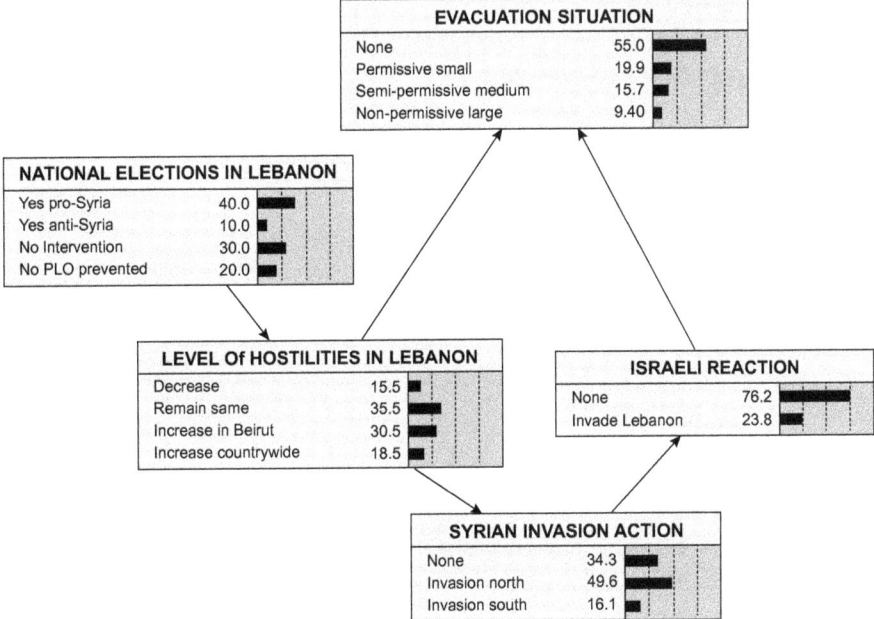

Figure 19.6

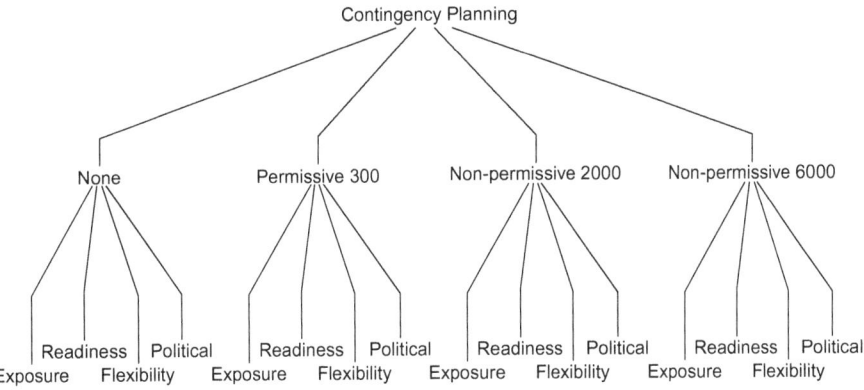

Figure 19.7

4.   Explore Results

The original model gives the result in Hiview shown in Figure 19.8.

   This was the result assuming the prior probabilities when the DDI team arrived, when NATO only knew that hostilities in Lebanon were getting worse. This result shows that a low profile for the fleet would be best, followed closely by a normal posture.

   Let's now see what would be recommended if elections in Syria favoured the current government. That might calm down the conflict in the country somewhat,

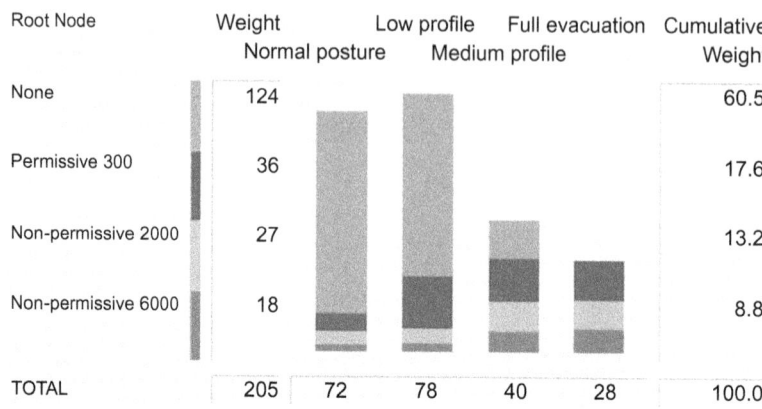

Root Node	Weight Normal posture	Low profile Medium profile	Full evacuation	Cumulative Weight
None	124			60.5
Permissive 300	36			17.6
Non-permissive 2000	27			13.2
Non-permissive 6000	18			8.8
TOTAL	205 72	78 40	28	100.0

Figure 19.8

but as it was getting worse, that might not have much effect. Here are the revised posterior probabilities for the Evacuation Situation, along with the results. Now, with a higher probability for None, the overall result is a tie between normal posture and low profile (Figure 19.9).

I was curious to know if elections did occur in Lebanon, but couldn't find any evidence of it, so I asked ChatGPT. Here is the reply:

As for the elections in Lebanon in 1976, I couldn't find any records or information indicating that elections took place in that year. The Lebanese Civil War, which began in 1975, brought about a significant disruption in the political and social fabric of the country. The conflict involved multiple factions and foreign interventions, which likely made holding elections difficult or infeasible at that time.

5.   Agree the Way Forward

So, what did happen in mid-1976? Again, evidence was difficult to find, so I asked ChatGPT: What was the reaction by Israel to Syria's invasion of Lebanon in June 1976? Did they invade Lebanon?

Yes, Israel did respond to Syria's invasion of Lebanon in June 1976, but they did not invade Lebanon themselves. Instead, Israel provided military assistance to Christian militias in Lebanon, particularly the Phalange Party, which was engaged in fighting against Syrian forces. This assistance included air support, artillery, and supplies, which helped the Lebanese Christians in their battle against the Syrian-backed Palestine Liberation Organization (PLO) forces. Israel's decision to intervene was driven partly by their desire to counter Syrian influence in Lebanon and protect their own northern borders.

Interesting that the model's options about the Israeli Reaction didn't include what actually happened, but it is more realistic to instantiate Invade Lebanon than None

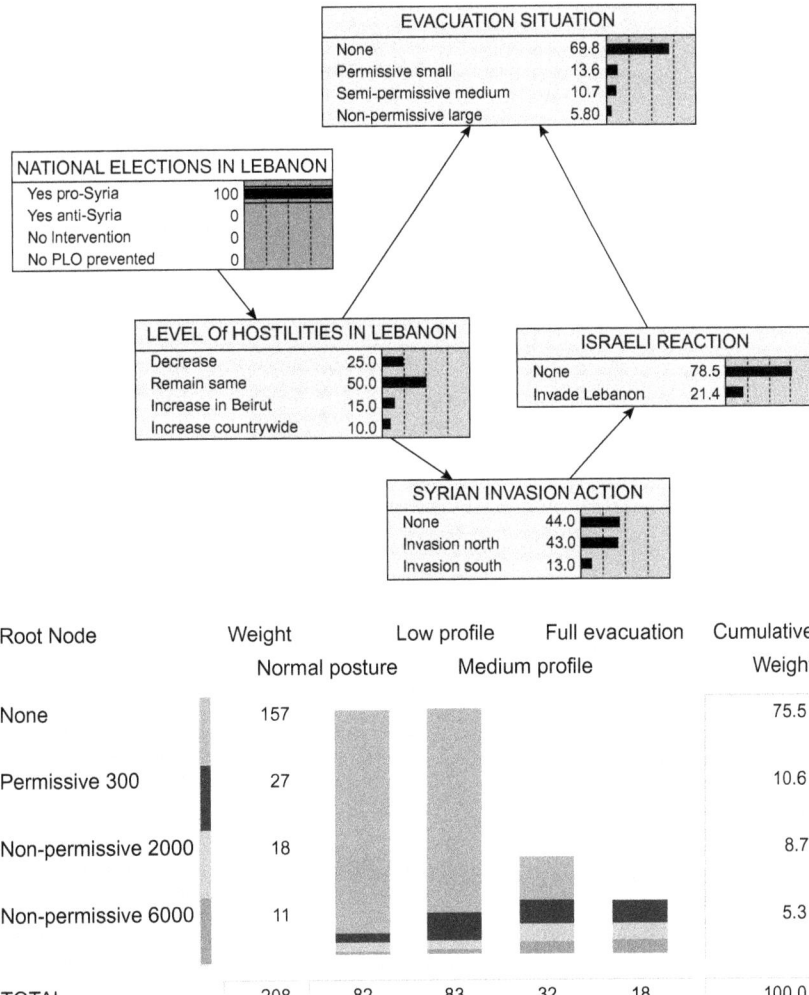

Figure 19.9

(Figure 19.10). The level of hostilities increased countrywide, and Syria invaded from the north.

Now it's a toss-up between a medium profile and full evacuation. And, indeed, the medium profile was adopted by the 6th Fleet. On 20 June, about 267 personnel were rescued from Beirut by a US Navy ship and taken to safety in Syria, followed by another evacuation on 26 July of 300 US and European personnel, with security at dockside protected by the PLO.[231]

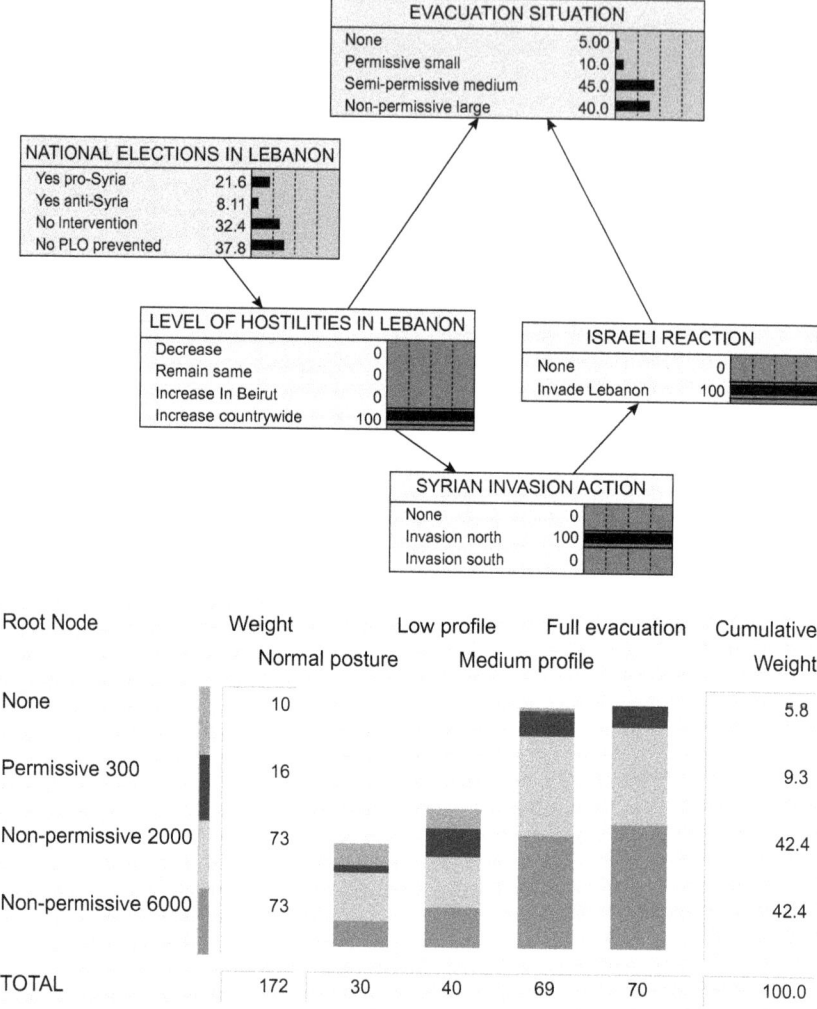

Figure 19.10

Conclusion

The two case studies in this chapter showed different ways in which decision analysis models can serve as transitional objects. The elements of strategic intent formed the context for the IFHF prioritisation model, which assisted in the transition to the forum two years later, and subsequently allowed Ken Groom to oversee progress in broadening the organisation's reach.

The OPINT software, with its three DA types, decision tree, MCDA and BBN, integrated the military objectives governing decisions by the military leaders of NATO and the Mediterranean operations with the operational intelligence experts, allowing a rapid and informed response to the unstable political situation.

Both strategic management and contingency planning make use of some or all elements of the strategic management cycle:

Mission: Why are we here? What is our reason for existing?
Vision: Where are we going?
Objectives: What do we wish to achieve?
Goals: Objectives expressed in measurable terms.
Strategies: What must we do to achieve the goals and objectives, and why?
Plans: How shall we do it, and by when?
Operations: Doing it!
Results: Judge outcomes against goals. Cycle back to a previous step as needed.

Many organisations engage a team of planners who use these elements and propose a way forward to their CEO, but as they were based on best guesses and were not owned by those who would carry out the plans, the plans may be felt to be unrealistic and unworkable. Other organisations hire a prestigious consultancy company to do the planning. Then when things work out differently from the plan, blame it on the consultants.

This cycle belongs to everyone in the organisation and is to be developed by those who must own it, as shown in the two case studies of this chapter. But that's a continuing theme of this book, that decision analysis can help an organisation to develop its mission, vision, goals and strategies, by capturing the capability, experience and knowledge of members of the organisation to create plans that can be adapted in a changing environment, and implement them to ensure a better future.

Epilogue to Part III

This third section made clear that structure and content are driven by process. Each of these three blocks includes unique features, but also interacts with the other two as decision-analytic modelling is applied to a practical problem. You might find places in your organisation that could benefit from some combination of the 10 ingredients, which you could deploy by applying the appropriate processes (Figure EP.2).

But how do you sell decision analysis to your boss?

I think the answer is, 'You don't.' Instead, where you see an opportunity, a problematic situation, a set of issues or a manager expressing a sense of unease, you engage the manager, saying, 'Perhaps I could help with that.' You ask a few questions, engage the manager in active enquiry by exploring any of the 10 elements of good decisions, structure and/or content, helping the manager to think afresh on the spot.

For example, answers to your questions might reveal that the manager's thinking is focused on options, so you ask, 'So what are you trying to accomplish, what are your objectives?' Or if the manager seems overwhelmed by uncertainty about the future, ask if there are any key uncertain events, or if they can be resolved sequentially, learning from initial outcomes to see what to do next. Or if you sense that unclear trade-offs might be preventing moving forward, ask, 'What do you see is pulling you forward and what is holding you back, more of this and less of that?'

In other words, you use your understanding of structure, process and content to ask questions, encouraging your manager to explore the issues. You might eventually be told, 'You've given me food for thought, which has been helpful.' Perhaps you stop at this point, thank the manager, and say you're available at any time to explore the issues further. In future interactions, apply the principles of process consultancy to develop a trusting, helping relationship. If you already have a good relationship, you might be more forthright by asking, 'I wonder if it might be possible to resolve the difficulties you are having by making explicit your main concerns in a decision model that can hold all the difficulties and complexities, and allows you to explore alternative futures. Just a thought; you might give it a try.' You could suggest that there isn't a right answer, but there certainly are better and worse answers, which the model might reveal. You say this if you think a requisite decision model could serve as a transitional object that will hold the major concerns without commitment, allowing your manager to explore the model and find at least a better way forward.

If you are part of a team of decision analysts in your organisation, then it is important to develop and maintain relationships with managers in all parts of the

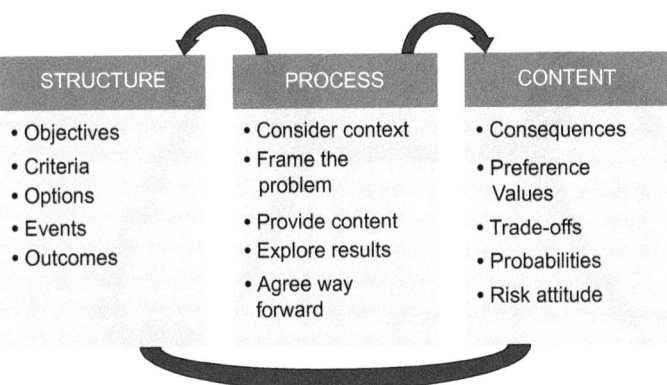

STRUCTURE	PROCESS	CONTENT
• Objectives	• Consider context	• Consequences
• Criteria	• Frame the	• Preference
• Options	problem	Values
• Events	• Provide content	• Trade-offs
• Outcomes	• Explore results	• Probabilities
	• Agree way	• Risk attitude
	forward	

Figure EP.2

organisation. Eating lunch together and chatting about current developments can highlight areas where decision analysis could be applied. Better yet, the organisation might specify accountability relationships between a centralised decision-analytic group and individual subordinate units, with authority for a member of the group to attend key meetings of each unit, to suggest ways decision modelling might help, and to report back to the central group how your suggestion was received. I've found that a centralised service group with no formal relationship to the other parts of the organisation may become an annoyance to other units, who consider it out of touch, and so it is eventually closed down.

By asking the question of what makes a good decision to hundreds of R&D decision makers, managers and executives in commercial organisations, Matheson and Matheson summarised their answers as focusing on six features they called 'decision quality', which they argued characterise better-performing organisations.[232] Decision analysis certainly incorporates these features, but it doesn't follow that if an organisation accepts and implements them, they will make better rather than worse decisions. And that isn't just because good decisions are not necessarily followed by good outcomes. My experience is that for decision analysis to flourish, the culture of the organisation must be open to change, accountability and authority should be well distributed throughout the organisation, a culture of problem solving should exist so that issues can be fully explored, and the style of decision making in the organisation should allow for consultation and deliberation, time allowing (Figure EP.3).

Some decision analysts use decision quality (DQ), smart decisions and the PrOACT-URL process, or even decision analysis (DA) itself, as a selling point. I haven't done that in this book because it's rarely not what the client wants. Yes, the CEO of Commercial Union wanted underwriters to make better decisions, but the application of the 10 ingredients of good decisions focused on modelling risk using Bayesian Belief Networks, which underpinned the series of stages from understanding the risk to making a final decision. Applying MCDA to modelling the harm of drugs involved no decisions at all; just the overall harms of 20 drugs on 16 harm criteria, all dis-value.

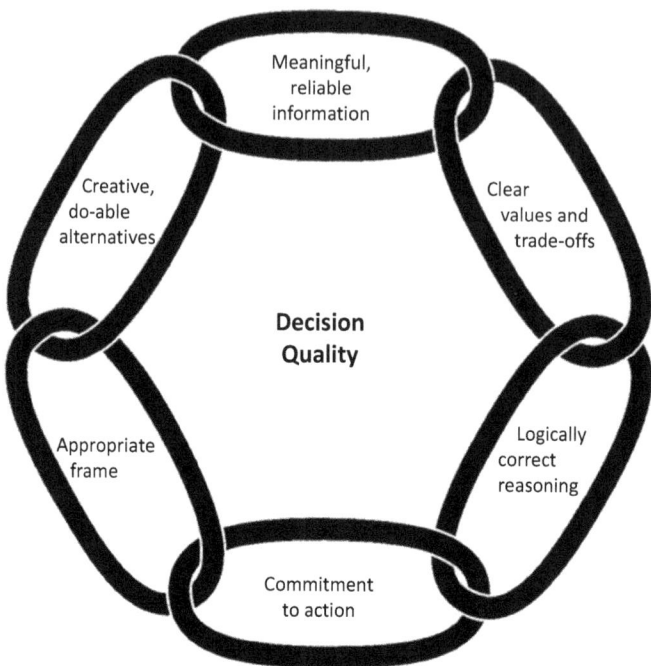

Figure EP.3

Drug Science adopted a strategy table approach to develop a multi-criteria template, which contained no decisions, that could help government policy advisers to devise severe or lenient policies for restricting the availability of psychoactive drugs such as alcohol, heroin and cannabis.[233] And modelling the benefit-safety balance of alternative drugs for a given medical condition left decisions to patients or prescribers. Indeed, you may have noticed that none of the 10 ingredients of good decisions is itself a decision, that word only appearing in the definition of 'options' along with alternatives, choices or courses of action for achieving objectives.

Of course, analysing decisions was very much on the mind of Howard Raiffa and Ron Howard in the 1960s, when they gave the name 'decision analysis' to our discipline. Dealing with uncertainty was the focus, so required careful analysis. Keeney shifted that focus to objectives and values, and analysis broadened to incorporate multiple objectives. By continuing to use DA and DQ as selling points, we are suggesting to clients that decisions are the focus of modelling, or that their current decisions are inadequate. But usually, neither is true. It will be more helpful to make the client's sense of unease the focus, using some combination of the 10 ingredients to resolve that feeling and enable the accountable decision maker to proceed confidently.

The 15 case studies in Part III illustrated how that process works, showing how a requisite decision model can serve as a transitional object, holding and containing the many elements of judgements and data, enabling the decision maker to explore the model, make changes and see what might happen, 'trying out the future before having to live it'. That to my mind is what decision analysis means in the twenty-first century. And I'm 100 per cent sure that well before 2050, AI will substantially complement decision analysis modelling for the future.

Notes

1 A Decision-Making Framework

1. Raiffa, H. (1968). *Decision Analysis*. Addison-Wesley.
2. A search of 'decision tree software' shows that some programs are just for the tree, but don't accept data or do any calculations. Of the software that support decision analysis, Excel add-on programs, like TreePlan, are relatively inexpensive, while stand-alone programs with full capabilities and capable of interacting with Excel, like DPL, are more expensive.
3. Kirkwood, C. W. (1997). *Strategic Decision Making: Multiobjective Decision Analysis with Spreadsheets*. Duxbury Press.
4. Lichtenstein, S. & Slovic, P. (eds) (2006). *The Construction of Preference*. Cambridge University Press. The introductory chapter provides an excellent overview of the 'enormous literature that is central to preference construction' (p. 3).
5. A good example is the eight-step PrOACT-URL framework: Problem, Objectives, Alternatives, Consequences, Trade-offs, Uncertainty, Risk attitude and Linked Decisions. See Hammond, J. S., Keeney, R. L. & Raiffa, H. (1999). *Smart Choices: A Practical Guide to Making Better Decisions*. Harvard University Press. This book presents decision theory as a narrative, requiring little or no mathematics, that could be applied to personal and organisational decisions. A more recent guide by Ralph Keeney elaborates the first six steps of the PrOACT-URL framework and draws on his extensive experience in applying decision analysis. See Keeney, R. L. (2020). *Give Yourself a Nudge: Helping Smart People Make Smarter Personal and Business Decisions*. Cambridge University Press.

2 The Foundations of Decision Theory

6. Nadler, S., (2020). Baruch Spinoza. In E. N. Zalta (ed.), *The Stanford Encyclopedia of Philosophy*, available at: https://plato.stanford.edu/archives/sum2020/entries/spinoza.
7. Raiffa, H. (1968). *Decision Analysis*. Addison-Wesley.
8. Ramsey, F. P. (1931). Truth and probability. In R. B. Braithwaite (ed.), *The Foundations of Mathematics and Other Logical Essays* (pp. 156–98). Kegan, Paul, Trench, Trubner & Co., Harcourt, Brace & Co. 1999 electronic ed.; 1926.
9. Ramsey, Truth and probability, p. 21 of the original essay.
10. Holroyd, M. (1994). *Lytton Strachey: The New Biography*. Head of Zeus, pp. 654–5.
11. Jeffreys, H. (1961). *Theory of Probability*. 3rd ed. Oxford University Press.
12. de Finetti, B. (1937). La prévision: ses lois logiques, ses sources subjectives. *Annales* de l'*Institut Henri Poincaré* 7, translated by H. E. Kyburg (Foresight: its logical laws, its subjective sources), in H. E. Kyburg & H. E. Smokler (eds) (1964). *Studies in Subjective Probability*. John Wiley & Sons.
13. de Finetti, B. (1990). *Theory of Probability: A Critical Introductory Ttreatment*, Vol. 1, translated by A. Machi and A. Smith from *Teoria Delle Probabilità*, 1970. John Wiley & Sons.

14. von Neumann, J. & Morgenstern, O. (1947). *Theory of Games and Economic Behavior.* 2nd ed. Princeton University Press.

15. Savage, L. J. (1954). *The Foundations of Statistics.* John Wiley & Sons.

16. Savage, L. J. (1972). *The Foundations of Statistics.* 2nd ed. Dover Publications.

17. French, S. (1994). Utility: probability's younger twin? In P. R. Freeman & A. F. Smith (eds), *Aspects of Uncertainty: A Tribute to D V Lindley* (pp. 171–80). John Wiley & Sons.

18. Edwards, W. (1954). The theory of decision making. *Psychological Bulletin* 51(4): 380–417; Kahneman, D. (2011). *Thinking, Fast and Slow.* Allen Lane.

19. For example: Luce, D. & Raiffa, H. (1957). *Games and Decisions: Introduction and Critical Survey.* John Wiley & Sons; Fishburn, P. (1970). *Utility Theory for Decision Making.* Defense Technical Information Center; Bell, D. E., Keeney, R. L. & Raiffa, H. (eds) (1977). *Conflicting Objectives in Decisions,* Vol. 1. John Wiley & Sons.

20. Schlaifer, R. (1959). *Probability and Statistics for Business Decisions.* McGraw-Hill.

21. Raiffa, H. & Schlaifer, R. (1961). *Applied Statistical Decision Theory.* Harvard University Press.

22. The case studies developed in the 1960s at the Harvard Business School, whose MBA has always been based on case-study material, were published in Brown, R. V., Kahr, A. S. & Peterson, C. (1974). *Decision Analysis for the Manager.* Holt, Rinehart & Winston. I used these case studies in teaching decision analysis on executive courses for many years.

23. Schlaifer, R. (1969). *Analysis of Decisions under Uncertainty.* McGraw-Hill.

24. I soon discovered Schlaifer had written an instructor's manual to accompany the book and another book *Computer Programs for Elementary Decision Analysis,* the MANECON programs, that could be ordered from Harvard. It was a remarkable collection of programs for the interactive assessment of probability distributions and utility functions, way ahead of its time and accessible only from interactive workstations connected to a mainframe computer. See Schlaifer, R. (1971). *Computer Programs for Elementary Decision Analysis.* Harvard University Press.

25. Howard, R. A. (1966). Decision analysis: applied decision theory. In D. B. Hertz & J. Melese (eds), *Proceedings of the Fourth International Conference on Operational Research* (pp. 55–71). Wiley-Interscience.

26. In a talk he gave in November 2014 at the 50th Anniversary celebration of the founding of the Decision Analysis Society.

27. Kepner, C. H. & Tregoe, B. B. (1965). *The Rational Manager.* McGraw-Hill.

28. Kepner, C. H. & Tregoe, B. B. (1981). *The New Rational Manager.* Princeton Research Press.

29. Brown, R. V. (1970). Do managers find decision theory useful? *Harvard Business Review* 48: 78–9; Ulvila, J. W. & Brown, R. V. (1982). Decision analysis comes of age. *Harvard Business Review* 60(5): 130–41.

30. Raiffa, H. (1969). *Preferences for Multi-Attributed Alternatives.* The RAND Corporation.

31. Keeney, R. L. & Raiffa, H. (1976). *Decisions with Multiple Objectives: Preferences and Value Tradeoffs.* John Wiley & Sons, republished in 1993 by Cambridge University Press (with some important new material).

32. Dyer, J. S. & Sarin, R. K. (1979). Measurable multiattribute value functions. *Operations Research* 27(4): 810–22.

33. Phillips, L. D. (1984). A theory of requisite decision models. *Acta Psychologica* 56(1–3): 29–48.

34. For example, Belton and Gear showed that after obtaining an ordering of options from applying Saaty's Analytic Hierarchy Process (AHP), if one of the alternatives were eliminated and the AHP process applied again, the new result could show that the ordering of the remaining options had changed (Belton, V. & Gear, T. (1983). On a short-coming of Saaty's method of analytic hierarchies. *Omega* 11(3): 228–30). Imagine, for example, you are in

a restaurant looking at the main-dish specials. You tell the waiter you would like the sirloin steak rather than the pork chops, when the waiter adds that fish has just been added to the specials. 'Oh, in that case,' you say, 'I'll have the pork chops.' These two examples demonstrate violations of the principles of ordering and transitivity working together.

35. As it did when I was called to give testimony in 1995 at a public enquiry to defend a multi-criteria model of potential underground sites for disposing of the UK's medium- and high-level nuclear waste. I was on the stand for a day and a half, showing the decision analysis model I had helped Nirex develop, and exploring it for the inspector by conducting several sensitivity analyses. The inspector, Greenpeace, and Friends of the Earth agreed that the multi-criteria model was the right approach to selecting a site. See: Phillips, L. D. *Multi-Attribute Decision Analysis for Recommending Sites to be Investigated for their Suitability as a Repository for Radioactive Wastes*; Proof of Evidence of Dr L. D. Phillips at the Public Local Inquiry into an Appeal to the Secretary of State for the Environment against the decision of Cumbria County Council to refuse Planning Permission for the construction of a Rock Characterisation Facility at Longlands Farm, Gosforth, Cumbria. Nirex Ltd; 1995. Report No.: App Ref.: DB/CD 8.5.1; LPA Ref.: 4/94/9011; DOE Ref.: APP/H0900/A/94/247019; Nirex Ref.: PE/NRX/18.

   For the UK, see Keeney, R. L. & von Winterfeldt, D. (1988). The analysis and its role for selecting nuclear repository sites. In G. K. Rand (ed.), *Operational Research '87* (pp. 686–701). Elsevier Science Publishers.

3   The Language of Numbers

36. Thompson, W. (2011). Electrical units of measurement. In *Popular Lectures and Addresses*, Vol. 1: *Constitution of Matter* (pp. 73–136). 1st ed. 1889. Cambridge University Press.
37. These questions are based on chapter 2, 'Psychological measurement theory', of Coombs, C. H., Dawes, R. M. & Tversky, A. (1970). *Mathematical Psychology: An Elementary Introduction*. Prentice-Hall, and on the elaboration in Krantz, D. H., Luce, R. D., Tversky, A. & Suppes, P. (1971). *Foundations of Measurement*, Vol. I: *Additive and Polynomial Representations*. Academic Press. A more accessible source is Krantz, D. H. (1972). Measurement structures and psychological laws. *Science* 175(4029): 1427–35.
38. Thaler, R. H. (2015). *Misbehaving: The Making of Behavioural Economics*. Penguin Books.
39. Edwards, W. (1954). The theory of decision making. *Psychological Bulletin* 51(4): 380–417.
40. Edwards, W. (1961). Behavioral decision theory. *Annual Review of Psychology* 12: 473–98.
41. Edwards, W. & Tversky, A. (eds) (1967). *Decision Making*. Penguin Books.
42. Tversky, A. & Kahneman, D. (1974). Judgment under uncertainty: heuristics and biases. *Science* 185(4157): 1124–31.
43. Kahneman, D., Slovic, P. & Tversky, A. (1974). *Judgment under Uncertainty: Heuristics and Biases*. Cambridge University Press.
44. Kahneman, D. (2011). *Thinking, Fast and Slow*. Penguin Books.
45. Peterson, C. R. & Beach, L. R. (1967). Man as an intuitive statistician. *Psychological Bulletin* 68(1): 29–46.
46. Peterson & Beach, Man as an intuitive statistician, p. 29.
47. Lejarraga, T. & Hertwig, R. (2021). How experimental methods shaped views on human competence and rationality. *Psychological Bulletin* 147(6): 535–64, 535.
48. A notable early integration, von Winterfeldt, D. & Edwards, W. (1986). *Decision Analysis and Behavioral Research*. Cambridge University Press, helpfully brought to the attention of decision analysts the extensive literature in psychology of methods that minimise bias in making subjective assessments of numerical quantities and of the effects of context on those judgements. A more recent book, French, S., Maule, J. & Papamichail, N. (2009). *Decision*

Behaviour, Analysis and Support. Cambridge University Press, shows how the 'rules of thumb' people use in making decisions and their associated errors and biases can be minimised by applying decision modelling.

49. Beach, L. R. (2016). *A New Theory of Mind: The Theory of Narrative Thought*. Cambridge Scholars Publishing.

4   Preference Values

50. As Ralph Keeney has so well elaborated in his important 1992 book, *Value Focused Thinking; A Path to Creative Decision Making*. Harvard University Press.

51. Collins, J. C. & Porras, J. I. (1996). *Built to Last: Successful Habits of Visionary Companies*. Century.

52. See the Business Roundtable statement signed by 222 executives of large US corporations at https://opportunity.businessroundtable.org/ourcommitment.

53. Keeney, R. L. (2007). Developing objectives and attributes. In W. Edwards, R. F. Miles Jr & D. Von Winterfeldt (eds), *Advances in Decision Analysis: From Foundations to Applications* (pp. 104–28). Cambridge University Press.

54. Moore, R., Crossley, A., Ng, B., Phillips, L., Sancak, O. & Rainsford, K. (2017). Use of multicriteria decision analysis (MCDA) for assessing the benefit and risk of over-the-counter analgesics. *Journal of Pharmacy and Pharmacology* 69(10): 1364–73.

55. Kelly, G. A. (1955). *The Psychology of Personal Constructs*. Norton.

56. Patrick went on to write the following article with Wendy McFadden: Humphreys, P. C. & McFadden, W. (1980). Experiences with MAUD: aiding decision structuring versus boot-strapping the decision maker. *Acta Psychologica* 45(1–3): 51–69.

57. Bond, S. D., Carlson, K. A. & Keeney, R. L. (2010). Improving the generation of decision objectives. *Decision Analysis* 7(3): 238–55.

58. Von Winterfeldt, D. & Edwards, W. (1986). *Decision Analysis and Behavioral Research*. Cambridge University Press, ch. 11.

59. The program, Hiview, enables any numerical input to be transformed into a piece-wise preference value function. It starts with a linear function whose (x, y) positions can be set to move in vertical, horizontal or any direction by clicking and dragging the points, thus creating a value function of any shape.

60. A quick overview is at https://en.wikipedia.org/wiki/Psychophysics. The method I describe is a variation on the Method of Limits. For more detail, see Kingdom, F. A. A. & Prins, N. (2016, 2010). *Psychophysics: A Practical Introduction*. 2nd ed. Academic Press.

61. Hunt, W. A. & Volkmann, J. (1937). The anchoring of an affective scale. *American Journal of Psychology* 49(1): 88–92.

62. Montibeller, G. & von Winterfeldt, D. (2015). Cognitive and motivational biases in decision and risk analysis. *Risk Analysis* 35(7): 1230–51.

63. Thurstone, L. L. (1959) *The Measurement of Values*. University of Chicago Press.

64. Fasolo, B. & Bana e Costa, C. (2014). Tailoring value elicitation to decision makers' numeracy and fluency: expressing value judgments in numbers or words. *Omega: the International Journal of Management Science* 44: 83–90.

65. Bana e Costa, C. A., De Corte, J. M. & Vansnick, J. C. (2012). MACBETH, *International Journal of Information Technology and Decision Making* 11(2): 359–87. If you wish to learn more, search the internet for M-Macbeth, which avoids thousands of hits for Shakespeare's play.

66. Clyde Coombs, a mathematical psychologist at the University of Michigan, originally called this an ordered metric scale, in Coombs, C. H. (1950). Psychological scaling without a unit of measurement. *Psychological Review* 57(3): 145–58. It was later changed to a higher ordered metric scale in Coombs, C. (1964). *A Theory of Data*. John Wiley & Sons.

67. Bana e Costa, C. A. & Vansnick, J.-C. (2008). A critical analysis of the eigenvalue method used to derive priorities in AHP. *European Journal of Operational Research* 187(3): 1422–8. Two of the examples reported in the paper show cases in which judgements were deemed by the AHP process to be inconsistent although MACBETH found consistency. See also Dyer, J. S. (1990). Remarks on the analytic hierarchy process. *Management Science* 36(3): 249–58. He considered that the AHP's axiom system, unlike that of decision analysis, was not empirically testable and that assuming 'weights' at higher levels of a value tree can be determined independent of the 'weights' at lower levels is incorrect. He concluded that the output rankings of alternatives are 'arbitrary'.

68. Strictly speaking, decision theory considers this number 80 as a utility or 'certainty equivalent' because it not only incorporates the assessor's preference value, but also his or her attitude towards risk. Many people are averse to the risk of a gamble, so they give an indifference value that is lower than their preference value, like a 70 or 75. Indeed, numbers greater than 80 would be possible if the assessor liked the thrill of a gamble! However, I've learned that it is better to treat 'risk' as a separate criterion (or collection of criteria, for example, financial risk, personal risk, reputation risk, etc.) so that direct assessment can focus on preference value.

5   Trade-Off Weights

69. Grey, J. (1996). *Isaiah Berlin*. Princeton University Press, p. 1.

70. The first use of this technique was applied to the assessment of probabilities as reported in Gustafson, D. H., Shukla, R. U., Delbecq, A. & Walster, G. W. (1973). A comparative study of differences in subjective likelihood estimates made by individuals, interacting groups, Delphi groups, and nominal groups. *Organizational Behavior and Human Performance* 9(2): 280–91. I have found it works well for assessing scores, weights, and probabilities, and helps to minimise bias.

71. Weinfurt, K. P. (2019). Clarifying the meaning of clinically meaningful benefit in clinical research: noticeable change vs valuable change. *JAMA* 322(24): 2381–2.

72. Johnson, F. R. (2006). *Measuring Conjoint Stated Preferences for Pharmaceuticals: A Brief Introduction*. RTI Health Solutions.

73. Nutt, D. J., King, L. A. & Phillips, L. D., on behalf of the Independent Scientific Committee on Drugs (2010). Drug harms in the UK: a multicriteria decision analysis. *The Lancet* 376(9752): 1558–65.

74. Dyer, J. S. (1990). Remarks on the analytic hierarchy process. *Management Science* 36(3): 249–58.

75. Keeney, R. L. (2002). Common mistakes in making value trade-offs. *Operations Research* 50(6): 935–45.

6   Uncertainty and Probability

76. *The Advancement of Learning*, Book I, ch. v, section 8.

77. Schlaifer, R. (1959). *Probability and Statistics for Business Decisions*. McGraw-Hill.

78. Lichtenstein, S., Fischhoff, B. & Phillips, L. D. (1982). Calibration of probabilities: the state of the art to 1980. In D. Kahneman, P. Slovic & A. Tversky (eds), *Judgment under Uncertainty: Heuristics and Biases* (pp. 306–34). Cambridge University Press.

79. O'Connor, M. (1989). Models of human behaviour and confidence in judgement: a review. *International Journal of Forecasting* 5(2): 159–69.

80. Griffin, D. & Brenner, L. (2004). Perspectives on probability judgment calibration. In D. J. Koehler & N. Harvey (eds), *Blackwell Handbook of Judgment and Decision Making* (pp. 177–99). Blackwell Publishing Ltd.

81. Mandel, D. R. & Barnes, A. (2014). Accuracy of forecasts in strategic intelligence. *Proceedings of the National Academy of Sciences* 111(30): 10984–9.

82. Fischhoff, B. & Beyth, R. (1975). I knew it would happen: remembered probabilities of once-future things. *Organizational Behavior and Human Performance* 13(1): 1–16.

83. As demonstrated in Phillips, L. D. (1999). Group elicitation of probability distributions: are many heads better than one? In J. Shanteau, B. Mellors & D. Schum (eds), *Decision Science and Technology: Reflections on the Contributions of Ward Edwards* (pp. 313–30). Kluwer Academic Publishers.

84. For example, Morgan, M. G. & Henrion, M. (1990). *Uncertainty: A Guide to Dealing with Uncertainty in Quantitative Risk and Policy Analysis*. Cambridge University Press, is an excellent practical guide, while O'Hagan, A., Buck, C. E., Daneshkhah, A., Eiser, J. R., Garthwaite, P. H., Jenkinson, D. J. et al. (2006). *Uncertain Judgements: Eliciting Experts' Probabilities*. John Wiley & Sons, provides a thorough review of literature, explains many examples of formal elicitation and includes a final chapter, Guidance on best practice.

85. Seaver, D. A., von Winterfeldt, D. & Edwards, W. (1978). Eliciting subjective probability distributions on continuous variables. *Organizational Behavior and Human Performance* 21(3): 379–91.

86. Nuclear Decommissioning Agency (2017). *Geological Disposal: Methods for Management and Quantification of Uncertainty*. Radioactive Waste Management Ltd, Report No. NDA/RWM/153.

87. Barclay, S., Brown, R. V., Kelly, C. W., Peterson, C. R., Phillips, L. D. & Selvidge, J. (1977). *Handbook for Decision Analysis*. Technical Report. Decisions and Designs, Inc. Report No. TR 77-6-30. Available at https://files.eric.ed.gov/fulltext/ED153329.pdf.

88. Wallsten, T. S. & Budescu, D. B. (1983). Encoding subjective probabilities: a psychological and psychometric review. *Management Science* 29(2): 151–73.

89. Phillips, L. D. & Wright, G. N. (1977). Cultural differences in viewing uncertainty and assessing probabilities. In H. Jungermann & G. de Zeeuw (eds), *Decision Making and Change in Human Affairs* (pp. 507–15). D. Reidel.

90. Wright, G. N., Phillips, L. D., Whalley, P. C., Choo, G. T., Ng, K-O. & Tan, I. (1978). Cultural differences in probabilistic thinking. *Journal of Cross-Cultural Psychology* 9(3): 285–99.

91. Yates, J. F., Zhu, Y., Ronis, D. L., Wang, D.-F., Shinotsuka, H. & Toda, M. (1989). Probability judgment accuracy: China, Japan, and the United States. *Organizational Behavior and Human Decision Processes* 43(2): 145–71.

92. A modern discussion of 'The utility of a probability distribution' can be found in Bernardo, J. M. & Smith, A. F. M. (1994). *Bayesian Theory*. John Wiley & Sons, section 2.7.2, pp. 69–75.

93. Beach, L. R. & Phillips, L. D. (1967). Subjective probabilities inferred from estimates and bets. *Journal of Experimental Psychology* 75(3): 354–9.

94. Winkler, R. L. (1996). Scoring rules and the evaluation of probabilities. *Test* 5(1): 1–60.

Epilogue to Part I

95. The phrase was first published in the 1666 edition of F. de La Rochefoucauld, *Reflections; Or Sentences and Moral Maxims*.

96. Miller, G. A. (1956). The magical number seven, plus or minus two: some limits on our capacity for processing information. *Psychological Review* 63(2): 81–97.

97. Cowan, N. (2001). The magical number 4 in short-term memory: a reconsideration of mental storage capacity. *Behavioural Brain Science* 24(1): 87–114; discussion 114–85.

7 Decision Conferences

98. Phillips, L. D. & Phillips, M. C. (1993). Facilitated work groups: theory and practice. *Journal of the Operational Research Society* 44(6): 533–49.
99. Phillips, L. D. (1982). Requisite decision modelling: a case study. *Journal of the Operational Research Society* 33(4): 303–11.
100. See Higgin, G. & Bridger, H. (1990). The psycho-dynamics of an inter-group experience. In E. Trist & H. Murray (eds), *The Social Engagement of Social Science*, Vol. 1 (pp. 199–220). Free Association Books.
101. 180 DDI works in 190 publications identified by OCLC World Cat Identities can be accessed by searching on Decision and Designs Inc. publications. Clicking on the names of DDI authors, lower left, shows additional titles to those on the initial pages. It is a treasure trove of downloadable materials about many aspects of military and civilian decision making.
102. Phillips, L. D. (1990). Requisite decision modelling for technological projects. In C. Vlek & G. Cvetkovich (eds), *Social Decision Methodology for Technological Projects* (pp. 95–110). Kluwer Academic Publishers.
103. Phillips, L. D. (1984). A theory of requisite decision models. *Acta Psychologica* 56(1): 29–48.
104. Gregory, R., Lichtenstein, S. & Slovic, P. (1993). Valuing environmental resources: a constructive approach. *Journal of Risk and Uncertainty* 7(2): 177–97.
105. See section 7.5 of Dodgson, J. et al. (2000). *Multi-Criteria Analysis: A Manual*. Department of the Environment, Transport and the Regions, republished 2009 by the Department for Communities and Local Government. Available at: http://eprints.lse.ac.uk/12761/1/Multi-criteria_Analysis.pdf.
106. Three papers: Schilling, M. S., Oeser, N. & Schaub, C. (2007). How effective are decision analyses? Assessing decision process and group alignment effects. *Decision Analysis* 4(4): 227–42; McCartt, A. T. & Rohrbaugh, J. (1995). Managerial openness to change and the introduction of GDSS: explaining initial success and failure in decision conferencing. *Organization Science* 6(5): 569–84; McCartt, A. T. & Rohrbaugh, J. (1989). Evaluating group decision support system effectiveness: a performance study of decision conferencing. *Decision Support Systems* 5(2): 243–53. See also the following PhD thesis: Chun, K.-J. (1992). *Analysis of Decision Conferencing: A UK/USA Comparison*. London School of Economics & Political Science.
107. See section 7.5 of Dodgson et al., *Multi-Criteria Analysis*.
108. Phillips, L. D. (2007). Decision conferencing. In W. Edwards, R. F. Miles & D. von Winterfeldt (eds), *Advances in Decision Analysis: From Foundations to Applications* (pp. 375–99). Cambridge University Press.
109. Forsyth, D. R. (2006). *Group Dynamics*. 4th ed. Thompson Learning.
110. Sommer, R. (1967). Small group ecology. *Psychological Bulletin* 67(2): 145–52.
111. See Schein, E. H. (1999). The concept of appreciative inquiry. In *Process Consultation Revisited: Building the Helping Relationship* (pp. 56–8). Addison-Wesley.
112. Tuckman, B. (1965). Developmental sequence in small groups. *Psychological Bulletin* 63(6): 384–99.
113. Stein, J. (no date). Using the stages of team development. MIT Human Resources. Available at https://hr.mit.edu/learning-topics/teams/articles/stages-development.
114. The first detailed discussion of this insensitivity was in ch. 11 of von Winterfeldt, D. & Edwards, W. (1986). *Decision Analysis and Behavioral Research*. Cambridge University Press.

115. According to the Statista.com website, between 200 and 300 deaths each year in England and Wales are from paracetamol poisoning.
116. Vermersch, P., Martinelli, V., Pfleger, C., Rieckmann, P., Alonso-Magdalena, L., Galazka, A. et al. (2019). Benefit-risk assessment of cladribine using multi-criteria decision analysis (MCDA) for patients with relapsing-remitting multiple sclerosis. *Clinical Therapeutics* 41(2): 249–60.
117. Friend, J. & Hickling, A. (1987). *Planning under Pressure: The Strategic Choice Approach*. Pergamon Press.
118. Phillips, L. D., Fasolo, B., Zafiropolous, N., Eichler, H.-G., Ehmann, F., Jekerle, V. et al. (2013). Modelling the risk-benefit impact of H1N1 influenza vaccines. *European Journal of Public Health* 23(4): 674–8.
119. Beach, L. R. & Wise, J. A. (2022). *The Theory of Narrative Thought*. Cambridge Scholars Publishing.
120. More about work preferences in Margerison, C. J. (2002). *Team Leadership: A Guide to Success with Team Management Systems*. Thomson.
121. Tufte, E. R. (2001). *The Visual Display of Quantitative Information*. 2nd ed. Graphics Press.

8   Behaviour in Organisations

122. Jaques, E. (1990). In praise of hierarchy. *Harvard Business Review* (January–February): 127–33.
123. Jaques, E. (1998). *Requisite Organisation: A Total System for Effective Managerial Organization and Managerial Leadership for the 21st Century*. Cason Hall & Co.
124. Jaques, E. (2002). *Social Power and the CEO: Leadership and Trust in a Sustainable Free Enterprise System*. Quorum Books.
125. Jaques, E. (1998). *Time-Span Handbook*. Cason Hall & Co. This is very detailed, probably unnecessarily so, as is suggested in the Introduction, but it does relate the initial difficulties an unfamiliar user of the concept may find in interviews with managers.
126. Richardson, R. (1971). *Fair Pay and Work*. Cason Hall & Co. Richardson developed a short questionnaire used by paid graduate students to elicit time-spans from managers of employees at Honeywell, but neither the students nor the managers were told why this was being done, simply that this was a research project under the direction of Marvin Dunnette, Professor of Industrial Psychology at the University of Minnesota. Results showed a correlation of 0.86 between time-span and the judgements of employees about what level of pay they considered to be fair for the work required of their role, which suggests that the single measure of time-span is capturing the level of work in a role.
127. Jaques, In praise of hierarchy.
128. Peter, L. J. & Hull, R. [1969] (1970). *The Peter Principle*. Pan Books.
129. Jaques, *Requisite Organisation*, p. 35.
130. Jaques, E. & Clement, S. C. (1991). *Executive Leadership: A Practical Guide to Managing Complexity*. Cason Hall & Co., p. 4.
131. Lee, N. R. (2017). *The Practice of Managerial Leadership*. 2nd ed. Xlibris.

9   Process Consultancy

132. Schein, E. H. (1999). *Process Consultation Revisited: Building the Helping Relationship*. Addison-Wesley (emphasis in the original).

133. Spetzler, C., Winter, H. & Meyer, J. (2016). *Decision Quality: Value Creation from Better Business Decisions*. John Wiley & Sons.

134. Keeney, R. (1992). *Value-Focused Thinking: A Path to Creative Decisionmaking*. Harvard University Press.

135. Schein, *Process Consultation Revisited*.

136. Fischhoff, B. (1980). Clinical decision analysis. *Operations Research* 28(1): 28–43.

137. Slovic, P. (1987). Perception of risk. *Science* 236(4799): 280–5.

138. The company has not completed their intended use of this model, so permission to identify them and the product has not been given.

139. Schein, E. S. (2009). *Helping: How to Offer, Give, and Receive Help*. Berrett-Koehler.

140. This TED talk is a quick summary of Onora O'Neill's views on trust: www.youtube.com/watch?v=1PNX6M_dVsk.

141. King, A. (1993). From sage on the stage to guide on the side. *College Teaching* 41(1): 30–5.

10   Facilitation Skills

142. Phillips, L. D. & Phillips, M. C. (1993). Facilitated work groups: theory and practice. *Journal of the Operational Research Society* 44(6): 533–49. The example is on p. 542.

143. Phillips & Phillips, Facilitated work groups, p. 543.

144. Bridger, H. (1990). Courses and working conferences as transitional learning institutions. In E. Trist & H. Murray (eds), *The Social Engagement of Social Science: A Tavistock Anthology*, Vol. I: *The Socio-Psychological Perspective* (pp. 221–45). Free Association Books.

145. Bridger, H. (2001). Foreword. In G. Amado & A. Ambrose (eds), *The Transitional Approach to Change* (pp. xi–xiv). Karnac Books, p. xii.

146. Winnicott, D. W. (2000). Transitional objects and transitional phenomena. In P. du Gay, J. Evans & P. Redman (eds), *Identity: A Reader* (pp. 150–62). Sage Publications. In this chapter, Winnicott reflects on his original 1951 publication that introduced transitional objects and provides two examples.

147. Franco, L. A. & Montibeller, G. (2010). Facilitated modelling in operational research. *European Journal of Operational Research* 205(3): 489–500.

11   Group Processes

148. Nutt, D., King, L. A., Saulsbury, W. & Blakemore, C. (2007). Development of a rational scale to assess the harm of drugs of potential misuse. *The Lancet* 369(9566): 1047–53.

149. Nutt, D. J., King, L. A. & Phillips, L. D., on behalf of the Independent Scientific Committee on Drugs. (2010). Drug harms in the UK: a multicriteria decision analysis. *The Lancet* 376(9752): 1558–65.

150. Bolger, F., Stranieri, A., Wright, G. & Yearwood, J. (2011). Does the Delphi process lead to increased accuracy in group-based judgmental forecasts or does it simply induce consensus amongst judgmental forecasters? *Technological Forecasting & Social Change* 78(9): 1671–80. The paper suggests that majority opinion is the major influence in a Delphi process and that change is more likely from a process that deploys reasoned arguments.

151. Kahneman, D., Sibony, O. & Sunstein, C. R. (2021). *Noise: A Flaw in Human Judgment*. William Collins.

152. Kahneman, D. (30 September 2025). Prize Lecture. NobelPrize.org. Nobel Prize Outreach 2025. Available at: www.nobelprize.org/prizes/economic-sciences/2002/kahneman/lecture/.

153. Phillips, L. D. (1999). Group elicitation of probability distributions: are many heads better than one? In Shanteau, J., Mellors, B. & Schum, D. (eds), *Decision Science and Technology: Reflections on the Contributions of Ward Edwards* (pp. 313–30). Springer Science+Business.

154. Reagan-Cirincione, P. (1994). Improving the accuracy of group judgment: a process intervention combining group facilitation, social judgment analysis, and information technology. *Organizational Behavior and Human Decision Processes* 58(2): 246–70.

155. Lichtenstein, S. & Slovic, P. (2006). *The Construction of Preference.* Cambridge University Press.

156. The Lancet. (2015). E-cigarettes: Public Health England's evidence-based confusion. *The Lancet* 386(9996): 829.

157. Nutt, D. J., Phillips, L. D., Balfour, D., Curran, H. V., Dockrell, M., Foulds, J. et al. (2014). Estimating the harms of nicotine-containing products using the MCDA approach. *European Addiction Research* 20(5): 218–25.

158. Phillips, L. D., Fasolo, B., Zafiropoulos, N. & Beyer, A. (2011). Is quantitative benefit-risk modelling of drugs desirable or possible? *Drug Discovery Today: Technologies* 8(1): e3–e10.

159. Meehl, P. E. (1954). *Clinical Versus Statistical Prediction: A Theoretical Analysis and a Review of the Evidence.* University of Minnesota Press.

160. Payne, J. W., Bettman, J. R. & Johnson, E. J. (1993). *The Adaptive Decision Maker.* Cambridge University Press.

161. Shanteau, J. (1992). Competence in experts: the role of task characteristics. *Organizational Behavior and Human Decision Processes* 53(2): 252–66.

162. Maier, N. R. F. & Solem, A. R. (1952). The contribution of a discussion leader to the quality of group thinking: the effective use of minority opinions. *Human Relations* 5(3): 277–88.

163. Phillips, L. D. & Phillips, M. C. (1993). Facilitated work groups: theory and practice. *Journal of the Operational Research Society* 44(6): 533–49.

164. Tuckman, B. W. & Jensen, M. A. C. (1977). Stages of small group development revisited. *Group and Organizational Studies* 2(4): 419–27.

165. Morton, A., Airoldi, M. & Phillips, L. (2009). Nuclear risk management on stage: the UK's Committee on Radioactive Waste Management. *Risk Analysis* 29(5): 764–79.

166. Chang, A. & Bordia, P. (2001). A multidimensional approach to the group cohesion-group performance relationship. *Small Group Research* 32(4): 379–405.

167. See the chapter on 'Cohesion and development' in Forsyth, D. R. (2013). *Group Dynamics.* 6th ed. Wadsworth, Cengage Learning. This comprehensive, excellent book shows how to put theory into practice with numerous practical examples.

168. This TED talk is a quick summary of Onora O'Neill's views on trust: www.youtube.com/watch?v=1PNX6M_dVsk.

169. Stoner, J. A. F. (1967). *A Comparison of Individual and Group Decisions Involving Risk.* Massachusetts Institute of Technology.

170. Phillips, Facilitated work groups.

171. Bion, W. R. (1961). *Experiences in Groups.* Tavistock Publications.

172. Turquet, P. M. (1974). Leadership: the individual and the group. In G. S. Gibbard, J. J. Hartman & R. D. Mann (eds), *Analysis of Groups: Contribution to Theory, Research, and Practice* (pp. 349–71). Jossey-Bass.

173. Lawrence, G., Bain, A. & Gould, L. (1996). The fifth basic assumption. *Free Associations* 6(Pt 1, No. 37): 28–55.

174. Klein, G. (1998). *Sources of Power: How People Make Decisions.* MIT Press.

175. See 'The Recognition Primed Decision Model' on YouTube for a short introduction.

176. This is my summary based on experience and reading about group processes. An internet search of 'high-performing teams' revealed many definitions and team characteristics, but there is substantial agreement that it is a group of experts with different skills and

capabilities committed to a single goal, collaborating productively to achieve the goal. The six items I've listed in the text are necessary, but not necessarily sufficient.

177. Margerison, C. J. (2002). *Team Leadership: A Guide to Success with Team Management Systems*. Thomson. I have found the emphasis on work preferences of the Team Management System (TMS), www.teammanagementsystems.com/, with its research base of several decades, to be more acceptable in creating high-performing teams than alternative methods emphasising personality types, such as the Myers-Briggs Type Indicator (MBTI), available at www.myersbriggs.org. However (potential conflict of interest), I should add that I am a qualified TMS practitioner in the UK.

178. Janis, I. L. (1982). *Groupthink: Psychological Studies of Policy Decisions and Fiascos*. 2nd ed. Houghton Mifflin.

Epilogue to Part II

179. Beach, L. R. & Wise, J. A. (2022). *The Theory of Narrative Thought*. Cambridge Scholars Publishing.

12   Types of Decision Models

180. Gregory, R., Lichtenstein, S. & Slovic, P. (1993). Valuing environmental resources: a constructive approach. *Journal of Risk and Uncertainty* 7(2): 177–97.

181. Named after the use of land held in common by England's farmers in the Middle Ages, when it was in each farmer's best interests to add more animals to their herds, which led to overgrazing. What is individually best is rarely collectively best. Today, the commons dilemma applies, for example, to overfishing in the seas. And it applies to all organisations that apply 'salami slicing', cutting a little here, adding a bit there, as their method of allocating resources. For more, see Hardin, G. (1968). The tragedy of the commons. *Science* 162(3859): 1243–8.

182. The theory behind this can be found in Raiffa, H., Richardson, J. & Metcalfe, D. (2002). *Negotiation Analysis: The Science and Art of Collaborative Decision Making*. PON Books.

183. Slovic, P. (1987). Perception of risk. *Science* 236(4799): 280–5.

13   Evaluate Options

184. Angelis, A. & Phillips, L. D. (2020). Advancing structured decision-making in drug regulation at the FDA and EMA. *British Journal of Clinical Pharmacology* 87(2): 395–405.

14   Allocate Resources

185. A modernised interpretation of his principles.

186. Based on the definition in Jaques, E. (2002). *Social Power and the CEO: Leadership and Trust in a Sustainable Free Enterprise System*. Quorum Books.

187. Named after the use of land held in common by England's farmers in the Middle Ages, when it was in each farmer's best interests to add more animals to their herds, which led to overgrazing. What is individually best is rarely collectively best. Today, the commons

dilemma applies, for example, to overfishing in the seas. And it applies to all organisations that apply 'salami slicing', cutting a little here, adding a bit there, as their method of allocating resources. For more, see Hardin, G. (1968). The tragedy of the commons. *Science* 162(3859): 1243–8.

188. Ostrom, E. (1998). A behavioral approach to the rational choice theory of collective action: presidential address, American Political Science Association, 1997. *American Political Science Review* 92(1): 1–22.

189. Koriat, A., Lichtenstein, S. & Fischhoff, B. (1980). Reasons for confidence. *Journal of Experimental Psychology: Human Learning & Memory* 6(2): 107–18. This statistically significant finding was discovered when participants in the experiments worked individually, but I suspect it would be even stronger in a group as individuals hear about possible failures they hadn't yet thought about.

190. Cardinal, L. B. (2001). Technological innovation in the pharmaceutical industry: the use of organizational control in managing research and development. *Organization Science* 12(1): 19–36.

191. The history is described in Phillips, L. D. (2011). The Royal Navy's Type 45 story: a case study. In A. Salo, J. Keisler & A. Morton (eds), *Portfolio Decision Analysis: Improved Methods for Resource Allocation* (pp. 53–75). Springer Science+Business Media.

192. Phillips, The Royal Navy's Type 45 story, p. 64.

193. Phillips, The Royal Navy's Type 45 story, p. 71.

194. Phillips, The Royal Navy's Type 45 story, p. 74.

195. A detailed history is available at https://en.wikipedia.org/wiki/Type_45_destroyer.

15 Bargain and Negotiate

196. So says Goodreads, but evidence is lacking.

197. A brief introduction to negotiation can be found in Ulvila, J. W. & Snider, W. D. (1980). Negotiation of international oil tanker standards: an application of multiattribute value theory. *Operations Research* 28(1): 81–96. The bible is Raiffa, H., with Richardson, J. & Metcalfe, D. (2002). *Negotiation Analysis: The Science and Art of Collaborative Decision Making*. PON Books. Clear, simple, practical and wonderful.

198. This example is adapted from the Lisa vs Williams case study, pp. 45–54, in Raiffa, H. (1996). *Lectures on Negotiation Analysis*. PON Books.

199. Ulvila & Snider, Negotiation of international oil tanker standards.

200. Ulvila & Snider, Negotiation of international oil tanker standards, p. 93.

201. Personal communication from Cam Peterson in the 1980s.

16 Choose and Decide

202. Morreau, M. (2019). Arrow's Theorem. *The Stanford Encyclopedia of Philosophy*. Metaphysics Research Lab, Stanford University.

203. Phillips, L. D. (1982). Requisite decision modelling: a case study. *Journal of the Operational Research Society* 33(4): 303–11, 307.

17 Manage Risk

204. No definitive source or date available.

205. Slovic, P. (1987). Perception of risk. *Science* 236(4799): 280–5. A more detailed discussion of the psychometric methods for measuring perceived risk is given in ch. 5 of Slovic, P., Fischhoff, B. & Lichtenstein, S. (2000). *Facts and Fears: Understanding Perceived Risk. The Perception of Risk*. Earthscan.
206. MacCrimmon, K. & Wehrung, D. (1986). *Taking Risks: The Management of Uncertainty*. Collier Macmillan.
207. Wikipedia's brief summary of event tree analysis provides the following overview: https://en.wikipedia.org/wiki/Event_tree_analysis.
208. Wikipedia provides a good summary of the principles and methods of fault tree analysis: https://en.wikipedia.org/wiki/Fault_tree_analysis.
209. Kay, J. & King, M. (2020). *Radical Uncertainty*. Bridge Street Press. A subtitle appears only on the paper cover: *Decision-Making for an Unknowable Future*. Here are two eminent UK economists who appear to be unaware of the Society for Decision Making under Deep Uncertainty (DMDU). Slides from meetings of the society for 2017–19 are available on their website, and their leadership team includes economists.
210. Schoemaker, P. J. H. (1991). When and how to use scenario planning: a heuristic approach with illustration. *Journal of Forecasting* 10(6): 549–64.
211. Schoemaker, P. J. H. (1993). Multiple scenario development: its conceptual and behavioral foundation. *Strategic Management Journal* 14(3): 193–213.
212. Collins, J. C. & Porras, J. I. (1996). *Built to Last: Successful Habits of Visionary Companies*. Century.

18   Revise Opinion

213. In classical statistics, x is fixed and d varies, so all inferences are about the data – for example, there is a 95 per cent chance that these data would not have arisen if the hypothesis of no difference were true.
214. Villejoubert, G. & Mandel, D. R. (2002). The inverse fallacy: an account of deviations from Bayes's theorem and the additivity principle. *Memory & Cognition* 30(2): 171–8.
215. Kruschke, J. K. (2015). *Doing Bayesian Data Analysis; A Tutorial with R, JAGS, and Stan*, 2nd ed. Elsevier.
216. See www.drugscience.org.uk.
217. See www.drugscience.org.uk/about-us.
218. Zafar, R. R., Schlag, A. & Nutt, D. J. (2020). Ending the pain of children with severe epilepsy? An audit of the impact of medical cannabis in 10 patients. *Drug Science, Policy and Law* 6: 1–6; Zafar, R. R., Schlag, A., Phillips, L. & Nutt, D. J. (2021). Medical cannabis for severe treatment resistant epilepsy in children: a case-series of 10 patients. *BMJ Paediatrics Open* 5: article e001234.
219. Schlag, A. K., Zafar, R. R., Lynskey, M. T., Athanasiou-Fragkouli, A., Phillips, L. & Nutt, D. J. (2022). The value of real world evidence: the case of medical cannabis. *Frontiers in Psychiatry* 13: article 1027159.
220. Phillips, L. D. & Wisniewski, T. K. (1983). Bayesian models for computer-aided underwriting. *The Statistician* 32(1): 252–63.
221. How did I select the five most important factors for the shop model presented here from the original 11-factor model? I invoked the Sensitivity Analysis function in Netica, after selecting the top Shops_risk node, then in the ribbon, Network → Sensitivity to Findings to analyse the variance reduction contributed by each of the 11 factors. I chose the first five listed in order of variance reduction, which accounted for nearly 80 per cent of the total reduction in variance.

222. Gillott, N., Carroll, P., Chamberlin, P., Hudson, B., Malde, S., Masters, G. et al. (1988). *Commercial Fire Insurance*, presented to the Staple Inn Actuarial Society, p. 7. Available at www.actuaries.org.uk/system/files/documents/pdf/fire_0.pdf.
223. Keeney, R. (2008). Personal decisions are the leading cause of death. *Operations Research* 56(6): 1335–47.
224. See, e.g., McElreath, R. (2020). *Statistical Rethinking: A Bayesian Course with Examples in R and Stan*. 2nd ed. CRC Press.
225. Lindley, D. (2006). *Understanding Uncertainty*. John Wiley & Sons.

19 Think Strategically

226. Hussey, D. E. (2000). *How to Manage Organisational Change*. 2nd ed. Kogan Page.
227. Hamel, G. and Prahalad, C. K. (1989). Strategic intent. *Harvard Business Review* May–June, President and Fellows of Harvard College.
228. See www.mindtools.com/amtbj63/swot-analysis.
229. Collins, J. C. & Porras, J. I. (1996). *Built to Last: Successful Habits of Visionary Companies*. Century.
230. Allen, J. J., Kelly, C. W., Phillips, L. D. & Stewart, R. R. (1976). *Computer-Assisted Option Screening and Intelligence Assessment: Software User's Guide*. Decisions and Designs, Inc.
231. The evacuation was known as Operation Fluid Drive; see https://en.wikipedia.org/wiki/Operation_Fluid_Drive.

Epilogue to Part III

232. Matheson, D. & Matheson, J. (1998). *The Smart Organization: Creating Value through Strategic R&D*. Harvard Business School Press.
233. Rolles, S., Schlag, A. K., Measham, F., Phillips, L. D., Nutt, D., Bergsvik, D. et al. (2021). A multi criteria decision analysis (MCDA) for evaluating and appraising government policy responses to non-medical heroin use. *International Journal of Drug Policy* 91: article 103180.

Index

For EU product safety concerns, contact us at Calle de José Abascal, 56–1°,
28003 Madrid, Spain or eugpsr@cambridge.org.

www.ingramcontent.com/pod-product-compliance
Ingram Content Group UK Ltd.
Pitfield, Milton Keynes, MK11 3LW, UK
UKHW052127280426
470499UK00020B/513